Intellectual Property Rights

Intellectual Property Rights

Innovation, Governance and the Institutional Environment

Edited by

Birgitte Andersen

Reader in the Economics and Management of Innovation, School of Management and Organizational Psychology, Birkbeck College, University of London, UK, where she is also Director of E-business Programmes

Edward Elgar

Cheltenham, UK • Northampton, MA, USA

Published by
Edward Elgar Publishing Limited
Glensanda House
Montpellier Parade
Cheltenham
Glos GL50 1UA
UK

Edward Elgar Publishing, Inc.
136 West Street
Suite 202
Northampton
Massachusetts 01060
USA

A catalogue record for this book
is available from the British Library

Library of Congress Cataloguing in Publication Data
Intellectual property rights : innovation, governance, and the institutional environment / edited by Birgitte Andersen.
p. cm.
Includes index.
1. Intellectual property. I. Andersen, Birgitte, 1967–

K1401.I5597 2006
346.04'8–dc22

2005052088

ISBN-13: 978 1 84542 269 1
ISBN-10: 1 84542 269 4

Printed and bound in Great Britain by MPG Books Ltd, Bodmin, Cornwall

Contents

List of contributors vii

Introduction 1
Birgitte Andersen

PART I INTELLECTUAL PROPERTY RIGHTS AND THE GLOBAL COMMONS

1 The market economy and the scientific commons 17
Richard R. Nelson
2 Public interest and the public domain in an era of corporate dominance 46
Fiona Macmillan
3 AIDS, TRIPS and 'TRIPS plus': the case for developing and less developed countries 70
Fabienne Orsi, Mamadou Camara and Benjamin Coriat

PART II THE RATIONALES FOR INTELLECTUAL PROPERTY RIGHTS REVISITED

4 If 'intellectual property rights' is the answer, what is the question? Revisiting the patent controversies 109
Birgitte Andersen
5 Why do small high-tech firms take out patents, and why not? 148
Lee N. Davis

PART III THE PERFORMANCE OF THE PATENTING PROCESS

6 Knowledge spillovers from the patenting process 179
Jesper Lindgaard Christensen
7 The determinants of patentees' use of 'continuation' patent applications in the United States Patent and Trademark Office, 1980–99 215
Stuart J.H. Graham

PART IV COORDINATING INSTITUTIONS OF INTELLECTUAL PROPERTY RIGHTS GOVERNANCE

8 Public and private institutions in the governance of intellectual property rights 243
Eric Brousseau and Christian Bessy
9 The exploration of knowledge networks through patent citations 278
Stefano Breschi, Lorenzo Cassi and Franco Malerba
10 Intellectual property rights for governance in and of innovation systems 311
Ove Granstrand

Index 345

Contributors

Birgitte Andersen

Birgitte Andersen is Reader in the Economics and Management of Innovation in the School of Management and Organizational Psychology, Birkbeck College, University of London, UK, where she is also Director of E-business Programmes (since October 2000). She has a PhD in Economics. Her research profile includes evolutionary economics and industrial dynamics with respect to innovation and institutions, and the economics and management of Intellectual Property Rights (IPRs). Selected research programmes include: (i) European Union funded Network of Excellence 2005–2010: *Dynamics of Institutions and Markets in Europe*, (*DIME*) where Andersen is Coordinator for the research area on the formal aspects of knowledge exchange, which has a special focus on IPRs; (ii) Convenor of *Global Network on IPR Research* (since 2004); (iii) Member of research network on *New Directions in Copyright Law* (2004–2007), funded by the Arts and Humanities Research Board (AHRB); and (iv) owner of research project, *The Rationales for IPRs*, funded by the British Academy (2003–2004). Publications include *Technological Change and The Evolution of Corporate Innovation: The Structure of Patenting 1890–1990* (Edward Elgar: Cheltenham, 2001). She has advised economists and policy makers of national governments inside and outside Europe, as well as leading interest organizations. She has also collaborated with leading researchers at the United Nations Conference on Trade and Development (UNCTAD) of the United Nations on IPR matters in relation to copyrights and cultural industries; and the United Nations International Labour Office (ILO), Employment and Strategy Department, on productivity measurement and performance matters in relation to the intangible service economy.

http://www.bbk.ac.uk/manop/management/staff/andersen.shtml

Christian Bessy

Christian Bessy graduated from the Ecole Normale Supérieure of Cachan (France) and is a laureate of the Agrégation d'Economie et de Gestion (1987). He received a PhD in Economics from the University of Paris-

Panthéon-Sorbonne (1991). He is currently Research Fellow at Institutions and Dynamics of Historical Economics (IDHE, Paris), affiliated to the CNRS (Centre National de la Recherche Scientifique), and is a lecturer at the Ecole Normale Supérieure de Cachan. He is also an Associate Researcher at the Centre d'Etudes de l'Emploi (CEE, Paris), where he has been working for several years. He has carried out research funded by the French Ministry of Social Affairs, Work and Solidarity. Until 2004, he was Associate Researcher at the Centre for Analytical Theory of Organizations and Markets (ATOM, University of Paris-Panthéon-Sorbonne) and a member of its scientific committee. He specializes in institutional economics, law and economics, recruitment and labour market intermediaries, knowledge transfer and intellectual property rights. He has published numerous books and articles on these subjects. He has been a Visiting Scholar at Washington University in Saint Louis (Missouri).

Stefano Breschi

Stefano Breschi has a PhD in Economics at the University of Pavia in Italy. He is Associate Professor and Fellow of Industrial Economics, Bocconi University, and Deputy Director of the Centre for Research on Innovation and Internationalization (CESPRI), Bocconi University. His main research interests include the economics of innovation and technical change, industrial organization and dynamics, economic geography and networks of inventors. He has carried out research and collaborations with the European Commission, the Italian Ministry of Science and Technology, ENEA (Italian Energy Agency), Lombardy Region, and Confindustria.

http://www.cespri.unibocconi.it/breschi

Eric Brousseau

Eric Brousseau is Professor of Economics at the University of Paris X, and Director of EconomiX, which is a joint research centre between the CNRS (French National Science Foundation) and the University of Paris X. He is also Co-Director of the GDR TICS (Research consortium Information Technologies and the Society) of the CNRS. His research agenda focuses on the economics of institutions and the economics of contracts, with two main applied fields: the economics of intellectual property rights and the economics of the Internet and digital activities. On this last issue he works both on digital business models and on the governance of the Internet and of the information society. He also works on the economics of technology licensing agreements and on intellectual property rights in the cultural industries.

http://www.brousseau.info

Mamadou Camara

Mamadou Camara is Associate Professor in Economics at the Centre for Distance Education in the University of Paris 13's Institute of Technology, and Researcher at the Centre d'Economie de Paris Nord–Institutions, Innovation et Dynamiques Economiques (CEPN-IIDE), Centre National de la Recherche Scientifique (CNRS) Research Unit, at the University of Paris 13. In 2004 he obtained a postdoctoral scholarship from the French association Sidaction on the topic of access to AIDS treatment in Sub-Saharan Africa. His aim was to proceed to an evaluation of the regional projects on the production of unbranded antiviral drugs in the Economic Community of West African States (ECOWAS) area. He obtained his doctorate in Economics in 2001, with a thesis entitled *Foreign Direct Investment and the Evolution of Domestic Inequalities in Emerging Nations in the 1990s*.

Lorenzo Cassi

Lorenzo Cassi gained a PhD in Economics at the University of Ancona in Italy. He is a Postdoctoral Fellow at the Centre for Research on Innovation and Internationalization (CESPRI), Bocconi University. His main research interests include the economics of innovation and technical change, networks analysis and the economics of knowledge. He has carried out research and collaborations with the European Commission and ENEA (Italian Energy Agency).

http://www.cespri.unibocconi.it/cassi

Jesper Lindgaard Christensen

Jesper Lindgaard Christensen has a PhD in Economics. He is Associate Professor at the Department of Business Studies at Aalborg University in Denmark, where he is also a member of the IKE research group (since 1989). He teaches both business administration education and economics education. His research includes various aspects of innovation theory and practice. He has a broad knowledge of innovation and innovation policy, and has specialized in the financial aspects of innovation. He is currently doing research on product innovation, the venture capital market, regional economics, IPR systems and inter-firm collaboration. He has experience with a number of innovation surveys, including the Community Innovation Survey (CIS). Previous projects include being the daily coordinator of a three-year research project on the Danish Innovation System in comparative perspective (DISKO). Similarly, he coordinated a large-scale project on product innovation, interactive learning and economic performance. He is now managing a research unit focusing on regional economics, and he is still researching various aspects of the venture capital market. He has been involved in the Danish Research Unit for Industrial Dynamics (DRUID) from the start of the network.

Benjamin Coriat

Benjamin Coriat is Professor of Economics and Director of the Centre d'Economie de Paris Nord–Institutions, Innovation et Dynamiques Economiques (CEPN-IIDE), Centre National de la Recherche Scientifique (CNRS) Research Unit, at the University of Paris 13. His areas of expertise include industrial economics, economics of organizations and innovation. In recent years he has worked extensively in different targeted socioeconomic research programmes on European firm capabilities and performances sponsored by the European Union. He is acting Chairman of the Coordinated Action "Economics of AIDS and Access to HIV Care in Developing Countries" at the French Agency for Research on AIDS (ANRS).

Lee N. Davis

Lee Davis is Associate Professor at the Department of Industrial Economics and Strategy, and Research Associate at the Centre on Law, Economics and Financial Institutions, both at the Copenhagen Business School in Denmark. In 2003–4 she was Visiting Scholar at the Faculty of Management, Dalhousie University, Halifax, Canada. She has conducted research on economic incentives to research and development and the role of intellectual property rights for the past two decades, and published widely in the field. She teaches courses on the management of innovation and intellectual property rights strategy and policy in the MSc and Law and Economics programmes at the Copenhagen Business School, and in executive MBA programmes. Her main research interests include: what motivates inventors to invent (including the role of alternative incentive systems such as prizes), how firms capture the profits from their investments in R&D, the appropriability aspects of university-business relationships in biotechnology, and the new perspectives on appropriability raised by advances in digital technologies.

Stuart J.H. Graham

Stuart J.H. Graham is Assistant Professor of Strategic Management, College of Management, Georgia Institute of Technology. Professor Graham teaches and conducts research on the management of innovation and technology, intellectual property strategies, technology transfer and the legal environment. He received his PhD in business economics at the University of California, Berkeley, holds advanced degrees in Law (JD), Business (MBA), and Geography (MA), and is an attorney, licensed to practice law in the State of New York, and is a member of the American Bar Association and the American Intellectual Property Law Association. A selection of his recent publications includes 'Prospects for Improving U.S. Patent Quality via Post-grant Opposition' in Stern, S., Jaffe, J. and Lerner, J. (eds) *Innovation Policy and the Economy IV*, NBER, 2004 (with B.H. Hall, D. Harhoff and D.C. Mowery), 'Submarines in Software? Continuations in U.S. Software Patenting in the 1980s and 1990s' in *Economics of Innovation and New Technology* 2004 (with D.C. Mowery), and 'Intellectual Property Protection in the U.S. Software Industry' in Cohen, W.M. and Merrill, S.A. (eds), *Patents in the Knowledge-Based Economy*, National Academies Press, 2003 (with D.C. Mowery). Professor Graham teaches courses in international management and law at the Georgia Institute of Technology.

Ove Granstrand

Ove Granstrand was educated at Chalmers University of Technology, Göteborg University, Sweden, and Stanford University, with graduate degrees in mathematics, economics and engineering and a PhD degree in industrial management and economics. His work experience includes teaching, research and consultancy in various Eastern and Western countries. He serves as Professor in Industrial Management and Economics at Chalmers University of Technology, and as Chairman of the Centre for Intellectual Property Studies. His research interest concerns the economics and management of technology and innovation. In particular, he has studied innovation, corporate strategy and diversification in multi-technology corporations in Europe, Japan and the USA, as well as various issues related to R&D, intellectual property and intellectual capital in general. He has authored and edited several books and articles on these topics.

Fiona Macmillan

Fiona Macmillan is Professor of Law and Pro-Vice Master at Birkbeck, University of London. She researches and publishes in the areas of intellectual property law, especially copyright, and World Trade Organization law. Her last sole-authored book was *WTO and the Environment* (Sweet and Maxwell, 2001). Her forthcoming book is *The World Trade Organization and Human Rights* (Hart Publishing, 2006), which includes a consideration of the effect of TRIPs-fuelled copyright law on cultural development and self-determination. Recent publications in the area of copyright law include 'How the Movie Moguls Learned to Stop Worrying and Love the New Technology' in Moran, L., Christie, I., Loizidou, E. and Sandon, E. (eds), *Law's Moving Image: Law and Film* (Glasshouse Publishing, 2004), 'Commodification and Cultural Ownership' in Griffiths, J. and Suthersanen, U. (eds), *Copyright and Free Speech: Comparative and International Analyses* (OUP, 2005), 'Artistic Practice and the Integrity of Copyright Law' in Rosenmeier, M. and Teilmann, S. (eds), *Art and Law: the Debate Over Copyright* (DJØF, 2005), 'What Might Hans Christian Andersen Say About Copyright Today?' in Porsdam, H. (ed.), *Copyright and Other Fairy Tales: Hans Christian Andersen and the Commodification of Creativity* (Edward Elgar, forthcoming). She is the convenor of the Arts and Humanities Research Council Network on New Directions in Copyright, and the editor of the series *New Directions in Copyright Law*, which is published by Edward Elgar.

Franco Malerba

Franco Malerba has a PhD in Economics from Yale University (USA). He is Full Professor of Industrial Economics, Bocconi University, and Director of the Centre for Research on Innovation and Internationalization (CESPRI), Bocconi University. He is Editor of the *Journal of Industrial and Corporate Change*; Associate Editor of the *Journal of Evolutionary Economics*; Advisory Editor of *Research Policy*; and Member of the National Technology and Science Board of the Italian Ministry of University and Scientific and Technological Research. His main research interests include industrial economics and organizations; technological progress; innovation; and industrial dynamics. He has carried out research and collaborations with the European Commission, the OECD, EUREKA, the American National Science Foundation, ENEA (Italian Energy Agency), the Italian Ministry of Science and Technology, the Italian Ministry of Industry, Confindustria, Lombardy Region of Assolombarda and the American Enterprise Institute.

http://www.cespri.unibocconi.it/malerba

Richard R. Nelson

Richard R. Nelson has taught at Oberlin College, Carnegie Mellon University, Yale University and Columbia University, where he has been George Blumenthal Professor of International and Public Affairs since 1986. He was Director of the Institute for Social and Policy Studies at Yale University, and has directed Columbia's Public Policy Doctoral Consortium. He has also served as research economist and analyst at the Rand Corporation, and at the President's Council of Economic Advisors. Nelson's central interests have largely been on the process of long-run economic change. Much of his research has been directed toward understanding technological change, how economic institutions and public policies influence the evolution of technology, and how technological change in turn induces institutional and economic change more broadly. His recent work has focused on the varied roles of government in modern mixed economies. His work has been both empirical and theoretical. Along with Sidney Winter, he has pioneered in developing a formal evolutional theory of economic change. Their joint book *An Evolutionary Theory of Economic Change* (Belknap Press of Harvard University, 1982) is widely recognized as a landmark in this field. Recent books include: *Technology, Institutions, and Economic Growth* (Harvard University Press, 2005), *The Limits of Market Organization* (Russell Sage, 2005) and *Ivory Tower and Industrial Innovation* (with David Mowery, Bhaven Sampat and Avids Ziedonis; Stanford Business Books, Stanford, 2004).

Fabienne Orsi

Fabienne Orsi is Researcher at the Centre d'Economie de Paris Nord–Institutions, Innovation et Dynamiques Economiques (CEPN-IIDE), Centre National de la Recherche Scientifique (CNRS) Research Unit, at the University of Paris 13. She specializes in the economics of intellectual property rights in the fields of biotechnology and the pharmaceutical industry. In 2003 she obtained a postdoctoral scholarship from the French Agency for Research on AIDS (ANRS) in order to work on the link between the new international patent laws and the market of generics anti-AIDS drugs in developing countries. In 2002 she began work with Benjamin Coriat and ANRS on the topic of access to HIV/AIDS drugs in developing countries in relationship to the World Trade Organization (WTO) agreement on Trade Related Aspects of Intellectual Property Rights (TRIPS). In December 2001 she obtained her doctorate in Economics, with a thesis entitled *Intellectual Property Rights and Financial Markets in the New Relationships between Science/Industry – the Case of Human Genome Research.*

Introduction

Birgitte Andersen

We have experienced a growing importance of intellectual capital and intangible assets and an increased tendency for firms and public institutions to privatize, by the use of patents or copyrights, their knowledge assets and creative expressions. Because control over the use of an intellectual property right (IPR) requires ownership or a licence, the growing importance of knowledge-based assets and creative expressions has been accompanied by recognition that patents and copyrights represent strategic assets for those who own and control them. It is therefore not surprising that, in recent years, the pace at which individuals, firms and the public sector are using IPRs to privatize knowledge-based assets and creative expressions has been accelerating. This trend has been enhanced by the view of many in industry, government and international agencies that the privatization of the intellectual capital and knowledge-based assets of individuals and firms provides many advantages (for example, competitive advantage), and we have seen an increased enforcement of IPR regimes worldwide.

At the international DRUID (Danish Research Unit for Industrial Dynamics) conference on *Industrial Dynamics, Innovation and Development*, held at Elsinore, Denmark, 12–14 June 2003, there was a round table discussion regarding the belief systems underpinning IPRs and the increased enforcement of IPR regimes worldwide. The fact that IPR policy has been largely based on the 'vision' of policy makers rather than on the findings of solid empirical research was discussed; and within the IPR research community, the social and economic effects of tightening the IPR systems are not considered obvious. Thus, this book, containing contributions presented at the DRUID 2003 summer conference, has emerged because many scholars within the IPR research community believe that there is a need for providing profound insights with respect to understanding the role of IPR regulation in achieving economic performance, growth and sustainable development at the corporate, sectoral and global levels, at the same time as providing a higher quality of life at the level of all groups of civilization in all regions of the world.

Furthermore, by addressing some of the conflicts, contradictions and trade-offs in IPR systems (both in terms of rationales, operation and effects) the contributions to this book challenge the existing mainstream thinking and analytical frameworks dominating the theoretical literature on IPRs within economics, management, politics, law and regulation theory.

This book is cutting edge in addressing current debates affecting businesses, sectors and society today, and in the way it not only focuses on the enabling welfare effects of IPR systems, but also puts special emphasis on some of their possible adverse effects. All contributors to this book share the same fascination, and see the same need, for understanding the dynamic role of IPRs for business and society.

INTELLECTUAL PROPERTY RIGHTS AND THE GLOBAL COMMONS

The global commons are in danger. This is partly due to the role of IPRs in the commodification of three separate areas: science, culture and healthcare. All three areas used to be regarded as important areas of the public domain or for public access. The first three chapters in this book suggest that we need to rethink whether such sectors perform best under the rules of markets and capitalism.

Professor Richard Nelson and Professor Fiona Macmillan have been invited as guest contributors to this book, due to their important contributions in the area of IPRs and the global commons in an era of corporate dominance and privatization of the public domain. Their contributions focus, respectively, on patents and markets for science, and copyrights and markets for creative cultural expressions. Fabienne Orsi, Mamadou Camara and Benjamin Coriat focus on patents and markets for healthcare under the effects of the Trade-Related Aspects of the Intellectual Property Rights Section (TRIPS) of the World Trade Organization (WTO), which came into force in 1994 as a part of the Uruguay Round to enforce intellectual property worldwide. Their contributions will now be described.

In Chapter 1 on *The Market Economy and the Scientific Commons*, Richard Nelson discusses the problem that even though scientific inventions are not in principle allowed to be protected by patents, there is still an increased propensity to patent very fundamental inventions. Thus, in practice, the divide between science and technology is very blurred. Nelson argues that this propensity is partly due to national policies encouraging universities to patent their scientific findings. As an example, he refers to the Bayh-Dole Act of 1980. This is an US Act encouraging universities to patent their scientific findings and discoveries, and similar types of policies are now adopted worldwide. In particular, he discusses some of the adverse effects of such policies. He basically argues that the increased privatization of scientific inventions or very fundamental knowledge is bad for the advance of both science and technology. The specific natures of science and technology, as well as their co-evolution, are the key to understanding the long-term effects of such policies. It is also important to understand the specific role of universities in this co-evolution. Nelson argues that, even if the Bayh-Dole Act helps certain ends (for example, helps universities and individuals to develop a clear strategy regarding how best to commercialize their ideas), it still has the effect of taking very basic knowledge out of the public domain.

Nelson advocates very strongly that basic scientific findings should be kept in the public domain. Very basic inventions tend to have broader patent scope. If they are patented, prohibiting general use, this can induce a direct welfare loss, as many firms will avoid scientific and technological trajectories where basic knowledge has been made scarce and expensive, or they will be excluded due to exclusive licensing. Nelson argues that it is the openness of basic inventions for multiple exploration paths in the market economy that makes the evolutionary process of technological advance more powerful. Furthermore, he recognizes that many universities today are keen subscribers to the patent system, and that their incentives are more for profit than for technological transfer. However, he argues that it is uncertain whether such policies have facilitated more technological transfer, and even whether they generate profit to universities. Nelson then discusses some strategies relating to the way we can protect the scientific commons. Basically, he rejects the view that universities should, like firms, be driven by profits in markets and therefore join the patent bandwagon which seems to be going on currently in the corporate world. Rather, he suggests a combination of (i) a policy encouraging universities to keep their results open, and letting them co-exist alongside, and compete with, the patented inventions in private firms, and (ii) a policy to roll back the invasion of privatization by discouraging all patenting activities of basic inventions by both public and private organizations. The latter would, however, involve a change in law.

The problem of markets, commons and capitalism continues in Chapter 2 on *Public Interest and the Public Domain in an Era of Corporate Dominance*. Fiona Macmillan maintains that our aim should be to understand the dynamic effects of the exploitation of the general profile of corporate power endorsed by copyrights, and the accountability of that power. She argues that copyright's commodification of creativity has established a structure that enables the domination of cultural output by multinational media and entertainment corporations. She examines this structure by describing how the current design of copyright regimes facilitates very strong copyrights, and she discusses the conflicting interests of stakeholders, wanting strong copyrights, and the public, needing user rights. She argues that the current structure of strong copyrights and dominance of the media and entertainment corporations over cultural output has had the effect of contracting the public domain, while at the same time undermining some of the rationales for the existence of copyright. In particular, Macmillan discusses the conflict between the economic and moral rationales for copyright. She stresses how it is the focus on, and the dynamic nature of, the economic rationales of copyright law that has caused a corporate dominance over cultural output.

The paper then lays out a strategy to overturn some of these adverse effects of copyright law. Macmillan discusses whether the importance of the economic rationales implemented into the functioning of copyright law can be counterbalanced by the implementation of some of the moral rationales underpinning the philosophy of copyright. Realizing that such a solution may not be sustainable in practice due to the spiralling power of the media and entertainment sectors over cultural products, she argues that we need to think holistically. She considers whether there are other legal approaches, either within the structure of copyright law or external to it, which might be capable of remedying the corporate dominance consequences of copyright's commodification of creativity and thus reclaiming a portion of the public domain. She turns to competition law, corporate law, and, regarding cultural products, media law, and she presents ways that those laws could be implemented to make private power more publicly accountable.

In Chapter 3 on *AIDS, TRIPS and 'TRIPS Plus': The Case for Developing and Less Developed Countries*, Fabienne Orsi, Mamadou Camara and Benjamin Coriat discuss some of the adverse effects of the TRIPS agreement of the WTO, which came into force in 1994 as a part of the Uruguay Round to enforce intellectual property rights worldwide. However, the agreement has been amended over time due to the situation of the less developed and developing countries. Because the latest revised version goes even further than the TRIPS requirements, it is often referred to as 'TRIPS plus'. Orsi, Camara and Coriat examine how TRIPS has provoked a radical change in the healthcare situation of the poorest countries, focusing on the situation created by TRIPS in the French-speaking countries of Sub-Saharan Africa. They argue that in this zone, where AIDS has struck most severely, the application of TRIPS, combined with existing regional IPR agreements (known as the Bangui Agreements), has created a legal situation particularly prejudicial to healthcare. Their paper argues that access to healthcare (in this case, the treatment of AIDS) is determined by a combination of market forces under particular patent governance structures, institutional capabilities (or lack thereof), strategic interaction, and the bargaining power of individuals, firms and countries. This situation is inherently disadvantageous for less developed and developing countries, which are those with the severest AIDS problems. Thus, if we support the view argued in this chapter that access to healthcare should be a global common good, we need to rethink whether this is a sector that should be ruled by markets and capitalism.

THE RATIONALES FOR INTELLECTUAL PROPERTY RIGHTS

It is important for an IPR regime to have a design which will enable it to achieve its objectives, and consequently an understanding and critical evaluation of the rationales underpinning the IPR system, in terms of policy and corporate goals, is urgently needed. This is important both for assessing the social and economic effects of the IPR systems and when designing policy which will foster a sustainable development of business and society, as discussed by Birgitte Andersen. It is also important for understanding why firms take out patents and why they do not, as researched by Lee Davis. Their contributions will now be described.

In Chapter 4, '*If Intellectual Property Rights' is the Answer, What is the Question? Revisiting the Patent Controversies*, Birgitte Andersen develops a typology of the rationales for IPRs. In this context, she discusses several policy goals or rationales for IPRs: why we have the IPR system, and what the objectives of the system are as well as how it operates. She then examines each of the IPR rationales or policy goals, discussing whether the IPR system really performs in relation to its objectives. In discussing the economic rationales for IPRs (that is, the IPR policy goals), the chapter provides an introduction to belief systems in the mainstream literature of law and economics. It argues that, as IPRs signal prospects for reward, they stimulate incentives to invest in invention and innovation, which in turn stimulate innovation-based competition. Furthermore, it is argued that IPRs facilitate markets for ideas and knowledge as well as creative expressions of ideas, by adjusting for the inherent problems of market failure normally attached to knowledge and intangible expressions of ideas. It is also believed that such commercial exploitation in markets facilitates the spillover of such knowledge-based ideas and creative expressions of ideas, as profit-oriented firms would spread their IPR-protected ideas and expressions as widely as possible for profit purposes. Moreover, as IPRs temporarily protect entrepreneurial talent from imitation (or offer market privileges to them), or facilitate market entry of products or services embodying their novel ideas and original creative expressions, it is believed that IPRs in this way facilitate sustainable development of firms and industries. Finally, there are also natural rights and a moral rationale attached to the IPR – basically a natural right to claim an intellectual property, and the moral right to compensation and reward if someone else exploits one's idea or expression of an idea.

However, Andersen concludes that belief systems in the mainstream literature of law and economics are inherently flawed, since their analysis assumes that all inventors are autonomous, rational, profit-maximizing agents whose collective behaviour maximizes both their own welfare and that of society in general. The very real effects of technological and creative interdependence, strategic interaction and collaboration in competitive IPR markets are largely ignored. This is problematic because, for example, the specific and rigid nature of productive knowledge applied in technological ideas can affect the efficiency of patent systems. The effectiveness of copyright systems can also be influenced by predominant norms, values and beliefs embedded in cultural expressions of ideas. Power relationships in IPR-related bargaining situations can have important impacts on behaviour and outcomes; and there are substantial opportunity costs associated with using the IPR system as a political instrument. Finally, whereas the current law and economics approach to IPRs equates competition with perfect competition and monopoly with pure monopoly, the actual architecture of the IPR system is a hybrid structure with both competitive and monopolistic dimensions. These 'real-life' forces should be considered when IPR policy is designed and implemented, because the interaction of micro-level units within IPR systems does not necessarily maximize social and economic welfare at the macro level; and IPR regimes (at the macro level) do not guarantee welfare for each (micro-level) participant within the IPR system. Basically, it is a major problem that the existing social contract and political expediency literature examining the objectives, operation and performance of IPR systems bases its analysis on the theoretical logic of mainstream law and economic theory, particularly since this literature has informed the belief systems regarding the social and economic effects and operation of IPR systems which underpin the design of IPR policy.

Chapter 5 moves on to discuss the rationales of the IPR system at a much more micro level. In a study on *Why do Small High-Tech Firms Take out Patents, and Why Not?*, Lee Davis seeks to add to our understanding of the strategic and economic effects of patents for small enterprises. She also illustrates how the rationales of small firms in taking out patents are linked to their broader business and technology strategies. The case study is based upon thirty-four small Danish firms in telecommunications, software and biotechnology. Studies of this character are extremely important to initiate, since IPR research tends to be on larger firms and major multinationals whose propensity to patent is much higher. However, it is also extremely important to understand the strategic and economic effects of the IPR system for smaller firms when informing IPR policy. Reading this chapter, it becomes clear that the rationales for smaller firms to patent, or not to patent, are very different from the major organizations within their industries. For example, a major reason for small high-tech firms not to patent is the high cost of detecting infringements, whereas large firms do not face the same resource problems in detecting if ideas similar to theirs are used elsewhere and deciding if infringement court cases should be initiated. Also, many small software firms often find patents irrelevant, whereas small telecommunications firms find them important, but in combination with other factors. Again, those results may not correspond to the major or dominating firms within their industries, as their strategies would presumably be driven by IPR incentives. Thus, the stakeholders in IPR systems and their interests depend both on sector and firm size. This also became apparent at the most recent *Conference on Patent Policy Making* regarding computer-implemented inventions. At this hearing the small and medium sized enterprises were very worried about the industry effects of a strong patent policy. The hearing was held in the European Parliament on 1 June 2005 and organized by FFII (the Foundation for a Free Information Infrastructure) and CCIA (the Computer and Communication Industry Association) of the United States.

THE PERFORMANCE OF THE PATENTING PROCESS

The efficiency and effect of IPR systems also depends on the local IPR offices. This is a hugely under-researched institution. Basically, IPR offices tend to be treated as a 'black box', both in theory and within empirical analysis, in the sense that what goes on within them tends to be assumed or given. However, Jesper Lindgaard Christensen and Stuart J.H. Graham have started to open this black box. In their contributions they discuss how IPR offices can make a difference, focusing on the performance of the patenting process between IPR offices and the patentees. Their contributions will now be described.

Focusing on a patent office in a small open economy (the Danish Patent and Trademark Office: DKPTO), Jesper Lindgaard Christensen maintains in Chapter 6 on *Knowledge Spillovers from the Patenting Process* that the success of the patent system is still locally or nationally rooted despite globalization in IPR legislation. His basic contention, based upon a survey of what firms used the local patent office for, is that the national patent and trademark offices enhance knowledge spillover from the patenting process. In particular, he shows how the interaction between the applicant firms and the patent office adds to the general competence of both parties. In turn, this has positive long-term effects on the ability of the firms to innovate and use IPR systems. It is also shown that well-organized national IPR offices play an important role in supporting and educating local users of international IPR systems, as well as developing a vibrant local IPR community by bringing users of the system and IPR service firms together. These activities bring down the barriers to entering IPR protection. Christensen therefore maintains that national IPR offices should not be abolished in the era of institutional internationalization. Although many firms would be able to do without a national patent office with regard to the granting of patents, there is still a role for national IPR institutions.

However, Stuart Graham examines a very different, and to him unconstructive, aspect of the patenting process within the United States Patent and Trademark Office (USPTO). In Chapter 7 on *The Determinants of Patentees' Use of 'Continuation' Patent Applications in the United States Patent and Trademark Office, 1980–99*, Graham describes and examines the use of the 'continuation' patent application procedure available in the United States, but not generally available elsewhere in the world. This study of a particular process in the USPTO is of general interest for several reasons. This office underpins the largest market in the world, and inventions that are successful in other countries are also most likely to be patented in the USA. Also, the USPTO has always led the way in organizing IPRs, and other countries have subsequently followed its procedures and policies. This 'continuation' scheme allows patent applications to be updated (re-filed) while they are being processed. A rationale of the scheme is to encourage patent application submissions at a very early stage of a discovery. However, Graham demonstrates some of the perverse effects of the scheme. The 'continuation' procedure allows a patent applicant to postpone the issue of a patent, affording inventors several strategic opportunities, among which are delay and secrecy. Graham discusses the effect of the scheme that has resulted in an intricate web of applications and patents that can be traced by reference (if not by invention) back several decades. In all such cases, the early effective filing dates of those original patent applications turn the use of all similar subsequent inventions into infringements. Patents processed in this scheme are therefore often termed 'submarine patents'. The chapter discusses how this scheme also allows patentees to extract extraordinary economic rents. Graham also examines who is likely to use the 'continuation' procedure, and he demonstrates how and why innovators in the semiconductor and pharmaceutical technologies in particular have employed the 'continuation' patent application procedure for strategic gains.

COORDINATING INSTITUTIONS OF INTELLECTUAL PROPERTY RIGHTS GOVERNANCE

Intellectual property right governance is much more than the law setting the rules of the game. Entire IPR systems of coordinating institutions must be in place in order to create and extract as much financial and non-financial value as possible from IPRs. In this context there are different types of coordinating institutions of IPR governance. Eric Brousseau and Christian Bessy identify the complementarities and optimal division of labour between public and private institutions in IPR governance activities relating to IPR protection and diffusion, whereas Stefano Breschi, Lorenzo Cassi and Franco Malerba identify corporate coordinating knowledge networks underpinning IPR governance at the sector level. Finally, Ove Granstrand reviews the interface between various innovation systems (namely, national, sectoral, corporate, university and military systems) and IPR governance at various levels. Their contributions will now be described in turn.

Eric Brousseau and Christian Bessy show in Chapter 8 on *Public and Private Institutions in the Governance of Intellectual Property Rights* that the governance of IPRs is complex. They show how IPR governance, when it comes to identifying the nature of the rights associated with a particular right (patent or copyright) and the enforcement of such rights, happens at many different levels, and that there are complementarities between public (state) and private (firm and sector) institutions in such governance activities. However, the optimal division of labour between public and private institutions in the governance structures of elements surrounding IPRs should not be assumed or given, as this may vary according to a range of variables, including the nature of the IPRs (patents or copyrights) in question, the country in which the governance takes place (their case study was on the US and France), the type of IPR protection and infringement and the diffusion strategy used by the owners of the IPRs. The paper demonstrates that the organization of IPR governance should be taken into account when designing IPR systems in order to solve the protection versus diffusion dilemma often associated with IPRs.

In Chapter 9 on *The Exploration of Knowledge Networks through Patent Citations*, Stefano Breschi, Lorenzo Cassi and Franco Malerba identify coordinating institutions underpinning IPR governance at the sector level. They identify knowledge networks at the level of organizations and firms using patent citation and co-citation data as relational data, and they identify companies' positions in such networks by developing a taxonomy of four different dimensions: the extent to which organizations and firms are technological leaders, technological followers, brokers of new technologies or isolated organizations. In developing the taxonomy, they also develop a measure of the crowdedness of a company's position in the technological space and a measure of its status. Although this type of research is mainly descriptive, I believe that it provides an important underpinning for understanding how the knowledge and technological landscape of dependence and interdependence amongst organizations and firms looks. This in turn reveals something about how strong a position a firm may hold within IPR systems. Basically, the free ticket granted by the patent system to use organizations' and firms' patented knowledge to develop the research frontier does not necessarily grant a ticket to produce or trade. In other words, even if development rights (the right to use an idea to develop another idea) are not directly protected under the patent system, the production rights (the right to use the patented idea to produce) and trade rights (the right to trade a commodity embodying the idea) are. This is what creates the huge dependency and inter-dependency between firms, as there is no point in developing an idea if it cannot be used for commercial purposes. It could even be argued that the productive efficiency of knowledge networks of citations and co-citations depends on the relationship between (i) the government's granting of open access to improve and develop patented ideas (part of patent law) and (ii) the granting of rights, by individual patent owners, to produce and trade a product embodying patented ideas. If the latter is not granted, the overall efficiency of the knowledge network may decrease, even if some individual firms may improve their relative technological position. This may argue for a compulsory licensing law, but it is still a very controversial question. The relationship between those two rights (that is, the right to improve or develop patented ideas, and the right to produce and trade products embodying such patented ideas) is briefly discussed in Chapter 4 of this book.

The fact that products and processes are increasingly complex, both in their knowledge bases and in the ownership of such, is an important starting point for Ove Granstrand in Chapter 10: *Intellectual Property Rights for Governance in and of Innovation Systems*. This chapter addresses the role of IPRs in different innovation systems (namely, national, sectoral, corporate, university and military systems) from a governance perspective. The focus is on the pro-intellectual property era of the 1980s, which has generally transformed and strengthened various forms of IPR governance in different innovation systems. Granstrand argues that the necessity of more inter-firm technology collaborations and various forms of technology trade have fostered quasi-integrated corporate innovation systems. This is basically due to the availability of enforceable and valuable IPRs, together with more large-scale research and development (R&D) and the emergence of complex new technologies. However, he also argues that the efficiency or success in using IPR systems as a governance tool for incentivizing and coordinating innovation activities is not self-evident, and that a re-evaluation of various approaches is needed for sustaining efficient and effective innovation systems.

INTELLECTUAL PROPERTY RIGHTS: INNOVATION, GOVERNANCE AND THE INSTITUTIONAL ENVIRONMENT

In conventional literature, as well as this book, the boundary between the institutional IPR environment and the IPRs governing institutions is blurred. In this book therefore, these are taken to include all ways in which individuals, firms, organizations and governments control and manage IPRs. The effect this has for individuals, firms and society is also a special concern addressed in the book.

However, for future research, I believe that clear definitions of the 'institutional IPR environment' and the 'IPRs governing institutions' are useful. Clear concepts will provide a common platform for communication. This will, for example, enable us to build theories about the productive potential and adverse effects of IPRs. As described below, a clear distinction between the 'institutional IPR environment' and 'IPR governing institutions' will also help us when designing policy fostering the new economy.

I believe that inspiration regarding clear definitions of the 'institutional IPR environment' and the 'IPRs governing institutions' can be found in the new institutional economics,[1] although this literature focuses on different areas of enquiry to IPR systems. Within new institutional economics the 'institutional environment' is the 'rules of the game' and the 'governing institutions' or 'institutions of governance' are the structures in which the 'playing of the game' is carried out.

In this context, this book addresses how IPR systems form a central part of the 'institutional IPR environment' in setting the 'rules of the game' for the commercial exploitation of scientific and technological inventions (protected by the patent system) as well as inventions in creative expressions of cultural ideas (protected by the copyright system).

The rules of the game set by IPR systems affect the design of IPR law. Design issues include: (i) length of IPR protection obtained, (ii) the type of knowledge or creative expression protected (for example, should basic procedures to obtain DNA codes, and non-technical business methods, be protected), (iii) scope of knowledge protected (for example, should we allow or encourage patent protection on fundamental inventions in universities with huge technological scope), (iv) inventive step (for example, how significant an inventive step is needed for patent protection and how much originality is needed for copyright protection), (v) licensing law (for example, should we allow the opportunity to block competition or should we opt for compulsory licensing), (vi) the costs of and procedures for obtaining and holding a right, and (vii) the type and costs of the remedies available for infringement.

The design of IPR systems, in terms of the law setting rules, depends of course on what we want (that is, the rationales and objectives) from the IPR systems.

Broader discussions of the 'institutional IPR environment' as a rule setter which affects the behaviour of firms and individuals is provided in Chapters 4 and 10, while specific fields of inquiry are addressed in Chapters 1, 2, and 3.

The 'institutional IPR environment' also includes the rules, norms and routines regarding patenting processes in IPR offices. Such processes also differ across countries, and they affect the behaviour of individuals and firms. For example, the use of a 'continuation' scheme in the US affecting the use of 'submarine' procedures is not allowed elsewhere, and the active role of IPR offices in enabling learning processes and knowledge spillover is not general, but a particular attribute of a specific successful IPR office. Those issues are discussed in Chapters 6 and 7.

The players in the game of commercial exploitation of scientific and technological inventions as well as inventions in creative expressions of cultural ideas, and where the 'institutional IPR environment' sets rules, can be defined as both public and private sector organizations and firms as well as individuals. The nature of the interaction between the players can be termed 'the playing of the game'. Each interaction is formed within a certain structure of contracts. At the individual or firm level they are usually in the form of different types of licensing agreements (for example, exclusive licensing, cross-licensing, patent pooling) or involve transactions of full IPRs. A central aspect of IPR governance at the level of the state is the original contract between the government and the possessor of a novel idea, with respect to the patent system. A written contract is not needed with respect to the copyright system. All original expressions of ideas are automatically protected. Such structures of contracts can be defined as 'institutions of governance' or 'governing institutions'. Whereas Chapter 5 discusses the incentive for firms to participate in this game, Chapters 8, 9 and 10 discuss some of the coordinating elements of such games, namely knowledge networks and innovation systems, as well as the complementary roles of state and sector organizations in IPR governance.

An important aspect of the nature of the 'playing of the game' is the influence of the 'rules of the game' on the quality of relationships among the players and IPR systems stakeholders. Basically, the 'rules of the game' influence the ways in which firms and individuals create financial and non-financial value from IPRs, and how this value is distributed. This remains an almost ignored topic in the existing IPR and institutional literature. IPR stakeholders can be defined to include those individuals and groups that have both an interest in how the IPRs are being used and a stake in how the value from IPRs is being distributed. Thus, they include those players who own or hold the rights associated with ownership and control, as well as those who aspire to become users of the ideas and expressions protected by the IPR systems. The identification of stakeholders in the IPR systems, how they interact, and what their interests and roles are, are important matters for direct or indirect inquiry in most chapters within this book. For future research we also need to understand the mechanisms by which stakeholder interests are prioritized, and the influence this might have on the ability to exploit fully the productive potential of the protected IPRs.

As will be clear from reading this book, the 'institutional IPR environment' and the 'IPR governing institutions', as well as their interaction, have implications for the social and economic effects of IPR systems, at the levels of individuals, firms, sectors, countries and civilizations. The increased enforcement of IPR regimes worldwide has brought up many debates and empirical research priority themes. For example:

1. Current debates surrounding the patent scheme include issues related to:

    - The Trade Related Aspects of the Intellectual Property Section (TRIPS) of the World Trade Organization (WTO).
    - Integration of new areas of protection into the patent system that grant protection even beyond science-based principles (for example, business methods patents and other computer-implemented inventions).
    - Exclusive rights also on fundamental inventions (for example, genetic codes, some mathematics, university patents).
    - Patenting of traditional knowledge and the problem of bio-piracy.
    - Increased privatization of the public domain.
    - Design of patent law and the problem of an increased period of protection historically.
    - Patent offices grant patents on trivial knowledge with very little inventive development.

- 'Continuation' and the 'submarine' patenting scheme in the US.

2. Current debates surrounding the copyright scheme include issues related to:

   - Corporate power and the problem of fair recognition.
   - Increased privatization of the public domain.
   - Copyright and cultural imperialism (the problem of (low) variety, (low) quality and (high) price).
   - Increased data base protection.
   - Copyrighting traditional cultural expressions that are fundamental elements of our culture.
   - Design of copyright law and an increased period of protection historically.

3. Current debates surrounding the trademark scheme include issues related to:

   - Brands and trademarks for consumer protection versus consumer exploitation.

There is no way a single book can profoundly address *all* the relevant issues. However, at least this book serves as a beginning. Also, from the contributions to this book we see how the IPR debates engage different problems regarding the operation of IPR systems and the social and economic effects of such systems for business and society. They therefore also engage different sets of theoretical and analytical inquiry.

Finally, we all agree that the role and effect of IPR institutions is important to understand. For this purpose, I will again emphasize that a clear distinction between the 'institutional IPR environment' and 'IPR governing institutions' is useful. In particular, it helps us to understand how such institutions can be changed when designing policy fostering the new economy. For example, it requires complex collective action by means of government intervention to change the 'rules of the game', whereas it requires less complex individual action between the players to change the 'playing of the game'. However, the nature of the 'playing of the game' can of course also be regulated by rules established by government.

NOTE

1. See for example Oliver Williamson (1998): 'Transaction Cost Economics: How it Works; Where it is Headed', *De Economist*, 146, 23–58.

PART I

Intellectual property rights and the global commons

1. The market economy and the scientific commons*

Richard R. Nelson

ABSTRACT

In principle there is a clear divide between science and technology. In practice there isn't. In principle, while practical inventions can be patented, scientific findings can't be. In practice, increasingly scientific findings are being patented. The argument of this paper is that this is bad for the advance of science and for the advance of technology. However, because of the blurry lines, it will not be easy to deal with. The paper lays out a strategy that at least has some promise.

Keywords: Markets, Commons, Capitalism

1 INTRODUCTION

Modern capitalism has proved a remarkably powerful engine of technological progress. Most of the attention to its workings has focused on the business firms and entrepreneurs, operating in a market setting, who are the central actors in developing and introducing new products and processes. At the same time it is widely recognized that the power of market stimulated and guided invention and innovation is often dependent on the strength of the science base from which they draw (Nelson, 1993, Mowery and Nelson, 1999). This science base is largely the product of publicly funded research, and the knowledge produced by that research is largely open and available for potential innovators to use. That is, the market part of the capitalist engine rests on a publicly supported scientific commons.

The message of this chapter is that the scientific commons are becoming privatized. While this privatization up to now has been relatively limited,

* Reprinted from *Research Policy,* **33**, Richard R. Nelson 'The market economy and the scientific commons', 455–71, (2004), with permission from Elsevier.

there are real dangers that unless halted soon, important portions of future scientific knowledge will be private property and fall outside the public domain, and that could be bad news for both the future progress of science, and for technological progress. The erosion of the scientific commons will not be easy to stop. Here I want to call the alarm, and to suggest a strategy that has some promise.

But before I get on with this task, I need to clear some intellectual underbrush. A number of influential philosophers and sociologists of science have put forth a set of views, a theory, about the scientific enterprise that until recently has served well to protect the scientific commons. However, this theory is no longer adequate to the task, because the way it characterizes the nature of the scientific enterprise does not fit modern perceptions and the reality. Also, under this theory, it is hard to understand why privatization and markets are encroaching on the commons, and if they are, what is the matter with that? It is important, therefore, to scrutinize that theory.

A key element of the theory is that, outside of industry, the work of scientists is and should be motivated by the search for understanding, and that the practical payoffs that often come from successful research are largely unpredictable. Vannevar Bush (1945) is one among many proponents of public support of science who put forth this theme, and argued that it would be a mistake to look to likely practical payoffs as a guide to where scientific funds should be allocated. Serendipity is the reason why scientific research often has practical payoff, and the chances of serendipity are greatest when bright and dedicated scientists are free to attack what they see as the most challenging scientific problems in the way they think most promising.

For this reason, decisions regarding what questions to explore, and the evaluation of the performance of individual scientists and broad research programmes, should mostly be in the hands of the scientists working in a field. Indeed for the government or the market to intrude too much into how scientific research resources are allocated would be to kill the goose that lays the golden egg. In the terms used by Michael Polanyi (1962), society should appreciate and protect 'The Republic of Science'.

An associated belief or ideal is that the results of scientific research are and should be published and otherwise laid open for all to use and evaluate. As Robert Merton (1973) argued, the spirit of science is 'communitarian' regarding access to the knowledge and techniques it creates. All scientists are free to test the results of their fellows and to find them valid or not supported, and to build on these results in their own work. Because the results of scientific research are laid in the public domain for testing and further development, the bulk of scientific knowledge accepted by the community is reliable (as John Ziman (1978) has emphasized) and scientific knowledge is cumulative. These are basic reasons why the scientific enterprise has been so effective as an engine of discovery. And economists have often argued that keeping science open is the most effective policy for enabling the public to draw practical benefits from it.

My argument in this chapter is that the part of the theory about good science that stresses the value of open science is basically correct, but is in danger of being forgotten, or denied. A good share of the reason is that, as originally put forth, this part seemed a natural consequence of the other aspects of the theory: that the practical payoffs from scientific research were not predictable, but largely came about through serendipity, and that the allocation of scientific resources should not be guided by anticipation of particular practical payoffs, but rather by the informed judgements of scientists regarding the most important problems to work on. Keeping scientific findings in the public domain, with reward to the scientist being tied to the acclaim of his or her fellows, along with public funding of research based on peer review of the scientific promise of the proposal and the scientist, would then seem to be an important part of an incentive and control system for fostering productive science (for a discussion along these lines, see Dasgupta and David, 1994).

However the notion that academic scientists have no idea and do not care about the practical problems that their research might illuminate has never been fully true. In this era of biotechnology it is obvious, if it was not before, that both the funders and the undertakers of research often have well in mind the possible social and economic payoffs from what they are doing. But if in fact, much of scientific research is consciously aimed, at least broadly, at problems the solution to which can have major, and broadly predictable, practical value, what is the case against harnessing market incentives to the undertaking of research and to the use of research results? In particular, why should the privatization of these kinds of research results be viewed as a problem?

The case for open scientific knowledge clearly needs to be reconstructed recognizing explicitly that much of scientific research is in fact oriented towards providing knowledge useful for the solution of practical problems, that the applications of new scientific findings are often broadly predictable, and that this is why control over scientific findings in some cases is financially valuable property. I think there is a case for keeping basic scientific knowledge open, even under these conditions. To privatize basic knowledge is a danger both for the advance of science, and for the advance of technology. I will develop my argument as follows.

Section 2 is concerned with how technological advance draws from science. I have already tipped my hand. Without denying the role of serendipity, I will argue that for the most part science is valuable as an input to technological change these days because much of scientific research is in fields that are oriented to providing knowledge that is of use in particular areas. These are the scientific fields that Donald Stokes (1996) saw, as in 'Pasteur's quadrant', where the research aims for deep understanding, but the field itself is oriented towards achieving practical objectives, like improving health, or achieving better understanding of the properties of materials, or achieving a powerful theory of computing. I acknowledge that this is a somewhat more expansive view of what science is than that contained in earlier characterizations of a 'Republic of Science'. But in fact a large fraction of what is well recognized as science always has been undertaken with practical objectives in mind or not far out of mind. Stokes' example of Pasteur is apt. And this fact is vital to keep in mind when trying to understand how science operates, and the controversy this paper is about.

In Section 3 I discuss the rise and erosion of the idea that public support of open science is warranted because the expected returns are high but the areas of return are so uncertain that market mechanisms will not suffice. I begin by briefly reviewing the ideological and political debates that occurred after World War II that led to a broad consensus regarding the value of public support of open autonomous science. As I noted, that rhetoric stressed that the payoffs from science were almost completely unpredictable, and thus the allocation of funds to science should not be influenced by perceptions of social needs. The publicly supported science system that actually developed was in fact much more oriented to facilitating progress on important practical problems than the rhetoric allowed, and this is now obvious.

I do not want to argue that most academic researchers working in, for example, the biomedical sciences, define their goals as dealing with particular diseases. Much of the most important work in such fields is quite fundamental in nature, in the sense that it explores basic processes and phenomena, without a clearly defined specific practical objective in mind. However, the fundamental questions and appealing lines of research in sciences in Pasteur's quadrant are strongly influenced by perceptions of what kind of knowledge is relevant to problem solving in a field. Thus one of the reasons why cell biology is now such a fashionable field is belief that basic understanding won here might just unlock the cancer puzzle, or enable us to understand better how receptors work.

This perception of how the modern science system actually works has eroded the notion that it is important to keep science open. My argument is that this is a serious mistake.

While perceptions of possible applications of research are not as vague as proposed in the earlier rhetoric about serendipity, the actual paths to the application of apparently promising scientific discoveries are in fact very uncertain. Understandings that come from science seldom lead immediately or directly to the solution of practical problems. Rather, they provide the knowledge and the tools to wrestle with them more effectively. I propose that for just this reason, that the findings of basic science set the stage for follow-on applications work, for society to get maximal benefit from its support of basic science requires that there be open access to scientific research results. Open access permits many potential inventors to work with new knowledge. Privatization closes off access to only those whom the owner allows to make use of it. This is why some of the recent developments are so worrisome.

In Section 4 I discuss the current situation and the dangers in more detail. Then I turn to a number of measures that I believe have some promise as attacks on the problem.

2 THE COEVOLUTION OF PRACTICE AND UNDERSTANDING

Virtually everybody these days appreciates that the power of modern technological innovation depends to a considerable extent on its ability to draw from modern science. But there is little general understanding, and some quite wrong beliefs, about the nature of the science-technology links. Understanding these correctly is a precondition, I believe, for having an effective discussion about what public policy towards science ought to be. This is certainly so regarding the current controversies about patenting in science. Thus this section discusses what scholars studying technological advance know about these issues.

Technologies need to be understood as involving both a body of practice, manifest in the artifacts and techniques that are produced and used, and a body of understanding, which supports, surrounds and rationalizes the former. For technologies that are well established, an important part of the body of understanding supporting practice is generally grounded in the empirical experience of practitioners regarding what works and what doesn't, things that sometimes go wrong, reliable problem solving methods, and so on. However in recent times, virtually all powerful technologies have strong connections with particular fields of science. These connections, of course, are central in the discussion of this essay.

There is a widespread belief that modern fields of technology are, in effect, applied science, in the sense that practice is directly drawn from scientific understanding, and that advancing technology is essentially a task of applying scientific knowledge to achieve better products and processes. This task requires scientific expertise, but in most cases is relatively routine once the target is specified. Indeed in his *Capitalism, Socialism, and Democracy*,

(1942) Schumpeter argued that by the mid-twentieth century that was largely the case, and the kind of competition among firms that had over the prior century made capitalism such a powerful engine of progress was no longer necessary. With strong science, technological advance could be planned. Schumpeter's views were in accord with those of many prominent scientists of his day, and today. Yet careful studies of how technological advance actually proceeds in this modern era clearly show that the process remains unplannable in any detail, and competitive exploration of multiple paths remains an essential part of it (see for example, Rosenberg, 1996, Nelson and Winter, 1982).

Virtually all empirically oriented scholarly accounts of how technology progresses have highlighted that the process is evolutionary in the following senses (see for example, Basalla, 1988, Constant, 1980, Dosi, 1988, Mokyr, 1990, Nelson and Winter, 1982, Petroski, 1992, Vincenti, 1990, Ziman, 2000). First, at any time there are generally a wide variety of efforts going on to improve prevailing technology, or to supersede it with something radically better. These efforts are generally in competition with each other, and with prevailing practice. And the winners and losers in this competition to a considerable extent are determined through an *ex-post* selection process. Second, today's efforts to advance a technology are informed to a considerable extent by, and take off from the successes and failures of earlier efforts. While there are occasional major leaps that radically transform best practice, for the most part technological advance is cumulative. And scholars of technological advance have also generally stressed that the advanced technologies of a given era are almost always the result of the work of many inventors and developers. Technological advance is a collective, cultural, evolutionary process.

The proposition that technological advance is an evolutionary process in the above sense in no way denies, or plays down, the often extremely powerful body of understanding and technique used to guide the efforts of those who seek to advance it, at least in modern times. A strong body of scientific understanding of a technology serves to enlarge and extend the area within which an inventor or problem solver can see relatively clearly and thus make informed judgements regarding what particular paths are promising as solutions, and which ones are likely to be dead ends. Also, the sciences and engineering disciplines provide powerful ways of experimenting and testing new departures, so that a person or organization who commands these can explore the merit of designs without going to full scale operational versions. Thus strong science enables the process of designing and inventing to be more productive and powerful than it would be were the science base weaker.

However, it does not change the fact that the process of advancing the technology remains evolutionary. Strong science provides tools for problem solving, but usually in itself does not solve practical problems. If anything, strong science increases the advantages to society of having many competent actors striving to improve the art.

The connections between the 'body of practice' aspect of a technology and the 'body of understanding' part need to be understood in this context. Virtually all modern technologies are supported by a strong body of science or science-like understanding that illuminates how the artifacts and techniques employed work, provides insight into the factors that constrain performance and provides clues as to promising pathways toward improvement. But at the same time, much of practice in most fields remains only partially understood, and much of engineering design practice involves solutions to problems that professional engineers have learned 'work', without any particularly sophisticated understanding of why. Medical scientists still lack good understanding of just why and how certain effective pharmaceuticals do their work, and theories about that can change from time to time.

Technological practice and understanding tend to co-evolve, with sometimes advance of understanding leading to effective efforts to improve practice, and sometimes advance in practice leading to effective efforts to advance understanding. Thus the germ theory of disease developed by Pasteur and Koch, by pointing clearly to a certain kind of cause, led to successful efforts to get certain diseases (now known to be caused by external living agents) under control. Maxwell's theory of electromagnetism led to Hertz, Marconi and radio. But in many cases advances in practice come first and lead to efforts to understand scientifically. Thus the discovery by Shockley and his team at Bell Laboratories that a semiconducting device they had built as an amplifier worked, but not in the way they had predicted, led him to understand that there was something wrong, or incomplete, about the theory in physics regarding the electrical characteristics of semiconductors, which in turn led to his own theoretical work, and a Nobel Prize. Rosenberg (1996) has argued that a number of the most challenging puzzles science has had to face have been made visible by or been created by new technologies, and the puzzles of why they work as they do.

Much of the development of modern science should be understood as the result of institutionalized responses to these challenges and opportunities. Quite often specialized fields of applied science or engineering developed out of the experience of more generally trained scientists working on the problems of a particular technology or industry. Thus the field of metallurgy came into existence as chemists worked on problems of quality control in the rapidly growing steel industry (Rosenberg, 1998). As the industries producing chemical products expanded, chemical engineering developed as a field of research, as well as teaching. The physics of mechanical forces had long been useful for civil engineers designing buildings and bridges.

But with the new physics of electricity and magnetism, a whole new set of science-based industries was launched. As complex electrical 'systems' came into place, the new field of electrical engineering grew up. Later on, the invention of the modern computer would spawn the field of computer science. Stronger knowledge in chemistry and biology led to the development of a collection of specialized fields involved in agricultural research. Fields like pathology, immunology and cardiology, grew up for teaching and research at medical schools.

All of these fields of science are in 'Pasteur's quadrant'. Research done here often probes for quite deep understanding. But the field as a whole, and broad programmes of research in the field, are dedicated quite explicitly to solving particular kinds of practical problems, and advancing bodies of practical technology. I have developed this story at considerable length because in much of the writings on science, and the institutions governing science, these applied sciences tend to be ignored. However, in the United States, Western Europe and Japan, they account for the lion's share of the resources going into the support of science.

Popper (1989), Campbell (1974), Ziman (1978), Kitcher (1993) and other scholars of the advancement of science have stressed that science is a system of knowledge. The test that guides whether new reported findings or theories are accepted into the corpus of accepted knowledge is 'Is it valid? Is it true?'. Popper and his followers have argued that there can be no firm positive answer to that question. Ability to stand up under attempts at refutation, or (probably more commonly) for apparent implications to hold up when they are explored, may be the best humans can do. But in any case, from this philosophical perspective, the quest in science is for understanding in its own right. And there certainly is a lot of truth to this position as a characterization of the nature of scientific debates.

On the other hand, as Vincenti and others who have reflected on the similarities and differences between technological and scientific knowledge have argued, the central test for technological knowledge is 'is it useful?' Technological knowledge is part of a cultural system that is concerned with achieving practical ends, rather than knowledge for its own sake. The objective is to get something that works, or works better, and 'understanding' is important only in so far as it helps in that effort.

However, the selection criteria for new science and for new technology cannot be kept sharply separate for sciences in Pasteur's quadrant. In these fields, an important and often stringent testing ground for science is provided by those who think they see how it might be applied in practice. And failure to understand why something works is a strong motivation for scientific research.

By far the lion's share of modern scientific research, including research done at universities, is in fields where practical application is central in the definition of a field. And, not surprisingly, these are the fields on which efforts to advance technology mostly draw. Two recent surveys (Klevorick, Levin, Nelson and Winter, 1995, Cohen, Nelson and Walsh, 2002) have asked industrial R&D executives to identify the fields of academic research that contributed most to their successes in R&D. The fields they listed were exactly those discussed above.

The most recent of these studies (Cohen, Nelson and Walsh, 2002) also asked about the kind of research output that was most valuable to industry, and the most important pathways through which industry gained access. Contrary to much of the current discussion, prototype technologies were not rated an important output of academic research for most industries (biotechnology is an exception), but rather general research results and research techniques (and even in biotechnology these kinds of research outputs were rated as useful much more often than prototypes). Relatedly, in most industries the respondents reported that the most frequent use of university research results was in problem solving in projects, rather than in triggering the initiation of projects.

In most industries the respondents said that the most important pathway through which people in industry learned of and gained access to what was coming out of public research was through publications and open conferences. Put another way, today industry gets most of its benefit from academic science through open channels. In their more narrowly focused but more detailed study of the pathways through which research results of the MIT departments of mechanical and electrical engineering get to industry, Agrawal and Henderson (2002) arrive at a similar conclusion.

I want to conclude this section by again stressing that in all the fields of technology that have been studied in any detail, including those where the background science is very strong, technological advance remains an evolutionary process. Strong science makes that process more powerful, but does not reduce the great advantages of having multiple paths explored by a number of different actors. From this perspective, the fact that most of scientific knowledge is open, and available through open channels, is extremely important. This enables there to be at any time a significant number of individuals and firms who possess and can use the scientific knowledge they need in order to compete intelligently in this evolutionary process. The 'communitarianism' of scientific knowledge is an important factor contributing to its productivity in downstream efforts to advance technology.

3 THE GOVERNANCE OF PUBLIC SCIENCE

World War II and the period just after marked something of a watershed in broad public and political recognition of the important role that public science plays in technological progress, particularly in the United States and the United Kingdom. To be sure, much earlier visionaries like Francis Bacon had argued for support of science as a means through which societies could progress materially. Scholars like Don Price (1962), David Hart (1998) and David Guston (2000) have described the earlier history of debate about science policy in the US. But it was the World War II experience, where government supported and focused R&D was so successful both in the development of weapons that won the war, and in the development of medical capabilities that greatly reduced casualties both from wounds and from infectious diseases compared with earlier wartime experiences, that gripped the public attention. The title of the Vannevar Bush report (1945) advocating a major postwar programme in the United States of support of science caught the spirit: *Science, the Endless Frontier*.

In both the US and the UK the discussion about the appropriate postwar role of public science was structured and constrained, for the most part, by recognition of the central role of companies with their own R&D capabilities in the process of technological advance; the point of view there was implicitly Schumpeterian. While there were exceptions, the discussion was not about contesting that role. Rather, the focus was on the system of public science, done in universities and public laboratories, that was separate from the corporate system but strongly complementary, and which needed public support. The argument of those who advocated stronger government support was that this would make the overall system of innovation more powerful.

In both the UK and the US the debate about the governance of public science squared off along much the same lines. In the UK, J.D. Bernal, a distinguished physicist and a socialist, argued (1939) for a government programme in which the allocation of public funds to science would be strongly guided by the weighing of social needs, and the support programme as a whole would be closely monitored by the government. To this point of view Michael Polanyi, a distinguished philosopher of science, took strong exception, advocating a largely self-governing 'Republic of Science' (1962), which would be publicly funded, but in which the scientific community itself would set priorities and decide on what was good science.

In the US, Vannevar Bush's manifesto *Science, the Endless Frontier* argued strongly for a self governing scientific community, but with national priorities playing a role in setting broad research directions, at least in certain areas. In particular, national security and health were singled out as areas where the overall research budget and broad research priorities needed to be made through political and governmental processes. But given the funding within those broad areas, the scientists themselves were to have basic discretion for devising the research programmes they thought most appropriate. Government non-scientists were not to meddle in this. Regarding the role of public science in supporting economic progress more broadly, Bush saw the government's role as supporting basic research, with the science system self-governing, both with respect to identification of the broad fields of greatest promise, and the details of allocating funds and carrying out research.

There is no question but that, like Polanyi's response to Bernal, Bush's articulation of a basically self-governing community of science was put forth in good part to counter, to block, proposals for a postwar publicly supported science system that would involve much more political and government control of the allocation of resources. Senator Harley Kilgore took much the same position, as did J. D. Bernal in the United Kingdom. Bush believed that this would destroy the creativity and power of science, and it would be far better to have the top scientists running the show.

There is also no question but that Polanyi and Bush felt it of extreme importance that government support fields like theoretical physics and mathematics, where perceptions of potential practical payoff have little to do with the way the fields unfold, yet which provided important knowledge and techniques that helped to win the war. Hence the emphasis on serendipity, and the unpredictability of areas of potential payoff. It is almost certain that both men knew well that much of scientific research was not of this kind, but rather was in fields where perceptions of practical problems played a significant role in defining the broad agenda, if not the short run priorities of resource allocation. However, the rhetoric of Polanyi and Bush obscured the fact that most of science is in Pasteur's quadrant.

It is not surprising therefore, that in both the United States and Great Britain it turned out that mission-oriented agencies became the primary government supporters of basic research. Thus in the United States the Department of Defense funded basic work in computer and materials science, and in electrical engineering. The Atomic Energy Commission (later the Department of Energy) has had principal responsibility for funding high energy physics. The National Institutes of Health became the primary funder of university research in the biomedical sciences. The National Science Foundation, the only significant research funding agency in the US without a mission other than support of science, has always been a small supporter relative to the mission-oriented agencies. The lion's share of the research done in the United States, funded by government and undertaken in universities and public laboratories, is in fields in Pasteur's quadrant.

This fact both removes the puzzle of why science has contributed so much to technological advance, and enables one to understand better why Vannevar Bush (and most of his science trained followers writing about science policy) had such strong faith in the ability of the scientific community to steer their efforts in socially productive directions. But this recognition also signals that the lines between basic science and applied science are fuzzy, not sharp, and it raises the question of where the publicly supported Republic of Science ought to leave off, and the market begin. It is fair to say that for the most part the postwar debates were somewhat *ad hoc* about this. Thus Bush recognized a central role for market organized and induced R&D, and saw public science as providing inputs to that market system, but being separate. But he provided little in the way of coherent argument about where the one stopped and the other began. Indeed, despite its obvious importance, outside of economics, this question has aroused little analytical interest.

Economists have grappled with the question of the appropriate spheres of government activity in the science and technology system using two theoretical concepts: externalities and public goods. The externalities concept is about benefits (and costs) of private economic activity that those who make the relevant decisions do not see as benefits (or costs) to them. Here economists have highlighted the 'spillovers' from industrial R&D: information and capabilities created by a firm's efforts to create better products and processes that it cannot fully capture, and hence which benefit other firms, including competitors. In general the analyses by economists oriented towards the externalities from R&D have not served as a base for arguments for a domain of public science, but rather for arguments that industrial R&D in some instances should be encouraged by favourable tax treatment, and perhaps subsidies of various kinds to reduce private costs. Indeed, the policy discussion proceeding under the conception that research yields externalities naturally tends to be pulled towards devising policies that will make the results of R&D more proprietary, less public. An important part of the current policy discussion is in fact oriented in just this way.

The public good concept of economists is much more directly relevant to analysis of the appropriate domain of public science, or at least the range where 'communalism of knowledge' should apply. For our purposes here, the most salient aspect of the economists' public good concept is that a public good is 'non-rivalrous in use'. By that it is meant that, unlike a standard economic good, such as a peanut butter sandwich, which either you or I can eat but not both (although we can split it), a public good can be used by all of us at the same time without eroding the quality for any of us.

Knowledge is a canonical case of something that is non-rivalrous in use in this sense, and this is not a proposition conjured up by economists. The notion that I can tell you what I know, and then you will know it, and I will too, has almost surely been widely understood by sophisticated persons for a long time. There is no 'tragedy of the commons' for a pure public good like knowledge. And to deny access, or to ration it, can result in those denied doing far less well than they could if they had access. In the case in point, if access to certain bodies of scientific knowledge or technique can be withheld from certain researchers, they may be effectively barred from doing productive R&D in a field.

Now the fact that something is non-rivalrous in use does not mean that its use cannot be restricted. However, until relatively recently it was broadly assumed that it was difficult to restrict access to scientific knowledge. Certainly scientific knowledge could not be patented. This effectively took science outside the domain where market incentives could work. Indeed the presumption that the returns to scientific research could not be appropriated was a central part of the argument why public funding was necessary.

However, over the last quarter of a century there have been two key developments that have challenged this view of basic science. First, the courts have ruled that at least some of the results of basic research can be patented. And about the same time that the implications of these rulings were becoming evident, Congress passed the Bayh-Dole Act of 1980, which strongly encouraged universities to take out patents on their research results where they could, on the basis of a (not well supported) argument that this would facilitate firms who could make practical use of the results to do so under a protective licence (for a detailed account, see Eisenberg, 1996). The first of these developments significantly increased the incentives for for-profit firms to engage in the areas of basic research where the results can be patented, and to try to make their living licensing patented research results to other firms that can make use of them. The second has brought about profound changes in the way universities give access to their research results. As a result, important areas of science are now much more under the sway of market mechanisms than used to be the case. And in particular, in some important fields of science important bodies of scientific understanding and technique are now private property rather than part of the commons.

A widespread reaction is 'So what is the problem with that?' There is a strong presumption these days that if market organization can and will do a job, that is obviously a good thing. From this point of view, the main argument that needs to be made for government support of basic research is that the long run benefits to the society are high, and that for-profit firms have little incentive to do much of it because of the difficulties in establishing property rights, and the long time lags and uncertainties involved in moving from research results to commercial product. If these barriers to market organization are lowered for some reason, let the market move in.

I note that knowledge of an effective product design or a production process, what is customarily considered as technological knowledge, shares with scientific knowledge the property of being non-rivalrous in use. Yet society relies largely on the market to induce R&D aimed at creating new products and production processes, and there is little dispute that granting patents on product and process inventions is reasonable social and economic policy. So why not allow patents on the stuff of basic science, if that will induce the market to move in?

My response is that the outputs of scientific research are almost never themselves final products, or even close, but have their principal use in further research, some of it aimed to advance the science farther, some to follow leads that may enable a useful product or process to be found and developed. But in both cases, the latter as well as the former, there is considerable uncertainty about the best paths to pursue. Progress calls for a number to be explored. My concern is not with patents on the outputs of scientific research that are directly useful or close to that, so long as the scope of the patent is limited to that particular use. It is about not hindering the ability of the scientific community, both that part interested in advancing the science farther, and that part interested in trying to use knowledge in the search for useful products, to work freely with and from new scientific findings.

I do not know of a field of science where knowledge has increased cumulatively and, through cumulative advance, dramatically, that has not been basically open. It is easy to argue that scientists have never fully followed the canons of science identified and laid out by Robert Merton: universalism, communitarianism, disinterestedness and organized scepticism. Scientists are well known to keep their work secret until they are ready to publish. There is certainly a lot of self interest, opportunism, hostility and downright deviousness and lying that one observes in the histories of the progressive sciences. A scientific paradigm held by the élite in a field can hold intellectual tyranny. It is valuable to bring new organizations into the basic research scene, and in some cases for-profit business firms have explored paths that the academic community snubbed.

But on the other hand, a careful reading of important scientific controversies, for example the argument about the nature of combustion at the start of the 19th century, or of the nature of the genetic code, or of whether the expansion of the universe is decelerating or accelerating, shows the importance and the power of a public science system where by and large all participants have access to much the same facts, and the debates about whether new proposed facts or theories are valid are open to all working in a field. One cannot come away from reading Horace Judson's *The Eighth Day of Creation* (1996), a history of the development of molecular biology as a field of science, without respecting the power of open science to progress.

This is equally true for sciences that are strongly in 'Pasteur's quadrant'. Roy Porter's history of medical knowledge and practice, *The Greatest Benefit to Mankind* (1997) gives case after case where progress was made through a system where researchers were free to try to replicate or refute the arguments and findings of others.

While my argument above has focused on the advantages of an open science for the advancement of science, much of my discussion in Section 2 was concerned with considering why open science is important to technological progress. These arguments of course are mutually reinforcing. Keeping the body of scientific knowledge largely open for all to use, in the attempts to advance science, and in the attempts to advance technology, is in my view an extremely important matter. Its importance is not recognized adequately in the current discussions.

I want to conclude this section by putting forth three views on what should be done about the encroachment of proprietary property claims into what had been the domain of public science. The first option is to cede the contested turf. If research findings can be patented, accept and embrace that. If universities can patent their results and limit access to the highest bidder, fine. And welcome the presence of private firms motivated to do research by the lure of patents and control of subsequent work in a field, or royalty incomes. Indeed, these developments diminish or even eliminate the need for public funding of certain fields of science.

The second is to coexist and compete on the contested terrain. This is pretty much the policy that developed regarding research on the human genome. The argument here is that publicly supported research, and keeping open the results of that research, provide useful competition to private research, even if some private firms do not like the competition (Eisenberg and Nelson, 2002).

A third position is to resist and try to roll back the invasion of privatization. This point of view sees that invasion not only as probably undesirable, but also as something that is occurring under a given set of policies, which can be changed. Thus if the movement of patentability upstream into the sciences, together with the expectations under the Bayh-Dole Act, are leading to for-profit companies engaging in research to identify the genetic code, and to the patenting of that code by them and by universities operating under public funding, maybe patent law and practice, and Bayh-Dole, need to be revised.

Above I have given my reasons for rejecting the first position. My position on this is a combination of the second and third. I believe it important to preserve as much of the commons as possible. However, doing so will not be easy.

4 THE IMPORTANCE OF PROTECTING THE SCIENTIFIC COMMONS

The major expansion of patents into what used to be the realm of science is well documented. I am persuaded that there is enough of a potential problem here to call the alarm. However, I confess that the evidence that there is already a problem, that access to scientific research results having high promise of enabling the solution of important practical problems is being sharply limited by patent holders, is presently very limited. The most detailed study is by Walsh, Arora and Cohen (2002). This study involved interviews with a number of researchers in the biomedical field, asking whether their research had been hindered by patent rights that blocked access to certain paths they wanted to explore.

Scholars studying this potential problem have identified at least two different kinds of situations where the presence of patents can hinder research (for a general discussion, see Merges and Nelson, 1990). One of these is the problem caused by patents on 'research tools' (see National Research Council, 1997) where research techniques of widespread use in a field, materials that are inputs to a wide range of research endeavours or key pathways for research (like the use of a particular receptor), are patented, and the patent holder aggressively prosecutes unlicensed use or reserves exclusive rights to further research using the tool. The second, highlighted recently by Heller and Eisenberg (1998) is focused on contexts where development of or advance towards a useful product or technique may involve transgressing on several patents held by different parties.

The Walsh, Arora and Cohen interviews and case studies found that the latter problem, that of the need to assemble a large number of permissions or licences before being able to go forward, was not yet particularly important. Regarding research tools, a number of the more important general purpose ones are available to all who will pay the price, and while in some cases there were complaints about the price, at least they were available.

On the other hand, the study did identify a number of instances where the holder of a patent on an input or a pathway (for example a receptor) that was important in a particular field of exploration did not widely license, and in some cases sought to preserve a monopoly on use rights. It is clear that in a number of the cases, the patented finding had been achieved through research at least partially funded by the government. This policy may well have been reasonable from the point of view of the patent holders, but the burden of this paper is that it is not good from the point of view of society, seeking to maximize the benefits of publicly funded research.

The authors of the study take a cautious position regarding the implications of their findings. I find them sufficient evidence to indicate that there is a real problem here, or there will be soon, and it is time to think about what can be done to contain it.

There are two broad policy arenas that bear on this issue, to which I want to call attention here. One is intellectual property rights law. The second is the policies of universities and public laboratories regarding their research findings, and government policy regarding the university research it funds. My discussion below is oriented to what is needed, in my view at least, to preserve an appropriately wide area of public scientific knowledge.

4.1 Can we protect the Republic of Science through Patent Law?

I find that many people are puzzled when they learn that patents are being taken out on genes or gene codes, or more generally are intruding into the realm of science. There is a widespread belief that scientific facts or principles or natural phenomena are not patentable. Indeed, the courts have endorsed this position strongly, as a general philosophical principle. But the problem is that the lines between natural substances and principles and man-made ones are blurry not sharp. Nearly a century ago a landmark patent law case was concerned with whether purified human adrenalin was a natural substance and hence not patentable (although the process for purification certainly was patentable) or whether the fact that adrenalin never was pure in its natural state meant that the purified substance was man-made and hence patentable. The decision was the latter, and while it can be argued that the decision was unfortunate, one can certainly see the logic supporting it. In any case, the precedent set here has held through the years (*Parke-Davis & Co. v. H. K. Mulford & Co.*, 1911). Recent patents on purified proteins and isolated genes and receptors are couched in terms that highlight something that man has created or modified from its natural state.

A recent article by Bar-Shalom and Robert Cook-Deegan (2002) is concerned with the consequences of a patent granted on a monoclonal antibody (antibodies are natural substances, but particular antibodies cloned by a particular process have been judged not to be natural) which binds to a particular antigen (a natural substance) on the outer surface of stem cells, and hence is capable of recognizing such cells and serving as a basis for processes that would isolate stem cells. The patent also claimed 'other antibodies' that can recognize and pick out that antigen. The latter part of the claim in effect establishes ownership of the antigen. The authors argue, correctly in my view, that the inclusion in the patent claims of all 'other antibodies' meant that the patent was unreasonably broad and should have been pruned back by the patent office and the courts. However, one can clearly see the blurry lines here between the natural and the artificial. And the patentee could well argue that the 'invention' was a method of recognizing a particular antigen (such a method would seem to fall within the bounds of patentability) and the particular antibody actually used was just an exemplar. In the case in question this patent was licensed exclusively to a particular company and, in turn, later used effectively to close down another company that had achieved a process capable of isolating stem cells earlier than the licensee using a method judged to infringe the patent.

Setting aside the issue of undue patent scope for the moment, the problem of determining the patentability of a research output whose future use is largely in further research seems almost inevitable for research in Pasteur's quadrant, for obvious reasons. The original work in question was done by an oncologist at Johns Hopkins University. The research was clearly fundamental, and at the same time was aiming for understandings and techniques that would be useful in dealing with cancer.

The problem becomes even more complicated in scientific fields that are concerned with advancing understandings of technologies, fields like computer science and aeronautical engineering. Thus Walter Vincenti (1990) describes at some length the research done at Stanford during the 1920s that aimed to develop good engineering principles (reliable if rough 'laws') that would guide the design of aircraft propellers. The results of this research were laid open to the general aviation design community and were not patented. But had the researchers had the motivation, they could probably have posed their results in terms of processes useful in propeller design, which might have been patentable then, and are likely to be today. A significant portion of the work within the modern field of computer science is concerned with developing concepts and principles that can help improve design. Until recently at least, little of this work seems to have been patented, but a portion of it clearly could be.

In each of these cases, the research outputs were (are) at once important inputs to a flow of future research, and useful inputs for those who are focused on solving practical problems. In much of this paper I have been arguing that, because of the latter, there are major general economic advantages if those understandings and techniques are part of the general toolkit available to all those working to advance practice in the area. The obvious objection is that the ability of the discoverer or developer of these understandings and techniques to control their use is an important incentive for the research that creates them. I would reply that, at least in the case of research at universities, funded by a government grant, this is usually not the case. I will discuss university policy shortly.

But to return to the present discussion, I am not optimistic about how much of the problem can be dealt with by patent law. The focus here is on patent law on research outputs that provide tools for advancing a science or technology, as contrasted with a final product or process *per se*. Here one can urge several things of the patent office and the courts. But the problem of innately blurry lines will remain.

First, one can urge more care not to grant patents on discoveries that are largely of natural phenomena, by requiring a strong case that the subject matter of the patent application or patent is 'artificial', and by limiting the scope of the patent to elements that are artificial (more on the patent scope problem shortly). Demaine and Fellmeth make a similar argument (2003) that patents should be allowed only on outputs of research that are a 'substantial transformation' from the natural. The lines here are blurry. But the slope is clearly slippery and a strong argument can be made that the dividing line has been let slip too far, and leaning hard in the other direction is warranted. In the case of purified natural substances, this would call for a greater proclivity to limit the patent to the process and not allow the purified product *per se* to be patented.

Second, one can urge a relatively strict interpretation of the meaning of 'utility' or usefulness. This issue is particularly important for patent applications and patents that argue very broadly that the research result in question can be useful in efforts to achieve something obviously useful – a case for usefulness once removed. But the problem here is that the direct usefulness is then as an input or a focus of research, and this is the kind of generic knowledge and capability which I have been arguing is important to keep open and in the public domain. A stricter interpretation here would require more compelling demonstration of significant progress towards a particular practical solution than seems presently required, and particularly if combined with the suggestion below about reining in patent scope, would be a major contribution to protecting the commons.

Third, there is the issue of the allowed patent scope. There is a strong tendency of patent applicants to claim practice far wider than they have actually achieved. The claim described above covering 'all antibodies' that identify a particular substance is a case in point. While there are obvious advantages to the patentee of being able to control a wide range of possible substitutes to what has actually been achieved, there are great advantages to society as a whole in not allowing such broad blocking of potential competitive efforts. I believe that getting the patent office and the courts to understand the real economic costs of granting too broad patents is of the highest priority.

I have argued the special importance of not allowing patents to interfere with broad participation in research going on in a field. One way to further this objective would be to build some kind of explicit research exemption, analogous to the fair use exemptions in copyright law, into patent law. Indeed there is a long history of statements by judges to the effect that use in pure research is not a violation of a patent. Universities have clearly been clinging to this theory to justify their freedom of research.

A recent decision of the US Federal Circuit (*Madey v. Duke*, Oct. 2002) has changed the situation. In a ruling on an infringement suit against Duke University, the court argued that doing research, basic or applied, was part of the central business of a university, and that the university benefited in terms of funding as well as prestige from the research it did. Thus university interests, not simply scientific curiosity, were at stake in the research. Therefore, it was quite reasonable under the law for a patent holder to require that the university take out a licence before using patented material in research. After this ruling, it is highly likely that patent holders will act more aggressively when they believe that university researchers may be infringing their patents. While there is a chance that the Supreme Court will reverse this, it is not a good bet. It now looks as if an exemption for use in basic research will come into place only if there is new law.

However, under current university policies, a case for such new law is not easy to make. Among other things, there is clearly a problem of how to delineate basic research. As I have been highlighting, much of university research is in Pasteur's quadrant, where in many cases there are practical objectives as well as the goal of advancing basic understanding. And in recent years universities have been patenting their research results.

Discussions with industry executives suggest that, until recently, industry often gave university researchers a *de facto* research exemption. However, they are often now very reluctant to do so. In many cases they see university researchers as direct competitors to their own research efforts aimed to achieve a practical result which is patentable. And they feel themselves burdened by the requirement to take out licences to use university research results that are patented, and see no reason why they shouldn't make the same demands on universities. In my view, the obstacles to a serious research exemption are largely the result of university policies.

Of the several proposals for a research exemption that have circulated recently, I find one of the most interesting to be that put forth by Rochelle Dreyfuss (2002). In what follows, I amend it slightly. Under the proposal a university or non-profit research organization (under one version of her proposal, any research organization) would be immune from prosecution for using patented materials in research if i) those materials were not available on reasonable terms (this is my amendment), and ii) if the university or other research organization agreed not to patent anything that came out of the research, (or if they did patent to allow use on a non-exclusive royalty-free basis – my amendment). Certainly there could be some difficulty in determining, if the matter was brought up, whether or not the patented material was available on reasonable terms, or just what 'reasonable' means, but in many of the most problematic cases which this proposal is designed to fix, the answer is that they are not available at all. In some cases it would not be easy to determine whether a patent emanated from a particular research project or from some other activity. But these problems do not seem unusually difficult compared with other matters often litigated. And it is likely that, for the most part, if a research organization proceeded under this law, there wouldn't be much litigation, and there would be much reduced fear of such.

After the Duke decision, the road to a university research exemption must almost surely go through Congress. The advantage of a proposal like that of Dreyfus is that it would trade open access to research results for university researchers for agreement of university researchers not themselves to add to the problem of patents in science. The principal obstacle to such a deal I believe is the universities themselves.

4.2 Will Universities Come to the Defence of the Scientific Commons?

I believe that the key to assuring that a large portion of what comes out of future scientific research will be placed in the commons is staunch defence of the commons by universities. Universities will almost certainly continue to do the bulk of basic scientific research. If they have policies of laying their research results largely open, most of science will continue to be in the commons. However, universities are not in general supporting the idea of a scientific commons, except in terms of their own rights to do research. In the era since Bayh-Dole, universities have become a major part of the problem, avidly defending their rights to patent their research results, and license as they choose.

Derek Bok (2003) has argued persuasively that the strong interest of universities in patenting is part and parcel of trends that have led universities to embrace commercial activities in a variety of areas, for example athletics as well as science. Earlier I proposed that Bayh-Dole, and the enhanced interest of universities in patenting, should be regarded as one aspect of a broad increased public acceptance of the importance of intellectual property rights. But these factors do not make the problem any less significant, only harder to deal with.

I note that the current zeal of universities for patenting represents a major shift from the universities' traditional support of open science. This does not mean that traditionally university research was largely distanced from practical applications. There have long been many university research programmes designed to contribute to economic development (see Rosenberg and Nelson, 1994, Mowery and Rosenberg, 1989). Since the late 19th century, university research has played a major role in the development of American agricultural technology. The hybrid seed revolution which was key to the dramatic increases in productivity made during the half century after 1930 in corn and other grain production was made possible by work at agricultural experimentation stations that explored basic concepts and techniques of hybridization. These basic techniques were made public knowledge. Universities also made available on generous terms the pure lines of seeds they developed to serve as the basis for commercial efforts to design and produce hybrids. University-based research on plant nutrition and plant diseases and pests helped companies identify and design effective fertilizers and insecticides. Very little of this university research was patented.

American engineering schools and departments have had a long tradition of doing research to help industry. As noted earlier, chemical and electrical engineering were developed as scientific fields largely within universities. Earlier I recounted Stanford's role in developing the principles of propeller design. Several universities played key roles in developing the early electronic computers. There was some patenting of devices that came out of university engineering research, but also an apparent continuing commitment to contribute to the advance of basic engineering understanding as the common property of the professions.

American medical schools have also long been contributors to technical advance in medicine and the enhanced ability of doctors to deal with human illness. Medical schools have occasionally been the sources of particular new medical devices and new pharmaceuticals, although this was not common prior to the rise of biotechnology and modern electronics. And while patents were sometimes taken out on particular products (streptomycin, identified by a team led by a Rutgers university scientist, is a good example) by and large until the 1980s there was little patenting, and many medical schools had an articulated policy of dedicating research results to the public commons.

The sea change, or the schizophrenia, began to emerge as a result of several developments (see Mowery *et al.*, 2001). First, during the 1970s and 1980s there was a broad general ideological change in the United States in attitudes towards patents, from general hostility in the 1930s and the early postwar years, to a belief that patents were almost always necessary to stimulate invention and innovation. Actually, several empirical studies provide evidence that in many industries patents are relatively unimportant as a stimulus to R&D (see Cohen *et al.*, 2000). However, much of the argument for Bayh-Dole concentrated on pharmaceuticals, and patent protection was and continues to be important for pharmaceutical companies.

There was, secondly, the rise of molecular biology as a field of science and the development of the principal techniques of biotechnology, which for a variety of reasons made university biomedical research a much more likely locus of work leading to pharmaceuticals or potential pharmaceuticals, and of techniques that could be used in such work. Third, as noted, several key court decisions made many of these developments patentable. The apparent possibility of substantial income from university research clearly attracted some university officials and scientists. The patenting of the Cohen-Boyer gene splicing process, and the quick flow of substantial revenues to the two universities that held the rights, provided a strong signal that there was now substantial money that could be brought in from licensing university inventions.

The Cohen-Boyer patent was granted prior to the passage of Bayh-Dole. Bayh-Dole legitimated, even warranted, university patenting. And universities have not been slow in adopting policies where patenting anything that can be patented is the rule.

In my view, there is nothing wrong *per se* with universities patenting what they can from their research output. In some cases such patenting may actually facilitate technology transfer, although in many cases it is a good bet that technological transfer is not enhanced but rather the university is simply earning money from what it used to make available for free (see the case studies in Colyvas *et al.*, 2002). The cases that worry me are the ones where the university is licensing exclusively or narrowly a development that is potentially of wide use; also, where it is limiting the right to take a particular development further to one or a few companies in circumstances where there is still sufficient uncertainty regarding how best to proceed to make participation by a number of companies in that endeavour socially desirable. The argument that if an exclusive licence is not given, no one will try to advance, seems particularly dubious for research tools of wide application, or for findings that appear to open up possibilities for new research attacks on diseases where a successful remedy would clearly find a large market. Thus the Cohen-Boyer patent was licensed to all comers, and there were plenty of them. The report by Colyvas *et al.* (2002) gives several examples showing the willingness of pharmaceutical companies to work from university research findings that appeared to point towards promising treatments, without receiving an exclusive licence.

I do not see a major problem if access to certain parts of the commons requires a small fee. What I want to see happen is that universities recognize that for research results of these sorts, if they patent them, they have an obligation to license them to all who want to use them at reasonable fees. (Similarly, with respect to 'research tools' created by industry research and patented, my difficulty is not so much with those where use is open but users are charged a fee, provided the fee is not too high, but with those that are not made widely available.) Bok (2003, p 143), recognizing the problem I am discussing here, proposes that the major universities come to an agreement to license widely and easily, and not grant exclusive licences to research results that are basically inputs to further research. However, a policy of open licensing of research results of certain kinds is not likely to be adopted voluntarily by universities, because this practice will not always be seen as maximizing expected revenues from intellectual property. And that is what many universities are aiming for now.

The recent report signed jointly by a number of university presidents, chancellors and foundation presidents (Atkinson *et al.*, 2003) shows the tension here. The authors (focusing on the field of agricultural research) clearly recognize the problem that can, and has, been caused by university patents that block or cause high transaction costs for downstream research to advance agricultural technologies, and announce the establishment of a 'Public Sector Intellectual Property Resource for Agriculture' which would make access easier. But the authors stop far short of agreeing to a general policy of open licensing of university research results that can set the stage for downstream applied R&D.

Universities will not give up the right to earn as much as they can from the patents they hold unless public policy pushes them hard in that direction. I see the key as reforming Bayh-Dole. The objective here, it seems to me, is not to eliminate university patenting, but to establish a presumption that university research results, patented or not, should as a general rule be made available to all who want to use them at very low transaction costs, and reasonable financial costs. This would not be to foreclose exclusive or narrow licensing in those circumstances where this is necessary to gain effective technology transfer. Rather, it would be to establish the presumption that such cases are the exception rather than the rule.

I note that there is nothing in Bayh-Dole that explicitly encourages exclusive or narrow licensing, but nothing discourages it either, and the rhetoric associated with the legislation pushed the theory that generally dedicating research results to the public commons did not encourage use. There is nothing in the legislation that says universities should use their patenting and licensing powers to maximize university income, but there is little in the language that discourages that. What is needed, I believe, is language that recognizes much better than the current language that much of what comes out of university research is most effectively disseminated to users if placed in the public domain, and that exclusive or restricted licensing may deter widespread use at considerable economic and social cost.

The Act as currently written does include the clause stating that the objective of the act is : 'to ensure that inventions made by nonprofit organizations ... are used in a manner to promote free competition and enterprise without unduly encumbering future research and discovery'. However, apparently this clause has no teeth at present. My proposal is that this statement of objective be highlighted and supplemented by the proposition that in general this objective calls for licensing that will achieve the widest possible use. Exclusive or narrow licensing by a university should require an explicit rationale. Willingness of firms to take up university research results without an exclusive license should be regarded as evidence that an exclusive license is not appropriate.

Such language would encourage universities to move in the right direction on their own, by strengthening the hand of those who believe that universities should be contributing to the scientific and technological commons. At the present time, such university researchers and administrators seem to be bucking the law as well as internal interests. It would also provide legitimacy to government agencies funding university research to press for licensing that gives broad access. The recent tussle between the National Institutes of Health (NIH) and the University of Wisconsin regarding stem cell patents illustrates the value of such an amended Bayh-Dole. In this case, the university originally had in mind arranging an exclusive licence for a firm, and that would have been very profitable for the university. The NIH in effect indicated that unless the university licensed widely and liberally, it would consider their licensing policies when evaluating research proposals. The university then went along with the licence policies advocated by the NIH. Several legal scholars have proposed that, under the current law, the NIH in this case was skating on thin ice. There is nothing in the law that explicitly calls for open licensing. And had the NIH been forced to follow its bark with a bite, they might well have been taken to court. Rai and Eisenberg (2001) make a similar argument for amendment of Bayh-Dole.

Or consider how the case analysed by Bar-Shalom and Cook-Deegan (2002) (see section 4.1) might have gone had the amendment I am proposing been in place. It is likely that the NIH recognized quite early in the game the value of allowing more than one company to work with the new technique for identifying stem cells, and of having widespread research use allowed, and would have balked at the exclusive licence that was given had it felt itself on a firm footing for doing so. Later in the game the NIH was asked to open use of the patented technique, under the 'march in' provisions of Bayh-Dole, but did not do so because according to the way the legislation is written such a step clearly is exceptional. It would have been in a far stronger position to accede to the request to open up use if the language I propose were in the legislation.

Many university administrators and researchers would certainly resist such an amendment, on the grounds that it would diminish their ability to maximize financial returns from their patent portfolio. As I observed above, the principal support for university patenting with freedom to license as they wish now comes from universities and is based on their perception of their own financial interests; the case for it on the grounds that this facilitates technology transfer is no longer credible. If pressed hard, the case that the current policy is against the public interest should carry the day. And it is interesting that, if universities were so constrained in their licensing policies, that might damp their resistance to a research exemption of the sort proposed by Dreyfuss (2002), since the financial costs to them of agreeing not to patent or not to charge for licences would be diminished.

I suggest that most universities actually have nothing to lose from adopting a policy of broad, more or less automatic, low price licensing. While the press calls attention to a number of cases where universities have in fact reaped significant financial returns from the licensing of particular inventions, informed observers are virtually unanimous in believing that only a small fraction of American universities have brought in more money from their patenting and licensing operations than they spend on them. If experience to date be a guide, it is a mistake for universities to think that they have a potential financial bonanza here, if they only got their policies and organization in order. Worse, by vigorously supporting this myth when they advertise their new policies, universities are encouraging the traditional public research support agencies to believe that, if a university research programme is effective, it can largely support itself from industry grants and licensing revenues. It is clear that in several countries Treasury officials are beginning to take this attitude.

The burden of this essay is that our scientific commons is in danger, the costs of having it eroded further are likely to be high, and that we ought to move to protect it. What I have proposed above is a strategy for protecting the commons.

ACKNOWLEDGEMENTS

The author wishes to thank John Burton, Wesley Cohen, Paul David, Rochelle Dreyfuss, Nathan Rosenberg, Bhaven Sampat, Marie Thursby and Eric von Hippel for very helpful comments and suggestions on earlier drafts. I hasten to add that none of the above necessarily agrees with all of the position espoused here.

BIBLIOGRAPHY

Agrawal, A. and Henderson, R. (2002), 'Putting patents in context: exploring knowledge transfer at MIT', *Management Science*, 48(1): 44–60.
Arora, A. and Gambardella, A. (1994), 'The changing technology of technological change', *Research Policy*, 23(5): 523–32.
Atkinson, R., Beachy, R., Conway, G., Cordova, F., Fox, M., Holbrook, K., Klessig, D., McCormick, L., McPherson, P., Rawlings, H., Rapson, R., Vanderhoef, L., Wiley, J. and Young, C. (2003), 'Public sector collaboration for agricultural IP management', *Science*, 11 July, 301(5630): 174–5.
Bar-Shalom, A. and Cook-Deegan, R. (2002), 'Patents and innovation in cancer therapeutics: lessons from CellPro', *Millbank Quarterly*, 80(4): 637–76.
Basalla, G. (1998), *The Evolution of Technology*, Cambridge University Press, Cambridge.
Bernal, J.D. (1939), *The Social Functions of Science*, Routledge and Kegan Paul, London.
Bok, D. (2003), *Universities and the Marketplace*, Princeton University Press, Princeton.
Bush, V. (1945), *Science, the Endless Frontier*, National Science Foundation, Washington D.C.
Campbell, D. (1974), 'Evolutionary Epistemology', in Schelpp, P. (ed.), *The Philosophy of Karl Popper*, Open Court Publishing Company, LaSalle, Illinois.
Cohen, W., Nelson, R. and Walsh, J. (2002), 'Links and impacts: the influence of public research on industrial R&D', *Management Science*, January, 48(1): 1–23.
Cohen, W., Nelson, R. and Walsh, J. (2000), 'Patenting their intellectual assets: appropriability conditions and why U.S. manufacturing firms patent or not', NBER paper 7522, National Bureau for Economic Research, Boston.
Colyvas, J., Crow, M., Gelijns, A., Mazzoleni, R., Nelson. R. and Sampat, B. (2002), 'How do university inventions get into practice?', *Management Science*, January, 48(1): 61–72.
Constant, E. (1980), *The Origins of the Turbojet Revolution*, Johns Hopkins University Press, Baltimore.
Dasgupta, P. and David, P. (1994), 'Towards a new economics of science', *Research Policy*, 23(5): 487–521.
Demaine, L. and Fellmeth, A. (2003), 'Natural substances and patentable inventions', *Science*, 30 May, 300(5624): 1375–6.
Dosi, G. (1988), 'Sources, procedures, and microeconomic effects of innovation', *Journal of Economic Literature*, 26(September): 1120–71.
Dreyfuss, R. (2002), unpublished manuscript.
Eisenberg, R. (1987), 'Proprietary rights and the norms of science in biotechnology research', *Yale Law Journal*, 97: 177–231.
Eisenberg, R. (1996), 'Public research and private investment: patents and technology transfer in government sponsored research', *Virginia Law Review*, 82: 1663–735.
Eisenberg, R. and Nelson, R. (2002), 'Public vs proprietary science: a useful tension?', *Daedalus*, 131(2): 89–101.
Gelijns, A. (1991), *Innovation in Clinical Practice*, National Academy Press, Washington, D.C.

Gelijns, A., Rosenberg, N. and Moskowitz, A. (1998), 'Capturing the unexpected benefits of medical research', *New England Journal of Medicine*, 339(10): 693–8.
Guston, D. (2000), *Between Politics and Science*, Cambridge University Press, Cambridge.
Hart, D. (1998), *Forged Consensus*, Princeton University Press, Princeton.
Heller, M. and Eisenberg, R. (1998), 'Can patents deter innovation? The anticommons in biomedical research', *Science*, 280: 698–701.
Judson, H. (1996), *The Eighth Day of Creation*, Cold Spring Harbor Press, Cold Spring.
Kitcher, P. (1993), *The Advancement of Science*, Oxford University Press, New York.
Klevorick, A., Levin, R., Nelson, R. and Winter, S. (1995), 'On the sources and significance of inter-industry differences in technological opportunities,' *Research Policy*, 24: 185–205.
Merges, R. and Nelson, R. (1990), 'The complex economics of patent scope', *Columbia Law Review*, 90(4): 839–916.
Merton, R. (1973), *The Sociology of Science: Theoretical and Empirical Investigations*, University of Chicago Press, Chicago.
Metcalfe, S. (1998), *Evolutionary Economics and Creative Destruction*, Routledge, New York.
Mokyr, J. (1990), *The Lever of Riches,* Oxford University Press, Oxford.
Mowery, D. and Nelson, R. (1999), *The Sources of Industrial Leadership*, Cambridge University Press, Cambridge.
Mowery, D., Nelson, R., Sampat, B. and Ziedonis, A. (2001), 'The growth of patenting and licensing by American universities', *Research Policy*, 30: 99–119.
Mowery, D. and Rosenberg, N. (1989), *Technology and the Pursuit of Economic Growth*, Cambridge University Press, Cambridge.
National Research Council (1997), *Intellectual Property Rights and Research Tools in Molecular Biology*, NAS Press, Washington D.C.
Nelson, R. (1993), *National Innovation Systems*, Oxford University Press, Oxford.
Nelson, R., Peterhansl, A. and Sampat, B. (2002), *Why and How Innovations Get Into Practice: A Tale of Four Models*, Mimeo, Columbia University.
Nelson, R. and Winter, S. (1982), *An Evolutionary Theory of Economic Change*, Harvard University Press, Cambridge, MA.
Petroski, H. (1992), *The Evolution of Useful Things*, Alfred Knoph, New York.
Polanyi, M. (1962), 'The republic of science', *Minerva*, 1: 54–73.
Popper, K. (1989), *The Logic of Scientific Discovery*, Basic Books, New York.
Porter, R. (1997), *The Greatest Benefit to Mankind*, W.W. Norton, New York.
Price, D. (1962), *Government and Science*, Oxford University Press, Oxford.
Rai, A. and Eisenberg, R. (2001), *The Public and Private in Pharmaceutical Research*, Mimeo.
Rosenberg, N. (1982), 'How exogenous is science?', in Rosenberg, N., *Inside the Black Box*, Cambridge University Press, Cambridge.
Rosenberg, N. (1996), 'Uncertainty and technological change', in Landau, R., Taylor, T. and Wright, G. (eds), *The Mosaic of Economic Growth*, Stanford University Press, Stanford.
Rosenberg, N. (1998), 'Technological change in chemicals', in Arora, A., Landau, R. and Rosenberg, N. (eds), *Chemicals and Long Run Economic Growth*, John Wiley, N.Y.

Rosenberg, N. and Nelson. R. (1994), 'American universities and technical advance in industry', *Research Policy*, 23(3): 323–48.
Sampat, B. and Nelson, R. (2002), 'The emergence and standardization of university technology transfer offices: a case study of institutional change', *Advances in Strategic Management*, 19.
Schumpeter, J. (1942), *Capitalism, Socialism, and Democracy*, Harper and Row, New York.
Stokes, D. (1996), *Pasteur's Quadrant: Basic Science and Technological Innovation*, Brookings Press, Washington D.C.
Vincenti, W. (1994), 'The retractable landing gear and the northrup anomaly', *Technology and Culture*, 35(1): 1–33.
Vincenti, W. (1990), *What Engineers Know and How They Know It*, Johns Hopkins Press, Baltimore.
Von Tunzelmann, G.N. (1995), *Technology and Economic Progress*, Edward Elgar, Aldershot UK.
Walsh, J., Arora, A. and Cohen, W. (2002), *The patenting and licensing of research tools and biomedical innovation*, paper prepared for the STEP Board of the NAS.
Ziman, J. (1978), *Reliable Knowledge*, Cambridge University Press, Cambridge.
Ziman, J. (2000), *Technological Innovation as an Evolutionary Process*, Cambridge University Press, Cambridge.

2. Public interest and the public domain in an era of corporate dominance

Fiona Macmillan

ABSTRACT

This chapter argues that copyright's commodification of creativity has established a structure that enables the domination of cultural output by multinational media and entertainment corporations. It argues that the primary tools of the commodification process have been the alienability of the copyright interest, the long duration of copyright, its strong distribution rights, and the apparent demise of some of the most significant user rights. The consequent dominance of the media and entertainment corporations over cultural output has had the effect of contracting the public domain, while at the same time undermining the rationale for the existence of copyright. The chapter concludes by considering whether there are legal approaches either within the structure of copyright law or external to it that might be capable of remedying the consequences of copyright's commodification of creativity and thus reclaiming a portion of the public domain.

Keywords: Public interest, Public domain, Corporate dominance, Copyright and culture

1 COPYRIGHT'S COMMODIFICATION OF CREATIVITY

I have argued in other places (Macmillan 1998, Macmillan 2002a, Macmillan 2002b) that copyright's relationship to the concepts of creativity and culture, with which it is often rhetorically associated (Waldron 1993, p. 853), is most accurately viewed as an instrumental rather than a fundamental one.[1] That is, copyright has been well used as an instrument for promoting trade in the cultural output that comes within its purview. Accordingly, copyright deals with works in relation to which it subsists as products or commodities, the importance of which is reflected in their impact on trade rather than in any value they may enjoy in their own right. A fundamental relationship between copyright, culture and creativity, on the other hand, would result in copyright stimulating and protecting cultural output on the basis that it has a non-economic value in itself as an expression of human creativity.

The negotiation and conclusion of the Agreement on Trade Related Aspects of Intellectual Property Rights (the TRIPS Agreement) is not only one of the best examples of the ascendancy of the instrumental approach, it has also introduced a shift in intellectual property discourse that further consolidates this approach. The conclusion of the TRIPS Agreement, as one of the multilateral trade agreements of the World Trade Organization (WTO), was formally driven by the United States. Lying however, behind the government of the United States as formal actor, was a formidable coalition of US-based multinational corporate interests (Sell 2003, especially chs. 5 and 6). Acting in concert with these corporate interests, the US used two tools in particular, to drive the TRIPS negotiations (Blakeney 1996, ch.1). First, it took on the burden of convincing the Council of the General Agreement on Tariffs ad Trade (GATT) that intellectual property rights were relevant to GATT. In 1983 and 1984 evidence was submitted to Congressional hearings by US trade associations on the economic loss that the members of those associations suffered internationally as a consequence of the non-enforcement or absence of intellectual property laws.[2] Amongst other things, evidence was presented at these hearings that the video industry was losing $6 billion annually (Blakeney 1996, p. 2). The International Intellectual Property Alliance, representing American trade associations in the copyright-related industries, produced a study in 1985 estimating that non-enforcement or absence of copyright laws in Brazil, Egypt, Indonesia, Malaysia, Nigeria, the Philippines, the Republic of Korea, Singapore, Taiwan and Thailand had caused annual losses of $1.3 billion to the US copyright industries.[3] The second tool used by the US to drive the TRIPS process was the amendment in 1984 to s 301 of the Trade Act of 1974 to make intellectual property protection explicitly actionable under s 301 (Blakeney 1996, p. 4). This was followed by the introduction in the Omnibus Trade and Competitiveness Act of 1988 of 'Special 301', enabling the US Trade Representative to put countries that failed to protect US intellectual property on a watch list with a view to investigation and possible trade retaliation (Blakeney 1996, p. 5). In operating the Special 301 watch list, the US Trade Representative was heavily dependent upon information supplied by US corporate interests (Sell 2003, p. 93).

The upshot of this activity was a multilateral agreement, the very name of which reflects its gestation and instrumentality. That is, since the arrival of the TRIPS Agreement, intellectual property law has been explicitly configured as being about 'rights' in relation to 'trade'. For those who would want to see copyright bolstering the fundamental rather than the instrumental role of culture, some comfort might be taken from the fact that the agreement refers to 'trade related aspects' of intellectual property and thereby suggests that there may be some other aspects – but it is cold comfort. Not only is the TRIPS Agreement the dominant normative instrument of international intellectual property law, its location within the suite of WTO agreements means that it is an integral part of what is emerging as the pre-eminent system of international law making (Kennedy 1995, Macmillan 2004a). These two aspects of the TRIPS Agreement are, of course, intrinsically related. The systemic legal dominance and concomitant strong enforcement procedures of the WTO are a large part of the reason that the TRIPS Agreement has acquired the ability to define the parameters of intellectual property law discourse.[4] While it is true that some of the most important steps down the instrumental/trade related road were taken before the advent of the TRIPS Agreement, at least in the Anglo-Saxon model of copyright law, the TRIPS Agreement has provided an authoritative consolidation and normalization of that approach.

In my earlier work (Macmillan 1998, Macmillan 2002a, Macmillan 2002b) I have argued that there are four interdependent aspects of copyright law that have been essential to the commodification process and to copyright's consequent instrumental approach to culture and creativity. The first and most basic tool of commodification is the alienability of the copyright interest. A second significant aspect of copyright law, making it an important tool of trade and investment, is its duration. The long period of copyright protection increases the asset value of individual copyright interests (Towse 1999). Thirdly, the strong commercial distribution rights,[5] especially those which give the copyright holder control over imports and rental rights, have put copyright owners in a particularly strong market position, especially in the global context. Finally, the power of the owners of copyright in relation to all those wishing to use copyright material has been bolstered by a contraction of some of the most significant user rights in relation to copyright works, in particular fair dealing/fair use and public interest rights. This has been accompanied by significant shifts in rhetoric. Not only have the monopoly privileges of intellectual property owners become 'rights', user rights have become 'defences' or 'exceptions'. The public domain is thus protected by 'exceptions' to 'rights'. Nothing could better encapsulate its current vulnerability.

It may be possible to justify a degree of commodification by reference to the need for creators to be remunerated in order to encourage them to create[6] and by reference to the need for cultural works to be disseminated in order to reap the benefits of their creation. This latter point would fit in with the argument that an important aspect of copyright is its communication role (van Caenegem 1995, Netanel 1996). Whether some degree of commodification is essential to the integrity of copyright law or not, the point is that we have allowed the process of commodification to take over copyright without adequately considering the costs and consequences of this commodification.

2 THE ACQUISITION OF PRIVATE POWER

2.1 Global Rights, Global Distribution, Global Dominance

One consequence of the commodification of creativity through copyright is the build-up of private power over cultural output (Bettig 1996, especially ch. 3, Towse 1999). The way in which the distribution rights attaching to copyright might be used by a multinational corporation to carve up the international market (Macmillan 1998) is a small part of a much bigger story about the way in which commodification can lead to global domination of a market for cultural output. The capacity to achieve a position of global power is a combination of the international nature of intellectual property rights, the fact that many of the corporations owning the rights operate on a multinational level, and the fact that many of the media and entertainment corporations are conglomerates that display a high degree of horizontal integration by operating in a number of different areas of cultural output (Towse 1999, pp. 97–98). Some are also vertically integrated with a high degree of control over the entire distribution process.[7] The oligopolistic nature of the media and entertainment sector is accentuated through the prevailing pattern of horizontal and vertical mergers.

The fashion for horizontal and vertical mergers and acquisitions in the media and entertainment sector began in the 1970s. It seems that one force driving these mergers is the desire to increase the level of corporate ownership over copyright interests. As Smiers puts it:

> The best way to acquire rights on huge quantities of entertainment and other artistic materials is through mergers. Synergy is the rationale for media conglomerates snatching up as much copyrighted material as they can (Smiers 2002, p. 120).[8]

Such activity is not only stimulated by the significant asset value of copyright interests,[9] it also reflects strategic business concerns. Bettig describes mergers and acquisitions in the media and entertainment sector as 'a process of reorganization around core and related lines of business along with an effort to establish alliances across national boundaries with market dominant firms in other countries' (Bettig 1996, p. 37). This process has been reflected in the activities of media and entertainment corporations such as Viacom Inc. (which owns Paramount Communications Inc.), Time Warner Inc., News Corporation Ltd and The Disney Corporation and Comcast Inc.,[10] so that the activities of these corporations involve diversified lines of business including film and television production and distribution, international ownership of cinema chains, broadcasting, cable networks, music and book publishing.[11] Beginning in the late 1980s there has also been a trend on the part of corporations that were primarily engaged in the production of technology used in the distribution of media and entertainment content to merge with or acquire interests in corporations producing that content. So, for example, Sony Corporation acquired Columbia Pictures Entertainment in 1989, and Matsushita Electric Industrial Company acquired MCA, the parent company of Universal Pictures in 1991. The most significant recent example of this tendency towards the integration of corporations owning rights over content and distribution of filmed entertainment and those owning rights over the technology of distribution is the merger of AOL and Time Warner.[12] Not only do these mergers increase the concentration of copyright ownership in the media and entertainment sector, they also place the ownership of the patent rights over the distribution technology in the same hands.[13] This process of concentration seems to be leading inexorably to the conclusion that 'a handful – six to ten vertically integrated communications companies – will soon produce, own and distribute the bulk of the culture and information circulating in the global marketplace' (Bettig 1996, p. 38).

An example of this type of concentration of corporate power, analysed by Anne Capling (1996), is the power that six[14] international entertainment corporations held over the Australian market for contemporary music. The companies in question were CBS (Sony), WEA (Time Warner), Polygram (NV Philips), EMI (Thorn EMI), BMG (Bertelsmann Music Group) and Festival (News Limited). All of these corporations operate as international conglomerates, some with substantial media interests, and between them they control 70 per cent of the world's recorded music market (Capling 1996, p. 22). Furthermore in Australia they also have control of the distribution system – EMI and CBS do this by virtue of a joint venture, as do BMG and WEA; Polygram and Festival have subsidiaries that act as their distributors (Capling 1996, p. 21). The specific copyright tool that they used to orchestrate their oligopoly was their control over the import of works to which they own the copyright (Capling 1996, p. 21). The right to control parallel imports with respect to recorded music was removed from Australian copyright law in 1998.[15] However, this appears to have done little so far to alter patterns of control and distribution in the Australian recorded music market.

It seems that even without the right to control parallel imports, copyright has been an essential tool in the orchestration of this type of global oligopoly because of the long period of control that it gives its owner over the distribution of content (Towse 1999). The market for filmed entertainment provides a particularly good example of this. In this market the copyright monopoly, allied with the vertical integration of the market, has allowed the major media and entertainment corporations to dominate, not only the market for first run cinema, but also the markets that have been created as a consequence of the development of new technologies for the distribution of filmed entertainment. That is, the same oligopolistic market structure controls the market for television feature films, cable transmission of films, videos and (now) digital versatile disks (DVDs) (Bettig 1996, pp. 39–42). The video market, now being superseded by the market for DVDs, has been a particularly significant market for the major media and entertainment corporations. Bettig estimates that in the early 1990s the video market for sales and rentals accounted for 35 to 45 per cent of the global revenues of the filmed entertainment industry (Bettig 1996, p. 40).[16] In 1992 six major filmed entertainment corporations accounted for 77 per cent of the total revenue of the North American video market. These were: Disney (21.3 per cent), Warner Home Video (18.1 per cent), FoxVideo (14.1 per cent), Columbia Tri-Star Home Video (9.7 per cent), Paramount (7.3 per cent), MCA/Universal Home Video (6.6 per cent) (Bettig 1996, p. 40). Making allowances for the processes of merger and acquisition that have characterized the media and entertainment sector, more or less the same majors dominate the video market in Europe.[17] For example, in 1987 the video-rental market in the United Kingdom was dominated by four US corporations: Warner (21.6 per cent), CBS/Fox (18.5 per cent), CIC Video handling distribution for MGM/UA, Universal and Paramount (12.7 per cent) and RCA/Columbia (11.6 per cent). By 1992, CIC Video had increased its share of the rental market to 20 per cent. So far as the video sale market in the UK was concerned, in 1992 Warner and Disney held approximately 50 per cent of this market between them. Other than Italy, in which there was a significant market in pirated videos, the story is more or less the same in the rest of Europe. In Spain, for example, four of the US majors (RCA/Columbia, CBS/Fox, CIC and Warner), accounted for 70 per cent of the video market in 1990 and they managed to increase this dominance to 78 per cent by 1991. It is perhaps worth noting, finally, that the implementation of the obligations in the TRIPS Agreement is likely to have increased the market dominance of the major filmed entertainment corporations in countries where a significant portion of the video market was represented by the sale or rental of pirate videos.

2.2 The Role of Technology

Technological developments tend to cause crises for the media and entertainment oligopolies by threatening their control over distribution. Copyright law, which is the key to the control of distribution, is intimately bound up with these technological developments because they raise questions about either the scope or the enforceability of copyright. Thus, the major music labels and music publishers leapt to the defence of their market control in a series of copyright cases in the US directed at preventing the distribution of music on the Internet by the use of MP3 files. The upshot of at least some of these proceedings is that the major record labels have entered (or are negotiating to enter) into distribution arrangements with online music providers (Macmillan 2002a, p. 108).

Another recent controversy, which has created alarm in the ranks of the filmed entertainment industry and has seen the majors jumping to the defence of their distribution monopoly, was the release of the DeCSS (Decrypted Content Scrambling System) source code. This source code allows the copying of DVDs and their transmission via the Internet. Not only did the eight US majors of the filmed entertainment industry take an action against the publishers of sites that had disclosed the code, they also commenced proceedings against *Copyleft* for reprinting the code on to a T-shirt.[18] Of the three Internet site publishers pursued by the film industry majors, two negotiated consent decrees. The third, who goes by the underground name of Eric Corley,[19] had published the code in his online journal, *2600: The Hacker Quarterly*, and chose to defend the case. On 17 August 2000 US District Court Judge Lewis Kaplan handed down a decision preventing *2600* from continuing to publish the DeCSS code on its website.[20] This decision, which may resonate in European jurisdictions as a result of Article 6 of the Copyright in the Information Society Directive, was affirmed on appeal.[21]

Judge Kaplan's original decision was based on a provision of the Digital Millennium Copyright Act.[22] This Act forms part of the amended US Copyright Act of 1976. The Act, in s 1201(a)(1), prohibits the circumvention of technological measures controlling access to a copyright work. Section 1201(a)(2) prohibits a person, amongst other things, offering to the public or providing 'any technology, product, service, device, component or part thereof' that:

(A) is primarily designed for the purpose of circumventing a technological measure,
(B) has limited commercially significant purpose other than circumvention of a technological measure, or
(C) is marketed with personal knowledge of use in circumventing a technological measure.

Corley was held to have breached this section. This was despite the fact that s 1201(c) of the Act provides that nothing in the section limits the rights of free speech for activities using consumer electronics, telecommunications or computing products, nor the rights of fair use with respect to copyright works. Taking the matter of free speech first, there is a reasonable argument to be made that merely posting and linking the DeCSS code, as opposed to making use of it, is purely expressive. If this is so, then injuncting such behaviour raises serious free speech concerns.[23] The US Court of Appeals for the Second Circuit accepted that the decryption code was constitutionally protected speech. However, it held that the right of the copyright holder to protect its property must be balanced against the right to free speech and that, as a result, the restraint imposed by the circumvention provisions of the Digital Copyright Millennium Act was not an undue restraint on speech.

So far as the issue of fair use/fair dealing is concerned, the consequences of the case are also serious. The Court of Appeals noted that Corley was not claiming to have made a fair use of the copyright material. However, it did observe that fair use does not involve a right to access to copyright material 'in order to copy it by the fair user's preferred technique or in the format of the original'.[24] Overall, the Court of Appeals seems to have brushed aside the combined result of its determinations on the free speech and fair dealing issues. If the publication and use of the DeCSS code is not permitted it will not be possible to copy any part of a film on DVD. Consequently, the right to engage in a fair use/fair dealing with the film, for example, for criticism or review, is meaningless. Thus, the effect of this case is to strengthen considerably the rights of the filmed entertainment corporations over their output and fatally undermine the cogency of the fair use/fair dealing defence. The case does more than merely maintain the exclusive distribution rights of the majors.

Hot on the heels of the decision of the Court of Appeals in the DVD case is a case that explores the legitimacy of film sharing software for the distribution of film over the Internet. The complaint in *Metro-Goldwyn-Mayer Studios Inc v Grokster Ltd*[25] was filed on behalf of the film studios making up the Motion Pictures Association of America (MPAA) in November 2001. It makes up one part of two closely associated actions, the other filed as a class action on behalf of all music publishers represented by The Harry Fox Agency,[26] against the same defendants in respect of the same activities. The activities complained of relate to peer to peer file sharing software provided by the defendants, which it is alleged amounts to 'a 21st century piratical bazaar where the unlawful exchange of protected materials takes place across the vast expanse of the Internet'[27] or 'a cybernetic Alice's Restaurant [where] the menu is our protected content'[28] – either way, a copyright infringement. The software in question, variously known as KaZaA, Grokster or Morpheus (but referred to as Morpheus hereafter), can be downloaded by the user from the defendant's website. Once the user has logged on to the defendant's server, it is connected to a so-called 'supernode', a more powerful computer operated by another user. Search requests are sent to the supernode, which searches the computers of other users in the Morpheus network and compiles search results. The user then selects and downloads the files that it wants directly from the other user.

The plaintiffs in the *Morpheus* case appear to have accepted that the issue is not about the software *per se*,[29] but rather about the behaviour of the defendants in relation to the use of the software.[30] That is, they argue that the defendants are 'knowingly and systematically, participating in, facilitating, materially contributing to, and encouraging'[31] infringing behaviour of the users. Concerns that the entertainment industry is not attempting to use copyright law in a fashion that is anti-innovation should not, however, be regarded as being allayed. The line between accepting the lawfulness of the programme, but not of its distribution, is a rather blurry (if not completely meaningless) one. This is particularly so when there is a good argument to be made that distribution is the only thing the defendants have actually done. The defendants draw the attention of the users to their obligations under copyright law.[32] Unlike the famous Napster programme, the Morpheus programme does not rely on a central server system to hold an index of all available files on the network.[33] This was crucial to the decision of the Central District Court of California,[34] affirmed by the Court of Appeals for the Ninth Circuit,[35] granting partial summary judgment to the defendants and denying it to the plaintiffs. It seems, therefore, that we may not yet have reached the position where innovations in the use of the Internet have to be approved by the entertainment industry before the rest of us can enjoy them. However, the fact that the entertainment industry uses its deep pockets to take such overreaching actions in order to protect its distribution monopoly is a cause for continuing concern.

2.3 The Exponentiality of Power

Despite the concern engendered by the new technologies, the general rule appears to be that the position of power that is enjoyed by media and entertainment corporations is self-reinforcing. By having such considerable power they are able to acquire more. Put simply, this is a consequence of the interdependence in most Western economies between the public and private sectors. The economic health of nations is dependent on the success of the corporate sector. This puts corporations in the position to demand of government that it take steps to protect their interests and thereby to reinforce their positions of private power.[36] It is important in this context not to forget that it was the US corporate sector that the US government was seeking to protect when it engaged in its various strategies to force the progress of the TRIPS Agreement. So far as the US government was concerned, looking after the interests of the multinational corporate sector would also involve addressing its concern about the trade deficit and the increasing economic might of Japan (Sell 2003, p. 76). Thus, the negotiation of the TRIPS Agreement is a clear example of the interdependence between public and private sectors. So far as the media and entertainment corporate sector is concerned, the upshot of both the TRIPS Agreement and of associated domestic policies[37] has been to allow the sector to increase substantially its stranglehold over international cultural output protected by copyright (Capling 1996). The fact that the government is so willing to act in the interests of the corporate sector – even if for its own reasons – shows the power that the sector wields.[38] It is not unreasonable to suggest that the degree of power of the private sector compares with that of government (Chayes 1959, p. 25), although of course it is exercised differently. One significant difference is that the power of government, at least in democratic societies, is legitimated through accountability mechanisms such as elections and the rules of administrative law (Macmillan Patfield 1995, pp. 7–15). The private sector has a free hand to use power in a way that government can only dream about.

3 THE SIGNIFICANCE OF PRIVATE POWER

3.1 Cultural Filtering and Homogenization

What are the consequences of this copyright-facilitated aggregation of private power? Returning first to the example of the contemporary music industry and the way it operates in Australia, according to Ann Capling, even though the then big six (now three) corporations control seventy per cent of the global market for music, they only release around twenty per cent of this music in Australia. Not only does this mean that these corporations act as a cultural filter, controlling what we can hear,[39] it also means that the music offered for retail sale has 'about as much cultural diversity as a Macdonald's menu' (Capling 1996, p. 22):[40]

> The domination by these global entertainment corporations of the Australian market facilitates the globalisation of a mass culture of mediocrity in a number of ways. It ensures, for instance, the prevalence of the top sellers to the detriment of other less mainstream overseas music ... The import restrictions also make it much more difficult for local Australian performers and composers to get airplay within Australia. Pop and rock account for close to ninety per cent of the Australian music market and, with the exception of a handful of Australian acts which have won an international following, this market is overwhelmingly dominated by North American and British artists. (Capling 1996, p. 22)

And, of course, Australia is hardly likely to be the only market where this happens. The processes that produce cultural homogenity and mediocrity are global.[41] It is interesting in this respect to note that one of the arguments that is made on behalf of the activities of MP3 Internet music file trading services, such as Napster, is that they give exposure and airplay to smaller artists and small independent labels.[42] If this is so, then it is a benefit likely to be lost if the major labels gain a distribution grip over the online music providers.

It is not just the music industry where the corporate sector controls what filters through to the rest of us. For example, the control over film distribution that is enjoyed by the major media and entertainment corporations means that these corporations can control to some extent what films are made, what films we can see, and our perception of what films there are for us to see. The expense involved in film production and distribution means that without access to the deep pockets of the majors and their vertically integrated distribution networks, it is difficult, but not impossible, to finance independent film making and distribution. This, naturally, reduces the volume of independent film making. The high degree of vertical integration that characterizes the film industry, especially the ownership of cinema chains, means that many independent films that are made find it difficult to make any impact on the film-going public. This is mainly because we don't know they exist. The control by the media and entertainment corporations of the films that are made is also a consequence of their habit of buying the film rights attached to the copyright in novels, plays, biographies and so on. There is no obligation on the film corporations to use these rights once they have acquired them but, of course, no one else can do so without their permission. Similarly, the film corporations may choose not to release certain films in which they own the exclusive distribution rights or only to release certain films in certain jurisdictions or through certain media. All these things mean that the media and entertainment corporations are acting as a cultural filter.[43] The problem of cultural filtering with respect to films appears to have received recent acknowledgement in the UK in the form of the UK Film Council's Digital Screen Network under which grants will be made to cinemas for the installation of digital cinema technology on the condition that they show a wider variety of specialized films.[44] It seems a pity that public money raised for good causes through the National Lottery must be used to remedy a privately created distortion.

A further example of the filtering function, if one is needed, is provided by the publishing industry. The economic power of publishers has, in its wake, conferred on them a broader power to determine what sort of things we are likely to read. Richard Abel is eloquent on this topic:

> Book publishers decide which manuscripts to accept; form contracts dictate terms to all but best-selling authors; editors 'suggest' changes; and marketing departments decide price, distribution and promotion. Sometimes publishers go further ... The Japanese publisher Hayakawa withdrew a translation of *The Enigma of Japanese Power* because the Dutch author had written that the Burakumin Liberation League 'has developed a method of self-assertion through 'denunciation' sessions with people and organizations it decides are guilty of discrimination'. Anticipating feminist criticism, Simon and Schuster cancelled publication of Bret Easton Ellis's *American Psycho* a month before it was to appear. (Abel 1994a, p. 52)[45]

There are a number of other examples of the same phenomenon in publishing. For example, it was reported that HarperCollins (UK), a member of the Murdoch Group, declined to publish Hong Kong Governor Chris Patten's memoirs in breach of contract because it was alleged that the memoirs included commentary on the Beijing government that might threaten Murdoch's substantial business interests in China.[46] It has also been suggested that the takeover of the British publisher Fourth Estate by HarperCollins (UK) was in some way related to a biography of Rupert Murdoch contracted to be published by Fourth Estate. The biography was not published by them.[47] On the other hand, a development that may have the effect of breaking down some of the power of publishers is the advent of electronic self-publishing. It seems, however, that any inroads that this makes in the power of publishers will be confined to publications by the very few authors who command sufficient market power to dispense with the promotional services of the publishers.[48]

3.2 Loss of the Commons

So the media and entertainment industry controls and homogenizes what we get to see, hear and read. In so doing it is likely that it also controls the way we construct images of our society and ourselves.[49] The scope of this power is reinforced by the industry's assertion of control over the use of material assumed by most people to be in the intellectual commons and thus in the public domain. The irony is that the reason people assume such material to be in the commons is that the copyright owners have force-fed it to us as receivers of the mass culture disseminated by the mass media. The more powerful the copyright owner, the more dominant the cultural image, but the more likely that the copyright owner will seek to protect the cultural power of the image through copyright enforcement. The result is that not only are individuals not able to use, develop or reflect upon dominant cultural images, they are also unable to challenge them by subverting them (Chon 1993, Koenig 1994, Macmillan Patfield 1996). This is certainly unlikely to reduce the power of those who own these images.

As an example of this type of concern Waldron (1993) uses the case of *Walt Disney Prods v Air Pirates*.[50] In this case the Walt Disney Corporation successfully prevented the use of Disney characters in *Air Pirates* comic books. The comic books were said to depict the characters as 'active members of a free thinking, promiscuous, drug-ingesting counterculture' (Waldron 1993, p. 753).[51] Note, however, that the copyright law upon which the case was based does not prevent this depiction only, it prevents their use altogether. Waldron comments:

> The whole point of the Mickey Mouse image is that it is thrust out into the cultural world to impinge on the consciousness of all of us. Its enormous popularity, consciously cultivated for decades by the Disney empire, means that it has become an instantly recognizable icon, in a real sense part of our lives. When Ralph Steadman paints the familiar mouse ears on a cartoon image of Ronald Reagan, or when someone on my faculty refers to some proposed syllabus as a 'Mickey Mouse' idea, they attest to the fact that this is not just property without boundaries on which we might accidentally encroach ... but an artifact that has been deliberately set up as a more or less permanent feature of the environment all of us inhabit. (Waldron 1993, p. 883)

Coombe describes this corporate control of the commons as monological and, accordingly, destroying the dialogical relationship between the individual and society:

> Legal theorists who emphasize the cultural construction of self and world – the central importance of shared cultural symbols in defining us and the realities we recognize – need to consider the legal constitution of symbols and the extent to which 'we' can be said to 'share' them. I fear that most legal theorists concerned with dialogue objectify, rarefy, and idealize 'culture', abstracting 'it' from the material and political practices in which meaning is made. Culture is not embedded in abstract concepts that we internalize, but in the materiality of signs and texts over which we struggle and the imprint of those struggles in consciousness. This ongoing negotiation and struggle over meaning is the essence of dialogic practice. Many interpretations of intellectual property laws quash dialogue by affirming the power of corporate actors to monologically control meaning by appealing to an

> abstract concept of property. Laws of intellectual property privilege monologic forms against dialogic practice and create significant power differentials between social actors engaged in hegemonic struggle. If both subjective and objective realities are constituted culturally – through signifying forms to which we give meaning – then we must critically consider the relationship between law, culture, and the politics of commodifying cultural forms. (Coombe 1998, p. 86)

If copyright has any hope of answering a criticism this cogent then a key aspect of copyright law is the fair use/fair dealing defence. It is this aspect of copyright law that permits resistance and critique (Gaines 1991, p. 10). Yet the fair dealing defence is a weak tool for this purpose and becoming weaker.[52]

3.3 Copyright and Development?

The utilitarian/development justification for copyright is overwhelmingly familiar. The general idea underlying this rationale is that the grant of copyright encourages the production of the cultural works, which is essential to the development process.[53] However, the consequences of copyright's commodification of creativity, as described above, seem to place some strain on this alleged relationship between copyright and development. This argument may be illustrated by reference to the World Commission on Culture and Development's concept of development as being about the enhancement of effective freedom of choice of individuals (World Commission on Culture and Development 1996).[54] Some of the things that matter to this concept of development are 'access to the world's stock of knowledge, ... access to power, the right to participate in the cultural life of the community' (World Commission on Culture and Development 1996, Introduction).[55] The edifice of private power that has been built upon a copyright law that seems to care more about money than about the intrinsic worth of the cultural product it is protecting, has deprived us all to some extent of the benefits of this type of development. As Waldron comments, '[t]he private appropriation of the public realm of cultural artifacts restricts and controls the moves that can be made therein by the rest of us' (Waldron 1993, p. 885). It seems worth noting briefly that increases in the duration of copyright protection, such as that which has occurred in the European Union countries[56] and in the United States[57] are hardly helping.

Things look no better if we focus on the World Commission on Culture and Development's fundamental approach to culture, which is the handmaiden of its wide concept of development. A fundamental approach to culture means valuing cultural output as an end in itself, a commitment to diversity and multiculturalism, and the control of power in the form of cultural domination (World Commission on Culture and Development

1996, Analytical ch. 9). Not only has copyright failed to effect these things in relation to cultural output, it is arguable that it has effected their opposite. Since copyright law dominates the production and distribution of many forms of creativity, its failure to take a fundamental approach to the cultural products that fall within its purview may be regarded as a factor in our failure to achieve development in the wide sense. What is more, the unaccountable and self-reinforcing power of the media and entertainment conglomerates suggests that this process of development failure is accelerating.

4 COULD COPYRIGHT DO BETTER?

4.1 Limiting Commodification?

The question of whether copyright could do better in protecting the public domain, or what Waldron calls 'the public realm of cultural artifacts' (Waldron 1993, p. 885), raises an issue about the extent to which commodification is essential to the concept of copyright. The idea that the copyright interest is and should be assignable goes hand in hand with the Anglo-Saxon conception of copyright as primarily an economic, and thus assignable, right (Bently 1994, especially pp. 980–981). This is important because, as argued above, assignability of the copyright interest appears to be necessary in order to commodify cultural and creative output. It has been argued in this chapter, however, that the degree of commodification of cultural products that has been created through the copyright instrument is not purely a consequence of assignability. Other aspects of copyright law that have a part to play are the strong distribution rights attached to copyright and the long period of copyright protection. Placing limits on the exclusive distribution rights and reducing the period of copyright protection would address some of the concerns raised in this chapter about the processes and consequences of commodification. It also appears to be the case that such alterations to the law would involve less conflict with the essential nature of Anglo-Saxon copyright law than attempts to limit the alienability of the copyright interest.

In the early life of English copyright law, much of the justification for increases in duration and in the exclusive rights of the copyright holder appear to be a manifestation of the influence of romantic conceptions of the author and the author's right to control the work (Bently 1994, Vaidhyanathan 2001, ch. 2).[58] Given that the process of commodification divorces the author from his or her work (Gaines 1991), so that the author has become a somewhat marginalized figure in copyright law, extensions of the copyright interest based upon the figure of the author seem to have little justification. Furthermore, the current fruits of long duration and strong distribution rights are, as argued in this chapter, so unpalatable that there are good reasons grounded in public interest to look at these issues again. It must be conceded, however, that the hope that such views were gaining some ground has been dashed by the recent US Supreme Court decision in *Eldred v Ashcroft*.[59]

4.2 Counterbalancing Rights?

It is often suggested that the provision of counterbalancing rights would do much to break down the power of the commodifiers. The rights being referred to here are moral rights and performers' rights. These rights are not a cure for the displacement of the author in the copyright system, rather they are a response to such a displacement (Gaines 1991, p. 26). As is well known, the introduction of both types of rights has been strenuously resisted by the media and entertainment sector. Opposition of this sector to moral rights was one of the reasons for the reluctance of the US to join the Berne Convention on the Protection of Literary and Artistic Works. The US film industry opposed moral rights, fearing that they would interfere with industry practices such as the alteration of screenplays, the release of the studio's rather than director's cut and the 'colorization' of black and white films (Bettig 1996, p. 222). The US eventually joined the Berne Convention as part of the process of securing the WTO TRIPS Agreement. The TRIPS Agreement incorporates all of the substantive provisions of the Berne Convention except, of course, Article 6*bis*, its moral rights provision.

The story with respect to the introduction of performers' rights is somewhat similar. Performers represent an area of creativity that is not well recognised by copyright law. As with moral rights, the media and entertainment industry, especially that part of it concerned with film production and distribution, has resisted an attempt to bring performers into the copyright fold through the introduction of performers' rights. Essentially, the industry sees such rights as conferring an undue amount of power on performers, whose relationship with the studios is currently governed by contract. When the WIPO Performers and Phonograms Treaty of 1996 was negotiated, the question of the extension of performers' rights to audiovisual performances was a matter of great contention. The US, representing the interests of Hollywood and its studio-based system of contractual relationships with performers, strongly opposed such an extension while the European Community took the opposite position. After much diplomatic wrangling, it was impossible to achieve a consensus on the question (Blakeney 2004, pp. 145–147). The result is that the Treaty protects the rights of performers in audio performances only. This means that the film industry remains untouched, not only by any treaty requirement, but also by any clear international consensus that performers' rights are desirable.

If we are going to keep copyright as an economic right then counterbalancing the power of the commodifiers with unassignable moral and performers' rights seems to be a reasonable idea. It is unclear, however, what weight such rights might have, given the extent of power enjoyed by the media and entertainment corporations. Both moral rights and performers' rights may be waived. That is, they can be bought off, if not bought. The uneven bargaining positions of the film industry and many participants, such as screenwriters, actors and directors, mean these waivable rights are inherently weak. In addition, there is a concern that where moral rights are enforced, they might also lead to the stultification of creativity (Smiers 2002).[60] For example, the right of integrity might interfere with fair dealing with a copyright work for the purpose of criticism or review.

4.3 Fair Dealing Rights?

Copyright's central tool for securing the public domain and protecting the intellectual commons has been the fair use/ fair dealing right. This right has, however, been subject to continual erosion. Early on in the history of copyright there was a transition in the application of the fair dealing right from a focus on what the defendant had added to what the defendant had taken (Bently 1994, p. 979).[61] That this transition appears to have owed much to the romantic concept of the, now marginalized, figure of the author (Bently 1994, p. 979) is not comforting. The contraction of the right has moved forward in leaps and bounds in more recent times. The determination in *Rogers v Koons*[62] that the fair use right only applies where the infringing work has used a copyright work for the purpose of criticizing that copyright work, rather than for the purpose of criticizing society in general, exposed a crucial flaw in the use of the defence as a tool of resistance and critique. The fact that the fair use doctrine did not entitle Koons to engage in an act of cultural pastiche and parody is of concern if one thinks that copyright law should be about the promotion of cultural activity and diversity. It is of serious concern if one subscribes to the postmodernist view that modern cultural products are all about pastiche or parody or both,[63] whether consciously referential or not.[64]

Optimists may argue that subsequent decisions on both sides of the Atlantic in cases like *Campbell v Acuff-Rose Music, Inc.*[65] and *Time Warner Entertainments Company LP v Channel 4 Television Corporation plc*[66] repair or mitigate some of the damage that *Rogers v Koons* has done to the vitality of the fair dealing/fair use right as a weapon for securing the intellectual commons. However, the more likely result of this mish-mash of case law is to create confusion about the scope of the right. The outcome of this confusion is to make users of copyright works reluctant to rely on the fair dealing/fair use rights, with a consequent increase in the power of the copyright owner over the work in question.

Even an optimist could hardly be sanguine about recent developments concerning the application of the fair dealing/fair use rights in the digital context.[67] The pressures that gave rise to the WIPO Copyright Treaty of 1996 have spawned a series of pieces of domestic or regional legislation that tip the copyright power balance even more strongly in favour of the commodifiers.[68] The legislation in question is designed to strengthen the position of copyright owners in the face of the perceived threat to copyright as a consequence of digitization and new forms of communication technology, such as the Internet. One of the ways in which these pieces of legislation typically seek to shore up the position of copyright holders is by removing or reducing the existence or practical utility of the fair dealing or fair use rights (Macmillan 1999, Vaidhyanathan 2001, ch. 5). This point could hardly be better illustrated than by *Universal Studios v Corley*.[69]

4.4 Public Interest Right?

As long as copyright law continues along its present path, it will continue to erode the public domain. Valuable suggestions have been made as to ways in which the commodification process might be limited, especially as it relates to duration (Netanel 1996, pp. 366–371) and to fair use/fair dealing (Netanel 1996, pp. 376–382), while still preserving the integrity of copyright as a means of encouraging speech and the dissemination of that speech. The question is whether the tools of copyright alone can ever repair the damage that copyright itself has done to the public domain. Other solutions may need to be broached. One of these might be a resuscitated public interest right to prevent the exercise of copyright in certain circumstances. There are precedents for the use of this right in relation to other private law rights governing speech (Macmillan 2004b). In relation to copyright, however, developments in common law jurisdictions have raised questions about the vitality of the public interest right. In Australia, for example, doubts about the existence of this right as a defence to an action for copyright infringement are relatively longstanding.[70] The decision of the US Supreme Court in *Eldred v Ashcroft*[71] is eloquent testament to the fact that public interest will rarely, if ever, trump the proprietary interests of the copyright holder. In the United Kingdom, even before the decision of the English Court of Appeal in *Hyde Park v Yelland*,[72] which appeared to have killed off the right in the United Kingdom, there was considerable evidence that the courts were unwilling to engage with the question of the relationship between copyright and the public interest.[73] However, the subsequent decision of the Court of Appeal in *Ashdown v Telegraph Group*[74] shows that the public interest right may yet have a spark of life in the United Kingdom, although it is unclear whether this decision will have much, if any, application apart from preserving the right to speak freely in the overtly party political arena.

4.5 Thinking Holistically?

This chapter has raised questions about whether the contraction of the public domain as a result of copyright's commodification of creativity and culture may be addressed by methods such as weakening the exclusive rights of the copyright holder, reducing the duration of copyright, introducing counterbalancing interests and reinvigorating the fair dealing and public interest defences. Perhaps, however, given the spiralling power of the media and entertainment sector, even these solutions are not enough on their own. The Report of the World Commission on Culture and Development recommended the promotion of media competition, access and diversity at an international level (World Commission on Culture and Development 1996, International Agenda, Action 5). It also suggests an international clearing house for national media and broadcast laws (World Commission on Culture and Development 1996, International Agenda, Action 5). These types of things are essential to reducing the power that the media and entertainment corporations exercise over cultural output. Clearly, being serious about making inroads into private corporate power means thinking about the role of media and competition law. However, this very small leap across boundaries is not enough on its own. If we want to legitimate the power of the corporate sector then we have to look for ways of making private power more publicly accountable. The area of law that needs work here if we are to have accountability in any structured and comprehensive fashion is, of course, corporate law. Thinking across intellectual property law, media law, competition law and corporate law sounds like a tall order, but it has been the failure of legislators, regulators, lawyers, academics and other commentators to do just that which has brought us the present era of cultural homogenization and domination.

NOTES

1. The fundamental/instrumental distinction drawn here is drawn from the World Commission on Culture and Development 1996. For a further discussion and application of that distinction in the context of copyright, see Macmillan 1998 and Macmillan 2002a.
2. *Possible Renewal of the Generalised System of Preferences - Hearing Before the Subcommittee on Trade of the US House of Representatives Commission on Ways and*

Means, 98th Congress 1st Session (1983); and *Unfair Foreign Trade Practices, Stealing American Intellectual Property: Imitation is Not Flattery*, 98th Congress 2nd Session (1984): both cited in Blakeney 1996, p. 2n.
3. International Intellectual Property Alliance, *Piracy of US Counterfeited Works in Ten Selected Countries* (1985), p. 7, cited in Blakeney 1996, p. 2.
4. Although, as Sell 2003, ch.3 shows, important changes in discourse, such as the move from intellectual property 'privileges' to intellectual property 'rights', began to occur much earlier than the Uruguay Round of trade negotiations.
5. See especially the TRIPS Agreement, Articles 11 & 14(4), which enshrine rental rights in relation to computer programmes, films and phonograms; WIPO Copyright Treaty 1996, Article 7; and WIPO Performances and Phonograms Treaty 1996, Articles 9 & 13.
6. See, however, Towse 2001, especially chs. 6 & 8, in which it is argued that copyright generates little income for most creative artists. Nevertheless, Towse suggests that copyright is valuable to creative artists for reasons of status and control of their work.
7. For further discussion of the way in which the filmed entertainment industry conforms to these industry features, see Macmillan 2002b.
8. See also Bettig 1996, pp. 40–42.
9. It was reported, for example, that Chrysalis, the music and broadcasting group, raised £60 million against its music publishing catalogue, which comprised 50 000 copyrights valued for the purpose of the securitization at £150 million and generating a revenue stream of £8 million per year: 'Chrysalis in £60m fundraising', *The Times*, 9 February 2001.
10. In February 2004, Comcast (in which Microsoft has a 7.4% holding) made a £35 billion hostile takeover bid for the Disney Corporation, after a merger proposition was rejected by the Disney board of directors. Some pundits suggest that this may mark the beginning of a period of more hostile activity in the media and entertainment sector: see 'The spirit of Mickey must survive', *The Guardian*, 14 February 2004.
11. For an example of this, see the description of the process of integration by Paramount Communications Inc. in Bettig 1996, pp. 37–38.
12. It has recently been reported that AOL Time Warner and EMI have revived merger talks, pursuant to which EMI would take a majority stake in Warner Music. This turns the table on previous merger talks between the two undertakings in 2000 that envisaged AOL Time Warner as the controlling partner in the merged entity. Clearly, this is a reflection of AOL Time Warner's recent reported annual loss of $98 billion: see 'EMI and AOL Time Warner Merger Back on the Table', *The Guardian*, 25 February 2003.
13. Thus returning us, strangely enough, to the origins of the filmed entertainment industry, which grew out of a need to exploit patents over cinematograph technology: see further, Vaidhyanathan 2001, pp. 87–93.
14. Such is the process of merger and acquisition in this industry that in less than a decade the six are now three with the most recent merger affecting this market being that between Sony & Bertelsmann.
15. Copyright (Amendment) Act (No 2) (1998).
16. According to one source, video rentals account for 46.6% of studio revenues: see 'Net Pirates Turn Sites on Hollywood', *The Guardian*, 23 February 2002.
17. The source of the following material on the European video markets is Bettig 1996, pp. 210–214.
18. See *The Wizard*, 7 August 2000, http://www.wizardfkap.com/page6.html and http://www.copyleft.net.
19. In homage to the character of the same name in George Orwell's *Nineteen Eighty Four*.
20. *Universal City Studios, Inc v Shawn C Reimerdes*, 111 F Supp 2d 294 (2000, SDNY).
21. *Universal City Studios, Inc v Corley*, US Court of Appeals for the Second Circuit, 28 November 2001, http://www.2600.com/news/112801-files/UniversalBrief_3.pdf.
22. Section 1201, Title 17 of the US Code.

23. 'Studios Score DeCSS Victory', *Wired News*, 17 August 2000.
24. Note 21 *supra*, 71.
25. US District Court for the Central District of California, Western Div, Case No: CV-01–08541 SVW.
26. *Leiber v Consumer Empowerment BV*, US District Court for the Central District of California, Western Div, Case No: CV-01–09923 GAF. The two cases were consolidated: see *MGM v Grokster* (Hearing Transcript, 4 March 2002) and *Leiber v Consumer Empowerment BV* (Hearing Transcript, 4 March 2002).
27. Complaint in *MGM v Grokster*, n 25 *supra*, para 1.
28. Hearing Transcript in *MGM v Grokster*, n 26 *supra*, 8.
29. The legality of which would appear to be protected on the basis that it has substantial non-infringing uses pursuant to the authority of *Sony Corp v Universal City Studios, Inc*, 464 US 417 (1984).
30. See Hearing Transcript in *MGM v Grokster*, n 26 *supra*, 6–9.
31. Complaint in *MGM v Grokster*, n 25 *supra*, para 52.
32. Although the plaintiffs argue that bulletin boards maintained by the defendants acknowledge that the software is for infringing purposes: Complaint in *Lieber v Consumer Empowerment BV*, n 26 *supra*, para 66.
33. The plaintiffs, of course, downplayed this difference between Napster and Morpheus, referring to it as being merely 'architectural': Hearing Transcript in *MGM v Grokster*, n 26 *supra*, 10.
34. *Metro-Goldwyn-Mayer Studios Inc v Grokster Ltd* (Order on Motions, 25 April 2003). This Order on Motion relates only to the Grokster and Morpheus software, no order is made in relation to the KaZaA software.
35. *Metro-Goldwyn-Mayer Studios Inc v Grokster Ltd* (United States Court of Appeals for the Ninth Circuit, 19 August 2004), http://www.eff.org/IP/P2P/MGM_v_Grokster/20040819_mgm_v_grokster_decision.pdf.
36. Not to mention the fact that the economic power of the media and entertainment sector gives it deep enough pockets to fend for itself in problematic cases like the DVD case, *Universal City Studios v Corley*, n 21 *supra*, & *MGM v Grokster*, nn 25–35 *supra*.
37. Such as those taken under s 301 of the Omnibus Trade & Competitiveness Act of 1988.
38. Bettig (1996) argues that the copyright laws follow the logic of capital.
39. For a more explicit application of the arguments in this chapter to the question of the relationship between copyright and free speech, see Macmillan (2004b).
40. The issue of release and promotion of recorded music is a big issue for many popular composers and performers. For example, popular music composer Michael Penn is quoted as saying: 'People disappear in this business not through drug abuse but because record companies sign them and then mess them around … They're very vengeful people. If you protest, like George Michael & Prince did, you're a whining rock star. In our case you're simply a loser … Epic put my album out but they won't spend a cent on promotion. The business is incredibly narrow now. The opportunities for flukes are zero. To escape this multinational hell, your only recourse is stuff like MP3': *The Evening Standard*, London, 12 July 2000.
41. Moran 1998.
42. See, for example, n 40 *supra*.
43. For further discussion of the issue of cultural filtering and homogenization in the film industry, see Macmillan 2002b, pp. 488–489.
44. See UK Film Council, Digital Screen Network, http://www.ukfilmcouncil.org.uk/funding/distributionandexhibition/dsn/, accessed 10 September 2004.
45. Ironically, in attempting to publish the monograph in which this passage appears, Abel himself was to feel the brunt of his publisher's attempt at censorship. He has subsequently defined this as an attempted exercise of private power to control speech: see Abel 1994b, p. 380.
46. Londoner's Diary, *The Evening Standard*, 11 July 2000.

47. *Ibid.*
48. In 2000 Stephen King decided to by-pass the electronic publishing division of his publishers, Simon and Schuster, & self publish his novel, *The Plant*, on the Internet: see 'King writes off the middleman', *The Weekend Australian*, 22–23 July 2000. King later abandoned this project: see *Metro* (London), 30 November 2000.
49. See further, for example, Coombe 1998, pp. 100–129, which demonstrates how even the creation of alternative identities on the basis of class, sexuality, gender and race is constrained and homogenized through the celebrity or star system.
50. 581 F 2d 751 (9th Cir, 1978), *cert denied*, 439 US 1132 (1979).
51. Quoting Wheelwright 1976, p. 582.
52. See further text accompanying nn 61–69 *infra*.
53. For a good example of a statement of this rationale, see the Preface to World Intellectual Property Organization 1978. For discussion of this rationale, see, for example, Waldron 1993, pp. 850ff; and Macmillan Patfield 1997.
54. For a detailed and persuasive account of this approach to development, see Sen 1999.
55. See further, Macmillan 1998 and Macmillan 2002a.
56. As a result of Council Directive 93/98/EEC, 1993 OJ L290/9.
57. As a result of the Bono Copyright Term Extension Act 1998, recently held to be constitutionally valid in *Eldred v Ashcroft* 123 S Ct 769 (2003).
58. Bently 1994, p. 979 makes reference to Wordsworth's support for Sergeant Talfourd's famous campaign to extend the duration of copyright.
59. Note 57 *supra*.
60. Vaidhyanathan 2001, pp. 160–162, takes the view that performers' rights could also have this effect.
61. Citing *Sayre v Moore* (1785) in *Cary v Longman* (1801) 1 East 358, 359n, 102 ER 138, 139n; *West v Francis* 5 B & Ald 737, 106 ER 1361; and *Bramwell v Halcomb* (1836) 2 My & Cr 737, 40 ER 1110, as examples of this transition.
62. 751 F Supp 474 (SDNY 1990), *aff'd*, 960 F 2d 301 (2d Cir), *cert denied*, 113 S Ct 365 (1992).
63. This is somewhat of an oversimplification. See further, for example, Hutcheon 1989 and Polan 1993.
64. With respect to postmodern art and copyright law, see Bowrey 1994.
65. 114 S Ct 1164 (1994). For a fuller discussion of this case in the context of the relationship between copyright and free speech, see Macmillan 2004b.
66. [1994] EMLR 1. For a fuller discussion of this case in the context of the relationship between copyright and free speech, see Macmillan 2004b.
67. On the need for strong fair dealing rights in the digital environment, see van Caenegem 1995.
68. See, for example, the Digital Millennium Copyright Act, the Australian Copyright Amendment (Digital Agenda) Act 2000, and European Parliament and Council Directive on the harmonization of certain aspects of copyright and related rights in the Information Society, COM (1999) 250 final.
69. Note 21 *supra*.
70. See Gummow J in *Corrs Pavey Whiting & Byrne v Collector of Customs for the State of Victoria* (1987) 10 Intellectual Property Reports 53, 70–77 and *Smith, Kline & French Laboratories (Australia) Ltd v Secretary, Department of Community Services & Health* (1990) 17 Intellectual Property Reports 545, 583.
71. Note 57 *supra*.
72. [2001] Ch 143, CA. See further Burrell 2000.
73. See, for example, *Secretary of State for the Home Department v Central Broadcasting* [1993] EMLR 253 and *Beggars Banquet Records Ltd v Carlton Television* [1993] EMLR 349. See also, Macmillan Patfield 1996, 223–225.
74. [2002] Ch 149, CA.

REFERENCES

Abel, R.L. (1994a), *Speech and Respect*, London: Stevens and Son/Sweet and Maxwell.

Abel, R.L. (1994b), 'Public Freedom, Private Constraint', *Journal of Law and Society*, **21**, pp. 374–91.

Bently, L. (1994), 'Copyright and the Death of the Author in Literature and Law', *Modern Law Review*, **57**, pp. 973–86.

Bettig, R. (1996), *Copyrighting Culture: The Political Economy of Intellectual Property*, Boulder: Westview Press.

Blakeney, M. (1996), *Trade Related Aspects of Intellectual Property Rights*, London: Sweet and Maxwell.

Blakeney, M. (2004), 'Part I – Commentary', in A. Ilardi and M. Blakeney (eds) *International Encyclopaedia of Intellectual Property Treaties*, Oxford: Oxford University Press, pp. 1–183.

Bowrey, K. (1994), 'Copyright, the Paternity of Artistic Works, and the Challenge Posed by Postmodern Artists', *Intellectual Property Journal*, **8**, pp. 285–317.

Burrell, R. (2000), 'Defending the Public Interest', *European Intellectual Property Review*, **22**, pp. 394–403.

Capling, A. (1996), 'Gimme shelter!', *Arena Magazine*, February/March. pp. 21–4.

Chayes, A. (1959), 'The Modern Corporation and the Rule of Law', in E.S. Mason (ed.) *The Corporation in Modern Society*, New York: Atheneum (reprinted 1980).

Chon, M. (1993), 'Postmodern "Progress": Reconsidering the Copyright and Patent Power', *DePaul Law Review*, **43**, pp. 97–146.

Coombe, R. (1998), *The Cultural Life of Intellectual Properties*, Durham, NC: Duke University Press.

Gaines, J. (1991), *Contested Culture: The Image, the Voice and the Law*, Chapel Hill, NC: University of North Carolina Press.

Hutcheon, L (1989), *The Politics of Postmodernism*, London: Routledge.

Kennedy, D. (1995), 'The International Style in Postwar Law and Policy: John Jackson and the Field of International Economic Law', *American University Journal of International Law and Policy*, **10**, pp. 671–716.

Koenig, D.M. (1994), 'Joe Camel and the First Amendment: The Dark Side of Copyrighted and Trademark-Protected Icons', *Thomas M Cooley Law Review*, **11**, pp. 803–38.

Macmillan, F. (1998), 'Copyright and Culture: A Perspective on Corporate Power', *Media and Arts Law Review*, **10**, pp. 71–81.

Macmillan, F. (1999), 'Striking the Copyright Balance in the Digital Era', *International Company and Commercial Law Review*, **10**, pp. 350–60.

Macmillan, F. (2002a), 'Corporate Power and Copyright', in R. Towse (ed.) *Copyright and the Cultural Industries*, Cheltenham, UK and Northampton, MA, USA: Edward Elgar, pp. 99–118.

Macmillan, F. (2002b), 'The Cruel ©: Copyright and Film', *European Intellectual Property Review*, **24**, pp. 483–92.

Macmillan, F. (2004a), 'International Economic Law and Public International Law: Strangers in the Night', *International Trade Law and Regulation*, **10**, pp. 115–24.

Macmillan, F. (2004b), 'Commodification and Cultural Ownership', in J. Griffiths and U. Suthersanen (eds), *Copyright and Free Speech: Comparative and International Analyses*, Oxford: Oxford University Press.
Macmillan Patfield, F. (1995), 'Challenges for Company Law', in F. Macmillan Patfield (ed.) *Perspectives on Company Law: 1*, London: Kluwer Law International, pp. 1–21.
Macmillan Patfield, F. (1996), 'Towards a Reconciliation of Free Speech and Copyright', in E. Barendt (ed.) *The Yearbook of Media and Entertainment Law 1996*, Oxford: Clarendon Press, pp. 199–233.
Macmillan Patfield, F. (1997), 'Legal Policy and the Limits of Literary Copyright', in P. Parrinder, W. Chernaik and W. Gould (eds) *Textual Monopolies: Literary Copyright and the Public Domain*, London: Arts and Humanities Press, pp. 113–32.
Moran, A. (1998), *Copycat TV: Globalisation, Program Formats and Cultural Identity*, Luton: Luton University Press.
Netanel, N.W. (1996), 'Copyright and a Democratic Civil Society', *Yale Law Journal*, **106**, pp. 283–387.
Polan, D. (1993), 'Postmodernism and Cultural Analysis Today', in E.A. Kaplan (ed.) *Postmodernism and its Discontents*, London/New York: Verso, pp. 45–58.
Sell, S.K. (2003), *Private Power, Public Law: The Globalization of Intellectual Property Rights*, Cambridge: Cambridge University Press.
Sen A. (1999), *Development as Freedom*, New York: Anchor Books.
Smiers, J. (2002), 'The Abolition of Copyrights: Better for Artists, Third World Countries and the Public Domain', in R. Towse (ed.) *Copyright and the Cultural Industries*, Cheltenham, UK and Northampton, MA, USA: Edward Elgar, pp. 119–39.
Towse, R. (1999), 'Copyright, Risk and the Artist: An Economic Approach to Policy for Artists', *Cultural Policy*, **6**, pp. 91–107.
Towse, R. (2001), *Creativity, Incentive and Reward: An Economic Analysis of Copyright and Culture in the Information Age*, Cheltenham, UK and Northampton, MA, USA: Edward Elgar.
Vaidhyanathan, S. (2001), *The Rise of Intellectual Property and How it Threatens Creativity*, New York/London: New York University Press.
van Caenegem, W.A. (1995), 'Copyright, Communication and New Technologies', *Federal Law Review*, **23**, pp. 322–47.
Waldron, J. (1993), 'From Authors to Copiers: Individual Rights and Social Values in Intellectual Property', *Chicago-Kent Law Review*, **69**, pp. 841–87.
Wheelwright, K. (1976), 'Parody, Copyrights and the First Amendment', *US Federal Law Review*, **10**, pp. 564–83.
World Commission on Culture and Development (1996), *Our Creative Diversity*, 2nd ed. Paris: UNESCO.
World Intellectual Property Organization (1978), *Guide to the Berne Convention for the Protection of Literary and Artistic Works*, Geneva: WIPO.

3. AIDS, TRIPS and 'TRIPS plus': the case for developing and less developed countries

Fabienne Orsi, Mamadou Camara and Benjamin Coriat

ABSTRACT

The signing of the TRIPS Agreement in 1995 (as part of the WTO Agreement) provoked a radical change in the healthcare situation of the poorest countries. It obliged these countries to comply with the intellectual property rights (IPR) legislation in force in the Northern countries. It ended a situation in which the poorest countries were able either to produce generic drugs locally or to import them at a low price. Given the development of the AIDS epidemic, the consequences of this agreement were dramatic. In this chapter, we shall examine the situation created by TRIPS in the French-speaking countries of Sub-Saharan Africa. In this zone (where AIDS has struck most severely) the application of TRIPS, combined with existing regional IPR agreements (known as the Bangui Agreements), has created a legal situation particularly prejudicial to healthcare.

Keywords: IPR, WTO, Generic drugs, Public Health, Sub-Saharan countries

1 INTRODUCTION

The World Trade Organization (WTO) Trade-Related Aspects of Intellectual Property Rights Agreement (TRIPS), signed in 1994, marked a turning point in public health, especially in the developing countries. By instituting a unique IPR regime for drugs on an international scale, closely copied from the regime existing in the most developed countries, TRIPS has created an additional series of barriers to access to treatment in the poorest countries.

This situation has provoked fierce debate and been the subject of numerous international forums.[1] However, until now, no solutions have been found that meet the acceptance of all the parties concerned.

This is the issue - the role of TRIPS in the access to healthcare in Southern countries – to which this chapter is devoted. We aim to show, using field surveys carried out in several countries, how and in what ways the signing of TRIPS has created a series of additional obstacles blocking access to treatment (in the form of anti-retroviral drugs – ARVs) for AIDS victims. Following on from other work on the same theme[2], we focus particularly on the question of access to treatment in the countries which need it the most, being the worst affected by the epidemic. These are the countries of Sub-Saharan Africa.

The chapter is structured as follows. In section 2, we present and analyse the transformations in the legal framework of access to drugs since the signing of TRIPS. We start by describing the ways in which TRIPS brought about a radical change in the prevailing international IPR and public health situation. We then show how the new framework enforced by TRIPS affected IPR legislation in Sub-Saharan Africa. The new IPR agreement enforced in this region, the 'Revised Bangui Agreement' signed in 1999, has created an extremely damaging situation in the countries concerned, even more deleterious in some respects than what would have resulted from the sole application of TRIPS. Because the Revised Bangui Agreement goes even further than the TRIPS requirements, it is often referred to as 'TRIPS plus'.

In section 3, we analyse the conditions of ARV supply in the countries in this zone. We present the functioning of the different players involved (multinational firms, local laboratories, international organizations, nongovernmental organizations). Using this presentation, we show how the constraints imposed by TRIPS and the Revised Bangui Agreement have affected both the regional supply of ARVs and, in consequence, the choice of local public health policies in the fight against AIDS.

In a brief conclusion, we sum up the main points established and raise some questions of general interest that come out of this study (section 4).

2 CHANGES IN THE INTERNATIONAL LEGAL SITUATION: FROM THE SIGNING OF TRIPS TO THE BANGUI AGREEMENT

The TRIPS agreement provoked dramatic changes (presented in section 2.2), which have in turn led to significant modifications in the regional IPR agreements in Sub-Saharan Africa (presented in section 2.3). One cannot appreciate the full impact of these changes without some background knowledge of the status of drugs in the legal framework of patents and IPR. We shall therefore start with a short description of this very particular status (section 2.1).

2.1 A Brief Survey of Drug Patenting

The creation of new drugs (in practical terms, this means the design of new molecules with proven therapeutic properties) is highly R&D intensive, and the 'productivity' (that is, the number of molecules discovered in proportion to the money invested) is relatively low.

For these reasons, economic theory, combined with the public welfare considerations involved in any reflection on healthcare, has always argued that research into new drugs and treatments should be supported and given different types of incentive. For a long time, the most important of these supports has been public aid. As for all research activities, the question of patent protection for pharmaceutical research discoveries has naturally arisen. Since Arrow (1962), or even earlier, it has been accepted that to ensure sufficient R&D investment by private firms, they must be protected from 'free riding' by their competitors. The attribution of patents – temporary monopolies granted to inventors – is one of the ways this protection can be ensured, thus encouraging private firms to invest in research. However, the fundamental theory underlying the patenting system also affirms that the protection (and the monopoly of exploitation) thus granted should not have too high a cost in welfare terms.

In the case of pharmaceuticals, such welfare considerations are even stronger, given that access to drugs and treatments is regarded as a 'basic need'. Furthermore, complex insurance systems (either private or public) are required to make the demand affordable and to guarantee public access to medicines. Moreover, in no other commercial activity is there so much public investment in research. Finally, as pointed out by Scherer, 'The public policy question, as a consequence, is how to balance the desire to make new drugs affordable to all those who need them, and yet retain strong incentives for inventing and developing new and better treatments' (Scherer and Watal, 2001: 4).

These are the reasons why, even in most developed countries, no patent system on molecules was introduced until the 1960s, or even (in the case of Switzerland) the 1970's[3] (Scherer 1993). Nevertheless, the pharmaceutical industry made spectacular progress. By the use of intense reciprocal reverse engineering, copying and 'inventing around' the molecules, the large Western firms were able to build enormous technological capabilities, whilst at the same time efficiently serving the public interest. It is worth noting that the pharmaceutical industry thrived during that period. One explanation for this is that firms can use a number of methods other than patents (secrecy, lead time, and so on) to ensure that they benefit from their innovations. In addition, the cost of entry into R&D-intensive industries is so high that it generally creates huge 'barriers to entry', under the protection of which innovative firms can enjoy the benefits of their innovations. Moreover, 'brand' names for established pharmaceutical firms provide a huge competitive advantage. Established firms, by segmenting the markets and raising the price of branded products, are generally able to maintain their profit levels, even after patent expiry and the entry of generic products (see FTC reports on this issue, available at http://www.ftc.gov; see also the recent survey conducted by Pammoli *et al.*, 2002).

Until the mid 1990s, patent systems in the pharmaceutical sector in less developed countries (LDC) were either weak or non-existent. This is not at all surprising. Many studies demonstrate the clear correlation between the level of economic development of a country and the strength of its patent system. It is obviously in the interest of most developed countries to grant patents to their pharmaceutical firms (to provide their 'national champions' with some institutional advantage). Most LDC, on the other hand, having no such firms and very limited resources to meet the basic needs of their populations, clearly have the opposite interest. In their case, the local production of 'similar' or 'generic' drugs is the only possible means to reduce the cost of treatment. It is worth noting that until the signing of TRIPS, the World Intellectual Property Organization (WIPO), through the Paris Convention, recognized the rights of countries with different levels of development to implement different patent systems (Zhang, 1994).

2.2 From Heterogeneous International IPR Laws to the TRIPS Agreement: Why the Public Health Conflict was Inevitable

With the signing of the TRIPS[4] in 1994, the international protection of IPR, until then organized exclusively under the aegis of the WIPO, moved into the sphere of competence of the WTO (Zhang, 1994). This adoption of IPR protection into the domain of the WTO was of considerable importance. It signified the enforcement, for and on behalf of the WIPO, of a new international standard, largely based on the standards of the most advanced countries. Coming after the considerable reinforcement of IPR in the Northern countries[5], the signing of the TRIPS heralded the enforcement of this new, stricter law on a worldwide scale (Reichman and Lange, 2000; Remiche and Desterbecq, 1996). From this moment, the adoption of the same IPR regime, covering all fields of activity, became mandatory for all member countries of the WTO. The signing of the TRIPS thus represents a radical break with some of the foundations and rules which had hitherto shaped international IPR protection.

We must underline the fact (mentioned briefly above) that before this agreement was signed, international treaties had recognized the right of different countries to implement different systems of protection, according to their level of economic development and according to the products concerned. Among these products, essential drugs, considered 'basic necessities', were ranked of the highest importance (Scherer and Watal, 2001). Thus Brazil, for example, dispensed with any form of IPR for drugs from 1971 to 1996 (the date of TRIPS implementation in this country). This made it possible to establish a large industry for the low-cost production of generic drugs, the only way to ensure access to treatment for the poorer segments of the population (Orsi et al., 2003).

One point cannot be emphasized too strongly: the possibility of implementing different IPR rules, according to the level of economic development and the products concerned, was accepted because international agreements were founded on priorities of welfare and equity. This differential regime was based on principles of public interest (access to healthcare or food), or the promotion of sectors of vital importance for the economic and technological development of the developing and least-developed countries (Coriat and Orsi, 2003).

Given this context, the advent of TRIPS could only result in major conflicts. The economic gap between developed and less developed countries has not evolved, over the last few decades, in any way that could justify the homogenization of international IPR rules[6]. Since its ratification, the TRIPS agreement, which had already provoked serious antagonisms between developing and industrialized countries during the Uruguay Round of negotiations (Zhang, 1994), has been the constant source of important discussions, the leading subject of which has been the issue of access to drugs in developing countries.

The Southern countries were quick to bring the issue of the impact of TRIPS on public healthcare to the forefront. Because it obliges these countries to introduce drug patenting legislation identical to that of industrialized countries, the debate has crystallized around the issue of access to certain generic drugs, hitherto produced cheaply by certain Southern countries. When these countries become TRIPS-compliant, all production of generic copies becomes impossible; consequently, the debate has centred on the question of access to HIV/AIDS treatments. This debate has been fuelled by the dramatic contrast between AIDS victims in the industrialized countries and those in the Southern countries that has appeared since the introduction (in 1996) of Highly Active Antiretroviral combination

Therapies (HAART),[7] which provide longer and improved conditions of life. While the great majority of people affected by the disease live in Southern countries, the high price of the treatments produced by patentee firms renders their purchase by these countries almost impossible. Before generic ARVs came into the market, the price of HAART was around ten to twelve thousand dollars per person per year. Obviously, this prohibited access to care for almost all AIDS sufferers in Southern countries, where no health insurance system, even where one does exist, can support such a cost for each patient.[8]

Nevertheless, the TRIPS Agreement contains certain exceptions to exclusive patent rights (TRIPS, 1994, Article 30) and makes provision for 'Other Use Without Authorization of the Right Holder' (TRIPS, 1994, Article 31). One example is compulsory licensing. This legal tool allows WTO members to authorize themselves or third parties to use the subject matter of a patent, for reasons of public policy, without the permission of the patent owner (Reichman and Hasenzahl, 2002). In other words, the patentee must tolerate the exploitation of his invention by a third person or by a government. In this case, as Reichman and Hasenzahl point out, 'the public interest in broader access to the patented invention is considered more important than the private interest of the right holder to fully exploit his exclusive right' (2002 p. 4). The practice of compulsory licensing is long established and has been used on numerous occasions by industrialized countries, including the United States.[9]

It should be noted that TRIPS does not define the grounds on which the issue of compulsory licences can be justified. It only recognizes such grounds as 'anti-competitive practices', 'national emergency or other circumstances of extreme urgency' or 'public non-commercial use' (TRIPS, 1994, Article 31b). Nevertheless, Article 31 of TRIPS stipulates the conditions governing the issue of compulsory licensing, including 'case-by-case authorisations, adequate remuneration based on the economic value of the license, prior negotiations with rights holders'. It should be noted that this last condition 'may be waived by a Member in the case of a national emergency or other circumstances of extreme urgency or in cases of public non-commercial use' (TRIPS, 1994).

However, another condition, specified in Article 31f, is of particular importance to us in this chapter. According to this article, compulsory licences should be granted 'predominantly' to supply the domestic market. This means that the use of compulsory licensing for export to countries without sufficient manufacturing capacity is very limited. Consequently, although the TRIPS Agreement does not prevent members from using compulsory licences for export purposes, in practice this use is highly limited by the restrictions on exporting goods produced under compulsory licence.

It is thus practically impossible for countries lacking technological capabilities to use compulsory licensing effectively, and this fact lies at the origin of the vast debate on the relationship between TRIPS and access to drugs. Initiated in 2001 by the Africa Group of the TRIPS Council, this debate aims explicitly to clarify the interpretation and application of TRIPS provisions in the context of public health. The move by Southern countries to provoke this debate within the TRIPS Council was motivated by a number of recent events illustrating the effects of TRIPS on public health policies. Among these, the most significant was clearly the lawsuit brought by the Pharmaceutical Industry Association and thirty-nine of its affiliate pharmaceutical companies against the Government of South Africa, alleging that its Medicines and Related Substances Control Amendment Act violated the TRIPS agreement.[10] Although the pharmaceutical industry finally withdrew its complaint, under the strong pressure of national and international public opinion, this lawsuit indicated the urgency with which Southern countries had to 'initiate discussions on the interpretation and application of the relevant provisions of the TRIPS Agreement, with a view to clarifying the flexibilities to which Members are entitled and, in particular, to establish the relationship between intellectual property rights and access to medicines.[11]

In June 2001, the TRIPS Council held its first session devoted to TRIPS and access to drugs and in November 2001, the fourth Ministerial Conference of the WTO in Doha adopted a Declaration on TRIPS and Public Health[12] (the Doha Declaration).

2.2.1 The Doha Declaration of 2001

In this chapter, we shall not go back over the negotiations that preceded the Doha Declaration. We simply observe that this declaration constitutes a 'compromise' text: the result of grim negotiations, most often pitting the Southern countries against certain industrialized countries which proposed that exceptions should be limited to cases of health crisis and not applied to health in general, arguing that exceptions made for the protection of public health would be inconsistent with TRIPS.

It should also be noted that this declaration has no legal status. However, many observers agree that it is of great importance, above all because, while accepting that protection of intellectual property remains a strong incentive for the development of new drugs, the Declaration explicitly acknowledges that IPR can damage public health through its effect on the price of drugs. It is on these grounds that the Declaration affirms the right of countries to interpret and apply the TRIPS in the best way to protect public health. Thus:

> We agree that the TRIPS Agreement does not and should not prevent Members from taking measures to protect public health. Accordingly, while reiterating our commitment to the TRIPS Agreement, we affirm that the Agreement can and should be interpreted and implemented in a manner supportive of WTO Members' right to protect public health and, in particular, to promote access to medicines for all (The Doha Declaration, 2001, Article 1).

The primary aim of the Doha Declaration is to reaffirm the possibility of recourse to the exceptions provided for in TRIPS by clarifying the way in which these exceptions can be used by WTO members. Thus the Declaration specifies notably that:

> Each Member has the right to grant compulsory licences and the freedom to determine the grounds upon which such licences are granted (The Doha Declaration, Article 5b)

> Each Member has the right to determine what constitutes a national emergency or other circumstances of extreme urgency, it being understood that public health crises, including those relating to HIV/AIDS, tuberculosis, malaria and other epidemics, can represent a national emergency or other circumstances of extreme urgency (The Doha Declaration, Article 5c).

In addition to the clarification of existing rules, the Doha Declaration set two specific new tasks. It extended the deadline for least-developed countries to apply provisions on pharmaceutical patents to 1 January 2016 (instead of 2006) and – acknowledging the problem posed by Article 31f for countries with little or no drug manufacturing capacity – mandated the TRIPS Council to find a solution to this problem. This is set out in the famous paragraph 6 of the Declaration:

> We recognize that WTO Members with insufficient or no manufacturing capacities in the pharmaceutical sector could face difficulties in making effective use of compulsory licensing under the TRIPS Agreement. We instruct the Council for TRIPS to find an expeditious solution to this problem and to report to the General Council before the end of 2002 (The Doha Declaration, Article 6).

For many observers, the Doha Declaration represented an important clarification of the issue and appeared to herald the relaxation of restrictions weighing on the least developed countries. These observers were to be heavily disappointed. The Declaration should have been incorporated into WTO rules by December 2002 at the latest. It never was. The negotiations held for this purpose in Geneva at the end of 2002 came to nothing. The United States vetoed a compromise which had been accepted by all the 123 other countries taking part in the negotiations. It was only in August 2003, after bitter negotiations, that a text specifying the conditions for the implementation of paragraph 6 of the Doha Declaration was approved by the TRIPS Council.[13] This text, criticized by the major nongovernmental organizations (NGOs) operating in this field (including Médecins Sans Frontières and Oxfam) set out, under very precisely defined and restrictive conditions, the circumstances under which least developed countries could import generic ARVs.

2.3 The impact of TRIPS on the Regional Bangui Agreement and its Revision: A 'TRIPS-Plus' Agreement in Contradiction to the Doha Declaration

As WTO members, the French-speaking African states in the Organisation Africaine de la Propriété Intellectuelle (OAPI – African Intellectual Property Organization, see Box 3.1) revised their joint law to bring it into compliance with the TRIPS Agreement. This revision resulted in the Revised Bangui Agreement of 1999,[14] which came into force on 28 February 2002. Labelled as 'TRIPS plus' because the provisions were even more constraining than those imposed by TRIPS, the Revised Bangui Agreement also rendered the Doha Declaration almost totally inoperative.

The OAPI was established in 1977 by the Bangui Agreement.[15] The aim was to create a body responsible for application of the joint administrative procedures resulting from a uniform regime of intellectual property protection. This Agreement has the value of national law for all the OAPI member states (Tankoano, 2002).

One of the key elements of the Bangui Agreement was the provision for a centralized procedure for the registration of patents (and other IPR) at the level of the OAPI. This body is responsible for granting patents which, through regional extension, automatically take effect in all the member states.[16] As for the measures applicable in each member state, Annex I of the Bangui Agreement defined those relating to patents for inventions. It should be noted that the Bangui Agreement of 1977 implicitly recognized patents on pharmaceutical products, as no distinction was made between patents on drugs and those on other products. However, certain provisions (relating notably to the duration of patents and the conditions governing recourse to compulsory licences) could be used as a legal basis to facilitate access to drugs, in the event that existing patents represented an obstacle to this access (Jourdain, 2002).

The provisions of Article 6 of the Bangui Agreement of 1977 stipulate that a patent be granted for a period of ten years counting from the registration date, with the possibility of extending this initial period by two further periods of five years upon request by the patentee. However, the duration of the protection thus granted is dependent on local exploitation

BOX 3.1 THE HISTORY AND MAIN CHARACTERISTICS OF THE OAPI

Until 1962, industrial property in most of the French-speaking member states of the OAPI was governed by French law. The Institut National Français de la Propriété Industrielle (INPI – French National Industrial Property Institute) was the National Office for each of these states, which were at the time grouped together in the French Union. When the majority of member countries of the French Union gained independence in 1960, it became necessary to create a specific structure in each of the new independent states, in accordance with international conventions on industrial property.

The legal foundation for the establishment of these structures lies in Article 19 of the Paris Convention for the Protection of Industrial Property, which stipulates that the signatory countries reserve the right to make particular separate arrangements amongst themselves, on the condition that these arrangements do not contravene the provisions of the said convention. On the basis of this provision, twelve French-speaking African countries agreed to create a joint structure that would function as a national office of industrial property for all twelve countries. The Office Africain et Malgache de Propriété Industrielle (OAMPI – African and Malagasy Office of Industrial Property) came into being on 13 September 1962, through an agreement known as the 'Libreville Agreement'.

The Libreville Agreement regime was founded on three fundamental principles:

- the adoption of uniform legislation through the implementation and application of common administrative procedures resulting from a uniform regime of industrial property protection.
- the creation of a joint office to carry out the organization's mission as national industrial property office for each of the member states.
- the centralization of procedures, made necessary by the introduction of uniform legislation and a joint office, so that any property rights granted could be split into independent national rights in every member country.

On the level of territorial competence, the Libreville Agreement covered African countries in which the French language and sphere of influence predominate. On the level of material competence, the objects governed by the Libreville Agreement covered patents for inventions, trade and production brand marks and industrial plans and models.

The following countries were signatories to the Libreville Agreement: the Federal Republic of Cameroon, the Central African Republic, the Republic of the Congo, the Ivory Coast, the Republic of Dahomey (now Benin), the Republic of Upper Volta (now Burkina Faso), the Gabon Republic, the Republic of Mauritania, the Republic of Senegal, the Republic of Chad, the Malagasy Republic (now Madagascar) and the Niger Republic.

A number of motives led the founding states to revise the Libreville Agreement. These included the withdrawal of the Malagasy Republic over questions of sovereignty; the desire to cover all objects of intellectual property, notably utility models, trade names, brand marks of products and services; the desire to involve intellectual property more closely in development; and the ambition to be the core of a wider expansion. This resulted in the creation of the African Intellectual Property Organization (OAPI), through the adoption of a new agreement signed in Bangui on 2 March 1977.

The Bangui Agreement, which formalized the revision of the Libreville Agreement, now governs industrial property law in each of the 16 member states currently comprising the OAPI zone. These 16 member states are Benin, Burkina Faso, Cameroon, Central Africa, Congo, Ivory Coast, Gabon, Guinea, Guinea-Bissau, Equatorial Guinea, Mali, Mauritania, Niger, Senegal, Chad and Togo.

Source: OAPI: www.oapi.wipo.net/fr/index.html

of the invention. Thus, the Bangui Agreement stipulates that if, in the five years following the granting of the patent, the patentee has failed, without 'legitimate excuse', to exploit his invention or to arrange to have it exploited, then 'no lawsuit for infringement of patent' will be receivable before a court (Bangui Agreement, 1977, Article 58.2). In other words, if there is no local exploitation of the patented invention within five years, the local production and import of this invention without the authorization of the patentee cannot be considered an infringement of the exclusive right of the patentee. This provision is essential in the specific case of access to drugs, as it implicitly authorizes not only the production of generic drugs before legal expiry of the patent but also the import of these drugs in the form of generic copies produced abroad. This measure, the primary objective of which is to make patents an effective tool for the industrial development of countries in the OAPI zone, is completed by measures concerning compulsory licensing.

On this point, the Bangui Agreement stipulates that any resident of an OAPI member state has the right to request the granting of a compulsory licence, three years after the granting of the patent and after prior negotiations with the patentee, if the patented invention has not been exploited industrially within one of the member states, or if existing local exploitation does not satisfy 'reasonable conditions of demand'. Two points here deserve particular attention: i) the Agreement stipulates that the recourse to compulsory licences is only possible in the perspective of local production – a compulsory licence cannot be granted to import a patented product (The Bangui Agreement, 1977, Article 47); ii) however, it provides that a member state can resort 'at any moment' to compulsory licensing, including for the purposes of import, 'for national defence or for public health or for the national economy' (The Bangui Agreement, 1977, Article 55). This measure does not define 'compulsory licences' but '*ex officio* licences', which differ from compulsory licences in that they can only be obtained by the state itself, even if a third party is then entrusted with exploitation of the licence on behalf of the state.

Finally, the Bangui Agreement of 1977, while establishing veritable intellectual property rights, contained a group of measures – in accordance with the spirit of patent law – that made it possible to protect the public interest. In particular, the clauses relating to compulsory and *ex officio* licences enabled the public authorities, whenever necessary and in well-defined circumstances, to release themselves from constraints likely to hinder their pursuit of the general interest.

However, some of the provisions of the Bangui Agreement of 1977 were not in accordance with the minimum standards defined by TRIPS. Notably, this concerned provisions relating to the duration of patent protection. The TRIPS agreement imposes a minimum patent duration of twenty years, whereas the Bangui Agreement of 1977 set a minimum of ten years. Since certain members of the OAPI[17] had to become TRIPS-compliant before 1 January 2001, the Bangui Agreement had to be revised.

Before presenting the main modifications introduced into the Bangui Agreement, we should explain why four of the member countries of the OAPI had to become TRIPS-compliant before the deadline of 1 January 2001, despite the fact that they are defined as developing countries. This obligation can largely be attributed to the recognition of drug patents by the Bangui Agreement of 1977. Although the TRIPS Agreement provided for an additional transition period for developing countries (the deadline was set for 2006), this period was only applicable to those countries that had yet to extend their patent laws to cover objects hitherto excluded from protection. Article 65.4 of TRIPS stipulates:

> To the extent that a developing country Member is obliged by this Agreement to extend product patent protection to areas of technology not so protectable in its territory on the general date of application of this Agreement for that Member, [...], it may delay the application of the provisions on product patents [...] to such areas of technology for an additional period of five years[18] (TRIPS, 1994, Article 65.4).

In addition, the transition period provided for by TRIPS for the least developed countries is not subject to any conditions (TRIPS, 1994, Article 66). With the exception of the four countries referred to above, this was the case for all the OAPI members. Thus, although these countries were theoretically granted a transition period for TRIPS compliance lasting until 2006 (indeed, the Doha Declaration provided for an extension of this period until 2016 for the least developed countries in the field of drug patents), the revisions of the Bangui Agreement were obligatory for all members of the OAPI. This extension was necessary because of the principle of 'common procedure' for all the OAPI countries, a principle that lies at the heart of the constitution of this organization.

So it was that this principle of 'common procedure', introduced to strengthen local cooperation and reduce exchange costs, with a view to constituting a unified zone that would be in a better position to face up to international competition, became highly detrimental to its initiators. When applied in the context of TRIPS, this measure turned into a sort of Trojan horse, by means of which measures highly prejudicial to the Southern signatory countries were introduced. This obviously raises a major subject for reflection, on the hierarchy of rules imposed by globalization and their likely consequences.

Besides the extension to the duration of patents, the main modifications of the Bangui Agreement concerned subjects as crucial as the cancellation of the possibility of resorting to compulsory licences in the event of non-exploitation of the patent locally by the patentee, as well as the abolition of the specific regime of *ex officio* licences enabling them to be used for import. Based on an interpretation of TRIPS which is not necessarily illegitimate, but certainly extremely strict, these new measures in the Revised Bangui Agreement resulted in the imposition of additional constraints on the access to generic drugs for the member countries of OAPI, constraints reaching well beyond those imposed by the provisions of the TRIPS Agreement, or at least beyond those recognized in the Doha Declaration. So in its expansion, the TRIPS Agreement – the severity of which for the least developed countries has often been stressed – has generated even greater restrictions than those it originally contained.

The principal modifications introduced in the Revised Bangui Agreement of 1999 concerned the following points:

- Article 9 (relating to the duration of patent protection), extended protection to a period of twenty years, on the sole condition that the patentee pays the taxes required to maintain the patent in force (The Bangui Agreement, 1999, Article 9). This new article stands in sharp contrast to the Bangui Agreement of 1977, which split patent protection into three periods (10 + 5 + 5 years) and subjected it to conditions of local exploitation of the patented invention. Consequently, according to the terms of the Revised Agreement, any import of the patented invention or its local production by a third party without the consent of the patentee is liable to a complaint of infringement, even if the patent is not being exploited locally by the patentee. Although nothing in the TRIPS Agreement explicitly obliges countries to implement such a measure, it seems likely that the condition of local exploitation was removed in application of Article 27.1 of TRIPS. However, the interpretation of this article, which stipulates that '[...] patents shall be available and patent rights enjoyable without discrimination as to the place of invention, the field of technology and whether products are imported or locally produced' (TRIPS, 1994, Article 27.1), remains the subject of fierce controversy.[19]
- It was doubtless in the same spirit that the measures relating to *ex officio* licences established in the Bangui Agreement of 1977 were modified to subject these licences to the same conditions as compulsory licences, including prohibition of the 'act of import'. This is because the Revised Bangui Agreement, contrary to the original Agreement of 1977, makes no distinction between *ex officio* and compulsory licences. Article 56a, nevertheless dedicated to *ex officio* licences, stipulates that

> when certain patents are of vital interest for the economy of the country, public health or national defence, or when the absence or inadequacy of their exploitation is seriously prejudicial to the satisfaction of the needs of the country, then these patents may be subjected to non-voluntary [compulsory] licensing through an administrative act by the competent Minister of the member state in question (The Bangui Agreement, 1999, Article 56a).

The same article goes on to specify that '*ex officio* licenses shall be subject to the same conditions as non-voluntary licenses'.

> Consequently, recourse to *ex officio* licences, as is also the case for compulsory licences, is no longer possible except under certain conditions, including prior negotiation with the patentee and 'only after expiry of a period of four years from the date of registration of the patent request or three years from the date of granting of the patent' (Bangui Agreement, 1999, Article 56a). Above all, the Revised Bangui Agreement also specifies, along the lines of the 1977 Agreement, that a licence 'cannot be extended to the act of import'.

Before we leave our examination of the texts, one final point must be made. The Revised Bangui Agreement makes it impossible to resort to compulsory licences for import from outside the OAPI zone. In practical terms, given that drug production capacities in the countries in this zone are limited or non-existent, this provision blocks all access to generic drugs, often supplied at very low prices by foreign producers such as India or Brazil. The paradox here is that, only a few months after the opening of the debate within the WTO (itself initiated by many African states) on the means of ensuring that the least developed countries could genuinely make use of the flexibilities provided for in the TRIPS Agreement, the members of OAPI found themselves obliged, by ratifying the Revised Bangui Agreement, to renounce all the flexibilities introduced in the previous version of their founding agreement.

Given these circumstances, it was inevitable that when the AIDS pandemic developed in this zone, the question of the supply of ARVs would be confronted under particularly difficult conditions.

3 THE SUPPLY OF ANTIRETROVIRAL DRUGS IN THE AFRICAN INTELLECTUAL PROPERTY ORGANIZATION ZONE: A SITUATION OF EXTREME CONSTRAINT

To appreciate fully the practical, public health consequences of the IPR measures presented above, it may be useful to start by giving some idea of the scale of the AIDS pandemic in Sub-Saharan Africa. We shall now focus on this question.

Table 3.1 gives a first idea of the dimensions of the problem. As the data show, Sub-Saharan Africa has suffered the most tragic developments of the epidemic. This is the worst affected zone in the world, with the highest rates of morbidity and mortality connected with the development of the AIDS epidemic. The average rate of infection in this region is seven to eight times

Table 3.1 Indicators of the HIV epidemic in different regions of the world in 2003

Region	Children and adults living with HIV/AIDS (millions)	New cases of HIV infection in children and adults (millions)	Prevalence among adults (%)*	Death of children and adults due to AIDS (millions)
Sub-Saharan Africa	25.0 – 28.2	3.0 – 3.4	7.5 – 8.5	2.2 – 2.4
North Africa and Middle East	0.47 – 0.73	0.43 – 0.067	0.2 – 0.4	0.035 – 0.05
South and South East Asia	4.6 – 8.2	0.61 – 1.1	0.4 – 0.8	0.33 – 0.59
East Asia and Pacific	0.7 – 1.3	0.15 – 0.27	0.1	0.032 – 0.058
Latin America	1.3 – 1.9	0.12 – 0.18	0.5 – 0.7	0.049 – 0.07
Caribbean	0.35 – 0.59	0.045 – 0.08	1.9 – 3.1	0.030 – 0.05
Eastern Europe and Central Asia	1.2 – 1.8	0.18 – 0.28	0.5 – 0.9	0.023 – 0.037
Western Europe	0.52 – 0.68	0.03 – 0.040	0.3	0.0026 – 0.034
North America	0.79 – 1.2	0.036 – 0.054	0.5 – 0.7	0.012 – 0.018
Australia and New Zealand	0.012 – 0.018	0.0007 – 0.001	0.1	0 – 0.0001
Total	35 – 46 (Average: 40.5)	4.6 – 5.5 (Average: 5)	0.9 – 1.3 (Average: 1.1)	2.7 – 3.3 (Average: 3)

Notes:
The margins around the estimations define the limits within which the real figures are located, based upon the best information available.
* Proportion of adults (aged between 15 and 49) living with HIV/AIDS, according to demographic statistics for 2003.

Source: UNAIDS (2003)

higher than the world average. In 2003, nearly 75 per cent of adult deaths from AIDS in the world occurred in Sub-Saharan Africa.[20]

Faced with this situation, the majority of countries have implemented preventive strategies, focused principally on programmes of awareness and the distribution of condoms. However, the increase in rates of infection over time – or their relative stability in some rare cases – together with the appearance of antiretroviral treatments have helped to shift AIDS policies away from the sole strategy of prevention and towards the treatment of infected people.

However, the introduction of ARV treatments rapidly came up against the obstacle of very high prices. The poverty of the majority of people needing treatment, the absence of social security systems and the low level of public resources devoted to the health sector explain why, to begin with, the ARV market was restricted to a minority of patients (notably high-ranking civil servants and expatriates). The handful of poor patients who obtained access to ARVs during the second half of the 1990s only did so thanks to the action of voluntary and humanitarian organizations such as Médecins Sans Frontières.

Today, out of the six million people living in developing countries who have immediate need of ARV therapies for their very survival, only 400 000 have access to them. Furthermore, more than one third of these 400 000 patients live in the same country, Brazil (World Health Organization, 2004a).

In the following paragraphs, we shall describe the key events and principal determinants of the drug supply policies adopted. By so doing, we propose to show how the IPR measures in force (presented in section 2) have raised huge obstacles to the access to treatment, in various ways.

Two series of events have played a key role in the evolution of ARV supply policies. The first was the introduction, in May 2000, of the Accelerating Access Initiative (AAI), born out of collaboration between several United Nations organizations and the main pharmaceutical companies. Unquestionably, for the countries concerned in this chapter, the launch of the AAI represented a major turning point (see section 3.2).

This event is of undoubted importance, but it can only be correctly interpreted by considering its context. The period during which the AAI was promoted was also the period when generic drugs started to arrive on the market in the countries concerned. These generic drugs were supplied by firms situated in the Southern countries which, for different reasons, were able to enter into the production of generic ARVs and offer them on the international market at greatly reduced prices, despite the TRIPS Agreement. The main producers were India, which took full advantage of its right not to comply with TRIPS until 2005 to launch the large-scale production of generic ARVs, and, to a lesser extent, Thailand.[21] This supply of generic ARVs was taken up all the more enthusiastically since, apart from the fact that it offered ARVs at prices much lower than those of the pharmaceutical companies, it came on the heels of an initiative by the Brazilian Ministry of Health which, by combining local production of generics and purchases from pharmaceutical laboratories, had succeeded in introducing a programme of free and universal access to HAART for all infected patients. This programme rapidly became a reference point on an international level (Orsi *et al.*, 2003; Coriat and Orsi, 2003).

In terms of supply, therefore, we can distinguish between two main periods. The first came before the introduction of the AAI. It was characterized by the exclusivity of the supply from pharmaceutical laboratories. The second period, following the introduction of the AAI, was marked by the multiplication of initiatives from international organizations and by the presence of strong, diversified supply from generic producers located in Southern countries.

3.1 Before the Accelerating Access Initiative: The Limited and Segmented Supply of Patented Drugs

Before the introduction of the AAI, most countries in Sub-Saharan Africa obtained supplies of ARVs by buying them (in the form of patented drugs) from the big pharmaceutical companies. The price was almost the same as that charged in the Northern countries (Dumoulin and Maville, 1999). Several lessons can be drawn from the data collected and presented by Dumoulin and Maville on wholesale prices of ARVs (that is, the price paid by trading groups for the patented drugs) in seven countries of Sub-Saharan Africa (Burkina Faso, Burundi, the Ivory Coast, Guinea, Mali, Niger and Senegal).

The first thing to note is the weak dispersion of prices throughout this group of countries. This low price dispersion (the prices are practically uniform, taking into account different transaction costs), testifies to the absence of 'preferential' agreements between the pharmaceutical companies and most of these countries, with the exception of Senegal and the Ivory Coast.[22] Table 3.2 illustrates the differences in terms of the price and availability of ARVs in the zone at the end of the 1990s.

Despite the very low levels of per capita income in the countries of the zone, and despite the fact that the most dramatic developments in the pandemic were occurring here, no specific offer was made by the pharmaceutical companies. They argued that the income from supernormal profits (extraordinarily high, as the subsequent evolution in the market prices of ARVs shows)[23] was indispensable for the maintenance of sufficient R&D activity to ensure the production of new drugs. During the whole of this

Table 3.2 Structure of ARV supplies and prices in US$ in certain countries in July 1999

ARV	**Burkina**	**Mali**	**Niger**	**Burundi**	**Guinea**	**Senegal**	**Ivory coast**	**Suppliers**
Rétrovir®-100mg	54.7	92.67	NA	92.67	NA	64.17	51.5	GSK
Rétrovir®-250mg	113.11	NA	NA	92.67	NA	NA	51.13	GSK
Epivir	94.56	NA	NA	160.67	NA	160.67	88.5	GSK
Videx®-150mg	98.24	111.67	131	89.52	NA	NA	NA	BMS
Videx®-100mg	73.9	75	433.30/6	59.68	76.28	59.68	60.0	BMS
Zérit®-40mg	144.0	149.33	158.78	131.22	166.67	131.22	131.6	BMS
Zérit®-30mg	154.23	144.5	152.98	126.43	162.95	NA	126.43	BMS
Crixivan®-200mg	NA	NA	NA	305	NA	NA	311.4	Merck
Crixivan®-400mg	372.79	345.58	NA	305	NA	311	311.1	Merck

Notes:
NA: not available
GSK: GlaxoSmithKline
BMS: Bristol-Myers Squibb

Source: Dumoulin and Maville (1999, p. 3)

period, spanning from the middle of the 1990s until the first half of 2000, the pharmaceutical companies refused to contemplate the possibility of a dual supply (high prices in the Northern countries, reduced prices in low-income countries). This was also the period when the big pharmaceutical laboratories, represented by a group of Northern countries (itself often led by the United States), were exerting very strong pressure to ensure that the TRIPS provisions on the development and import of generics (notably measures concerning compulsory and *ex officio* licences) were interpreted in the most restrictive possible manner, by emptying them of all practical effects. The Johannesburg lawsuit, coming after the opening of a lawsuit before the WTO against Brazil (t'Hoen, 2003), and the multiple pressures exerted on Thailand (Guennif and M'Fuka, 2003), bear witness to the severe character of the strategy adopted by the big international pharmaceutical laboratories during this period. This was also the period during which the Bangui Agreement was 'revised'.

In addition to this first observation, which is central to our thesis, the following characteristics can also be drawn from deeper analysis of the local ARV market.

1. The supply, only available in the form of patented drugs proposed by the big pharmaceutical laboratories, was limited to the following five ARVs: Retrovir® (Zidovudine); Epivir® (Lamivudine); Videx® (Didanosine); Zerit® (Staduvine); Crivixan® (Indinavir).
2. This supply, already limited in range in terms of patented drugs, was not available in all the countries concerned. For instance, in July 1999, Retrovir® (Zidovudine) – in its 250 mg box presentation – was only available in three out of seven countries (Burkina, Burundi and the Ivory Coast). Likewise, Epivir® (Lamivudine) was only available in four countries (Burkina, Burundi, the Ivory Coast and Senegal). As for Crivixan® (Indinavir), this was only available in Burkina and the Ivory Coast. Only Videx® (Didanosine) and Zerit® (40 mg) (Staduvine) were available in all seven countries.
3. Lastly, the supply of ARVs in the zone was both concentrated and segmented. Three firms shared the market in a relatively balanced way in terms of products. Out of the five proprietary drugs supplied, the firm Glaxo supplied two (Retrovir® and Epivir®), Bristol-Myers also supplied two (Videx® and Zerit®) and the fifth was supplied by the firm Merck.

This monopolistic structure of a market for products covered by patents explains the high prices that were charged until 2001, and thus goes some way towards explaining the very low number of patients gaining access to antiretroviral therapy.

However, this situation could not continue indefinitely. The Brazilian programme of universal and free access to ARVs, based partly on the supply of locally produced generic copies, the powerful rise in the supply from Indian (and Thai) generic producers, rising pressure from public opinion and NGOs,[24] within a context of a worsening pandemic, led the international organizations in charge of fighting the epidemic to promote initiatives to provide sustainable solutions. This time, as we shall see, the pharmaceutical companies, after having long demonstrated their lack of enthusiasm, joined in the effort. However, as we shall also see, the price reductions agreed by the laboratories, of limited scale and subject to many conditions, still did not constitute the hoped-for solution. So, despite the legal obstacles which remained – and which the Revised Bangui Agreement of 1999 had reinforced – the supply from generic producers retained all its importance.

3.2 After 2000: The Role of International Organizations, the Accelerating Access Initiative and the Rise of Generic Producers

After a brief summary of the contents and importance of the AAI, we shall return to the present and potential future role of generic producers.

3.2.1 The Accelerating Access Initiative reconsidered

Within the context, described above, of a multiplication in the number of national and international initiatives for the establishment of national programmes to combat the disease,[25] a partnership with the big pharmaceutical firms (Boehringer Ingelheim, Bristol-Meyers Squibb, GlaxoSmithKline, Merck and Co. and Hoffmann-La Roche, later joined by Abbott) was set up in 2000, under the aegis of major United Nations Organizations (the UN Population Fund, the UN Children's Fund (UNICEF), the World Health Organization (WHO), the World Bank and the UN Joint Co-sponsored Programme on HIV/AIDS Secretariat (UNAIDS)) with the precise aim of providing access to treatment in the least developed countries. Within this framework, all the countries classified as least developed (using the human development indicator) could benefit from a large reduction in the price of ARVs. Most of the countries in Sub-Saharan Africa were eligible for this initiative, which was developed under the name of AAI[26] (Lucchini *et al.*, 2003).

Senegal, Burkina Faso and Gabon were among the first countries to subscribe to this programme, in April, June and September of the year 2001 respectively. However, although this programme constituted the major source of supply for the majority of member countries of the OAPI until the end of 2002 or even the beginning of 2003, (Lucchini *et al.*, 2003, p. 190), it was neither a universal success nor the sole source of supply of ARVs at reduced prices.[27]

Nevertheless, the implementation of these agreements was accompanied by a significant fall in prices in the signatory countries. The data collected and presented by Lucchini *et al.* concerning more than 1000 transactions clearly testifies to this fall. However, it should be borne in mind, for a clear understanding of the situation, that during this period the preferential offers of the big pharmaceutical firms were in competition with those of the Indian generic producers. Lucchini *et al.* demonstrate that the largest price reductions were achieved by those trading groups which managed to develop 'hybrid' strategies, placing pharmaceutical laboratories in competition with generic producers. Table 3.3 shows the scale of the ARV price reductions achieved by the CAMEG,[28] the Burkina Faso trading group.

Table 3.3 Comparison of ARV prices before and after the price reductions of June 2001 (CAMEG data for Burkina Faso)

Types of ARV	**Price in CFA***		**Price reduction in %**
	Before June 2001	**After June 2001**	
Retrovir	55 055	34 060	38.13%
Epivir	56 733	14 460	74.51%
Combivir	110 835	46 375	58.15%
Videx	28 060	10 245	63.48%
Zerit	80 289	2 975	96.29%
Zerit	83 292	3 375	95.94%
Stocrin	139 349	35 705	74.37%
Crixivan	199 662	42 840	78.54%

Note: * 1 Euro = 650 CFA

Source: Bansee, Zigani and Traoré (2003)

3.2.2 The Indian generic supply and its effects

Producers of generic ARVs, notably Indian producers, started to penetrate the Sub-Saharan African market at the beginning of 2000, whilst the AAI was being negotiated and implemented. The pressure exerted by NGOs and the undertaking by bodies like the World Bank to fund programmes for the purchase of ARVs 'at the best price', on the condition of guaranteed quality (therefore irrespective of whether or not the drugs were patented), has encouraged the trading groups to place orders with these generic producers.[29]

In addition, the unavailability of patented proprietary combinations of ARVs, in the form of fixed-dose tritherapies, imposed a significant limit on the supply on offer within the framework of the AAI, compared with that offered by the generic producers. In fact, no laboratory held patents on all three of the ARVs required to produce such combinations.[30] These fixed-dose tritherapies, combining three different ARVs in the same pill, are highly recommended by the World Health Organization, as they present the advantages of simpler administration, reduced exposure to the risk of drug-resistance and lower cost[31] (World Health Organization, 2004a).

Putting supplies of preferential-price proprietary drugs in competition with supplies from generic producers has created a new situation, opening up more favourable perspectives for ARV supply. The data given in Table 3.4 illustrate the scale of this effect.

This table calls for several observations:

1. It shows that the proprietary ARV supply offered within the zone has diversified greatly compared with the situation in 1999. The number of different molecules sold in the form of proprietary drugs has more than doubled. The number of proprietary suppliers has also grown from three (Glaxo, Bristol-Myers, Merck & Co Inc.) to five, the other two being Boehringer and Roche. However, the greater availability of proprietary ARVs, though a positive element, is not the essential factor.
2. The real novelty, of considerable import, is the strengthening of the supply from generic producers (notably Indian, like Cipla or Ranbaxy Hetero, or Thai, with GPO). This signifies, for almost all the existing drugs,[32] a supply at distinctly lower prices than those proposed by the pharmaceutical laboratories. Nevertheless, it should be noted that the molecules that have undergone the strongest relative price reductions are generally those supplied by more than three different firms. This is the case for Lamivudine, Nevirapine and Zidovudine, for which there are five generic producers.
3. By comparing the data on the annual cost of preferential-price proprietary brand ARVs available in the least developed African countries with the annual cost of the cheapest generic treatments, we obtain very large differences in price levels. Indeed, given constant financial resources, if ARVs were supplied exclusively by the most competitive generic producers, the number of patients treated could be multiplied by a factor of between four and five, depending on the combinations administered.

Table 3.4 Comparison between proprietary brand preferential supplies offered to countries in Sub-Saharan Africa within the framework of the AAI and the general market price of generic copies (in US $).

ARV	**Patentee suppliers**	**Price per patient per year**	**Generic suppliers (The supplier with the most competitive price is listed in bold)**	**Lowest price of generic ARV**	**Difference between generic drug price and patented drug price (%)**
Abacavir	GSK	986	**Cipla**	821	20.10
Didanosine	Bristol-Myers	310	**Aurobindo,** Cipla, GPO	197	57.36
Lamivudine	GSK	234	**Aurobindo** Cipla, GPO, Hetero, Ranbaxy	66	254.55
Stavudine	Bristol-Myers	55	**Aurobindo** Cipla, GPO, Ranbaxy	31	77.42
Zidovudine	GSK	438	**Aurobindo** Cipla, GPO, Hetero, Ranbaxy,	140	212.86
Nevirapine	Boehringer	438	**Hetero** GPO, Cipla, Ranbaxi	105	317.14
Efavirenz	Merck & Co Inc.	500	**Cipla**, Ranbaxi	462	8.23
Indinavir	Merck & Co Inc.	600	**Hetero** Cipla, Ranbaxy	387	55.04

Source: Compiled by the authors from Médecins Sans Frontières (2003a).

3.2.3 The current situation and perspectives for the future

The year 2003, with the launch of the 'Three by Five' (3x5) Initiative by the WHO, aiming to supply HAART to three million people by the year 2005, was marked by new developments. The WHO carried out considerable clarification work, with the aim of reinforcing its action.

Firstly, treatment recommendations were updated, taking into account all the experience acquired. Thus, the WHO suggested, in particular, 'that countries should choose, with a view to large scale use, one sole first-line treatment and a limited number of second-line treatments'[33] (World Health Organization, 2004a).

The drugs recommended in the treatment guidelines are now the most widely prescribed initial treatment combinations in the world.[34] The committee which drew up these recommendations took into account the clinical experience obtained of the effectiveness and toxicity of the molecules used, the availability of fixed combinations[35] and the fact that the cold chain[36] could not necessarily be respected, as well as the availability and cost of the drugs. In addition, the WHO carried out a considerable operation of ARV 'pre-qualification'[37] (World Health Organization, 2004b). As Table 3.5 illustrates, this list shows that whenever a drug exists in a generic form, its availability is ensured.

If we compare the data presented in this table with the WHO recommendations for first-line treatments, we can see that:

1. The three ARVs recommended by the WHO for first-line use – Lamivudine, Staduvine and Zidovudine – all exist in the form of generic copies (Lamivudine (patented by GSK) is supplied by Hetero, Ranbaxy and Cipla; Staduvine (patented by BMS) is supplied by Hetero; Zidovudine (patented by GSK) is supplied by Cipla, Ranbaxy and Hetero).
2. At least one fixed-dose combined tritherapy (recommended by the WHO) exists in generic form: the combination Lamivudine/Stavudine/Nevirapine, supplied by Cipla and Ranbaxy.
3. The fixed-dose combined bitherapies, corresponding to the combination of the two ARVs recommended by the WHO, are supplied in the form of generic copies (these are the combination Lamivudine/Stavudine supplied by Ranbaxy and the combination Lamivudine/Zidovudine supplied by Ranbaxy, Cipla and Hetero).

It should be noted that when we consider not only first-line but also second-line treatments, as well as the treatments for HIV2 and the O group, similar observations can be made. All the recommended molecules are supplied in the form of generic copies.[38] So, today, we find ourselves in a situation of potential competition, not only between brand products and generic

Table 3.5 List of generic ARVs pre-qualified by the WHO and their producers (as of 23 April 2004)

Molecules	Strength	Dosage form	Suppliers	
			Brand	Generic
Indinavir	400mg	Capsule		Hetero Drugs Ltd Ranbaxy Laboratories Ltd
Lamivudine	150mg	Tablet	GlaxoSmithKline	Ranbaxy Laboratories Ltd Cipla Ltd Hetero Drugs Ltd
Lamivudine	50mg/5ml	Solution		Cipla Ltd
Nevirapine	200mg	Tablet	Boehringer Ingelheim	Ranbaxy Laboratories Ltd Cipla Ltd Hetero Drugs Ltd
Stavudine	30mg	Capsule	Bristol Myers Squibb	Hetero Drugs Ltd Ranbaxy Laboratories Ltd
Stavudine	40mg	Capsule	Bristol Myers Squibb	Hetero Drugs Ltd
Zidovudine	100mg	Capsule	GlaxoSmithKline	Combino Pharm S.L. Cipla Ltd
Zidovudine	300mg	Tablet	GlaxoSmithKline	Cipla Ltd Ranbaxy Laboratories Ltd Hetero Drugs Ltd
Zidovudine	50mg/5ml	Solution	GlaxoSmithKline	Cipla Ltd Combino Pharm

Table 3.5 continued

Molecules	Strength	Dosage form	Suppliers	
			Brand	Generic
Fixed dose combined tritherapies				
Lamivudine/ Stavudine/ Nevirapine	150 mg/ 40 mg/ 200 mg	Tablet		Cipla Ltd Ranbaxy Laboratories Ltd
Lamivudine/ Stavudine/ Nevirapine	150 mg/ 30 mg/ 200 mg	Tablet		Ranbaxy Laboratories Ltd
Fixed-dose combined biotherapies				
Lamivudine/ Stavudine	150mg/ 40 mg	Tablet		Ranbaxy Laboratories Ltd
Lamivudine/ Stavudine	150mg/ 30mg	Tablet		Ranbaxy Laboratories Ltd
Lamivudine/ Zidovudine	150mg/ 300mg	Tablet	GlaxoSmithKline	Ranbaxy Laboratories Ltd Cipla Ltd Hetero Drugs Ltd

Note: The drugs in this table are those chosen in the WHO recommendations for first-line treatments. The patented ARVs supplied by multinational firms which have obtained WHO pre-qualification, but which are not available in generic form, are nct included in this list.

Source: World Health Organization (2004b)

copies, but also, in most cases, between different generic copies of the same molecule, and this is true for almost all the recommended drugs.

However, this competition can only be effective for access to drugs that are not protected by patent in the territory of the purchasing countries. Otherwise, the import of generics is impossible and the only way to acquire reduced-price drugs involves the signing of contracts with the proprietary brand firms. Now, as Table 3.6 demonstrates, in the OAPI zone, five ARVs are patented, together with the two fixed-dose combinations of GSK. These five patented ARVs – Lamivudine, Nevirapine, Lopinavir/r, Saquinavir and Nelfinavir – are all essential components of the treatment guidelines recommended by the WHO. Even worse, Lamivudine (the patent for which was obtained within the OAPI zone by GSK) is the key element of first-line treatments and cannot be replaced by any other drugs. Likewise, Nevirapine (patented by Boehringer Ingelheim) is, along with Efavirenz, the indispensable non-nucleoside reverse transcriptase inhibitor for first-line treatment. As for the three other patented ARVs, these are the three main protease inhibitors recommended by the WHO guidelines for second-line treatment.

Table 3.6 ARVs currently patented in the OAPI zone (on 28 April 2004)

Molecule name (abbreviation)	**Brand name (Manufacturer)**	**USPTO Patent Holder**	**FDA Approved Date First – Last***
Lamivudine (3TC)	Epivir (GSK)	GSK	November 1995 – June 2002
Nevirapine (NVP)	Viramune (Boehringer Ingelheim)	Boehringer Ingelheim	June 1996 – September 1998
Saquinavir Mesylate (SQV)	Fortovase Invirase (Roche)	Roche	Invirase: December 1995 Fortovase: November 1997
Indinavir Sulfate (IDV)	Crixivan (Merck & Co.)	Merck & Co.	March 1996
Nelfinavir Mesylate	(Viracept (Agouron)	Agouron	March 1997 – April 2003
Lopinavir/Ritonavir (LPVr)	Kaletra (Abbott)	Abbott	September 2000
Zidovudine/Lamivudine	Combivir (GSK)	GSK	September 1997
Zidovudine/Lamivudine/ Abacavir	Trizivir (GSK)	GSK	November 2000

Note: This is a function of the dosage form of the drugs

Sources: Compiled by the authors from Food and Drug Administration Orange Book (www.fda.gov); US Patent Office (www.uspto.gov) and Médecins Sans Frontières, (2003b).

One point must be emphasized here. On a legal level, these patents also prevent the members of the OAPI from buying fixed-dose combinations supplied by Indian generic producers, as these all contain Lamivudine for the bitherapies and both Lamivudine and Nevirapine for the fixed-dose tritherapies.

Consequently, if current laws are strictly enforced, the IPR regime governing the Revised Bangui Agreement zone (an agreement which was itself imposed because certain countries in the zone were obliged to comply with the TRIPS Agreement), does indeed constitute a major obstacle to access to reduced-cost AIDS treatment.

This situation calls for certain observations, with which we propose to conclude this chapter.

4 CONCLUSIONS

Three issues arise from this survey.

4.1 The Key Role of Generic Producers and Supply-side Competition in Reduced-cost ARVs.

Contrary to what some observers had maintained, it is now obvious that the conditions of application of the TRIPS Agreement do indeed raise a series of obstacles to access to reduced-cost molecules.

Let us examine the arguments against this proposition. The foundation of these arguments, presented particularly vigorously by Attaran and Gillespie-White (2001) consists in maintaining that considering the low number of ARVs actually patented in the least developed countries (no more than 12, compared with a total of 150 to 171 ARV variants for which patents have been registered in developed countries), this could hardly represent an obstacle to access to treatment. The survey we have carried out clearly shows that in the case of the OAPI zone, with only five patents registered, access to every single first-line and second-line combination treatment at low costs is severely hindered: not one first-line combination can be acquired at generic prices.

In the same spirit, our survey demonstrates that the first significant price reductions agreed by pharmaceutical firms (in the context of the AAI) were made in 2000, concurrent with the arrival of generic producers. Until 1999, before the establishment of the Indian generic supply, the prices charged in this zone by the pharmaceutical companies were similar to those in the Northern countries. The data presented also shows that it is precisely in those areas where a generic supply is actually available that the large laboratories propose the most significant reductions. More generally, it is in those places where competition is the most lively, including competition between the generic producers themselves (when several of them are present in the market), that the lowest prices are offered.[39]

Another observation, which we believe to be of great significance, must be made on this point. The development of fixed-dose tritherapies, which constitutes a key advance in the treatment of AIDS, could only be achieved by generic producers. Because they were free of the prohibitions imposed in respect of IPR, only generic producers have been able to design and supply these drugs, the many advantages of which (convenience, price, and so on) have been universally recognised.

More generally, on a theoretical level, our survey clearly shows how difficult it is to find the right balance between efficiency and equity in the domain of IPR. For several reasons, patent protection constitutes an efficient way of encouraging firms to search for and develop new molecules. However, our survey of the conditions under which the TRIPS Agreement has been applied in Sub-Saharan Africa shows what terrible damage can be caused by inappropriate legislation. The dramatic impact of the TRIPS Agreement on access to healthcare in the poorest countries is all the more deplorable when we consider that, at the prices charged in the North (ten to twelve thousand dollars for tritherapy) there is no affordable demand and therefore no market in the South. Consequently, the maintenance (or reintroduction into international agreements) of measures enabling low-cost generics to be produced in or imported into these countries, would in no way reduce the incentive to research that patents represent in the Northern countries. Given their standards of living and social security systems, the industrialized countries are by themselves quite capable of covering the 'rents' levied by patented drugs. Extending patent protection to the Southern countries (as the TRIPS Agreement does) exacerbates existing situations of inequality in the access to healthcare, while doing nothing to increase the effectiveness of incentives to research.

4.2 The TRIPS Agreement and the Hierarchy of International Agreements

The situation we have presented, in which application of the TRIPS Agreement has blocked access to reduced-cost generic copies for many years, should never have arisen. The TRIPS Agreement provided for an extension of the compliance deadline in the least-developed countries (first to 2006, and then, after Doha, to 2016). So how did this situation arise? As we have seen, the essential reason lies in the fact that four countries in the zone were obliged to comply with the provisions of the Marrakech agreement as early as 2001. When the four countries met this obligation, the whole zone had to follow suit, because of the regional agreements to which they were signatories. Thus, long before the compliance deadline, all these countries had to comply with an IPR regime (copied almost exactly from that of the most developed countries), that was totally inappropriate to local conditions. When the Bangui Agreement was revised in 1999, the rule of 'common procedure' adopted in the original agreement of 1977 (see section 2.3) thus worked to the disadvantage of the poorest countries in the OAPI, transforming the revised treaty into a 'TRIPS plus' type agreement.

This raises serious questions about the hierarchy and 'rigidity' of the legal rules that prevail in these matters. Should flexibility and specific provisions be introduced to put an end to this situation?

In practical terms, the least developed countries in the OAPI zone found themselves faced with the following choice:

- They could forego the advantages of 'common procedure', in order to benefit from the extension of the deadline for compliance to 2006 (and subsequently to 2016). In this case, they would lose the advantages provided by the establishment of 'common markets' (at a time when large trading blocs were being constituted throughout the world).
- Alternatively, they could keep the benefits of 'common procedure', but at the price of having to introduce IPR regimes of the 'TRIPS plus' type, particularly prejudicial for access to healthcare.

Under these conditions, the introduction of appropriate legal measures to put an end to this dilemma would be very welcome.

4.3 After 2005

The situation described above is even more preoccupying when we consider that by the deadline of 2005, new, major changes will occur in the production and international circulation of generic copies. By 2005, the 'intermediate' countries which have benefited from an extension to the deadline, first among which is India, must become TRIPS-compliant. This means, especially for India, the end of production by national firms of drugs that are considered legal copies of the active anti-AIDS molecules. When this occurs, firms such as Cipla, Hetero and Ranbaxy, which today play a decisive role in the supply of generic copies, will have to fall into line.

What will happen then? The last agreement signed at the WTO in August 2003, concerning implementation of §6 of the Doha Declaration, provides for the possibility, in the event of national emergency, for the least developed countries to resort to compulsory licences for the import of generic drugs. This raises at least two questions: i) from a practical point of view, how will the cumbersome machinery required by this new agreement function? ii) which firms will have the required know-how and be prepared to satisfy this demand rapidly and at low cost?

Finally, will the solemn proclamation of Doha, according to which

> We agree that the TRIPS Agreement does not and should not prevent Members from taking measures to protect public health. Accordingly, we affirm that the Agreement can and should be interpreted and implemented in a manner supportive of WTO Members' right to protect public health and, in particular, to promote access to medicines for all...

be followed by tangible effects?

It is too early to give a verdict on these questions, but past experience shows that the 'facilities' provided for by the TRIPS Agreement, even when they have been put into practice, have never been easy to implement. Will anything be different after 2005? Only the future, now very near, will tell.

ACKNOWLEDGEMENTS

This research forms part of a set of studies of the generic antiretroviral drugs industry carried out (under the direction of Benjamin Coriat) with the support of the National Agency for AIDS Research (ANRS). In addition, some of the data on Sub-Saharan Africa presented here were collected through a survey conducted in the region by Mamadou Camara with a research grant funded by the French association SIDACTION. The authors wish to thank these two institutions for their efficient and generous support.

NOTES

1. See t'Hoen (2003) and debates of the WTO TRIPS Council, available at www.wto.org/english/tratop_e/trips_e/trips_e.htm
2. This paper is part of a series of studies sponsored by ANRS (Agency for Research on AIDS). Previous publications on this issue include Coriat and Orsi (2003), Orsi *et al.* (2003) on the Brazilian anti-AIDS policy as well as the various contributions published in Moatti *et al* 2003.
3. Although patents on production processes are long established in the pharmaceutical industry (as in other sectors), the adoption of patents *on molecules* is a recent development in most countries.
4. Agreement available at www.wto.org/english/docs_e/legal_e/legal_e.htm
5. The different directions and domains of this extension of the law are presented in Coriat and Orsi (2002). For the specific case of the human genome, see Orsi (2002).
6. On this point, see the very complete report of the Commission on Intellectual Property Rights set up by the UK government: *Integrating Intellectual Property Right and Development Policy*, London, September 2002, available at www.iprcommission.org.

7. This treatment is called 'tritherapy', as it combines three different ARVs.
8. In the year 2000, with the arrival of generic copies, this cost fell to around 300 dollars per person per year, and it has continued to fall ever since.
9. As Carlos Corréa points out, 'tens of thousands of patents have been compulsorily licensed in the United States, in more than a hundred cases. In one single case (US Manufacturers Aircraft Associations Inc.), about 1500 patents were compulsorily licensed (Corréa, 1999).
10. For details of the history, see t'Hoen (2003).
11. TRIPS Council report (2001) available at www.wto.org/english/tratop_e/trips_e/trips_e.htm
12. WTO document number: WT/MIN(01)/DEC/2 available at www.wto.org/english/thewto_e/minist_e/min01_e/mindecl_trips_e.htm
13. WTO document number: WT/L/540 available at www.wto.org/english/tratop_e/trips_e/implem_para6_e.htm
14. Agreement available at http://www.iprsonline.org/legalinstruments/regional.htm
15. See note 11.
16. However, it should be noted that 'downstream' questions concerning patent infringements or compulsory licences do not lie within the competence of the OAPI. These are matters for the civil court of each member state. In other words, complaints about infringement of patent and compulsory licence requests are dealt with at a national level. However, decisions pronounced by the court of one country must be respected by all OAPI members (Tankoano, 2002).
17. These were Cameroon, the Ivory Coast, Gabon and Senegal.
18. On this topic, it should be noted that measures relating to the protection of intellectual property in the field of genetic resources have not yet been incorporated into the Bangui Agreement, in complete compliance with Article 65.4 of TRIPS, as this field had never been protected in the OAPI zone.
19. On this point, see Reichman and Heisenzal (2002).
20. Despite the safety campaigns, new cases of infection in 2003 represented between 12 and 15% of the total number of adults living with HIV.
21. Unlike India, Thailand had, under strong American pressure, become TRIPS-compliant during the middle of the 1990s, long before the deadline. Nevertheless, this situation enabled Thailand, through its public laboratory GPO, to produce in the form of generic copies – as was also the case in Brazil – the ARVs that had not been patented in the country before the introduction of national TRIPS-compliant legislation. The Thai experience is recounted in Guennif and M'Fuka (2003); the Brazilian experience in Orsi *et al.* (2003).
22. Before 2000, as Senegal and the Ivory Coast had signed agreements with the suppliers, they benefited from reduced prices for the purchase of certain ARVs, such as Zidovudine. This negotiation contributed to a price reduction of 60% between 1997 and 1999.
23. Remember that while the cost of ARVs covered by patents stood at around ten to twelve thousand US dollars per person per year, in the year 2003 the same treatment with generic ARVs was offered for 300 US dollars per person per year by Indian generic manufacturers. This price itself was falling rapidly.
24. This was expressed notably in the withdrawal of the Johannesburg lawsuits and in 2001 by the Doha Declaration.
25. The scale of the sums allocated to the fight against AIDS undoubtedly explains the establishment of national strategies to combat AIDS by most of the countries in Sub-Saharan Africa. At the end of 2002, the World Health Organization listed nearly 40 countries in Sub-Saharan Africa that had adopted strategic plans to combat AIDS. This generally involved a document of political intention which: 1) identified the players involved in the strategy, 2) described the way in which the initiatives to be taken by these players would be coordinated and 3) proposed different methods of funding the national programme.
26. The founding agreement of the AAI stipulated notably that each government should negotiate bilaterally with each of the firms that were signatory to the initiative. This

multiplication of bilateral transactions is regrettable, because it is unfavourable to the formation of a homogeneous and transparent supply. Indeed, the available data show certain disparities in the selling prices practised by companies, according to the contexts and the negotiators. Furthermore, it should be noted that orders at preferential prices had to be paid before delivery.

27. The example of Gabon illustrates the difficulties that have been encountered in applying this programme. On this point, see Dégui (2002).
28. The CAMEG is the body responsible for managing supplies of generic drugs in Burkina Faso. This structure, which comprises three types of associate (the state, foreign development partners and the group of prescribers and patients representing different local committees) is endowed with the status of a private, non-profit-making association. This status of private association was adopted because it provides the CAMEG with greater flexibility than the same type of public body, such as economic interest groups or public industrial and commercial establishments, would have.
29. This pressure from international organizations for best-price purchase appears to be unflagging. The World Bank, with its MAP programme (Multi-countries AIDS Programme for Africa, disposing of a fund of one billion dollars to be invested in Southern countries in the fight against AIDS) does not intend to favour the exclusive purchase of patented proprietary drugs. Likewise, the Clinton Foundation has just signed an Agreement (April 2004) with the IMF, the World Bank and UNICEF, with the aim of enabling developing countries to buy ARVs at prices on average 50% lower than those currently in force. This agreement accepts ARV supplies from generic producers in South Africa (Aspen Pharmacare Holdings) and India (Cipla, Hetero, Ranbaxy and Matrix laboratories).
30. The only fixed-dose tritherapy produced by a patent-holding firm is Trizivir from GlaxoSmithKline, as this firm possesses the patents on all three ARVs in this combination: Zidovudine, Lamivudine and Abacavir. But this very specific combination is not included in the WHO recommendations for first-line treatments.
31. Fixed-dose tritherapies combining Staduvine, Lamivudine and Nevirapine are supplied by Indian generic producers (Triomune for Cipla and Triviro for Ranbaxy). They are sold at a price of 270 dollars (per person per year), as compared with 562 dollars when bought as three separate drugs from a patent-holding firm, even at preferential prices.
32. With the exception of protease inhibitors, which, in 2004, are being offered at lower prices by pharmaceutical firms (Médecins Sans Frontières, 2004).
33. Four first-line treatment guidelines have been defined. They are the following combinations:
    Zidovudine/Lamivudine/Efavirenz
    Zidovudine/Lamivudine/Nevirapine
    Stavudine/Lamivudine/Evafirenz
    Stavudine/Lamivudine/Nevirapine
34. These treatments are powerful and relatively simple, but they are ineffective against HIV-2 and HIV-1, O group, for which other combinations of molecules are proposed (see note 35).
35. These are combinations of bi- or tritherapies administered by unique dose.
36. Cold chain refers to the fact that the drugs must be kept at a very low temperature in order to maintain intact their therapeutic properties.
37. This is only a *pre*-qualification in that the countries that wish to distribute the molecules concerned must carry out the 'qualification' of these molecules themselves. 'Pre-qualification' process refers to a series of inspections conducted by the OMS aiming at verifying the quality of the drugs offered by genetic suppliers; the drugs which bioequivalence was considered identical to the ones of the originators were thus 'qualified' to be marketed and exported on external markets.
38. With the exception of Tenofovir, which is the newest drug, all the recommended ARVs are manufactured by several producers and available in both proprietary brand and generic form.
39. Note that these results, compiled from field research data, are in complete harmony with those of the survey conducted by Lucchini *et al.* (2003), and obtained by the econometric processing of 1030 transactions.

BIBLIOGRAPHY

Arrow, K. (1982), 'Economic welfare and allocation of resources for inventions', in R.R. Nelson (ed.) *The Rate and Direction of Inventure Activity*, Princeton, NJ: Princeton University Press.

Attaran, A. and Gillespie-White, L. (2001), 'Do patents for antiretroviral drugs constrain access to AIDS treatment in Africa?' *JAMA*, **286**, pp. 1886–2001.

Bansee, L., Zigani, W. and Traoré, V. (2003), 'Expérience de la CAMEG du Burkina Faso dans la distribution des antirétroviraux', available at www.remed.org/ZIGANI.rtf.

Boulet, P. and Forte, G.B. (2000), *Les brevets de médicaments dans les pays d'Afrique francophone*, report of the joint Mission MSF-WHO-ONUSIDA, available at http://www.accessmed-msf.org.

Camara, M. (2003), *Le difficile accès des pays d'Afrique Francophone aux ARV: l'exemple du Burkina Faso*, mission report, CEPN-IIDE, November.

Conseil National de Lutte contre le SIDA (2003), *Plan stratégique 2002–2006 de lutte contre le SIDA*, Republic of Senegal.

Coriat, B. and Orsi, F. (2002), 'Establishing a new regime of intellectual property rights in the United States: origins, content and problems', *Research Policy*, **32**, pp. 1491–507.

Coriat, B. and Orsi, F. (2003), 'Brevets pharmaceutiques, génériques et santé publique: le cas de l'accès aux traitements antirétroviraux', *Revue d'Economie Publique, Etudes et Recherches*, **12**, pp. 153–77.

Corréa, C. (1999), *Intellectual property rights and the use of compulsory licenses: options for developing countries*, Geneva: South Centre.

Dégui, H. (2002), 'Les limites du programme ACCESS, l'exemple du Gabon', *Remed*, no. 26, pp. 4–5, available at http://www.remed.org/remed262.pdf.

Dumoulin, J. and Maville, G. (1999), 'Prix et accès aux ARV dans les pays du sud: que peuvent faire la communauté internationale et les laboratoires pharmaceutiques', *Réseau Médicaments et Développement*, No. 22, available at http://www.remed.org/campagne_Medicaments.rtf.

Guennif, S. and M'Fuka, C. (2003), 'Impact of intellectual property rights on AIDS public health policy in Thailand' in J.P. Moatti, B. Coriat, Y. Souteyrand, T. Barnett, J. Dumoulin and Y.A. Flori (eds) *Economics of AIDS and Access to HIV Care in Developing Countries: Issues and Challenges*, ANRS editions, pp. 137–49.

Jourdain, R. (2002), 'Les droits de la propriété intellectuelle et la santé publique dans l'Accord de Bangui révisé: défis majeurs en santé publique pour les pays africains', in *Commerce, PI & Développement Durable vus de l'Afrique*, ICTSD, Enda, Solagral, pp. 106–13.

Love, J. (2002), 'Comment on the Attaran /Gillespie-White and pharma surveys of patents on antiretroviral drugs in Africa' available at www.cptech.org/ip/health/africa/dopatentsmatterinafrica.html.

Lucchini, S., Cisse, B., Duran, S., Cenival, M. de, Corniti, C., Gaudry, M. and Moatti, J.-P. (2003), 'Decrease in prices of antiretroviral drugs for developing countries: from political 'philanthropy' to regulated markets?', in J.P. Moatti, B. Coriat, Y. Souteyrand, T. Barnett, J. Dumoulin and Y.A. Flori (eds) *Economics of AIDS and Access to HIV Care in Developing Countries: Issues and Challenges*, ANRS editions, pp. 169–211.

Médecins Sans Frontières (2003a), Untangling the web of price reduction: a pricing guide for the purchase of ARVs for developing countries, 3rd edition, available at: www.accessmed-msf.org.

Médecins Sans Frontières (2003b), Drugs patents under the spotlight, available at www.accessmed-msf.org.

Médecins Sans Frontières (2004), Deux comprimés par jour pour sauver des vies: combinaisons à dose fixe de médicaments, available at www.accessmed-msf.org.

Moatti, J.P., Coriat, B., Souteyrand, Y., Barnett, T., Dumoulin, J. and Flori, Y.A. (eds) (2003), *Economics of AIDS and Access to HIV Care in Developing Countries: Issues and Challenges*: ANRS editions.

Orsi, F. (2002), 'La constitution d'un nouveau droit de propriété intellectuelle sur le vivant aux Etats-Unis: origine et signification économique d'un dépassement de frontière', *Revue d'Economie Industrielle*, no. 99, 2nd trimester, pp. 65–86. (Special Issue on 'Intellectual Property Rights' coordinated by Benjamin Coriat.)

Orsi, F., Hasenclever, L., Fialho, B., Tigre, P., Coriat, B. (2003), 'Intellectual property rights, anti-AIDS policy and generic drugs: lesson from the Brazilian public health program', in J.P. Moatti, B. Coriat, Y. Souteyrand, T, Barnett, J. Dumoulin and Y.A. Flori (eds) *Economics of AIDS and Access to HIV Care in Developing Countries: Issues and Challenges*. ANRS editions, pp. 109–35.

Pammoli, F., Magazzini, L. and Orsenigi, L. (2002), 'The intensity of competition after patent expiry in pharmaceuticals: a cross country analysis', *Revue d'Economie Industrielle*, no. 99, 2nd trimester, pp. 107–32. (Special Issue on 'Intellectual Property Rights' coordinated by Benjamin Coriat.)

Reichman, J. and Hasenzahl, C. (2002), *Non-voluntary licensing of patented inventions: historical perspective, legal framework under TRIPS, and an overview of the practice in Canada and the United States of America*, UNCTAD/ICTSD.

Reichman, J. and Lange, D. (2000), 'Bargaining around the TRIPS Agreement: the case for ongoing public-private initiatives to facilitate worldwide intellectual property transactions', *Duke Journal of Comparative and International Law*, **9** (11), pp. 11–68.

Remiche, B. and Desterbecq, R. (1996), 'Les brevets pharmaceutiques dans les Accords du GATT: l'enjeu?', *Revue Internationale de Droit Economique*, **1**, pp. 7–68.

Scherer, F.M. (1993), 'Pricing, profits and technological progress in the pharmaceutical industry', *Journal of Economic Perspectives,* **7** (3), pp. 97–115.

Scherer, F.M. and Watal, J. (2001), *Post-TRIPS option for access to patented medicines in developing countries*, World Health Organization, Commission on Macroeconomics and Health, CMH Working Paper Series, no. WG4: 1.

Tankoano, A. (2002), 'Les importations parallèles et les licences non volontaires dans le nouveau droit des brevets des Etats membres de l'OAPI', in *Commerce, PI & Développement Durable vus de l'Afrique,* ICTSD, Enda, Solagral, pp. 115–23.

t'Hoen, E. (2003), 'TRIPS, pharmaceutical patents and access to essential medicines: Seattle, Doha and beyond', in J.P. Moatti, B. Coriat, Y. Souteyrand, T. Barnett, J. Dumoulin and Y.A. Flori (eds) *Economics of AIDS and Access to HIV Care in Developing Countries: Issues and Challenges*, ANRS editions, pp. 39–67.

UNAIDS (2003), *Report on the global AIDS epidemic*, available at www.unaids.org.

World Health Organization (2004a), *Scaling up antiretroviral therapy in resource-limited settings: Treatment guidelines for a public health approach 2003,* Revised version, available at www.who.org.

World Health Organization (2004b), *Pilot procurement, quality and sourcing project: access to HIV/AIDS drugs and diagnostics of acceptable quality*, 14th edition, 28 April 2004, available at www.who.org.
Zhang, S. (1994), *De l'OMPI au GATT – La protection internationale des droits de propriété intellectuelle*, Paris: ITEC.

PART II

The rationales for intellectual property rights revisited

4. If 'intellectual property rights' is the answer, what is the question? Revisiting the patent controversies*

Birgitte Andersen

ABSTRACT

A typology of the rationales for intellectual property rights (IPRs), primarily in relation to patents, is developed. The focus is on natural rights and moral rationales, economic incentive rationales, increased competition and 'market protection of entrepreneurial talent' rationales, and the economic rationales of organizing science, technology and creativity. Whilst reviewing the controversies surrounding IPR legislation, the importance of this typology is justified. It will provide a good conceptual underpinning and analytical framework for achieving a finer empirical understanding of the social and economic effects of IPRs, and this understanding is urgently needed when designing policy fostering the knowledge-driven techno-economic paradigm in the twentieth first century.

Keywords: Intellectual property rights (IPRs), Patents, Rationales, Typology, Policy

1 INTRODUCTION

Capturing value from intellectual capital and knowledge-based assets has become the new mantra. The battles are not for control of raw materials, but for the control of the most dynamic strategic asset, namely 'productive knowledge'. Finding ways in which institutions can help firms with this increasingly important practice has become an explicit agenda for many governments.

* Reproduced from Birgitte Andersen, (2004), "If Intellectual Property Rights" is the answer, what is the question? Revisiting the patent controversies', *Economics of Innovation and New Technology*, **13** (5), 417–42, http://www.tandf.co.uk/journals.

Meetings in industry, national governments and international agencies as well as consultants seem to indicate a consensus or belief that increased privatization and recognition of the intellectual capital and knowledge-based assets of firms will better enable them to capture the value from their productive knowledge assets. See, for example the hearing regarding patent policy on business methods patents (EU 2002) (which is still being discussed and on which a decision is due to be taken in July 2005);[1] OECD (1999) regarding measuring and reporting intellectual capital; the Trade Related Aspects of Intellectual Property Section (TRIPS) of the World Trade Organization (WTO) which came into force in 1994 as a part of the Uruguay Round to enforce intellectual property worldwide; the Bayh-Dole Act in the US in 1980 to create incentives for transferring new technology from university laboratories to the private sector[2] and the new financial frameworks from the 1980s, where unprofitable firms can be listed on Nasdaq as long as they are able to report intangible assets.[3] Furthermore, entering a new economy, or techno-economic paradigm, in which knowledge assets rather than physical assets are the primary sources of wealth generation and economic growth, we have experienced a tightening of the intellectual property rights system in terms of (i) integrating new areas of protection (even beyond science-based principles, for example business methods patents),[4] (ii) exclusive rights also on pure ideas (for example genetic codes[5] and some mathematics),[6] (iii) an increased period of protection, as well as (iv) the introduction of the 'continuation' or 'submarine patenting' scheme in the U.S.[7]

Innovation policy is designed around some IPR legal regimes. The current tightening of such policy is obviously based upon a 'vision' of why this might provide the answer. However, we cannot base our policy on visions alone. Firstly we need to address the question to which IPR systems supposedly provide the answer. Secondly, we need to assess whether the IPR really is the best instrument for our political (that is, social and economic) objectives.

The current need for setting out clear objectives for the IPR system, and for understanding the operation and social and economic effects of IPR policies, is due in part to the emergence of new types of science and technologies, and the changing ways in which IPRs are governed within sectoral systems, as products and processes have become increasingly complex both in their knowledge bases and in the ownership of such. This need has also increased in importance as a consequence of the harmonizing effect of globalization policies.

Thus, this chapter aims to review critically and classify the rationales for IPRs, drawing upon past and current academic scholarship. Applying theoretical logic, speculations on the effects of IPRs will also be discussed. The controversies surrounding IPR legislation will form the central part of the discussion. Emphasis will be on natural rights and moral rationales (section 2), the economic incentive rationales (section 3), the increased competition and 'market protection of entrepreneurial talent' rationales (section 4), and the economic rationales for organizing science, technology and creativity (section 5).[8] Finally, based upon the critical review in sections 2–5, this paper develops a 'typology' of the rationales for IPRs. The overall design, use and justification for the typology will be described in section 6.

As is clear from this chapter, most of the theoretical contributions to the debate are historically rooted, although the focus in recent times has changed from 'the role of the entrepreneur and invention protection' towards 'appropriation from IPRs and the increasing importance of the venture capitalist as well as strategic interaction in the market place for ideas'. For the earlier classics on the early history of IPRs and patent grants, including a thorough exploration of the underpinning economic logic, see Machlup and Penrose (1950), Machlup (1958) and Kaufer (1989).

In some respect the typology in this paper can be compared to the functional approach[9] and categorizing of theories on the benefits and costs of patents proposed by Mazzoleni and Nelson (1998a, 1998b). However, in a crucial respect the typology proposed in this paper is different. Whereas Mazzoleni and Nelson's proposed categories (1998a, 1998b) can be considered as empirically grounded theory in the sense that they are grounded on empirical data and analysis, the typology proposed in this paper is grounded on theoretical logic already proposed in various theoretical and philosophical frameworks of analysis. Thus, whereas their categorizing of theories (including the breadth and depth in which they are discussed) is mainly in relation to economic incentive rationales[10] where empirical analysis has taken place, the theoretically grounded approach in this chapter aims to be 'all-inclusive'. In Mazzoleni and Nelson's approach (1998a, 1998b) we also learn how different IPR uses apply to different industries and different firm sizes, and how the individual versus public (for example university) versus private ownership of IPRs matters. The typology proposed in this paper does not aim to discuss the specificities of industries and firms in relation to the IPR rationales. That is, instead of focusing on empirical relationships or results from empirical surveys, it aims to discuss the theoretical (social and economic) logic regarding the operation and performance (that is, dynamics) of the IPR system.

Of course, it would be best to integrate the two, that is, the all-inclusive approach to the rationales for IPRs and the empirical results of the worth of the rationales in relation to the specificities of firms, industries and individual and public ownership. However, despite important contributions, much empirical research still needs to be done on just about *all* aspects of the rationales for IPRs. Also, the state of the art regarding many of the essential empirical contributions is well summarized and discussed in Mazzoleni and Nelson (1998a, 1998b). There are also numerous other outstanding empirical single contributions adding to the IPR debate that I cannot do justice to in the limited space allocated to this chapter. Thus, I have decided to discuss mainly the essential theoretical contributions to the IPR controversies, and to be selective and brief on empirical contributions to the debate.

With respect to the IPR context, I illustrate in previous work (Andersen *et al.* 2000, Andersen 2003) that, although protection of symbolic material and creative expression have increased the scope for copyrights and trademarks in the electronic age, the patent system protecting product and process inventions is still of primary importance, and even increasing in application for most service and manufacturing sectors in the new economy. This paper focuses on such IPRs designed to protect knowledge embodied in mainly industrial, product and process innovations. Although such protection mainly takes the form of patents (which are the focus of analysis in this chapter), trade secrets and design rights are also used on occasion for such purposes. Many copyright rationales regarding protection of creative expressions of ideas embodied in symbolic material are similar to those for patent protection, so they are somewhat implicitly addressed. However, I do not include any special attention to the specificities of the operation and performance of the copyright system. The rationales for trademarks are of a very different nature and impossible to incorporate in the short space of this chapter. Protection of 'effort' (an important part of copyright law for data base protection) will also not be discussed.

2 SOCIAL CONTRACT THEORY: NATURAL RIGHTS AND MORAL RATIONALES

John Locke [1632–1704] (1690/1980) argued for a 'natural rights theory of the social contract'. In this context ideas are protected under the principle of natural law, in the sense that somebody's idea is a 'natural right'. It follows that governments do not create property rights but are instituted to serve as their objective guardians. Jean-Baptiste-Ambroise-Marcellin Jobard (who, in the beginning of the nineteenth century, wrote on the natural aspects of rights) was a prolific advocator of perpetual patent protection. He believed that the IPR system provides the answer to protecting human creativity and personality from unfair exploitation. He introduced the term 'monautopoly' (meaning monopoly of oneself). Basically, in accordance with the 'natural rights theory of the social contract' everyone has a permanent and inalienable natural right to the sole disposal of themselves and their work.

This normative aspect of social contract is contested by a 'positive theory of the social contract'. The first advocator for this was Thomas Hobbes [1588–1679] (1660/1968) who contended that there is nothing natural about a right if we need the power of government to enforce it. That is, it is impossible for government to enforce a right without implementing its views on the notions of rights and wrongs, justice and injustice, so to claim that the rights are natural is a contradiction in terms. Thomas Hobbes changed the very essence of the concept of natural rights to the assumption that humans have a natural inclination to preserve themselves. Assuming the rationality of humans, and to avoid a 'war of all against all' Thomas Hobbes argued for the necessity of government. The utilitarian philosopher Jeremy Bentham [1748–1832] also drew a distinction between normative theory and positive theory, and adamantly opposed the theory of natural rights. He introduced ethical principles or morals into property right theory and laid the responsibilities for identifying and enforcing these in the hands of the state. In this context, it is not only society's duty to protect the inventor, but also to secure the inventor a fair share of the reward when exploiting the inventor's knowledge and ideas. The idea is that it would be immoral if the law let everybody freely use the work of inventors without their consent and without compensation or equivalent in return. The rationale is basically that justice requires that society compensate and reward its people for their services in proportion to what they cost and how useful they are to society. Those believing in the IPR system here consider that the most appropriate way to secure inventors is by issuing IPRs.[11]

However, the arguments against the view that the IPR system is designed to protect the inventor, are manifold.

2.1 Rights versus Privileges

Sened (1997), who is a devoted advocate of positive theory, takes a critical view and contends that we need to pay more attention to how social contracts (through which governments protect the individual rights of their citizens) emerge and evolve. Governments also reflect the interests of social groups. Ideas based upon 'natural rights' need to be seen in contrast to the positive origin of property and individual rights, where it could be claimed that society gives one some kind of 'privilege'.

This reflects the alternative view that our IPR regime cannot be approached with a functional problem-solving approach, in the sense that there is nothing rational about it. This puts the aim of this chapter on the rationales for IPRs into a different light. The critical theorists, Sell and

May (2001), present a number of key 'moments' in the history of IPRs that eventually led to particular IPR agreements (TRIPS being one of them). They maintain that these key 'moments' are not final improvements to legislation governing IPRs or the culmination of a history of legal rationalization. Rather, the design of an IPR system at any one time is based upon a particular constellation of political power, and when the power relations change, the IPR arguments become contested and open to amendment through political engagement.

Machlup and Penrose (1950) also maintained that the term 'intellectual property right', based upon the origin of a natural or moral right (as opposed to intellectual monopoly privilege), was a very deliberate choice on the part of politicians working for the adoption of a patent law in the nineteenth century. This period was for liberty and equality and against privileges and monopolies[12] of any sort.

2.2 The Social Origin of Inventions and the Existence of Technological Interdependence

A basic contention against IPRs in the context of natural rights and moral rationales is that technological inventions are mostly a social creation of collective, cumulative and interrelated work to which we all contribute, and, therefore, no one person or firm should be able to claim the property. Ownership of technological inventions here might be immoral, and actually against the principle of natural rights, as the IPR system in this case may prevent inventors from using or appropriating from ideas that they have collectively been a part of creating if someone else is granted the IPR. Thus, it is proposed that the IPR system decreases the moral rights for most subscribers to the system.

The social origin of inventions argument (which can also be termed distributed innovation processes) was put forward by Plant (1934). Research on patent scope by Merges and Nelson (1990) (discussed in section 4.1.1) revealed how inventions happen along multi-product trajectories that are cumulative, path-dependent and complex, in the sense that each innovation along the trajectory relies on its own or others' current or past ideas. I have used patent statistics to illustrate how technological trajectories increasingly rely on broader knowledge bases, and have also become less concentrated in the sense that a range of different firms now participate in the same technological evolution (Andersen 2001).

Furthermore, from the 'social origin of inventions' argument suggesting that the next novelty on the road can be hit on by a range of inventors, it follows that we should not reward those 'lucky' enough to be the first to hit on the technological solution which is of sufficiently novel character to merit IPR protection. Due to the randomness of the system it is almost impossible for the rewards to go to those who deserve it. This may in turn have a negative impact on the IPR incentive rationale (discussed in section 3.1.1). In addition, it can be argued that the patent system on average causes more losses than profits even to inventors, as they have to pay for using the ideas they have contributed to when other people have patented them. This problem of inventors paying to use their own ideas could in principle be solved by rewarding them with cash prizes rather than temporary exclusive property rights (Davis 2004). This reward system would however not solve the problem surrounding the social origin of inventions where everyone deserves a fair share for their effort, as it is impossible to calculate the effort-share that has been conducted on an individual basis. Basically, the patent system can here be viewed as inflicting injury upon others as it is impossible to compensate or pay rewards in proportion to the effort put in and the service provided to society.

2.3 The Reward may not Reflect the Value Created by the Inventor

According to the moral rationale of IPRs, justice requires that society compensate and reward its people for their services in proportion to what they cost and how useful they are to society. However, I would assert that it is very unlikely that the economic or money value (reflected in the reward system) of the idea is entirely created by the inventor. Money value tends to be circumstantial and indeed also a product of the external environment (notice the analogy with housing markets), and does not reflect the 'true' value created by the inventor. Circumstantial and external elements include economic climate and investment confidence, other inventors making complementary inventions in the 'region' of the invention and strategic interaction in markets for ideas where inventors are locked in to (or out of) technological webs. The belief that society, or the market economy by its own working, ensures that the 'reward system' generates rewards based upon the true value of the invention, or solely the value created by the inventor, is doubtful.

2.4 The IPR system is 'General' and Compensates and Rewards Equally all Novel Technological Ideas

It can be argued that it is a problem that the IPR system is 'general' and compensates and rewards equally all novel technological ideas, whether they are the result of great effort or a by-product of accidental inventive activity. However, history has revealed that most often inventions are generally not accidental, but that to invent the unthinkable and complex, scientists must specialize. Also, in patent law today, inventions are not patentable if they are 'obvious', meaning discoverable at low cost. Yet the troublesome question of which ideas are novel enough to be granted patent protection is often faced with great challenges. At one extreme, there is nothing new under the sun. At the other extreme, every different new combination of knowledge, creative expression or technology constitutes a new idea. In specifying the criteria of novelty sufficient for IPR protection, the designers of any IPR system must go through the difficult process of selecting a position somewhere on the spectrum marked by these extremes (Cheung 1986), and the problem solving for this seems to become even more ambiguous within digital and microelectronics, where new combinations are produced more easily or with very little effort (Andersen 2003; see also the discussion on the European E-Commerce Emergency, where e-commerce patents on trivial inventions have been granted, distorting the nature of competition: http://webshop.ffii.org/).

2.5 The Schumpeterian Theory of the Innovator's Head-start Profit

'The Schumpeterian theory of the innovator's head-start profit' can be used against the reward rationale for industrial inventions. The argument is that if an inventor is really ahead of other inventors, then the time interval before catching up and imitation have happened (which is difficult as it requires learning) should already secure the inventor profit and rent; thus there is no need for government to compensate or reward inventions in the first place. However, book publishing or pre-recorded music, for example, where imitation is easy, would still need to be protected under 'the theory of innovator's head-start profit' principle. The essential issue is the rate at which new ideas spread (that is, the rate of imitation and catching up): the faster the speed, the more protection is needed to ensure reward, and the slower the speed, the less IPR protection is needed. Large rewards from the innovator's head start can especially be obtained without IPR protection when the inventor experiences increasing return dynamics and 'lock-in to their particular technological trajectories'. This can happen by random events or due to strategic corporate interaction in markets for ideas (see section 4.1.1 for a brief discussion; and see Andersen, 2003 for a detailed discussion).

A related consequence is that IPR incentive rationales may not be necessary to induce inventive activities (discussed in section 3.1.1). Scherer *et al.* (1959), Mansfield (1986), Levin *et al.* (1987) and Cohen *et al.* (2000) indicate that in many industries, and in many large established firms, a head start on commercialization of an idea is enough to yield profit from the invention, and that patents in those cases are not needed to induce inventive activities or further development of those inventions.

3 ECONOMIC INCENTIVE RATIONALES: THE SOCIAL BENEFITS FROM PATENTS

That we have seen an increasing incentive to patent is an established fact. In an empirical study of patenting records in the US, I have shown empirically that patenting records have steadily increased (with small periodic disturbances) since the 1890s in all broad technological sectors, including chemicals, electrical/electronics, mechanicals, transport and non-industrial (Andersen 1998, 2001). The only exception is the period surrounding and just after World War II. This illustrates an increasing incentive for firms and individuals as well as the public sector to privatize knowledge-based assets. Furthermore, that there is a relationship between research and development (R&D) (that is, inventive and innovative effort) and patenting is well documented (Scherer and Ross, 1990). However, whether this relationship is based upon patents stimulating some incentives to conduct R&D, or whether patents are merely the outcome of organized R&D conducted, or both, has been a matter for enquiry.

Since the early days of the creation of the patent system the classical view has been that patents are an incentive mechanism. The rationales for the IPR system are here based upon 'political expediency'. It is believed that placing IPRs on knowledge-based ideas provides the answer to stimulating a variety of different 'economic incentives' in the strategic behaviour of inventors. Basically, the efficiency of an incentive system is that it drives people to do things they would not otherwise have done, and these incentives will thus result in some benefit to society as a whole. The incentive arguments in the IPR literature are threefold: incentives to invent, be creative and innovate, as well as motivating the direction of such (section 3.1), incentives to use and allocate resources more efficiently (section 3.2) and incentives to disclose ideas in libraries and trade (this will be discussed in section 5.1 in relation to knowledge spillover from IPRs).

3.1 Incentives to Invent, be Creative and Innovate, as Well as Motivating the Direction of Such

The basic proposition of utilitarian classical economists[13] (including Jeremy Bentham [1748–1832], Adam Smith [1723–1790], Jean-Baptiste Say [1767–1832], John Stuart Mill [1806–1873] and John Bates Clark [1847–1938]) is that, as IPRs provide 'the prospect of reward', this in turn encourages creative and technological advance by providing increased incentives to invest in invention and further develop new ideas, and that without such incentives the invention inducement would be weakened. Douglass North (1981) also points out that sustained inventions and innovations first began after the establishment of IPRs to raise the private rate of return. However, the 'IPR-induced incentives to invent' rationale for the IPR system rests on two assertions:

1. Not enough inventions will be made without effective incentives: neither invention nor exploitation of inventions will take place unless inventors and capitalists believe they will yield profits which make it worth their while to make their efforts and risk their money, and
2. IPRs are the cheapest and most effective way for society to hold out these incentives.

Along similar lines, it has been argued that even if the IPR system is *not the most essential ingredient* to make people invent and innovate, it helps when it comes to motivating the direction of such invention and innovation. That is, only the inventions with most commercial opportunities will be explored for profit purposes, so in that sense it promotes 'useful inventions' (that is, those that people want). Basically, according to the classical economists, as mentioned above, as IPR privileges offer prizes to creative minds they arouse the mental powers and give them a direction.

However, while there is agreement that industrial progress is desirable and inventions are necessary for industrial progress, there is less support for the above-mentioned two assertions. The arguments are outlined below.

3.1.1 Challenging assumption (i) above: Not enough inventions will be made without effective incentives

(a) Inventive activity is inborn from childhood and often accidental Many classical economists[14] (including Frank William Taussig [1859–1940] and Arthur Cecil Pigou [1877–1959]) maintained that IPRs are superfluous and unnecessary, as inventive activity is inborn from childhood, and as inventions are often accidental. However, as put forward in section 2.4, much evidence suggests that inventions are generally not accidental and scientists must specialize to invent the unthinkable.

(b) The problem of 'uncertainty', 'indivisibility' and 'appropriability' According to Arrow (1962), although property rights on ideas are clearly useful or necessary when it comes to creating a market of ideas, they are nonetheless inferior to direct government investment when it comes to

stimulating inventive activity. His contention is that even under patent law basic research is bound to be under-rewarded. The reasons are: 'uncertainty', 'indivisibility' and 'appropriability'.

Arrow (1962) notes that invention production is inherently uncertain in the sense that the inventor cannot calculate the risk as in many other risk-bearing or risk-spreading activities, so the risk-averse may decide against using resources on research and invention. Hence, due to risk-averse behaviour, he maintains that the patent system will not create optimal inventive effort, but under-investment.

Appropriability problems are also that the owner of an idea may not be able to exploit the idea as effectively as others, and due to uncertainty this risk is unknown, so the risk-averse entrepreneurs may decide against patenting their inventions in the first place. Furthermore, investing in knowledge production for market exploitation may not be as efficient as other investments. Due to the indivisible nature of ideas, once the idea is shared or sold there is no need for the user of the idea or information to come back for more. That is, the use of an idea or information is infinite and it never faces decreasing returns to scale or is used up, so the nature of sharing or trading ideas on the market is very different from other intermediates or commodities. Use of ideas or information does not depend on the rate of production as with other intermediates, such as oil. Thus, although Arrow in principle agrees with the transaction cost argument that the only way to trade or share intangible ideas and information is by protecting them by a property right, he still argues that such protection is inefficient for market creation as the inventor may lose control of its use. Arrow (1962) also contends that the legal protection is only a partial barrier, because information can flow despite patent protection (for example, mobility of personnel among firms is suggested). A related problem mentioned by Arrow is the disclosure problem, where the demand for information cannot be optimally defined, as the value for the purchaser is not known until it has been partly revealed. However, when revealed in a patent document, a patent does not prevent anyone from thinking about the patented idea, and through pure inspiration producing a different competitive product not embodying or rewarding the original idea.

According to Arrow (1962), these phenomena have negative implications for the 'incentive rationale' for patents. This will be seen to be in sharp contrast to the 'social origin of inventions' argument where the patent system is inefficient because it over-rewards the patentee, resulting in a variety of individual and social costs (see sub-section 3.1.2 below). That is, in a completely different type of appropriability argument put forward by Arnold Plant (1934), although inventions are socially created from a bundle of cumulative past and current ideas (see section 2.2), the patent is granted on the grounds of the full invention. That is, marginal patents do not exist, but the person who hits the right note at the right time gets the full monopoly reward on the particular invention, and the rest participating in the social activity of inventing are left out. It could also be speculated that this lottery version of the patent system might lead to under-investment in inventive activity for the risk-averse. It is interesting to see how Arrow (1962) focuses on how the IPR system under-rewards the one who has been granted the patent right, while Plant (1934) focused on how the IPR system over-rewards the patentee. Hence, the appropriability problems mentioned by Arrow and Plant are for different parties.

In an empirical study of the data from the 1993 EU-conducted Community Innovation Survey, Arundel (2001) showed how the probability of firms rating secrecy as more valuable than patents declines with an increase in firm size for product inventions, while there is no such relationship for process inventions. Regarding the controversies on appropriating the returns from research and development, and the role of patents in inventions protection, as well as inventive incentives from patents, Scherer *et al.* (1959), Mansfield (1986), Levin *et al.* (1987) and Cohen *et al.* (2000) showed that incentives from patents in the US manufacturing sector depend upon the nature of the industry and are positively correlated with firm size (see section 2.5).

Finally, appropriability problems for the inventor also include the problems of management and transaction costs in enforcing the system. Such costs are not trivial (see next section 3.1.2) and they may reduce or undermine the efficiency of the IPR system as an incentive mechanism. In Chapter 5 of this book, Davis shows how this is in fact is the case for small and medium sized enterprises.

(c) Incentive to joint ventures or venture capitalists More recently, Cohen *et al.* (2000) showed in an empirical survey that the motives to patent often extend beyond directly profiting from the patented innovation through either its commercialization or licensing (see section 4.1.1 on corporate strategies). Along similar lines Teece (1986) points out that if a firm can get a strong patent, it may be in a good position to bargain a joint venture or licence deal with another firm that has the production and marketing capabilities. Coriat and Orsi (2002) explain how changing financial regulatory frameworks in the 1980s allowed unprofitable firms to include a whole range of intangible assets in their financial statements (the most important being their IPR assets in general and their patent portfolios in particular) in order to be listed on the Nasdaq for venture capital generation. This model, together with a series of other institutional

complementaries, was very successful, but also central to the creation of the dot.com or new economy bubble.

However, Machlup and Penrose (1950) maintained that in situations where the inventors are employed by a manufacturer or capitalist, or are manufacturers themselves, they often find themselves in a bargaining situation where they have no option but to sell their patents or copyrights at a price below their value. These bargaining situations often go against the reward system idea (see for example Andersen *et al.* (2005) regarding revenue distribution from copyrightable material in the music industry). In this paper we argue that, although the author of a copyright work has the exclusive control over a bundle of rights (such as the right to perform, reproduce and distribute the copyrighted work) these rights (either separately or together) may be transferred to another party, mainly in order to get the music product to the market. The reasons for this transfer of ownership or control of copyrights, or the right to revenue from copyrights, is to maximize income through: (i) the economics of complementary assets, which include all best means of adding value to the copyright product or service; (ii) risk management in volatile copyright markets; and (iii) as a means to raise venture capital. However, when sectoral collaboration and competition surround ownership or control of the copyrights, there is a possibility for conflict when bargaining power sets the rules. It is often argued how 'majors' in industries seem to hold the bargaining power. Asymmetry in bargaining power is often a reflection of asymmetries in financial dominance. Thus, in the words of Machlup and Penrose (1950):

> If the inventors could not hope to reap the fruits of their work, ... another theory could be substituted for the weakened theory of the patent as an incentive to invent: a theory of the patent as an incentive to venture capital for the financing of the development and pioneer exploitation of inventions.

Basically, it is less risky to finance the implementation of an idea into products for markets if the idea is covered by an IPR. The Bayh-Dole Act of 1980 in the US encourages public universities to patent their knowledge bases. This Act came about mainly as an incentive mechanism to enhance knowledge spillover, by encouraging venture capitalists to invest in commercializing the (now IP-protected) knowledge bases of public universities (see section 5.1.3. for a critical discussion of this spillover rationale).

The function of the patent as a stimulus to the inventor's financier has been given more emphasis.

3.1.2 Challenging assumption (ii) above: IPRs are the cheapest and most effective way for society to hold out incentives to invent, invest in and further develop productive knowledge

The innovation incentives argument is based upon the idea that the IPR system costs nothing or only imposes trivial costs. In that sense society gets something for almost nothing. However, a range of thinkers claim that heavy social costs are unavoidable. There are several social costs:

(a) The opportunity cost of investment in arbitrary technological trajectories Diversion of activity caused by the patent reward system can be into less productive channels. The diversion could be in moving from one field of research into other less productive pursuits, just because patent protection can more easily be obtained or be enjoyed to a higher extent in that field. Plant (1934) asserted that the patent system provides specific favourable conditions for certain types of inventions and thereby diverts the activities in society into arbitrary solutions. Thus, technological trajectories will become arbitrary. Within corporate strategic management, it has also been argued by Rivette and Kline (2000) that R&D and branding tend to be pursued in those areas in which patents can help to establish a market share. These are not necessarily the 'best' product or process innovations. The strength of the potential patent position is a leading factor in deciding what research to pursue.

(b) Administration and enforcement costs Bureaucracy concerning administering and enforcing the IPR system includes costs of court personnel, lawyers, IPR portfolio managers, others engaged in patent applications and litigations and royalty management, and such costs are not trivial.

(c) The monopoly or anti-competition costs of 'blocking patents' or setting territories The extension of monopoly power over individual firms often goes way beyond the scope of an individual patent. The issue of strategic patent blocking put forward by Rivette and Kline (2000) becomes relevant here. Basically, since the strength of the potential patent position is an important factor in deciding what research to pursue, it is important to consider how patent positions are strategically established. Building a wall of patents around category-leading products can help companies defend against imitators and can secure market share. An example of the importance of patent walls around technological webs is in the strategies of firms. Firms are afraid of specializing too narrowly. Many firms adopt the policy of always being at 'all platforms'.

Patent walls can be used to impose threats of patent infringement suits to block potential rivals. This is increasingly common practice. The money currently paid to IPR lawyers is unprecedented, as IPRs protect the key competitive strategic asset (or intellectual capital) of many firms. However, as pointed out by Rivette and Kline (2000), building a patent wall around the product or process is not the only way to hold back competitors. If your competitor has patented an invention, but has not patented the surrounding application innovations, a corporate strategy can be to patent these, so your competitor is locked out of further developing the market, or is at least totally dependent on you. This is the essence of bracketing. It should not need to be explained that such forms of patent blocking reduce competition and hence social welfare.

Owning IPRs lets companies develop favourable partnerships and licensing relationships. Also, as one firm is not powerful enough to set standards alone, and to avoid the existence of mandatory standards, cross licensing (often based upon strategic choice of partners) has often been the solution. Collaboration is also often around open-architecture patent pools (that is, each participant contributes something to the development trajectory on a royalty-free basis) in which all participants include their relevant patents. When it comes to the specificities of the cross-licensing agreements, or sharing the royalties (from external contracts) in patent pools, bargaining power can play a role.

(d) Opportunity costs in depriving others from using the most efficient solution However beneficial the patent may be for the inventor who receives the privilege, the community will not always automatically benefit from an idea if it is protected by an IPR, and this in turn deprives society of the benefits that would flow from the more widespread use of these ideas. That is, although development rights are free of royalties (so spillover is in principle free), the subsequent production and trade rights embodying the ideas are not free (Cheung 1986).

Thus the temporary prevention, or high cost, of the use of the most efficient processes by most other producers can be considered as a welfare loss or social cost.

(e) Opportunity costs of depriving inventors of what they had before (assuming invention is a social process) Assuming that invention is a social or collective process to which many contribute (see section 2.2), the opponents of the IPR system (basing their views upon Plant 1934) would argue that a patent or copyright deprives others of what they had before (that is, the opportunity to use the same idea or expression that they have been part of developing but which the patentee or copyright holder now owns).

(f) The welfare cost of broad patent scope Along the lines of the arguments in *(d)* and *(e)*, Merges and Nelson (1990) note that the higher the scope of the protected idea, the higher the potential costs to society. In a similar context, Winter (1993) focuses on the social costs of non-free exploration of ideas, where society specializes in expensive innovation rather than cheaper imitation, in order to avoid the region occupied by the patent holder. To reduce such costs, Merges and Nelson argued for an IPR policy of 'compulsory licensing' (see section 4.1.1). F.M. Scherer *et al.* (1959) also proposed forced licensing in antitrust cases as a remedy against monopolization.

(g) The cost of patent panic As argued in section 2.1.2, the patent system can be compared to a lottery in the sense that most inventive activity is a social process, yet those who hit the next novelty on the road get the monopoly while the rest are excluded. This might be one of the reasons for patent panic where everyone patents everything they come across, despite the consumption of financial resources this entails, rather than sensible patenting strategies. Another reason for patent panic is also the fear that competitors will establish patent walls or conduct bracketing, so firms try to patent everything to avoid such situations. Some firms interviewed for an EU fifth framework project ('Patents and services'; contract no ERBHPV2-CT-1999–06) expressed concern regarding the huge resource costs involved with such patent panic, triggered mainly to protect against constant threats of infringement cases or problems regarding being locked out of the development trajectory.

Moreover, according to Kingston (2001), for complex technologies, patents are now used as much as a bargaining currency to prevent 'lock out' from use of state-of-the-art components developed by competitors, as they are as stimulus to research and development. He then discusses the need for patent reforms towards compulsory licensing and open architecture patent pools.

(h) Royalties as social costs A standard static efficiency argument against the IPR system is that, as the manufacturer also has to pay royalties R to the inventor of the product that they produce, the price of the good exceeds marginal costs ($MC + R = P$), and this therefore reduces welfare. However, those believing in the IPR system would here contend that R necessarily reflects the costs of having a property right system enforcing more efficient allocation of resources (see section 3.2 below). However, the answer from the system disbelievers presented here would naturally be that the social costs should not be treated as 'trivial'.

3.2 Incentives to Use and Allocate Resources more Efficiently

When understanding the economics of IPR law Posner (1992) focuses on the static and dynamic effects with respect to resource allocation. Just as with property rights on land, it should follow that with intellectual property rights, ideas are used or owned by the most efficient entrepreneurs, as it make sense for the less efficient inventors to license or sell their ideas. This is the static efficiency argument. Posner's dynamic efficiency argument (1992) reads that in a world without IPRs, where anyone is free to use others' ideas, inventive activity would be biased towards inventions that could be held secret, as well as towards activities that involve minimum preparatory investment. An implication is that, in the absence of IPR protection, inventors are not encouraged to conduct their inventive activities, as without an IPR they will not be able to recover the costs of research and development (that is, pricing at marginal production costs in order to compete with imitators means that the inventor or entrepreneur will not recover R&D costs) or expect any special reward. The main dynamic point in this context is that legal protection of property rights creates incentives to use resources more efficiently through investment in planning and development of resources. Innovation-enhanced competition here encourages inventors to come up with the most competitive product or process that either uses resources most efficiently, or holds a desired new attribute, or both. Both the static and dynamic efficiency arguments rest on the assumption that ideas are scarce, just as land resources are.

However, there are many arguments against IPRs as an incentive to use and allocate resources more efficiently.

3.2.1 The deliberate creation of statute that creates scarcity

Plant (1934) maintained that, whereas the system of property rights on land under property law is useful as it creates more efficient use of scarce resources, property rights on ideas are of a very different nature. Plant suggested that patents are not the consequence of scarce resources as in the case of property rights on land, but they are the deliberate creation of statute that creates scarcity. Along similar lines, David (2001) also argues that the creation of scarcity within information and knowledge spaces is inefficient, as their dynamic nature (facing increasing returns to scale) is very different from physical land spaces (facing decreasing returns to scale). Basically, information or knowledge spaces are likely to be enriched and rendered more accurate and more fully documented, the more researchers are allowed to participate. According to David, it is through wide and complete disclosure and the sceptical efforts to replicate novel research findings that scientific communities build bodies of reliable knowledge.

However, whereas David and Olsen (1992) contend that spillover occurs best through patented ideas (which speeds up knowledge diffusion through licensing, see section 5.1), the later David (2001, presented above) argues that knowledge is best developed though little IPR protection. A question that can be raised here is whether there is a trade-off between the speed of knowledge diffusion through patented ideas, and developing the best science (that is, the best trajectories) through very little protection or through a different type of open disclosure. Perhaps little protection is needed at an early state of the trajectory to allow for free exploration (as also suggested by Winter (1993) and Nelson (2004)), and clearer codification in patent disclosures is needed at a later stage to allow for diffusion.

3.2.2 Implications of avoiding a technological region occupied by an IPR holder

Winter (1993) contends that although it might be true that patents lead to more innovative effort, from a social welfare point of view, the IPR system does not necessarily lead to more efficient allocation of resources. He notes that inefficiencies might occur if patents are granted to inventors at an early stage of a technological trajectory. When a new trajectory is still being explored by a variety of inventors, an early granting of patents might disrupt and deprive the free exploration phase, and we might be diverted in an inefficient direction. It follows that Winter would not be a great supporter of the US scheme on 'continuation' or 'submarine' patents encouraging patent application submissions at a very early stage of the discovery (see Chapter 7 of this book as well as Mowery and Graham (2004) for a detailed account of the scheme).

Furthermore, a system with strong IPR protection may result in more resources devoted to expensive inventive and innovative R&D effort (in order to avoid a technological region occupied by a patent holder) rather than to cheaper imitative effort. This need for an inventor to avoid a technological region occupied by a patent holder will not only increase the cost of making a new economically comparable invention (as first noted in section 3.1.2*(f)*), but it might also result in inefficient technological trajectories.

3.2.3 Disincentives created by the inventor's pre-invention monopoly profits

Arthur (1988) argues that in industries where the fixed set-up costs are high in comparison to the cost of reproduction, individuals and organizations have a strong incentive to identify and stick with a single option. This certainly also applies to knowledge and information-based products and services. Once the costs of development have been recouped, every single additional reproduction (or re-application) of intangible ideas is pure profit. Thus, in this fashion, IPRs may encourage investment in arbitrary or sub-optimal technological trajectories and thereby create inefficient use of resources. Along similar lines, Arrow (1962) suggests that the patent system results in under-allocation of resources to invention. He argues that under monopolistic situations the incentive to innovate will be lower than under competitive conditions. Although monopoly situations will increase appropriability possibilities, Arrow maintains that this is offset by the disincentives created by the inventor's pre-invention monopoly profits.

However, even under competitive conditions Arrow (1962) argues that allocation of resources to invention is less than socially desirable due to uncertainty, indivisibility and appropriability problems (see previous section 3.1). To solve this allocation problem, he proposes government involvement and government expenditures, and he even suggests thinking about alternative methods of compensation and reward systems. However, David and Olsen (1992) discuss how Arrow's argument on 'loss from monopolies' rests on the assumption that monopolists are actively using their patented ideas, but that this is only the case for a short period. David and Olsen (1992) then emphasize how licensing is a fact of life in most industries, and how the knowledge spillover gains from such activities are underrated (see section 5).

4 INCREASED COMPETITION AND 'MARKET PROTECTION OF ENTREPRENEURIAL TALENT' RATIONALES: INDUSTRIAL DEVELOPMENT FROM PATENTS

That many patented inventions actually progress to innovation is an established fact, although this depends on industry and is negatively correlated to firm size (Sanders 1964, Napolitano and Sirilli, 1990). As illustrated in the sections below, some believe that property rights on ideas (that is, creating rivalry among) are the most efficient answer to stimulate innovation and industrial development from patents. Here it is believed that innovation, industrial development and social welfare happen through enhanced competition (section 4.1) or through market protection of entrepreneurial talent (section 4.2). Thus, the rationales for IPRs can also here be regarded as 'political expediency'.

4.1 The Innovation-enhanced Competition and 'Nature of Ideas' Argument

The fact that knowledge can be consumed jointly, reproduced very cheaply, and does not decrease in value (i.e. size or quality) by use, means that it has some of the qualities of a public good (usually referred to as the 'non-rival' aspect of a public good). But, unlike a public good, it is possible for the creator of an idea to exclude others from using it in production and trade, by the use of an IPR. This rival aspect of ideas embodied in the production and trade of goods and services is believed to stimulate innovation-enhanced competition by providing incentives to innovate in using scarce resources more efficiently (that is, process invention) or inventing the next new thing (that is, product invention). Thus, IPRs are here believed to stimulate a competitive dynamic environment as well as to strengthen continuous innovators.

However, there are many contrary arguments in the literature.

4.1.1 The problem of patent scope and corporate strategic behaviour

It is clearly debatable whether society experiences more competition by creating temporary monopolies (or exclusive rights on ideas). The whole argument of corporate strategies surrounding IPRs and strategic patent blocking becomes relevant here. Whereas Arrow (1962) maintained that patent grants lack sufficient blocking power for the inventors who cannot fully appropriate from their ideas (see section 3) so there is too little rivalry, others, such as Plant (1934), contended that patent monopolies provide such extreme privileges and appropriation opportunities to the inventor against other producers and even the consumers (see section 3) that rivalry becomes reckless. Both cases are competition-distorting. Like Plant (1934), Merges and Nelson (1990) suggest that inventive rivalry is good for inventive progress, but that too strong patent protection will distort such progress due to patent blocking slowing down cumulativeness. The basic contention is that most innovations take place in a social context, in the sense that complex and multi-component products are the norm in many industries, and individual patents often cover only a single component or sub-component. Essentially, there is no simple 'one to one' mapping of products and property rights, but each product includes a variety of patents of different types and with different scopes and durations. The breadth of the patent scope is very important for understanding the monopoly effects of the patent system. Due to cumulativeness in the innovative processes, a more narrow protection favours secondary inventions, but sacrifices the economic incentives that would otherwise be offered for breakthrough inventions, whereas broad protection has the opposite effect (as knowledge has become scarce and costly for secondary inventions). Merges and Nelson (1990) illustrate how history has shown that strengthening patent protection will not increase invention, due to the increased costs of the patent scope. Maintaining that patents do help to reach certain ends, Merges and Nelson (1990) discuss the idea of compulsory licensing to eliminate some of the problems with too broad patent scope enabling blocking power, and to enhance more inventive rivalry.

Hence, it is argued that patent blocking done to a patent with a broad scope destroys competition. This is also why 'pure ideas' – that is, laws of nature (physics laws), theoretical principles (for example, some mathematics), and natural species (an exemption being the controversial right to patent gene codes in some regions of the world)[15] – are not normally eligible for patent protection. Patenting such 'pure ideas' would block innovation and competition due to too broad patent scope, and thereby also block progress for industrial development and social welfare.

Blocking actions can also be channelled through patent or copyright assignments (that is, outright transaction or transfer/sale of rights) or through cross licensing. Such blocking actions are also often used to produce immunity from litigation because of the high (and increasing) costs of infringement suits. Thus, the value of patents essentially depends on its blocking power. Therefore, as illustrated in Rivette and Kline (2000) in section 3.1.2, firms lay out their patent portfolios when making long term investment decisions regarding which products to commercialize and which technological trajectories to participate in. It is essentially about positioning, but signalling is also important in this game. Cohen *et al.* (2000) have also showed in an empirical survey that, in addition to prevention from imitating or copying, the most prominent motives for patenting include the prevention of rivals from patenting related inventions (that is, 'patent blocking' actions), as well as the use of patents in negotiations and the prevention of infringement suits. The specific strategies are however industry-specific. Thus, commercialization or strategic licensing has become more important for corporate value creation than direct protection from imitation.

Granstrand (1999) also sheds light on the strategic use of intellectual property rights by companies holding large portfolios of such rights. He formulates different IPR-based anti-competition strategies (such as strategic patent searching and patent blocking as well as patent walls or fencing and so on), by which companies set their territories and appropriate revenues from intellectual property rights well beyond the recovery of their R&D costs.

The historical evidence cited by David (1985) and Arthur (1988, 1996) suggests various circumstances that make a technological idea prone to increasing returns and lock in and therefore competition distorting. David and Arthur emphasized how lock in can occur from random events. However, in a study of IPRs in the electronic age, I show how IPRs can enforce such lock-in mechanisms. Basically, as IPRs on a locked-in idea generate profit over time, this encourages corporate strategies to take advantage of such increasing returns dynamics to generate lock-in situations (Andersen, 2003). The basic assumption is that the increasing returns dynamics of

IPR-based sectors enforced by corporate strategic interaction (especially in the intangible economy where many products are purely knowledge-based) have implications for the value of IPRs, which thus encourages anti-competitive behaviour. In this manner, I show how firms' intellectual capital or inventive ideas are informally protected even without the formal IPR legal framework. The situations are those in which the following dynamics play a role: (i) learning effects and increasing returns to adaptation, (ii) network externalities, (iii) technological webs, (iv) informational increasing returns to adaptation, and (v) knowledge-based intangibles underpinning increasing returns to scale. Hence, in this context IPRs serve mostly as a means by which knowledge embodied in products and processes can be exploited for excessive rent creation. Therefore, one should reconsider how legitimate the market protection rationale of the IPR system is during increasing returns dynamics. This in turn also has implications for not only a winner takes all dynamics, but also the existence of sub-optimal technological trajectories or arbitrary technological solutions.

4.1.2 Production and trade rights versus development rights

When discussing patent blocking, we need to consider what the patent protects and what it does not protect. Development rights (that is, the right to use the idea to develop another idea) are not directly protected. However, production rights (that is, the right to use the idea to produce) and trade rights (that is, the right to trade a commodity embodying the idea) are protected through a patent. Yet it could be suggested that the development rights are indirectly protected by the production and trade rights, as there is no point in developing an idea if you cannot use it for commercial purposes. According to Cheung (1986), the exclusive rights to produce and trade a product also imply exclusive rights to improve a patented idea:

> In short, the rule for improvement would seem to read: You may tinker with my patent any way you please, but plan to pay me when you produce any commodity over which I have some claim; moreover, to avoid my possible excessive demands, it may be wise for you to obtain a license from me in advance.

Hence, a patent does imply some exclusive rights on development to the extent that the improvement is dominated by the original invention.

4.2 The 'Market Protection of Entrepreneurial Talent' for Industrial Development Rationale

It is proposed that efficient IPR protection allows profit-oriented firms to enter (or develop) an industry or market. This rationale of IPRs has also been compared to that of tariff protection. Just as with tariffs, a patent protects against market entry. The idea is that a temporary production and trade privilege will allow a firm or industry to develop and mature. This, in its turn, causes (or opens space for) industrial development and progress.

Kitch (1977) suggested that IPRs allow breathing room for the inventor to invest in development without fear that another firm will steal the idea. Furthermore, the temporary trade privilege in the form of an IPR should, just as with a tariff, help a firm or an industry to cover the fixed costs of inventing and setting up the production of a new product and thereby enhance the incentive to invent and innovate (see section 3 on incentive rationales).

4.2.1 The tariff protection analogy debate

Comparing patent protection with tariff protection and comparing exclusive rights (in the form of a patent) with monopoly privileges in general tends to help patent opponents and weaken patent defenders. Against patent protection during the final shaping of the patent system in the nineteenth century was the free trade argument. Those against tariffs were also generally against patents. However, those for tariffs were for patents. It was contended that IPRs were important for entrepreneurial talent to create and develop a market, just as tariffs were for firms and industries.

However, Jeremy Benthan [1748–1832], one of the advocators for patent protection, argued that the exclusive rights given to inventors have nothing in common with general monopolies which are so justly decried. Along similar lines, Adam Smith [1723–1790], a prolific advocator for free trade, suggested that although monopolies in trade deranged the more or less natural distribution of stock in society and were therefore hurtful to society, a temporary monopoly granted to an inventor of a new machine could be justified as a means of rewarding risk and expense and thereby encourage new ventures (cited in Machlup and Penrose 1950).

Rivera-Batiz and Romer (1991) point out that patents combined with free trade would reduce costs and enhance efficiency, as economic agents can use more efficient technology developed elsewhere, as well as specialize in areas in which they have the comparative advantage. Section 5 discusses further the view that the incentive to share ideas in trade is stimulated through patent legislation. However, I do not think that it would be wrong to assert that global free trade in ideas based on science and technology does not make sense to a country which has no such ideas whatsoever, or which is at a development stage and tries to break out of the traditional raw materials supplier role in order to step on to the next development stage and specialize in manufacturing. For such countries licensing fees can act as a cost and barrier to entering global markets. That is, developed or industrialized countries benefit from the IPR system, in the sense that (always being first) they have been able to use it as a way of financing development, whereas the less developed countries (being the followers) mainly experience it as a development cost and barrier to entering global markets.

Also, the free trade supporters did not take into account how the efficiency of the market for ideas also depends on the efficiency of the local IPR offices, whose role is also to educate the users of the system and enforce the system (see Chapter 6 in this book as well as Christensen (2004) in section 5.1.3 as regards the role of the patent system in knowledge spillover). With respect to cultural industries and creative expressions (which all countries have), I (Andersen *et al.* 2005) co-studied the global music industry, where we found how the efficiency of the local copyright system, local collecting societies and other local support institutions play an immensely important role for the gain from trade.

Basically, in many cases the gain from trade in the IPR system depends on how organized countries are in protecting their knowledge base. This is especially the problem regarding the issues related to:

- Patenting of traditional knowledge and the problem of bio-piracy: traditional knowledge in the form of plant breeding, rice breeding, knowledge about natural medicine from plants and herbs and so on (for example, from natives in Borneo, the Amazon, Thailand and so on) have increasingly become patented by large firms for profit exploitation purposes. This is easily done as many less developed regions do not have the capabilities to convert their productive practical knowledge (developed over centuries) into scientific knowledge for patenting purposes, and they do not have the patent institutions in place to protect and enforce their intellectual property.
- Copyrighting of traditional cultural expressions: traditional cultural expressions in the form of art and music (for example, from natives in Australia, Africa, the Caribbean and so on) have increasingly become copyrighted by large firms for profit exploitation purposes. This is easily done as many less-developed regions do not have the copyright institutions in place to protect and enforce their intellectual property.

The situation has become even worse, as there is no mechanism in place for the major companies which are patenting or copyrighting such knowledge or cultural expressions, to return some of the profit back to the communities which have provided the traditional knowledge or cultural expressions. Rather, the regions have been requested to pay licensing fees to produce or export goods in which their traditional knowledge or cultural expressions are embedded.

Finally, the existence of corporate strategic interaction in the marketplace for ideas also distorts the free trade ideology in practice.

These are some of the critical issues that can be raised in relation to the TRIPS of the WTO. An aim should be to understand the dynamic effects of the exploitation of the general profile of corporate power endorsed by IPRs, and the accountability of that power. An aim should also be to understand the dynamic effects of the exploitation of IPRs on less developed regions that have expressed problems with the global IPR system in its current form.

5 THE ECONOMIC RATIONALE OF ORGANIZING SCIENCE, TECHNOLOGY AND CREATIVITY: INCREASED INFORMATION SPILLOVER

In order to secure a stream of inventions and innovations it is important that new ideas become generally known to society. The argument is that, in the absence of protection for novel ideas, inventors will keep their inventions secret and they will die with them. Hence, it is in the interests of society to induce inventors to disclose their secrets for the use of future generations, and some believe that IPRs provide the answer here (see discussion in section 5.1 below). The economic rationale of organizing science, technology and creativity also includes the institutional aspects of the IPR system as an underpinning technology-support system reducing transaction costs with respect to information spillover in technological development and trade (see discussion in section 5.2 below).

Hence, the rationale is that IPRs should help to facilitate the sharing of ideas, creative efforts and new technologies nationally and worldwide. It is believed that this creates faster knowledge spillover and a more coherent technological and industrial development, which in turn will strengthen the national or global economy. Thus the IPR rationale for increased information spillover can be regarded as a 'political expediency' rationale.

However, even if it is debatable whether IPRs create more spillover (see 5.1 for discussion), patent statistics have often been the means by which spillover or technology diffusion or transfer have been measured. These data have been taken from patent citations (see Jaffe, Trajtenberg, and Henderson 1993, Jaffe and Trajtenberg 2002, Almeida, 1996), licensing agreements and the outward transfer of patent ownership.

5.1 'Incentives to Disclose Ideas' Rationale

Granting exclusive rights to inventors for their innovations in terms of efficient IPR protection can be regarded as a contract the inventor gets from government if the inventor agrees to disclose the idea in question (see (a) below). As an idea or information good is non-rival by nature, exclusive rights on such will also help the inventor to exploit directly, or appropriate from the idea as a value-driven intellectual capital, which in its turn will provide an incentive to share the idea in trade (see (b) below).

(a) Negotiated incentive to disclose ideas in libraries Patents and copyrights, when filed, provide immediate information to rivals who can incorporate it into their own knowledge bases even though they cannot make direct commercial use of it. The rationale here is that IPRs are necessary as incentives to induce inventors to disclose their new inventions instead of keeping them secret. That is, perhaps there would be enough incentive to invent without patents, but the invention would not be disclosed because the inventor would not wish to lose control of the idea. Hence, by issuing patents protecting the inventions, inventors agree to disclose their inventions that thus become part of society's knowledge base. To avoid interpretation of patents as 'privileges' this assertion has been developed as part of 'social contract theory'. In this statute a patent is not regarded as a privilege granted by society, but as a bargain between society and the inventor.

(b) Incentive to disclose ideas in trade Secondly, a rationale is that IPRs provide direct incentives for sharing ideas through trade in the sense that knowledge, by definition, faces increasing returns to scale. It can be claimed that, although knowledge is not a new feature of capitalist production, it takes on a greater weight in the globalizing economy when protected by an IPR. This trend is complemented by the public good nature of knowledge or ideas themselves. But, unlike a public good, it is possible for the creator of an idea to exclude others from using it by use of IPRs, opening the possibility for wider commercial exploitation (Rivera-Batiz and Romer, 1991). In this context, IPRs are in principle able to create a market for knowledge, and as ideas face increasing return to scale by nature, this give rise to increasing rent or profit as markets expand.

The information spillover effects from patents is taken seriously in the formal modelling of neoclassical economic literature. Rivera-Batiz and Romer (1991) build upon Arrow's (1962) notion of perfect knowledge spillover once ideas are disclosed in a patent document (it was argued that owners of ideas have thereby lost control of appropriation from such ideas; see 3.1.1). It can be said that Rivera-Batiz and Romer thereby consider the communication rationale of the patent system. Basically, they incorporate perfect knowledge spillover and knowledge accumulation from patents directly into an endogenous growth model:

> Holders of patents on previous designs have no technological or legal means of preventing designers of new goods from using the ideas implicit in the existing designs. The stock of A [knowledge or ideas] that can be put to use, with no compensation, by any individual researcher is therefore the entire stock of knowledge about the previous designs, provided that there exists a communication network that makes this information available.

However, although an IPR does not involve any research and development rights, Rivera-Batiz and Romer (1991) did not envisage it as a problem that the production and trade rights also have knock-on effects on the research and development right. Basically, there is no point in developing if you cannot exploit your idea, so the spillover may not be so perfect after all (see Cheung, 1986, in section 4.1.2, for a discussion of this).

David and Olsen (1992) emphasize how patent grants may improve economic welfare when there are learning externalities or spillover. The basic contention is that patents improve economic efficiency by speeding up learning by doing and quickening the diffusion of existing innovation. David and Olsen criticize the fact that the national patent systems require patent holders to pay a significant amount of annual fees, even after they stop directly using their patented idea but keep the IPR for licensing purposes. They believe that this fee-paying system reflects the view that patent monopolies are simply imposing a deadweight welfare burden upon the economy.

However, many do not believe in the 'incentives to disclose ideas' rationale of patents.

5.1.1 The complexity of bargain agreements in social contracts

As discussed by Machlup and Penrose (1950), there are many (conflicting) objections to such bargain agreements in social contracts that challenge the information disclosure and spillover rationales from IPRs:

- If inventors chose to keep inventions secret, society will not lose much because usually similar ideas are developed elsewhere (due to the social or collective nature of inventions; see section 2.2).
- It is practically impossible to keep ideas secret so the idea will be revealed even without an IPR. Eager competitors will find a way to find out (for example, reverse engineering, espionage). This argument resembles the appropriability problem in section 3.1.1.
- Where inventors think that they will succeed in guarding a secret, they will not take out a patent. Patents are only taken out where the secret is difficult to keep or where others develop similar ideas. There is therefore a net loss in the system since rational inventors would

only use the patent system to restrict access to markets, and would not cause disclosure of unique inventions.

- Since patents are only granted at a certain stage of an invention, the patent system encourages secrecy in the development stage. Without patents, inventors would quickly publish their ideas under development to secure recognition and fame. Thus, patent systems encourage secrecy and when patent disclosure finally comes about, it is at a huge social cost in terms of 'lost past disclosure at the development stage'. It might even be argued that if ideas were published before they had developed into patentable inventions, they would ripen more quickly and would become available for practical application elsewhere much sooner.

5.1.2 Invention diffusion and high barriers to imitation

According to Winter (1993), as resources for advancing or using knowledge are scarce and expensive in a patent system, more R&D is spent on innovative effort. However, in the absence of a patent system, R&D spent on innovative effort is very expensive compared to the less expensive imitative effort. Furthermore, he argues that this rival-based patent system, where each firm develops its own competitive trajectory, may result in too many sub-optimal solutions and arbitrary technological trajectories. Thus, Winter states that best practice productivity levels in most firms would be higher in a system without patents. He concludes that three-year patents are sufficient to allow a small role for imitation, but that a longer period would reduce imitation entirely and raise non-optimal R&D effort. The length of a patent is 20 years in most countries today. Despite Winter's contribution, it is evident that we know more about how the patent system affects invention and innovation from a supply side perspective (see sections 3 and 4), than the role it plays in the adoption of ideas and spillover from a knowledge-demand side perspective.

5.1.3 The role of public institutions in knowledge spillover to, or within, the private sector

The IPR system is also said to enhance knowledge spillover to the wider private community through several public institutions. Firstly, there is the most obvious (but under-researched) role of the patent office. Christensen (2004; see also Chapter 6 of this book) maintains that the success of the patent system is still locally rooted despite globalization in IPR legislation. In a current debate on the issue, his basic contention (based upon a survey of what firms used the local Danish patent office for) is that the national patent and trademark office enhances knowledge spillover from the patenting process, and should therefore not be abolished in the era of institutional internationalization. Well-organized local IPR offices provide an important role in educating and supporting the local users of the international IPR system, as well as developing a vibrant local IPR community by bringing users of the system and IPR service firms together.

The Bayh-Dole Act of 1980 in the US is another institution that encourages spillover. This Act is mainly an incentive to encourage universities to patent their ideas, which in turn should have a knock-on effect on venture capitalists who would then invest in commercializing the protected knowledge bases of public universities. The Bayh-Dole Act (summarized by Mowery *et al.* 1999 and Mazzoleni and Nelson, 1998a, b) rests on the assumption that inventions serve no economic purpose unless and until they are developed into commercial use, and that a company would be unlikely to engage in the development of a university invention unless it controls the property rights (that is, unless universities are in a position in which they can sell or license their invention, or, if government holds them, they have a commitment to non-exclusive licensing agreements). Although there is evidence that the Bayh-Dole Act has led universities to advertise and push their inventions more actively, Mazzoleni and Nelson (1998a, b) argue that we know very little about whether this has facilitated more technological transfer. The discussions presented in this chapter can explain some of the controversial elements of the Bayh-Dole Act. For example, even if the Act helps certain ends (that is, helping universities and individuals to develop a clear strategy regarding how best to commercialize their ideas), it is still an Act about taking very basic knowledge out of the public domain. Very basic inventions tend to have broader patent scope, which can induce welfare loss (see Merges and Nelson (1990) in section 3.1.2*(f)* and 4.1.1), or welfare loss from firms avoiding technological trajectories where basic knowledge has been made scarce and expensive (see Winter, 1993, in sections 3.1.2*(f)*, 3.2.2, and 5.1.2). Nelson (2004; see also Chapter 1 of this book) advocates very strongly that basic scientific findings should be kept in the public domain. In a range of empirical examples, he illustrates that inventions produced by universities are generally so basic that firms have plenty of opportunities to commercialize the ideas and patent follow-up inventions. It is the openness of basic inventions for multiple exploration paths in the market economy that makes the evolutionary process of technological advance more powerful. It follows that the necessity of the ownership of a basic invention as the incentive to create follow-up inventions for commercialization is overrated. Furthermore, the objectives of firms' and universities' knowledge bases, as well as their role in society, are very different. The market positioning of firms and universities are also very different, and this may affect the bargaining situation.

In a somewhat different light and different context, it is also (controversially),[16] suggested that public money spent on military research does not need to be a dead-weight burden to society if patented. Patents in the military can enhance spillover to the civil and commercial knowledge base (Molas-Gallart *et al.* 2000). It should however be noted that military inventions are often protected by trade secrecy, and that (when patented) patents containing national security-sensitive information (as is often the case with the military) are protected by special secrecy acts (for example, the Invention Secrecy Act of 1951 in the US case) that restrict disclosure of the invention and withhold the grant of a patent. This requirement can even be imposed when the application is generated and entirely owned by a private individual or company.

5.2 Rationale of Uniformity, Order, Increased Information, Increased Spillover and Better Advice

A central 'political expediency' rationale of organizing science and technology at the macro level is that an IPR system not only provides economic incentives, but also offers information on new trajectories, structural changes in technological development, and the technological capabilities of firms, industries, sectors and nations. That is, patents granted in specific fields of activity often follow identifiable trajectories or paradigms associated with the use of particular patent classes. An understanding of the trajectories being followed at a particular time may yield qualitative predictions about the nature of the improvements that are likely to be forthcoming in the near future. The information provided through the IPR system allows governments to be more effectively advised on science and technology policy matters. For example, so far, patent statistics have shown promise and some success in analysing international patterns of innovative activities in relation to trade and production; patterns of innovative activities amongst firms, and their effects upon competence as well as performance and industrial structures; rates and directions of innovative activities in different technical fields and industrial sectors; and links between science and technology. For the European contribution, see for example the numerous works of Pavitt and Patel and colleagues at the Science and Technology Policy Research Unit (SPRU), Cantwell and colleagues at the University of Reading, as well as Verspagen, Soete and colleagues at Maastricht Economic Research Institute on Innovation and Technology (MERIT), as well as a previous research project by me (summarized in Andersen, 2001). In a recent contribution from the US, Jaffe and Trajtenberg (2002) emphasize the direct information and communication rationales from patent grants and associated citations. Also, a national and international IPR system brings in national and international uniformity in the way the knowledge base is organized into scientific classes, increasing the scope of analysis and comparison.

The transparency of systems of organized knowledge also seeks to promote cross-country trade in IPRs, and hence international integration of science, technology and creative efforts, stimulating prosperity worldwide. Basically, the transaction cost rationale for the IPR system is manifold:

1. A standardized system simplifies contracts in buying and selling knowledge.
2. It also reduces information asymmetry and increases trust since the full idea is disclosed in a patent document.
3. The transparency of knowledge helps to prevent the duplication of creative effort and encourages coordination and broadening of activities, allowing inventive resources to be used more efficiently. Patents are therefore granted early (before invention has been carried to the point of commercial feasibility) in order to head off costly duplication of expensive development work. (The very early granting of patents is, however, controversial; see Winter (1993) in section 3.2.2 and Nelson (2004) in section 5.1.3).
4. Through open disclosure (that is, reduced information asymmetry), IPRs also provide an informal or formal way of collaborating around technological trajectories.

No one really objects to the usefulness of the information spillover rationale for promoting information on science and technology matters, as well as for promoting trade in ideas and standard-setting.

6 CONCLUSION

The complexity surrounding IPR systems is manifold, and we cannot take the effect or efficiency of any IPR regime for granted. The IPR regime should therefore be used cautiously. In this chapter I have illustrated that IPR systems are not neutral; they set the rules of the game in which individuals and organizations interact, and in which corporate leaders and stakeholders are shaped and technological trajectories selected or reinforced. As the nature of IPR systems is not neutral, I agree with the view of 'positive theory of the social contract' (in section 2), that it is impossible for a government to enforce a right without implementing its views on the notions of rights and wrongs, justice and injustice. I would suggest that the existence and design of IPR law have implications on wealth distribution in society. I therefore maintain that the rationales and social and economic effects of the IPR system are vital and must be addressed at the political level. For policy design it is important to state the aims and objectives with respect to what we wish to achieve from IPR systems.

Based upon the views of those who believe in the IPR system (as reviewed in sections 2–5), a typology of the complexity of IPR rationales has evolved in this chapter. This is presented in Figure 4.1.

The typology can help policy makers, analysts and academics when designing and analysing the IPR system. That is, the gain from stronger IPR protection is far from axiomatic. As shown in this chapter, there are many controversies in the theoretical literature regarding the aim, operation and effects of the IPR system. By illuminating the conflicts, contradictions, and trade-offs in the IPR system in this chapter, the proposed typology, mapping out the rationales for IPRs, will help policy makers, analysts and academics not just to 'assume' the IPR system, but to use the typology to address critically why we have it, how it works, and what effects from the system we will aspire to.

With respect to why we have the IPR system, there may be trade-offs between the moral or ethical aspects of the IPR system with respect to protecting the inventor, and the economic performance effects of the IPR system for certain sectors or society as a whole. With respect to the operation of the IPR system and its effects, it is evident that there are many different views in the theoretical literature. In summary, many of the social contract and political expediency rationales (based upon mainly theoretical logic) are problematic as they assume that all inventors (individuals or firms) are autonomous rational profit-maximizing agents, and that the aggregate of their behaviour maximizes their own as well as social welfare. The arguments do not take into account the effects of technological interdependence, strategic interaction and collaboration in competitive markets, the specific nature of productive knowledge, power relationships in bargaining situations, or the opportunity costs of using the IPR system as a political instrument.

However, understanding the social and economic effects of the legal exclusive rights created by IPR regimes is a challenging task, especially if we wish to include realistic assumptions of the governance of IPRs at the corporate and sectoral level. This includes considering different structures of ownership, taking into account portfolios of rights (not single rights) in innovation systems, as well as taking into account licensing possibilities, and considering modes of interaction. In this context it is a problem that the current law and economics agenda on IPR equates competition with perfect competition and monopoly with pure monopoly. The architecture of the intellectual property system is a hybrid structure of them both.

It is difficult to advance the understanding of the specific operation of the IPR system without more empirical research. We know little about the

Social contract theory	Natural rights and moral rationales	➢ The natural and moral right to claim the intellectual property.
		➢ The moral right to compensation and reward.
Political expediency as a means to affect economic behaviour, as a mechanism to obtain welfare goals	Increased competition and 'market protection of entrepreneurial talent' rationales: industrial development from patents	➢ The innovation-enhanced competition and 'nature of ideas' argument.
		➢ The 'market protection of entrepreneurial talent' for industrial development rationale.
	Economic incentive rationales: the social benefits from patents	➢ Incentive to invent, be creative and innovate, as well as motivating the direction of such.
		➢ Incentive to use and allocate resources more efficiently.
		➢ Incentive to disclose ideas.
	Economic rationale of organizing science, technology and creativity: increased information spillover	➢ Rationale of uniformity, order, increased information, increased spillover and better advice.

Figure 4.1 Typology of the rationales for IPRs

empirical social and economic effects. We need to establish more empirical research to explore further and more genuinely the social and economic effects of such systems. The typology developed in this chapter (see Figure 4.1) can assist in guiding empirical research when addressing the issue of whether IPR systems operate in accordance with their rationales, which should be set out in our political aims and objectives. The results may differ across technological sectors, industries, perhaps even across regions and over time.

Basically, we should not decide on IPR policy before knowing if, and under what conditions, IPR really is the appropriate policy instrument to achieve our goals in the first place. However, here I do not suggest that the performance of an IPR system can, or should, only be evaluated on the grounds of whether its existence is beneficial or creates social costs. For reasons of policy, we need more insight regarding the most appropriate design (or legal structure) of the IPR system. 'What type' and 'how many' exclusive rights should the system confer? Design includes issues like: (i) length of protection obtained, (ii) type of knowledge protected (for example, should basic procedures to obtain DNA codes, some mathematics, non-technical business methods, be protected?), (iii) scope of knowledge protected (allowing or encouraging IPR protection of basic ideas in university laboratories or not), (iv) amount of inventive steps required for patent protection (that is, the problem of patenting of trivial ideas, such as paying via credit card over the Internet and the like: see http://webshop.ffii.org/ for an overview of trivial patents), (v) licensing law (opportunity to block or compulsory licensing), (vi) costs and procedures of obtaining and holding a right, and (vii) type and costs of the remedies available for infringement.

Thus, it is suggested that the proposed typology will provide a good conceptual underpinning and analytical framework for critically addressing the rationales, operation and performance of IPR regimes in order to achieve a finer empirical understanding of the social and economic effects of IPRs, an understanding which is urgently needed when designing policy fostering the knowledge-driven techno-economic paradigm in the twenty-first century.

ACKNOWLEDGEMENTS

Many suggestions and profound comments have helped me to develop and further advance this chapter. In this respect I would especially like to thank Lee Davis, Giampaolo Garzarelli, Bronwyn Hall, Fiona Macmillan,

Jonathan Michie, Richard Nelson, Klaus Nielsen, Theo Papaioannou and F.M. Scherer for their valuable comments. Furthermore, I would like to acknowledge the British Academy for providing me with funding for a research project on the *Rationales for Intellectual Property Rights*, of which this particular study forms a part. In this connection I am indebted to Maria da Graca Derengowski Fonseca for support and thought-provoking discussions while I was a visiting fellow at the Institute of Economics at Universidade Federal do Rio de Janeiro.

NOTES

1. For a critical discussion and to catch up on the current debate, check the web site of the Foundation of Free Information Infrastructure: http://swpat.ffii.org/.
2. See Mowery *et al.* (1999) and Mazzoleni and Nelson (1998a) for an overview and discussion of the Bayh-Dole Act. See also Chapter 1 of this book for a profound discussion.
3. Coriat and Orsi (2002) argue that the most important intellectual assets in this respect are portfolios of patents and other IPRs.
4. See EU (2002), as well as Andersen (2003) for discussion of the EU's hearing on business methods patents.
5. See the special issue of *Academic Medicine* (December 2002) and *Bulletin of Medical Ethics* (December 1996 / January 1997) for discussion on human genome patents, which is one of the most controversial topics in the current debate.
6. See Besen and Raskind (1991) and Coriat and Orsi (2002).
7. Mowery and Graham (2004) present and discuss this scheme, which allows patent applications to be updated (refilled) while they are being processed, encouraging patent application submissions at a very early stage of the discovery. See also Chapter 7 of this book for a profound discussion.
8. The rationales have also been discussed elsewhere with respect to IPR policy implications in the electronic age (Andersen 2003).
9. Since all activities have costs and benefits attached to them, an important issue for a functionalist approach to property rights is to attach the costs and benefits to the owners of the property relative to the non-owners, as well as relative to social and economic efficiency (Sell and May 2001; and Demsetz 1967).
10. Mazzoleni and Nelson's, catalogue of patent theories (1998a, 1998b) is mainly constructed around economic incentive theories including (i) invention motivation theories, (ii) induce commercialization theories, and (iii) induce information disclosure theories. The fourth group of theories presented by Mazzoleni and Nelson, that is, (iv) exploration control theory, can also be considered as economic incentive theories as they are related to how patents can provide incentives to allocate resources more efficiently.
11. The classical writings on the theories of the origin of rights and social contracts are comprehensively reviewed in Sened (1997) and Richards (2002).
12. See further section 4.2.1 for the discussion on whether patents confer economic monopolies or merely competitive properties.
13. Cited in Plant (1934), Machlup and Penrose (1950), Cheung (1986), as well as Towse and Holzhauer (2002).
14. Cited in Plant (1934), Machlup and Penrose (1950), Cheung (1986) and Towse and Holzhauer (2002).
15. See section 1 for references regarding other aspects of the controversial debate.
16. See John Alic *et al.* (1992) for a critical reappraisal of traditional military/industry relationships.

REFERENCES

Academic Medicine (2002), Special issue regarding human genome patents 77 (12).

Alic, J., Branscomb, L., Brooks, H., Epstein, G. and Carter, A. (1992), *Beyond Spinoff: Military and Commercial Technologies in a Changing World.* Cambridge MA: Harvard Business School Press.

Almeida, P. (1996), 'Knowledge sourcing by foreign multinationals: patent citation analysis in the US semiconductor industry'. *Strategic Management Journal*, **17**, 155–65, also published in Cantwell, J. (ed.) (1998) *Foreign Direct Investment and Technological Change*, Vol. 2. Cheltenham, UK and Northampton, MA, USA: Edward Elgar.

Andersen, B. (1998), 'The evolution of technological trajectories 1890–1990', *Structural Change and Economic Dynamics*, **9** (1), 5–35.

Andersen, B. (2001), *Technological Change and the Evolution of Corporate Innovation: The Structure of Patenting 1890–1990*, Cheltenham, UK and Northampton, MA, USA: Edward Elgar.

Andersen, B. (2003), 'The rationales for intellectual property rights in the electronic age', in Jones, D. (ed.) *The New Economy Handbook*, San Diego: Elsevier Academic Press, 987–1024.

Andersen, B, Kozul-Wright, Z. and Kozul-Wright, R. (2005), 'The social and economic effects of copyrights in the music industry: a contribution to the convergence versus divergence debate', in Macmillan, F. (ed.), *New Directions in Copyright Law*, Vol. 1. Cheltenham, UK and Northampton, MA, USA: Edward Elgar.

Andersen B., Howells, J., Hill, R., Miles, I. and Roberts, J. (eds) (2000), *Knowledge and Innovation in the New Service Economy*. Cheltenham, UK and Northampton, MA, USA: Edward Elgar.

Arrow, K. (1962), 'Economic welfare and the allocation of resources for inventions', in *The Rate and Direction of Inventive Activity: Economic and Social Factors*, Princeton, N.J.: National Bureau of Economic Research, 609–25.

Arthur, B. (1988), 'Competing technologies: an overview', in Dosi, G., Freeman, C., Nelson, R., Silverberg, G. and Soete, L. (eds) *Technical Change and Economic Theory*. London: Pinter Publishers, 590–607.

Arthur, B. (1996), 'Increasing returns and the new world of business', *Harvard Business Review*, July–August, 101–109.

Arundel, A. (2001), 'The relative effectiveness of patents and secrecy for appropriation', *Research Policy*, **10**, 611–24.

Bessen, S. and Raskind, L. (1991), 'An introduction to the law and economics of intellectual property'. *Journal of Economic Perspectives*, **5** (1), 3–27.

Bulletin of Medical Ethics (1996/1997), Special issue regarding ethics and patenting of human genes, 124, January.

Cheung, S. (1986), 'Property rights and invention', *Research in Law and Economics*, 8, 5–18.

Christensen, J.L. (2004), Inter and intra-organizational learning processes in the interaction between firms and patent offices, in Christensen, J.L. and Lundvall, B.-A. (eds), *Product Innovation, Interactive Learning and Economic Performance*. Cheltenham, UK and Northampton, MA, USA: Edward Elgar.

Cohen, W. Nelson, R. and Walsh, J. (2000), *Protecting Their Intellectual Assets: Appropriability Conditions and Why U.S. Manufacturing Firms Patent (or Not)*. NBER Working Paper, No. w7552, Princeton, NJ: NBER.

Coriat, B. and Orsi, F. (2002), 'Establishing a new intellectual property rights regime in the United States: origins, content and problems', *Research Policy*, **31**, 1491–507.
David, P. (1985), 'CLIO and the economics of QWERTY', *American Economic Review*, **75** (2), 332–37.
David, P. (2001), *Will Building 'Good Fences' Really Make 'Good Neighbours' in Science*, report to European Commission (DG-Research) STRATA-ETAN workshop on IPR aspects of internal collaborations. Brussels, 22–23 January 2001.
David, P. and Olsen, T. (1992), 'Technology adoption, learning spillovers, and the optimal duration of patent-based monopolies', *International Journal of Industrial Organization*, **10**, 517–43.
Davis, L. (2004), 'Intellectual property rights, strategy and policy', *Economics of Innovation and New Technology*, **13** (5), 399–415.
Demsetz, H. (1967), 'Towards a theory of property rights', *American Economic Review*, **57** (2), 347–59.
EU (2002), *EU's hearing on 'Industrial Property' and 'The Economic Impact of Patentability of Computer Programs'*, see http://europa.eu.int/comm/internal_market/en/indprop/studyintro.htm
Gilbert, R. and Shapiro, C. (1990), 'Optimal patent length and breadth', *RAND Journal of Economics*, **21**, 106–12.
Granstrand, O. (1999), *Economics and Management of Intellectual Property*, Cheltenham, UK and Northampton, MA, USA: Edward Elgar.
Hobbes, T. (1660/1968), *Leviathan*, New York: Penguin Classics.
Jaffe, A. and Trajtenberg, M. (2002), *Patents, Citations and Innovations: A Window on the Knowledge Economy*, Cambridge, MA: MIT Press.
Jaffe, A.B., Trajtenberg, M. and Henderson, R. (1993), 'Geographical localisation of knowledge spillovers, as evidenced by patent citations', *Quarterly Journal of Economics*, **58** (3), 577–98.
Kaufer, E. (1989), *The Economics of The Patent System*. Chur: Harwood Academic.
Kingston, W. (2001), 'Innovation needs patents reform', *Research Policy*, **30**, 403–23.
Kitch, E. (1977), The nature and function of the patent system', *Journal of Law and Economics*, **20** (1), 265–90.
Levin, R., Klevorick, A., Nelson, R. and Winter, S. (1987), 'Appropriating the returns from industrial research and development', *Brookings Papers on Economic Activity*, **3**.
Locke, J. (1690/1980), *Second Treatise on Government*, Indianapolis: Hackett.
Machlup, F. (1958), *An Economic Review of the Patent System: Study of the Subcommittee on Patents, Trademarks, and Copyrights of the Committee on the Judiciary*, US Senate, 85th Congress, 2nd Session, Study Number 15, Washington: United States Government Printing Office, 1–86.
Machlup, F. and Penrose, E. (1950), 'The patent controversy in the nineteenth century', *Journal of Economic History*, **10** (1), 1–29.
Mansfield, E. (1986), 'Patents and innovation: an empirical study', *Management Science*, **32**, 173–81.
Mazzoleni, R. and Nelson, R. (1998a), 'The benefits and costs of strong patent protection: a contribution to the current debate', *Research Policy*, **27**, 273–84.

Mazzoleni, R. and Nelson, R. (1998b), 'Economic theories about the benefits and costs of patents', *Journal of Economic Issues*, **32** (4), 1031–52.

Merges, R. and Nelson, R. (1990), 'On the complex economics of patent scope', *Columbia Law Review*, **90** (1), 839–961.

Molas-Gallart, J., James, A. and Rigby, R. (2000), National Case Study of Civil-Military Interface: The UK's Defence Evaluation and Research Agency – In Search of a Successful Model of Technology Transfer, Section of *a Report to the Royal Swedish Academy of Engineering Sciences*, September.

Mowery, D. and Graham, S. (2004), 'Submaries in software? Continuations in U.S. software patenting in the 1980s and 1990s', *Economics of Innovation and New Technology*, **13** (5), 443–56.

Mowery, D., Nelson, R., Sampat, B. and Ziedonis, A. (1999), 'The effects of the Bayh-Dole act on U.S. university research and technology transfer', in Branscomb, L., Kodama, F. and Florida, R. (eds), *Industrializing Knowledge: University-industry Linkages in Japan and the United States*. Cambridge, MA: MIT Press.

Napolitano, G. and Sirilli, G. (1990), 'The patent system and the exploitation of inventions: results of a statistical survey conducted in Italy', *Technovation*, **10** (1), 5–16.

Nelson, R. (2004), 'The market economy, and the scientific commons', *Research Policy*, **33**, 455–71.

North, D. (1981), *Structure and Change in Economic History*, New York: W.W.Norton & Company.

OECD (1999), *Measuring and Reporting Intellectual Capital*, Amsterdam, 9–11 June 1999.

Plant, A. (1934), 'The economic theory concerning patents for inventions', *Economica*, **1**, New Series, 30–51.

Posner, R. (1992), 'The economic theory of property rights: static and dynamic aspects', extracts from Property in R. Posner, *Economic Analysis of Law*, 4th edition, Toronto: Little, Brown and Company, 32–9.

Richards, D. (2002), 'The ideology of intellectual property rights in the international economy', *Review of Social Economy*, **18** (4), 521–41.

Rivera-Batiz. L. and Romer, P. (1991), 'Economic integration and endogenous growth', *The Quarterly Journal of Economics*, May.

Rivette, K. and Kline, D. (2000), *Rembrandts in the Attic: Unlocking the Hidden Value of Patents*, Cambridge, MA: Harvard Business School University Press.

Sanders, B. (1964), 'Patterns of commercial exploration of patented inventions by large and small corporations into commercial use', *Patent, Trademark, and Copyright Journal* **8**, 51–92.

Scherer, F.M., Herzstein, S.E., Dreyfoos, A.W., Whitney, W.G., Bachman, O.J., Pesek, C.P., Scott, C.J., Kelly, T.G. and Galvin, J.J. (1959), *Patents and the Corporation*, 2nd ed. Boston, MA.

Scherer, F.M. and Ross. D. (1990), *Industrial Market Structure and Economic Performance*, 3rd ed. Boston, MA: Houghton Mifflin.

Sell, S. and May, C. (2001), 'Moments in law: contestation and settlement in the history of intellectual property', *Review of International Political Economy*, **8** (3), 467–500.

Sened, I. (1997), *The Political Institution of Private Property*, Cambridge: Cambridge University Press.

Teece, D. (1986), 'Profiting from technological innovation: implications for integration, collaboration, licensing and public policy', *Research Policy*, **15**, 285–305.

Towse, R. and Holzhauer, R. (eds) (2002), *The Economics of Intellectual Property*, Vols I, II, III and IV (The International Library of Critical Writings in Economics). Cheltenham, UK and Northampton, MA, USA: Edward Elgar.
Winter, S. (1993), 'Patents and welfare in an evolutionary model', *Industrial and Corporate Change*, **2**, 211–31.

5. Why do small high-tech firms take out patents, and why not?

Lee N. Davis

ABSTRACT

This chapter seeks to add to our understanding of the strategic and economic effects of patents by exploring why small firms take out patents, and why not, and how these choices are linked to their broader business and technology strategies. To this end, we interviewed patent experts in thirty-four small Danish firms in telecommunications, software and biotechnology. The major reasons to take out patents, we determined, were to protect against imitation and to signal strategic intent. The major reasons not to patent were that the invention was not patentable, and the high costs of detecting infringements. Generally speaking, biotech firms found patents essential to create value, software firms often found patents irrelevant, and telecommunications firms found them important, but in combination with other factors. Much depended on the type of innovation, and previous experiences with patents. Many respondents had developed fine-tuned, 'contextual' patent strategies, focusing patent resources in areas important to them.

Keywords: Patent motivations, Small firms, Biotechnology, Software, Telecommunications

1 INTRODUCTION

While there is an extensive literature on the benefits and costs of patenting for innovating firms, including empirical surveys (for example, Cohen *et al.*, 2000, Levin *et al.*, 1987), and accounts of the strategic use of patents (for example, Grindley and Teece, 1997, Rivette and Kline, 2000a,b), the analytical focus is typically large firms (principally US firms) from a variety of industries. Few scholars explore the patent strategies of small high-tech enterprises (exceptions include Arundel and Steinmueller, 1998, Audretsch, 2002, Mogee, 2000 and Morkel and Willoughby, 1992). This chapter seeks to add to our understanding of the strategic and economic effects of patents by exploring why small high-tech firms take out patents, and why not, and how these choices are linked to their broader business and technology strategies.

Existing studies show that common reasons to take out patents include preventing imitation, earning licence royalties, strategic signalling and attracting external capital. Common reasons not to patent include problems associated with the application process, with preventing imitation and enforcing patent rights, as well as the unsuitability of patents for the inventions concerned, and a desire to use other means to appropriate value. But how fully do these results reflect the patent choices of small high-tech enterprises? How important to patent choices are factors like industry affiliation and the nature of the invention?

In much of the debate about small and medium-sized enterprises (SMEs), both among academics and policy makers, it is often assumed that small firms behave differently from large firms due to resource differences (for example, Eisenhardt and Schoonhoven, 1990, Meyer and Lopez, 1995). Small enterprises have fewer resources than large firms, yet they are often better at spotting new technological opportunities and responding to changing market needs. Large firms have greater resources, but may be less flexible. With regard to patents, large firms typically have greater experience, often in the form of in-house patent experts, better enabling them to cover the costs and leverage the benefits of patents. Due to resource constraints, one might expect that small firms would find it more difficult than large firms to devise and implement effective patent strategies and to link these to their overall business and technology strategies. Yet there has been little concrete empirical data to inform this discussion. To this end, we conducted a series of in-depth, semi-structured interviews with patent experts in thirty-four small firms (under 250 employees) in Denmark in three industries: telecommunications, software and pharmaceutical-related biotechnology.

This chapter starts with a review of the literature on how firms use and view patents. Section 3 presents the empirical data used in this study. Section 4 explores how important various potential benefits and costs of patenting were for the respondents in our empirical data. The implications of these findings are discussed in Section 5, followed by the conclusion.

2 LITERATURE REVIEW

2.1 Theoretical and Empirical Background

Under the patent system, inventors obtain the legal right to exclude others from making, selling or using a new product or process for a given period, now typically twenty years. In return, they agree to disclose the details of the invention in the patent document, so that others can build on and use this knowledge, furthering technological progress. Literature on the economics of the patent system (for example, Andersen, 2004, Granstrand, 1999), comprises three approaches: (1) analyses of the problem of appropriability and welfare effects of patents (for example, Arrow, 1962, Besen and Raskind, 1991, Kitch, 1977, Nelson, 1959, Scotchmer, 1991), (2) empirical studies of patent effectiveness and importance (for example, Cohen *et al.*, 2000, Harabi, 1995, Levin *et al.*, 1987, Mansfield *et al.*, 1981), and (3) studies of firms' strategic use of patents (for example, Davis, 2001, 1998, Grindley and Teece, 1997, Rivette and Kline, 2000a,b). This study draws primarily on the latter two approaches.

Two seminal articles from the mid-1980s investigate how firms profit from investments in R&D (Levin *et al.*, 1987, Teece, 1986). These scholars argued that patents were often ineffective, and that if so it was the owners of valuable complementary assets that received the greatest economic benefits, since they could improve upon the original invention and dominate its subsequent production and distribution. Other analysts (for example, Cohen *et al.*, 2000, Rivette and Kline, 2000 a, b) have argued that traditional motivations to take out patents – to prevent imitation, or to earn licence royalties – should be supplemented by others, like patents as strategic signals. The benefits and costs of patenting are explored in Section 2.2 below.

In this chapter, we examine firm patenting activities in telecommunications, software and pharmaceutical-related biotechnology. Most of the leading empirical studies of the economic effects of patents (for example, Cohen *et al.*, 2000, Harabi, 1995, Kingston, 2001, Levin *et al.*, 1987) have found striking industry differences in patent importance and effectiveness. Patents are far more valuable in pharmaceuticals and speciality chemicals than other sectors. The Cohen *et al.* (2000) survey, in particular, emphasizes the differences in patenting behaviour between 'discrete' and 'complex' industries. In the former, patents serve primarily to exclude other firms, whereas in the latter, they function mainly as trading currency. But these studies only touch briefly on how small enterprises use and view patents. While there has been some work on the role and function of patents in electronics (for example, Grindley and Teece, 1997, Hall and Ham Ziedonis, 2001), software (for example, Blind and Edler, 2003, Conner and Rumelt, 1991, Graham and Mowery, 2004) and biotechnology (for example, Merges and Nelson, 1994, Ramani and De Looze, 2002, Sabourin and Pinsonneault, 1997), there has been little work on the special barriers and opportunities faced by small high-tech enterprises in these industries.

Several studies have considered the use of patents by small firms. For example, Arundel and Steinmueller (1998) investigate how small and medium sized enterprises (SMEs) use patent databases as a source of information. Morkel and Willoughby (1992), in a case study, explore the barriers faced by Orbital Engine Corporation, a small Australian company, in commercializing their inventions in fuel injection technology. Mogee (2000) analyses differences in patenting behaviour by large and small US firms. Audretsch (2002) shows that while large firms often take out more patents than small firms, the patenting rate of small firms, measured on a per-employee basis, is usually higher. Other studies use the size of the patent portfolios of small firms as indicators of their technological strength (Kelley and Rice, 2002) and innovative efforts (Lefebvre and Lefebvre, 1993). Some analyses have discussed the problems faced by small enterprises in a broader context. They point out, for example, that small firms experience particular difficulties regarding the costs of the application process and prosecuting or defending patent infringement actions (Cohen *et al.*, 2000, Kingston, 2001, Lanjouw and Schankerman, 2004). This paper seeks to contribute to this literature by focusing on the opportunities and problems faced by small firms in using patents.

As regards Denmark, two recent reports, based on interview results, have illuminated how Danish SMEs use patents and other IPRs. The first (IFO, 2000) explores the barriers faced by manufacturing SMEs in product development and patenting. Here, it was determined that the costs of patenting, particularly the fees for patent agents and lawyers, formed a substantial barrier to patenting. The second (IFO, 2002) analyses how Danish SMEs in a broad range of sectors in manufacturing, services and IT experience the IPR system, and what problems they have had. It found that IPRs only played a modest role in these firms' overall business strategies. Only a few informants spontaneously mentioned the value of IPRs (mainly in pharmaceuticals and biotechnology). The main problems were that they didn't believe they could enforce these rights, and they preferred to focus on immediate market needs.

2.2 Why Take out Patents?

On the basis of the leading empirical studies of firm patent strategies, as cited in the previous section, along with the author's earlier interviews with patent experts reported in previous work (for example, Davis, 1998), it is possible to identify a number of possible reasons why firms might find it to their advantage to take out a patent. These are summarized in Table 5.1 (next page) and discussed in the remainder of this section. In Section 4.1, we will investigate how our respondents viewed them.

2.2.1 Patents to protect against imitation

When a firm invests in R&D, it has no assurance that the investment will actually lead to a commercial product. To cover these costs and risks, it needs to charge a higher price than would prevail under competition. Once the innovation comes on the market, a rival might be able to copy the good and market it at a lower price which only has to cover production costs, thereby out-competing the innovator. In this sense, the patent monopoly is justified, in that it enables innovators to raise imitation costs (for example, Mansfield *et al.*, 1981).

Firms can also use patents more aggressively, not just to raise imitation costs, but to prevent rivals from pursuing their own, related development activities. Several empirical studies have found evidence of this strategy. According to Oppenländer (1977), blocking patents were typically used by firms in chemicals and precision instruments. Bertin and Wyatt (1988) determined that 12.4 per cent of their respondents utilized blocking patents.

Table 5.1 Possible reasons to take out patents

Reason	Variants
1. Protect against imitation	• Prevent competitors from imitating one's products or processes • Block competitors in their development activities
2. Establish legal basis for cooperation	• Earn royalties • Obtain a strong patent portfolio to strengthen one's position in licence negotiations
3. Patents as strategic signals	• Signal to competitors that technology is protected • Strengthen negotiating position in connection with a possible patent dispute
4. Patents as indicators of value	• Attract capital from external investors • Measure the results of the firm's R&D staff

2.2.2 Patents to establish the legal basis for cooperation

The exclusive right provided by the patent can also provide the legal basis to license out the rights to the invention. There can be many reasons to license. Perhaps the firm does not have the resources to develop the invention itself, or has other priorities, or wishes to promote the rapid dissemination of the invention. When licensed out, patents may provide a crucial source of royalty income. The amount of money that can be gained from licensing can be enormous. Rivette and Kline (2000a) point out that IBM earned nearly $1 billion per year from its patent-licence royalties, and Texas Instruments earned some $800 million per year. According to Bertin and Wyatt (1988), 22 per cent of the multinational enterprises in their survey agreed that this was an important reason to use patents. The use of patents to provide the legal basis by which to license out the rights might be particularly applicable to small firms, which often lack the resources to commercialize new goods.

Another advantage of patents might be to enable the firm to build up a strong patent portfolio to strengthen its position in licence negotiations. For innovations in electronics and semiconductors, patents function not so much to exclude others as to control the terms of access, as 'bargaining chips' in complex cross-licensing arrangements (for example, Grindley and Teece, 1997, Hall and Ham Ziedonis, 2001). In biotechnology and software, a strong patent portfolio might count not for cross-licensing, but to strengthen the firm's general bargaining position in negotiating for a licence with a larger enterprise.

2.2.3 Patents as strategic signals

As stated earlier, part of the social contract implied by the patent system is that the invention be published. As soon as the patent application is received, the subject matter is posted by the patent office. This provides a first indication as to what the firm is seeking to protect. After eighteen months, the application itself is laid open for public inspection. While the justification for this is to enable others to read and learn from the application, the patent can thereby also serve as a signal that the invention is protected, even warn others away. Leveraging patents as strategic signals has become more prevalent in recent years, as firms increasingly integrate patents into their overall competitive strategy (for example, Rivette and Kline, 2000 a,b).

Another manner in which patents might be used as signals is to enable firms to strengthen their negotiation position in connection with a possible patent dispute (for example, Cohen *et al.*, 2000). Suppose a company is facing a patent infringement suit from one of its rivals. If it has a strong patent portfolio, it will often be able to find an area where this competitor is infringing one of its own patents, thereby paving the way for settling the dispute before it reaches court. We were curious to learn whether small high-tech enterprises had adopted the same 'signalling' approach to patents.

2.2.4 Patents as indicators of value

If a firm bases its R&D largely on an idea, and hopes to attract capital from external investors, the patent might play a valuable role as an indicator of value. Otherwise, it might be difficult to gauge the value of a company whose primary assets are intangible (for example, Granstrand, 2000, Teece, 2000). A strong patent portfolio both clarifies the nature of the invention, provides the legal basis on which the patentee can develop the invention or license it out to others, and guarantees that the invention has not been patented by someone else. Patent holdings can serve as the basis of assessing stock market value, evaluating candidates for joint venture participation or an acquisition, and the like (Rivette and Kline, 2000a).

Finally, some of the multinationals Bertin and Wyatt (1988) interviewed also mentioned that patents could be used to measure productivity, either for the firm as a whole, or for individual researchers. Since we believed that the role of patents to attract external capital basically did not reflect these findings, we decided to ask our respondents whether or not they saw patents as a means to measure the results of their R&D staff.

2.3 Why not Patent?

There are also many reasons why firms might choose not to take out a patent. These are summarized in Table 5.2.

Table 5.2 Possible reasons not to take out patents

Reason	Variants
1. Problems associated with application process	• Product or process cannot be patented • Costs of applying for and maintaining patent are too high
2. Problems relating to preventing imitation	• Competitors can 'invent around' their inventions • Firm must reveal too much information in the patent application
3. Problems relating to patent infringement	• Too difficult to determine if patent is being infringed • Too expensive to pursue firms that infringe patent
4. Patents are not suitable given nature of information concerned	• Technology is developing so rapidly that patents are irrelevant • More advantageous to publish the information
5. Firms prefer to use other means to appropriate value	• More advantageous to keep the innovation secret • More advantageous to use other strategies of appropriability

2.3.1 Problems associated with the application process

To be patented, an invention must be new, non-obvious, and industrially applicable. The specific nature of these requirements may be defined somewhat differently in different patent systems (for example, Glazier, 1995, Kingston, 2001). Scientific discoveries, mathematical equations, marketing plans, customer service innovations and the like, typically cannot be patented. We wished to determine the extent to which the participants in our survey felt that their inventions did not fulfil the criteria of patentability.

Another disadvantage of patenting might be that the costs of applying for and maintaining the patent are too high. These costs include drawing up the application and paying the relevant fees. To avoid future difficulties with patent validity and reduce the risk of lawsuits, companies typically either employ patent experts in-house or hire external patent agents. To obtain effective international protection, the patent must be filed in all countries in which the inventor intends to do business. Arguably, given their resource constraints, small firms might find this a substantial barrier in using the patent system, as previously observed (Section 2.1).

2.3.2 Problems relating to preventing imitation

Competitors, by reading the patent, can identify 'gaps' in the protection sought, areas with commercial potential that they can use as the focus of their own patent applications, enabling them to appropriate a portion of the benefits for themselves. The empirical studies by Levin *et al.* (1987), Harabi (1995), and Cohen *et al.* (2000), all found that the chance that competitors might 'invent around' their patents was viewed by firms as the most substantial reason not to patent, especially for process inventions.

Empirical studies have shown as well that innovators may be reluctant to patent in that they must reveal too much information in the application (for example, Arundel, 2001, Arundel and Kabla, 1998). According to Harabi (1995), this is the second most important limitation on patent effectiveness, after concerns about 'inventing around' described above. Cohen *et al.* (2000) state that concerns over information disclosure have grown since the Levin *et al.* survey (1987), and that secrecy now appears to be more common, again particularly for process innovations (see Section 2.3.5).

2.3.3 Problems relating to patent infringement

The costs of patenting include not only the application costs, but also the costs of enforcement (Cohen *et al.*, 2000, Kingston, 2001). A study by Lanjouw and Schankerman (2004) found that small firms faced a higher litigation risk than large firms. The Danish IFO (2002) study reported that the primary problem for small firms was enforcing their IPRs. Small firms lacked the resources to enforce these rights, and tended to believe that large firms would infringe their patents anyway if they wanted to, knowing that a small firm would be unable to defend itself.

There are two aspects of the enforcement problem. Firstly, it may be quite difficult to determine if the patent is being infringed, particularly as regards patented processes where the imitator restricts access to its plant premises. If the good is sold in international markets, it may simply be too costly to check this. Secondly, even if infringement is known to occur, it may be too expensive to pursue the infringer. Litigation consumes enormous resources in both time and money. Arguably, the limited financial resources of small firms might make it especially difficult to bear these costs.

2.3.4 Patents are not suitable given the nature of the information concerned

In some industries, technological developments may proceed so rapidly that inventions are outdated within a short time (for example, Cohen *et al.*, 2000). Since the patent application can take several years, by the time patent authorities reach their decision, the firm may have moved on to a new area. If so, any resources spent on the application will be wasted.

Alternatively, it might be more advantageous to the firm to publish the information, for example in a journal article (for example, Merges, 2004). To be patented, an invention must not have been described in any commonly available written source, anywhere in the world. This means that if a firm simply publishes the information instead of patenting it, it not only saves the time and expense of patenting, but also prevents anyone else from patenting the invention.

2.3.5 Firms prefer to use other strategies of appropriability

Finally, firms might not take out patents because it is more advantageous to keep the innovation secret (for example, Pooley and Bratic, 1999, Sullivan, 1999). Key aspects of a firm's R&D are often kept secret, both to prevent rivals from 'inventing around' the patent, or due to the restrictions on what may be patented. Moreover, the patent expires after twenty years. Secrecy may be maintained indefinitely, at least in theory. Secrecy is considered especially effective for process innovations (Arundel, 2001, Arundel and Kabla, 1998).

Apart from secrecy, a range of additional appropriability strategies are available. According to leading empirical studies (Cohen *et al.*, 2000, Harabi, 1995, Levin *et al.*, 1987), respondents often evaluated lead time, learning curve and superior sales and service efforts as more effective than patents. Thus the availability of alternative means of protecting the knowledge may be a reason not to patent.

3 THE EMPIRICAL DATA

In identifying suitable potential participants for our analysis, we used three main criteria. In February 2002, we consulted one of the Copenhagen Business School's databases, called 'The Business World's Information Bureau',[1] which lists all firms in Denmark. Of these, we selected firms that

- employed up to 250 people
- were located in the greater Copenhagen area (postal addresses 1000–4000)[2]
- possessed the industry code for telecommunications, software or biotechnology.

This list was then further refined. We eliminated from our inquiry all firms that did not conduct R&D according to their home pages, to exclude firms that only engaged in production, marketing or distribution. For biotech firms, we restricted our inquiry to those engaged in pharmaceutical-related R&D. We eliminated all Danish subsidiaries of multinational corporations, since we believed that their patent policies might be too reflective of the policies of their mother corporations. For all the firms chosen, we double-checked to make sure that they were still in business at the time of the survey.

On this basis, we identified a population of ninety-three relevant firms in the three industries (twenty-two in telecommunications, thirty-five in software and thirty-six in biotechnology). We wrote letters to each of these firms, and then telephoned them to try to set up a meeting. Thirty-four firms agreed to participate. Seven of these were in telecommunications (31.8 per cent of the telecommunications firms we contacted), nine in software (25.7 per cent) and eighteen in biotechnology (50 per cent). In all, our response rate was 36.6 per cent. This, we feel, is reasonable, since we were asking our firms not only to fill out a questionnaire about their patent choices to form the basis of our discussion, but also to spend an additional one to two hours talking with us to explain the reasons behind these choices. The average number of employees for our sample firms was 36. The smallest firm had one employee, the largest had 227. The biotech and software firms in our sample had an average of about 40 employees; the telecommunications firms were smaller. The biotech and software firms in our sample were also somewhat larger than the firms in the overall population. The telecommunications firms, by contrast, were only about half as large.[3]

We left it up to our respondents to determine with whom we should speak, specifying that it should be the person who knew most about the firm's patent policies. For the very small firms, this was often the CEO, or one of the engineers who had developed an expertise in patent-related issues.

Others had appointed a patent specialist. Sometimes both the CEO and the patent specialist participated. We used a loosely structured interview protocol to ensure that we asked the same questions of each company, but encouraging our respondents to add their own further insights.

First we asked about the characteristics of their firm, the industry, the technologies used, and what factors influenced how they implemented patents. We then asked them to rate the importance of the eight possible reasons as to why to take out a patent, and the ten possible reasons why not, as summarized in Tables 5.1 and 5.2. We provided extra time in the interviews for our respondents to go into depth, in an effort both to capture the complexities of the factors surrounding firm choices, and ensure that our respondents understood the questions. We also asked supplementary questions, such as whether they differentiated between product and process patents, and whether small size had influenced their use of patents. The interviews were conducted between the spring of 2002 and the spring of 2003, and the conversations were recorded by dictaphone.[4]

We are aware that such an approach can have drawbacks. There might be systematic differences in the attitudes of firms that agreed to participate in this survey and those that refused. Informants working as patent experts within the firm would *ceteris paribus* have a more positive view of patents than, for example, the CEO or the director of R&D. There is always the risk that we might, through the phrasing of the questions, nudge our respondents in a particular direction. We also recognized that our respondents might be less willing to be candid in a face-to-face interview. We made every effort to ensure that we did not influence how our respondents answered the questions, but this is clearly not always possible to control. Our mere presence might, for example, have led them to be more positive about their strategic use of patents than they were in practice. For example, our respondents expressed few complaints that large firms were using patents to beat them into place. Possibly this reflects their confidence in their own choice of strategies. Possibly, however, they refrained from saying this in the interviews in order to place themselves in the best possible light. We agreed to keep the names and identities of all of our respondents confidential, and many participants made this a condition of their willingness to talk with us.

While we realize that this is a relatively small sample of firms, we believe that our findings are representative for high-tech SMEs more generally. Denmark is well-known as a country with numerous SMEs, and small high-tech firms are critical to its economic base. Denmark has an open, technologically advanced economy, subjecting domestic enterprises to the pressures of international competition. Almost all of the participants in our survey developed inventions intended for use in international markets.

The exceptions were several of the software enterprises that specialized in customer-tailored software solutions, where the innovator did not operate outside of the country. It should also be noted that our findings for software firms may not be applicable in countries where software inventions are easier to patent, notably the United States.

4 RESULTS OF THE EMPIRICAL STUDY

4.1 Why Take out Patents?

4.1.1 Patents to protect against imitation

Our respondents were virtually unanimous in agreeing that a critical reason to take out patents was to protect against imitation. Nearly two-thirds (twenty-two firms) assigned this the highest marks. Many exclaimed that this was obvious, it was what the patent system was all about. A few disagreed. One stated that it was too small to hope to use its patents to prevent imitation. Two others pointed out that while product patents might be leveraged to this end, this was not necessarily true for processes, since it could be difficult to know whether a rival had imitated a process.

There was considerably more disagreement as regards the use of blocking patents. Many biotech innovators used their patents, at least to some degree, to block others in their development efforts. One was particularly graphic:

> To prevent them from doing it to us, we have to do it to them. There is unfortunately a tendency to take out patents on the use of a particular principle for a particular illness, and one can do this in all kinds of ways, so one in reality prevents others from working in large areas.

Other biotech firms disagreed. Two observed that for a small enterprise, new to the market, the costs of doing this would rarely justify the benefits. This reflects earlier findings by Bertin and Wyatt (1988) and Oppenländer (1977), that blocking patents are used more by large than small firms. Several respondents in software and telecommunications opined that such a strategy simply would not work, since there was almost always a way around such a patent. A software informant asserted that firms in this sector often do not respect each other's patents, and might not feel blocked, even if they were (blocking works only if the patentee is willing to pursue infringers). Others objected on moral grounds. A software respondent called this practice destructive. A biotech interviewee stated that even if his firm could do this, it was unethical. Innovators should patent their research to advance technological development, not block it.

4.1.2 Patents to establish the legal basis for cooperation

Nearly half of our interviewees (sixteen firms, all but two of which were in biotechnology), gave this motivation the top ranking. 'That's what it's all about!' exclaimed one. Another stressed that 'all our future earnings are based on patent royalties, and it is our only long-term source of income'. A third described how they individually tailored the conditions of their licence contracts to the patent holdings and market strategies of the customer. Yet many noted that while earning licence royalties clearly mattered, it was not a prime reason to take out patents. This might be termed a luxury, or a side benefit. At least one respondent in all three industries stated that earning licence royalties was never a reason to take out patents.

As regards building up a strong patent portfolio to strengthen its negotiating position in licence negotiations, twenty-two of our respondents assigned this the highest marks, again especially in biotechnology. One called this 'essential, the basis of our existence.' But the reasons differed according to industry, as predicted in Section 2.2.2. Our biotech firms felt that a strong patent position was essential as a platform on which to negotiate with a large pharmaceutical firm. Our telecommunications firms, likewise, stressed the importance of patents as bargaining chips. As one put it, they took out patents not to protect the technology, or even to earn royalties, but to lay the basis for them to get together with their competitors and divide the market between them through cross-licensing. A second stressed that they needed to accumulate a patent portfolio to 'fight' against their rivals. The area in which they worked was 'patent-infected', rendering it impossible to operate without patent protection. Curiously, another telecommunications patent holder dismissed this entirely. They never used patents as trading currency in their portion of the industry. Four of our software participants also termed this completely 'irrelevant' for their needs. One exclaimed that they, like all the other firms they knew, felt no need to trade patent rights, they simply 'ignore those ridiculous patents'.

4.1.3 Patents as strategic signals

The value of patents as signals that the technology was protected received high marks from our respondents in all three industries, for several reasons. The patent application indicated that the innovator was seriously committed to a particular line of research. It was a way to get one's name in the databases, where others searched and tried to find out what was going on. The patent could alert other market actors who might seek to enter into cooperation. About a fourth of our respondents leveraged patents as signals not only to competitors, but also to customers, potential partners and investors. Yet there was also a recognition of the limitations of this approach. Respondents stressed that patents were only one of many ways to denote value, since your competitors typically knew what you were doing anyway. The signalling function could also be more useful for firms operating in broad technological areas than in niche markets.

The use of patents to help patent holders strengthen their negotiation position in connection with a possible patent dispute was emphasized by many participants in our survey, again especially in biotechnology. Five of our eighteen biotech participants mentioned that they had direct experience with this, since their patent holdings made it possible to solve potential conflicts without going to court. As one expressed it:

> Technology often develops in the same direction. You cannot, at some point or other, avoid getting into conflict with another patent. Firms can try to resolve the situation before it becomes a lawsuit. You might contact the other firm and evaluate the costs and benefits, including to your reputation, perhaps leading to a licence agreement. You can use your patent to threaten the other party to reach agreement.

Three others pointed out that while such signalling was not vital now, it could be so in the future. Our software participants, by contrast, either asserted that this was not relevant in their industry, or that they had heard of this strategy but had never themselves encountered it. A telecommunications patentee maintained that such a strategy was not an option for small firms, since it would be difficult to enforce their claims.

4.1.4 Patents as indicators of value

Twenty-one of our thirty-four respondents found this highly relevant, notably in biotechnology, but also about half of our telecommunications and software respondents. Patent holdings made it easier to obtain finance and measure value, not only to investors, but also to customers and potential partners. Some biotech interviewees contended that it was the only way to attract capital. One telecommunications respondent, organized under a holding company, exclaimed:

> This is the top scorer, and the probable reason why management never questions how much money we use on patents. It is simply never discussed.

But others stressed that while this naturally mattered, it was not the only factor. Two software firms scoffed at this as irrelevant. One had formed an alliance with another company even though they had had no patents, and patents had played no role in the discussion. The other argued that patents in software said nothing about the earning potential of the innovation. Even if you had a clever invention, unless you had a solid customer base, no one would believe in its potential. Even some biotech informants characterized this as unimportant. One noted that this might count in the early phases, especially for start-up enterprises. But for more established firms, what investors cared most about was how you planned to use your patents, not simply whether or not you had them.

Of all of the possible reasons to take out patents, the use of patents to measure the results of R&D staff received the lowest scores. Respondents in software and telecommunications typically scoffed that they would never do this. One software respondent said that he 'would rather see one good patent than ten half-good ones'. A second declared, 'If you did this, you would be a bad leader'. Even so, some respondents, particularly in biotechnology, noted that the number of patents could serve as an indication of the general productivity of R&D staff.

4.1.5 Other reasons to patent

Several respondents additionally emphasised that patents could be key to ensuring that others do not patent in their area, blocking them (see Section 4.1.1). In other words, they sought to ensure 'freedom to operate'. Investors, partners, and customers had to be confident that the company would not suddenly have to stop producing the good because another firm held the patent rights. In the literature, there are similar reports of firms concerned that a rival would apply for patents on incremental improvements of their own core technology, 'enclosing' their patents so that they could not proceed in further developing the innovation, possibly forcing them to cross-license their original patent to the rival (Glazier, 1995). Firms can thus feel compelled to apply for patents in order to avoid being blocked, a practice which Cohen *et al.* (2000) found had accelerated in recent years. Other respondents emphasized the branding effect of patents in creating the firm's identity and image.

The findings presented in Section 4.1 are summarized in Table 5.3 (next page) arranged in terms of a selection of representative comments according to industry.

4.2 Why not Patent?

4.2.1 Problems associated with the application process

A third of our software interviewees, and half of those in telecommunications, agreed that it could be very difficult to fulfil the criteria of patentability. For the former, this was because they generally felt their inventions were not unique enough to be patented. For the latter, it was because there were so many patents in their area that there was not much new to patent. In biotechnology, on the other hand, most participants seemed confident that they could patent their inventions. As one put it, 'it is almost always possible

Table 5.3 Results of the empirical study: possible reasons to take out patents

Reason	Some illustrative comments from telecommunications	Some illustrative comments from software	Some illustrative comments from biotechnology
1. Protect against imitation	Blocking patents may not work	Blocking patents can be destructive	Blocking patents carries both advantages and disadvantages
2. Establish legal basis for cooperation	Licences can be useful for cross-licensing	Licences are generally not used	Licence royalties are an essential source of income
3. Patents as strategic signals	Signalling about a possible patent dispute harder for small firms	Signalling about a possible patent dispute not used	Had direct experience with signalling about a possible patent dispute
4. Patents as indicators of value	Often important but in combination with other factors	Other factors mattered more than patents	Patents the only way to attract external capital

to describe something in a way that can be patented'. Several conceded that it could be difficult to patent processes, since they were not new and different enough. Another remarked that incremental inventions could not be patented (for example, when the innovator was scaling up production). A third noted that an invention could sometimes be patented in the US but not in Europe.

As regards the costs of applying for and maintaining the patent, most of our software respondents complained that they were too high, particularly given the costs involved in obtaining effective international protection. Also, the application process was too bureaucratic. The costs of patent application and enforcement, declared one, made this 'completely unrealistic' for an enterprise of their size. This finding accords with that of the IFO (2000) report. The firms they interviewed found the costs of applying for and maintaining the patent to be a fairly large barrier, though this was mainly in terms of the costs of patent agents and attorneys, and the costs of patent enforcement, not the patent application and renewal fees *per se*. But in the other two industries in our study, most respondents stated that while of course the patent application process was expensive, this was not an argument not to patent. 'If you spend over a hundred million Euro on development costs', as one expressed it, 'the costs of the actual patent are not that great'.

4.2.2 Problems relating to preventing imitation

Opinions were divided as to how crucial problems of preventing imitation were. A software respondent observed that the possibility of competitors 'inventing around' their patents was the prime reason they did not patent. Another said that even if this might happen, it was not a reason not to patent. Respondents in telecommunications and biotechnology emphasized that this could well be a disadvantage, mainly for process inventions, since it could be so difficult to detect and prove infringements (see Section 4.2.3 below). But again, it was not a reason not to patent. This finding is intriguing in that it contradicts the empirical results mentioned earlier (Section 2.1). It suggests that most small firms, while cost-conscious, now accept that if it is necessary to patent, the related costs must be incurred. Perhaps earlier, when patents were not so central to business strategy, a different attitude could prevail. Three biotech interviewees stressed the difficulties of preventing imitation. If the patent was not essential to you, or if you believed the patent would be too easy to design around, you might not want to patent. But generally speaking, our biotech participants were not concerned about this. Over half rated it as of no import. Several noted that this was the whole point of the patent system, and at any rate was not a reason not to patent.

With regard to revealing too much information, our respondents answered similarly that of course this happens, it is the 'rules of the game' of the patent system. Yet as a telecommunications enterprise observed, if the patent is formulated properly, it is not necessary to reveal that much:

> You describe the bare bones ... and it's possible that you leave out some 'small tricks'. So even though the others tried to copy it, they would run into problems, because it was not so straightforward.

One software respondent who saw this as a problem noted that it takes a great deal of time to complete an application. If the application is turned down after publication, the information is out for all to read. The applicant cannot retract the information and keep it secret. A few survey participants, on the other hand, stressed the benefits of information disclosure. A software firm noted that they were glad to inform customers of what they could do. A biotech firm said that if potential partners were aware of their work, they might approach them for a licence.

4.2.3 Problems relating to patent infringement

Many participants in our study, especially in software and telecommunications, agreed that it could be very difficult to determine whether their patents were being infringed. In the words of one software respondent: 'With a firm our size, it would really only be by chance that we would find out about it'. A telecommunications firm commented:

> It's almost impossible to prove that a competitor is infringing a process patent. Clearly, if we have a terrific idea, but could never prove infringement, that would be a crucial argument not to patent. If it is a process where we would be 90 per cent sure that we could prove to a judge that someone had infringed the patent, then we would apply for a patent. These are the arguments we would weigh in relation to each other.

A software participant, on the other hand, observed that the technology was changing so rapidly that patent holders did not even try to check for infringements. Another insisted that it was not a problem because 'it is part of the software business to copy each other'. In biotechnology, several of our respondents concurred that this was a barrier to using patents, particularly for processes. Some said that this kept them from patenting processes, while others insisted it was not a reason not to patent.

Interestingly, pursuing patent infringements was generally considered less of a problem than detecting them. Pursuing infringers was of most concern to software firms, five of whom dubbed it severe. In telecommunications, by contrast, there was a wide disparity in attitudes. Three respondents characterized it as critical. The remaining four felt it mattered little. Among the latter, one did not go after infringers unless the market was of a certain minimum size. Another insisted that it was not a problem since they were part of a larger corporate group. Among our biotech participants, it was typically seen as a concern but not relevant to them, since by that time they would have sold the rights to a larger corporation. Yet generally speaking, our biotech respondents did feel that rivals respected each others' patents.

4.2.4 Patents are not suitable given the nature of the technology concerned

Clear industry differences emerged as regards whether the technology was developing so rapidly that patents were irrelevant. No biotech interviewee found this to be a barrier to patenting, mainly due to the very long product development times in this industry. Four of our seven telecommunications firms also dismissed this. As one noted, even though technology develops quickly, an innovator cannot just change production methods overnight. There is a time lag between developing something and patenting it and then producing it. Nearly all of our software informants, by contrast, assessed this as a major reason not to patent. Product life cycles were very short, often under one year. What counted most was speed to market and flexibility, none of which were supported by what one termed the 'heavy' patenting process. One software firm disagreed, arguing that it was still selling software developed five years previously. Another observed that if the product life cycle was expected to be three years or more, they might consider patents.

As regards publishing the information instead of patenting it, many software and telecommunications respondents were unaware of this option. Our biotech respondents were well aware of it. Some had actually exercised it, others had not. One made decisions from case to case. Usually, this firm would patent, but they might publish information such as the details of a production process. Another maintained that they might publish if they feared that the patent application would be rejected. Two software participants stressed that they deliberately published information, not to prevent others from patenting but to signal to customers and competitors what they could do.

4.2.5 Firms prefer to use other strategies of appropriability

Most of our respondents used some form of secrecy, either alone or in combination with patents. Secrecy costs less, they said, and is administratively easier than patenting. It was more prevalent in telecommunications than in the other two sectors. As one respondent from this sector exclaimed:

> I am a believer in secrecy. It is better to earn some money before they enter the market after us, better to have the technological lead.

It was also easier to enforce employee secrecy than to detect patent infringements.

Several software firms pointed out that they tried to keep the source code secret. One said that they would deliver programs in binary format, which was more difficult to reverse engineer. Another described how they utilized secrecy in their production tools, which could not be discovered by reverse engineering. For our biotech firms, a reason to use secrecy might be difficulties of determining whether others had infringed their patents, or simply because they preferred to include this as supplementary 'know-how' in the licence agreement. Some respondents did not use secrecy. A telecommunications firm argued that it was vital to get input from customers and tailor their products to customer needs, rendering it difficult to use secrecy. Several biotech interviewees asserted that they needed to reveal information about the process anyway as part of the clinical testing process.

As regards other appropriability strategies, five of our nine software firms gave this the highest rating. What was crucial, they contended, was to deliver a high quality product to customers, and to develop strong, lasting customer ties. In all of these respects, good service mattered more than anything else. Interviewees in both software and telecommunications also stressed the value of trademarks, particularly as a guarantee of quality, and the role of marketing. Two thirds of our biotech enterprises, by contrast, typically had little use for alternative strategies of appropriability.

Table 5.4 (next page) gives an overview of these comments.

5 DISCUSSION

Several patterns in our empirical data could be observed. Firstly, there were considerable industry differences as regards how patents were used and viewed. In particular:

- Our biotech firms restricted their work to the pre-commercial phases of development, and tailored their patent policies accordingly. Patents were especially prized to prevent imitation, strengthen the firm's position in relation to a possible patent dispute, form the basis of a licence agreement, signal that the technology was protected, and attract external capital. Blocking patents were used by some (to enable comprehensive coverage of the research area they were exploring) but not others, who called them unethical. Licences were viewed

Table 5.4 Results of the empirical study: possible reasons not to take out patents

Reason	Some illustrative comments from telecommunications	Some illustrative comments from software	Some illustrative comments from biotechnology
1. Problems associated with application process	There were so many patents in their area there was little left to patent	Inventions were not unique enough to be patented	No choice but to patent, and patented everything they could
2. Problems relating to preventing imitation	It was particularly difficult to prevent the imitation of process patents	This could be a main reason not to patent	Not much concerned about the possibility of imitation
3. Problems relating to patent infringement	It could be very difficult to detect infringements	The technology was changing so rapidly they never bothered to check infringement	Not a problem, since the invention would be licensed or sold to a larger firm
4. Patents are not suitable given nature of information concerned	Even though the technology develops quickly, cannot just change production methods overnight	Very short product life cycles a major reason not to patent	Not a problem due to the long product development times
5. Firms prefer to use other means to appropriate value	Easier to enforce employee secrecy than detect patent infringements	Keep source codes secret, tailor products to customer needs	Patents far and away the most effective appropriation strategy

as an essential source of income, and patents were fundamental to attracting external capital. No reasons not to patent really counted. Many participants asserted that they had no choice but to patent. While they recognized that there could be some disadvantages to patenting, none outweighed the advantages.

- Our software firms, by contrast, primarily engaged in product development and sales. They had no interest in adopting the kind of proactive patent strategy pursued by giants like Microsoft. The main reason they applied for patents was strategic signalling. Other potential advantages were largely considered unimportant or irrelevant. Blocking patents, for example, were seen as destructive. Licence agreements were not much used. Essentially, our respondents emphasized the reasons why they did not patent: the technology was moving so rapidly that patents were irrelevant, the invention couldn't be patented, and the high costs of patent application and enforcement. They preferred to keep the source code secret and appropriate rents through tailoring products to customer needs.
- Our telecommunications firms generally pursued the same kinds of patent strategies as their larger competitors. While they found patents important, they realized that certain patent strategies were not available to them, given their limited resources. They primarily applied for patents to strengthen their position in connection with licence negotiations, to protect against imitation, to block competitors, and as strategic signals. The major reasons not to patent included concerns that competitors would invent around their patents, and the costs of detecting infringements, particularly for process patents. A further factor was the possibility of using secrecy, which avoided the costs of applying for and enforcing patents.

There were also differences among the firms within the three industries. In some cases, respondents were sharply divided as to whether a reason was highly critical, or of no concern whatsoever. This was true, for example, of our telecommunications interviewees as regards the difficulties of pursuing infringers, of our software firms in relation to the value of patents to attract external capital, and of our biotech firms regarding using secrecy.

Many respondents stressed the role of the market in which they were operating. One telecommunications firm remarked that in areas where they were competing with American corporations, it was better to patent, while if the competitors were Asian, it was better to keep the invention secret, since it could be quite difficult to enforce patents in Asia. A software innovator emphasized that they were exclusively focused on the Danish market, and did not know of any other firms that only sold on the Danish market that used patents. But if they tried to enter the American market, their patent policies might change.

Attitudes towards patents also differed. The majority of our software interviewees were quite dismissive of the whole idea of patenting, complaining that it slowed down technological progress rather than promoting it. They were critical of developments in the United States, which permitted patents on software. Many such patents, particularly for computer-implemented business methods, were in their eyes both trivial and unnecessary. We did not encounter similar negative attitudes in our interviews with biotech and telecommunications informants.

Finally, our data provides some insights as to the patenting policies of very small enterprises. In our data, there were only two areas where differences emerged between the smallest of our respondents (those with twenty employees or less) and the rest (21–250 employees). The smallest were more likely than the others to use their patents to earn royalties, and less concerned about the chance competitors might 'invent around' them. The former is not particularly surprising, since the smallest firms typically lack resources to commercialize inventions themselves. The latter is puzzling, however, given that the costs of preventing imitation would arguably place especially heavy burdens on very small enterprises. Several reasons for this lack of concern emerged in our interviews. Two firms emphasized that they could always turn for support to their parent company. Others, typically in software, observed that one advantage of being small was that the larger companies took no notice of what one was doing.

6 CONCLUSION

In this chapter, we have sought to determine the extent to which small high-tech firms agree with commonly cited motivations to take out patents, and the reasons not to seek patent protection. Since existing studies of these issues are largely based on data from large enterprises, we were curious as to whether the same patterns could be observed among small firms.

The main reasons to take out patents, we found, were to protect against imitation, and as strategic signals. The main reasons to refrain from doing so were because the invention was not patentable, and the high costs of detecting infringements. Distinct industry differences emerged. In telecommunications, patents were typically viewed as important, but in combination with other factors, and the disadvantages were recognized. In software, patents were mainly seen as costly, irrelevant and ineffective. In biotechnology, there was a clear consensus. Patents were the only effective means of protection, and were essential to create value from their investments in R&D. Generally speaking, respondents were aware that large firms, given their greater resources, could act in ways not available to them, especially as regards the accumulation of large patent portfolios, the use of blocking patents, and the ability to enforce their patents effectively. But this also forced them to tailor their use of patents to their own R&D, production and marketing strategies.

Our findings have implications for both management and policy. Firstly, our respondents emphasized the role of patents not only to prevent imitation, but also as signals to denote that the invention was protected, and in connection with a possible patent dispute. That they fully embraced the 'strategic signalling' function of patents is intriguing, reflecting a similar trend among larger firms in recent years. But while large firms often employ signalling to warn would-be competitors away, our small firms seem to have done so more for quite another reason: to alert potential partners and customers (both firms and individual consumers) to what they were doing. This differs from the patent policies pursued by large firms, which would be more on the receiving end of signals from would-be suppliers.

Secondly, while small high-tech enterprises naturally operate under resource constraints, this is not necessarily a disadvantage, and might well spur them to develop an approach to patents tailored to their special circumstances. Lack of resources compelled our informants to focus on what they could do best, and to weigh, very carefully, whether the benefits of patents justified the costs. One of the primary effects of patents for small enterprises, they stressed, was to give them the freedom to manoeuvre in their chosen patent area, to prevent others from taking out patents to block their own development activities.

Many respondents had developed their own fine-tuned, 'contextual' patent strategies, which sometimes resembled, and sometimes differed from the patent strategies pursued by larger firms in the same industry. Telecommunications firms, for example, realized that they couldn't blanket a technological area with patents in the same way as large firms. Sometimes they tried to 'disguise' what they were doing by not patenting, as one respondent put it. Sometimes they utilized patents for cross-licensing like their larger counterparts. Our biotech firms, as specialized suppliers to the large pharmaceutical firms, tailored their patent policies to the needs of these firms.

This 'contextual' approach is not necessarily positive. It may indicate an appropriate use of resources, but it may also reveal ignorance of how patents might be leveraged to best ensure their commercial survival over the longer term. In particular, the highly negative view of patents by our software enterprises, while it saves costs in the short term, may leave them defenceless in the face of the patenting activities of larger competitors that compete in the same markets.

There were two major reasons our participants did not take out patents. Firstly, they believed that their inventions were not patentable. It may well be, however, that their inventions *were* patentable, and that they simply were not aware of this. Secondly, they felt it would be difficult to detect infringements. Large corporations can draw upon in-house patent expertise in both regards. A policy implication here is that small firms could benefit from assistance from the public R&D infrastructure on both counts, since both problems are grounded in a lack of information.

A third disadvantage, the difficulties of pursuing infringers, was frequently mentioned in interviews, but not often listed as a major reason not to seek patent protection. This may be because our respondents realized that pursuing infringers would in practice be impossible for them, and thus (perversely) did not even count as a reason not to patent, but as a given. This, too, might fruitfully be an area for public intervention to help small enterprises. More specifically, our findings support the establishment of a common European patent insurance policy to cover the costs of patent suits, should a firm later have its patent infringed. Lanjouw and Schankerman (2004), for example, argue that private patent litigation insurance can help small firms mitigate the adverse effects of high enforcement costs.

Future research could address several interesting questions raised by this study. Firstly, we found considerable industry differences among our respondents' views of patents. It would be worthwhile to learn more about the reasons underlying these differences. We also did not explore the degree to which small high-tech enterprises utilize patents strategically in other manners, such as the development of sophisticated patent data mining techniques to analyse competitor market positions and the patent holdings of target acquisitions. Patent intelligence is increasingly gathered to help firms to stay on the forefront of developments in their own fields. Small enterprises, one might hypothesize, can similarly not afford not to gather this information, but may not have the resources to do so.

An additional area for future research concerns the patenting process. Virtually nothing has been written about this, as far as I am aware, yet it is a key element of patent strategy. Should a firm patent early in the development process, or wait? There are costs and benefits for both approaches. How many patents should a firm apply for in a product area, and when should it apply for these patents? Should it seek to protect its products, or processes, or both? The application process tends to be relatively inexpensive at the beginning. For most Danish firms, the major expense comes when they seek patent protection under the European Patent Office, and must pay to have the patent translated into the languages of the countries in which they intend to do business.

Finally, our use of semi-structured in-depth interviews enabled us to achieve a more subtle understanding of the reasons why small high-tech enterprises choose to patent, and why not, than can be gleaned from the existing empirical studies. But we limited our sample to small firms. What we have thereby not been able to determine is the degree to which medium-sized and large enterprises, too, have developed their own contextual approaches to patents. Future studies could enable fruitful comparisons along these lines.

ACKNOWLEDGEMENTS

I would like to thank the Danish Social Sciences Research Council for providing the funding for this research, which is part of an international research project, *Mobilizing Knowledge in Management of Technology*, under the Centre for Interdisciplinary Studies in Technology Management programme (CISTEMA), under the leadership of Jens Frøslev Christensen at the Copenhagen Business School. I would also like to thank my research assistant, Kirsten Kjaer, MSc in Economics and Business Administration, Copenhagen Business School, for helping with gathering the data and conducting the interviews. Thanks are due as well to Birgitte Andersen for her thorough and helpful comments on a previous version of this chapter. An earlier draft of this paper was presented at the Summer Conference of the Danish Research Unit for Industrial Dynamics (DRUID): *Industrial Dynamics, Innovation and Development* (Copenhagen/Elsinore, Denmark, 12–14 June 2003). Here, I am grateful for the feedback provided by my two discussants, Benjamin Coriat and Birgitte Andersen. Further feedback was graciously provided by another DRUID participant, Naubahar Sharif, and by Jerome Davis, Roskilde University/Dalhousie University.

NOTES

1. The Danish title is *Købmandsstandens Oplysningsbureau*.
2. We were interested in interviewing firms in the greater Copenhagen area because of the many SMEs that are located here in the three industries, and because Copenhagen has a strong R&D infrastructure. We wished to eliminate from our inquiry any differences in patent policies that might be attributable to differences in access to R&D infrastructure resources. The city boasts three science-based universities (the Technical University of Denmark, the University of Copenhagen and the Royal Agricultural University), three science parks (Symbion, CAT and the Danish Science Park at Hørsholm), the Danish Technological Institute and the Danish Patent and Trademark Office. Directly across the

sound, in southern Sweden, is another science-based university, the University of Lund, and two additional science parks. See http://www.copcap.com.

3. As regards the number of employees in the telecommunications firms, the sample mean was 15.4 (std. dev. 6.6), the population mean was 36.6 (std. dev. 32.5). For software, the corresponding figures were 39.2 (std. dev. 52.6) for the sample and 31.5 (std. dev. 48.5) for the population. For biotechnology, the corresponding figures were 40.7 (std. dev. 56.1) for the sample and 36.8 (std. dev. 44.1) for the population. Most of the firms in our population were quite small (the median number of employees for telecommunications was 17, for software it was 15 and for biotech, 23).
4. It should be noted that our survey is not strictly comparable with the two other Danish studies mentioned in Section 2.1 (IFO 2000, 2002). The former is based on 451 telephone interviews, the latter on 75 face-to-face interviews (of which two-thirds were with firms with up to 250 employees). The sources interviewed, the questions asked and the sectors included also differed.

REFERENCES

Andersen, B. (2004), 'If 'Intellectual Property Rights' is the Answer, What is the Question? Revising the Patent Controversies', *Economics of Innovation and New Technology*, **13** (5), July, pp. 417–42.

Arrow, K.A. (1962), 'Economic Welfare and the Allocation of Resources for Invention', in Nelson, R.R. (ed.) *The Rate and Direction of Inventive Activity: Economic and Social Factors*. (Princeton, NJ: Princeton University Press and National Bureau of Economic Research).

Arundel, A. (2001), 'The Relative Effectiveness of Patents and Secrecy for Appropriation', *Research Policy*, **30**, pp. 611–24.

Arundel, A. and Kabla, I. (1998), 'What Percentage of Innovations are Patented? Empirical Estimates for European Firms', *Research Policy*, **27**, pp. 127–41.

Arundel, A. and Steinmueller, E. (1998), 'The Use of Patent Databases by European Small and Medium-sized Enterprises', *Technology Analysis and Strategic Management*, **10** (2), pp. 157–73.

Audretsch, D.B. (2002), 'The Dynamic Role of Small Firms: Evidence from the U.S.,' *Small Business Economics*, February–May, **18** (1–3), pp. 13–40.

Bertin, G.Y. and Wyatt, S. (1988), *Multinationals and Industrial Property* (Harvester Wheatsheaf).

Besen, S.M. and Raskind, L.J. (1991), 'An Introduction to the Law and Economics of Intellectual Property'. *Journal of Economic Perspectives*, Winter, **5** (1), pp. 3–27.

Blind, K. and Edler, J. (2003), 'Idiosyncrasies of the Software Development Process and Their Relation to Software Patents: Theoretical Considerations and Empirical Evidence', *Netnomics: Economic Research and Electronic Networking*, **5** (1), May, pp. 71–96.

Cohen, W.M., Nelson, R.R. and Walsh, J.P. (2000), *Protecting their Intellectual Assets: Appropriability Conditions and Why U.S. Manufacturing Firms Patent (or Not)*. NBER Working Paper (Cambridge, Mass: NBER).

Conner, K.R. and Rumelt, R.P. (1991), 'Software Piracy: An Analysis of Protection Strategies', *Management Science*, February, pp. 125–39.

Davis, L.N. (1998), 'Patents and Innovation: a Strategic Perspective', in Riis, Thomas and Nielsen, Ruth (eds), *Law and Economics: Methodology and Application* (Copenhagen: DJØF Publishing), pp. 11–31.

Davis, L.N. (2001), 'R&D Investments, Information and Strategy', *Technology Analysis and Strategic Management*, **13**, p. 3.
Eisenhardt, K.M. and Schoonhoven, C.B. (1990), 'Organizational Growth: Linking Founding Team, Strategy, Environment, and Growth among U.S. Semiconductor Ventures, 1978–1988', *Administrative Science Quarterly*, September, **35** (3), pp. 504–30.
Ellis, L.W. and Honig-Haftel, S. (1992), 'Reward Strategies for R&D', *Research Technology Management*, **35** (2), March–April, pp. 16–20.
Glazier, S. (1995), 'Inventing Around Your Competitors' Patents', *Managing Intellectual Property*, July/August, pp. 10–14.
Graham, S. and Mowery, D. (2004), 'Submarines in Software? Continuations in US Software Patenting in the 1980s and 1990s', *Economics of Innovation and New Technology*, **13** (5), July, pp. 443–56.
Granstrand, O. (1999), *The Economics and Management of Intellectual Property*, Cheltenham, UK and Northampton, MA, USA: Edward Elgar.
Granstrand, O. (2000), 'The Shift Towards Intellectual Capitalism – the Role of Infocom Technologies', *Research Policy*, **29**, pp. 1061–80.
Grindley, P.C. and Teece, D.J. (1997), 'Managing Intellectual Capital: Licensing and Cross-licensing in Semiconductors and Electronics', *California Management Review*, **39** (2), pp. 8–41.
Hall, B. and Ham Ziedonis, R. (2001), 'The Patent Paradox Revisited: An Empirical Study of Patenting in the U.S. Semiconductor Industry, 1979–1995', *The Rand Journal of Economics*, **32** (2), pp. 101–28.
Harabi, N. (1995), 'Appropriability of Technical Innovations: An Empirical Analysis', *Research Policy*, **24**, pp. 981–92.
IFO – Institute for Opinion Analysis (2000), *Small and Medium-sized Manufacturing Firms: Barriers to Product Development and Patenting*, report to the Danish Patent and Trademark Office, 19 October (in Danish).
IFO – Institute for Opinion Analysis (2002), *Investigation of Firms' Use of Intellectual Property Rights*, report to the Danish Ministry of Industry and Trade, 17 December.
Kelley, D.J. and Rice, M.P. (2002), 'Leveraging the Value of Proprietary Technologies', *Journal of Small Business Management*, **40** (1), pp. 1–16.
Kingston, W. (2001), 'Innovation Needs Patent Reform', *Research Policy*, **30**, pp. 403–23.
Kitch, E.W. (1977), 'The Nature and Function of the Patent System', *The Journal of Law and Economics*, **20**, pp. 265–90.
Lanjouw, J. and Schankerman, M. (2004), 'Protecting Intellectual Property Rights: Are Small Firms Handicapped?', *The Journal of Law and Economics*, **47**, pp. 45–74.
Lefebvre, L.A. and Lefebvre, E. (1993), 'Competitive Positioning and Innovative Efforts in SMEs', *Small Business Economics*, **5** (4), pp. 297–306.
Levin, T.C, Klevorick, A.K., Nelson, R.R. and Winter, S.G. (1987), 'Appropriating the Returns from Industrial Research and Development', *Brookings Papers on Economic Activity*, **3**, pp. 783–820.
Mansfield, E., Schwartz, M. and Wagner, S. (1981), 'Imitation Costs and Patents: An Empirical Study', *The Economic Journal*, **91**, December, pp. 907–18.
Merges, R.P. (2004), 'A New Dynamism in the Public Domain', *The University of Chicago Law Review*, **71** (1), Winter, pp. 183–203.

Merges, R.P. and Nelson, R.R. (1994), 'On Limiting or Encouraging Rivalry in Technical Progress: the Effect of Patent Scope Decisions', *Journal of Economic Behavior and Organization*, **25**, pp. 1–24.

Meyer, M.H. and Lopez, L. (1995), 'Technology Strategy in a Software Products Company', *The Journal of Product Innovation Management*, September, **12** (4), pp. 294–307.

Mogee, M.E. (2000), 'Foreign Patenting Behaviour of Small and Large Firms', *International Journal of Technology Management*, **19** (1, 2), pp. 149–64.

Morkel, A. and Willoughby, K. (1992), *Orbital Engine Corporation*, Teaching Case.

Nelson, R.R. (1959), 'The Simple Economics of Basic Research', *Journal of Political Economy*, June, **67**, pp. 297–306.

Oppenländer, K.H. (1977), 'Patent Policies and Technical Progress in the Federal Republic of Germany', *IIC*, **8** (2), pp. 97–122.

Pooley, J. and Bratic, W. (1999), ' The Value of Trade Secrets', *Managing Intellectual Property*, October, issue 93, pp. 66–9.

Ramani, S. and De Looze, M.-A. (2002), 'Country-specific Characteristics of Patent Applications in France, Germany and the UK in the Biotechnology Sectors', *Technology Analysis and Strategic Management*, December, **14** (4), pp. 457–80.

Rivette, K.G and Kline, D. (2000a), 'Discovering New Value in Intellectual Property', *Harvard Business Review*, January–February, pp. 54–66.

Rivette, K.G and Kline, D. (2000b), *Rembrandts in the Attic: Unlocking the Hidden Value of Patents* (Boston, Mass: Harvard University Press).

Sabourin, V. and Pinsonneault, I. (1997), 'Strategic Formation of Competitive High Technology Clusters', *International Journal of Technology Management*, **13** (2), pp. 165–78.

Scotchmer, S. (1991), 'Standing on the Shoulders of Giants: Cumulative Research and the Patent Law', *Journal of Economic Perspectives*, Winter, **5** (1), pp. 29–41.

Sullivan, C.G. (1999), 'Trade Secrets and Other R&D Capital Preservation Techniques', *Pharmaceutical Science and Technology Today*, **2** (6), pp. 253–5.

Teece, D.J. (1986), 'Profiting from Technological Innovation: Implications for Integration, Collaboration, Licensing and Public Policy', *Research Policy*, **15**, pp. 285–305.

Teece, D.J. (2000), *Managing Intellectual Capital* (Oxford: Oxford University Press), pp. 135–55.

PART III

The performance of the patenting process

6. Knowledge spillovers from the patenting process

Jesper Lindgaard Christensen

ABSTRACT

This chapter highlights and investigates potential knowledge spillovers from a patent office. It furthermore discusses if such spillovers are localized within the nation. It researches if the interaction between the applicant firms and the patent office, in this case the Danish Patent and Trademark Office (DKPTO), adds to the general competence of both parties. In turn, this may have positive long-term effects on the ability of the firms to innovate and use the intellectual property rights (IPR) system.

Patent offices are often regarded as performing relatively standardized processing of applications without much interaction with other parties in the innovation system. On the contrary, the research reveals that the DKPTO not only grants patents and sells business services, but also has a complementary role as a knowledge-diffusing organization.

A survey was implemented to explore this role in the innovation system further. The general impact of the DKPTO on knowledge diffusion is, according to the survey, primarily to increase the awareness of IPR among firms and to bring together the IPR branch by constituting a central focus point for common interests. Additionally, the DKPTO serves a role in facilitating easy access to the patent system for firms by lowering the cultural and linguistic barriers of IPR protection. Moreover, the DKPTO educates patent engineers who after a period in the DKPTO are employed in other organizations. The role of the DKPTO in terms of stimulating innovation directly is modest, but the above-mentioned complementary functions are likely to produce considerable knowledge spillovers. On the basis of the results the organization of a European patent system is discussed, specifically whether a centralization of the patenting process would deprive nation states of the knowledge spillovers from a national location of patent offices. The conclusion from the study is that although many Danish firms would be able to do without a national patent office with regard to the patenting process, there is still a role for national IPR institutions.

Keywords: Innovation system, Knowledge spillovers, Patent system, Patent offices

1 INTRODUCTION

The organization of the patent system has been subject to discussions during many years both in policy circles and in academia. One of the issues in this discussion is an intense debate on the consequences of centralizing patent casework in the European Patent Office (EPO). The present research may have valuable insights for this discussion. For many years, probably for the past 25, there has been a broad agreement that a common European patent system would be beneficial. While it was decided (Lisbon Council in 2000) that by the end of 2001 a community patent should be launched, there has (until 3rd March 2003 when many of the most severe barriers were removed) been little progress in efforts to actually get the organization of the system in place. In fact, the negotiations on this issue have proven immensely difficult. One of the obstacles was agreement on language, another the juridical question regarding, for example, settling disputes and in harmonizing procedures. A third issue in the debate is particularly relevant in the present context, that is whether the centralization of patent casework, as prescribed by the European Patent Convention (EPC), would deprive national offices of knowledge and competencies concerning patenting. This knowledge, it is argued, may diffuse through the innovation system if a national patent casework is upheld.

The role of knowledge generation and diffusion in the economy is nowadays high on the agenda of innovation studies. In particular, a number of earlier and contemporary studies have looked into possible knowledge spillovers[1] from university-industry interaction, and other types of knowledge institutions are analysed as well. However, patent offices[2] are most often regarded as different from other knowledge institutions. The actual operation of national patent offices is rarely discussed; mainly they are seen as part of the regulatory framework together with standard-setting agencies – they are thus often regarded as only performing the necessary tasks in relation to granting a patent. Reviews for improving the dynamics of a national patenting system disregard the technology diffusion potential of the institutions themselves and their activities. The contribution of this chapter lies in highlighting and investigating potential knowledge spillovers from a patent office. It furthermore discusses if such spillovers are localized within the nation. The latter may have implications for the rationale for the political decision with regard to harmonizing and centralizing the patent system in Europe.

This aspect of the patent system is often overlooked and scarcely researched as an issue in itself. The study investigates in particular the competence building and knowledge diffusion resulting from a) the processing of the patent application and b) the provision of services related to patenting. This analysis contends that the interaction between the applicant firms and the patent office, in this case the Danish Patent and Trademark Office (DKPTO), may add to the general competence of both parties. In turn, this may have positive long-term effects on the ability of the firms to innovate and to use the intellectual property rights (IPR) system on the one hand, and on the other hand the competence of the patent office. The internal competencies resulting from processing applications are likely to spill over to other activities of the DKPTO, thus enhancing other departments' abilities to provide services, not only to firms directly (the main focus in this study), but also indirectly through various types of intermediaries such as patent agents and technological institutes. Additionally it is discussed if there are other channels of knowledge diffusion from the patent office. The chapter focuses upon the possible knowledge spillovers to firms, disregarding the possible internal knowledge development within the DKPTO. The latter is analysed specifically in Christensen (2004).

The research is not on patents *per se* or on the economics of patenting. Rather, it is on the institutional role of the patent office in innovation. Thus, the research question is to what extent are there knowledge spillovers from patent offices? In this analysis it is important to consider the spatial dimension, that is whether a national location of patent offices is of importance (as is implicit in the argument above about potential knowledge drain from centralized patent casework).

The chapter proceeds in section 2 with a more thorough theoretical discussion of the rationale for the research question. Section 3 presents key activities of the patent office in Denmark. This section discusses important complementary institutions in the innovation system and their place in the overall national innovation system. A survey was undertaken to determine if the services provided in relation to patenting contributed to a build-up of innovative capabilities in Danish firms. Results from this survey are reported in section 4. The concluding section 5 summarizes the findings and points to perspectives based on the research findings.

2 POTENTIAL LEARNING PROCESSES FROM THE INTERACTION BETWEEN KNOWLEDGE INSTITUTIONS AND FIRMS

It is widely believed that knowledge is a critical asset in the present mode of production. The move from production based mainly on land use and machinery to a mode of production heavily dependent on human skills has even been compared to the transformation which occurred during the industrial revolution.[3] Terms like 'information society,' 'the knowledge-based economy' and even 'the learning economy' are now part of the daily vocabulary of academics and policy makers alike. Modern economic theory now emphasizes strongly that knowledge is the most important asset and learning the most important process in production.[4] A policy strategy for promoting economic development is consequently often said to be to increase the knowledge base of the economy and the speed of knowledge diffusion in the economy. One of the most prominent policy strategies in many countries is to stimulate the interplay between key actors in the innovation system. Specifically, a number of governments have now put the knowledge exchange between industry and knowledge institutions high on the agenda.

In spite of the general agreement on the importance of knowledge and learning, our understanding of the process of knowledge creation and diffusion remains limited. Likewise, the indicators used to measure knowledge and knowledge flows are underdeveloped. With the case of DKPTO-firm interaction in mind, this section sets out to point to important advances in the theory of innovation and knowledge creation and diffusion relevant for the research in this chapter. It discusses in sequence the transmission and transformation of knowledge. The spatial dimension of knowledge spillovers is then briefly discussed by considering whether the national innovation system is a relevant geographical entity in the present research.

2.1 The Transmission of Knowledge

The development of situations beneficial for learning implies among other things trust and various kinds of proximity. The latter has several dimensions, spatial, cultural, and historical. Similar to the situations beneficial for generating knowledge, the transmission of knowledge may have several dimensions: spatial, over time and between people.

To some extent a one-time/first-time exchange of knowledge is different from a situation where the parties know each other. The transmission of information is easier when relationships have been established and ways of communication, which are understandable by both parties, have been worked out. Once established through a process of learning, one is unwilling to invest in building up new relationships, implying a new series of learning processes.

> A communication system has some cost of initial investment which is irreversible. In particular, a communication channel is used to greatest capacity when it has

> an optimal code for transmitting messages. This 'code' need not be interpreted literally; the term refers to all patterns of communication and interaction within an organization, patterns that make use of conventional signals and forms that have to be learned. Once learned, however, it is cheaper to reuse the same system than to learn a new one; there is a payoff on the initial learning investment but no way of liquidating it by sale to others. (Arrow, 1974, p. 19)

A prerequisite for efficient information exchange is common channels and codes of information, effectively distributed and understood. The specific channels and codes will reflect the cultural, geographical and organizational differences between the parties. Established relationships will be kept when satisfactory exchange of information (through interactive learning processes) has developed together with an establishment of competence on both sides. The establishment and maintenance of relationships between users of business services, like the process of producing the final patent application, and producers of these services is facilitated by a social and cultural coherence. However, there may be difficulties in the ability to process information. Therefore the interaction must lead to ways of pooling the information in a manner suited to the receivers' organizational structure and ability to process informational signals.

The recent upsurge of social network theory builds upon and extends these insights (Podolny *et al.*, 1996, Shane and Cable, 2002, Sorensen and Stuart 2001, Stuart and Sorensen, 2003). Parts of this literature add a spatial dimension claiming that these processes are best facilitated in close geographical proximity. For example, Stuart and Sorensen explain spatial concentrations of start-ups by the social networks of potential entrepreneurs. The social capital to mobilize resources for start-ups is tied to the relationships of the entrepreneur. Both the potential entrepreneurs and the social and professional ties of these entrepreneurs tend to cluster in space, these authors claim. Debate prevails as to whether the social ties are more important or if the geographical proximity *per se* is the decisive factor. Breschi and Lissoni (2003) maintain that social ties rather than geographical proximity are important when analysing knowledge spillovers by mapping patent citations, thus contrasting the Jaffe, Trajtenberg and Henderson (1993) analysis. Later we shall return to this discussion about localized knowledge spillovers.

Implications of this understanding with respect to our case are not only confined to the alleviation of information problems related to the specific treatment of one patent application. The process is not only a development and accumulation of knowledge about a single patent application. As the one party, a firm or entrepreneur, becomes better at articulating requirements concerning the process, the other might be able to develop new procedures to meet these needs.

There are, however, limits to the benefits of such 'relational' transactions. Their primary disadvantage is probably the costs such as the time invested in the relationship. Also, it has been pointed out that these relationships or 'strong ties' (Granovetter, 1973, Hansen, 1998), may produce inertia and lack of innovation because new, and perhaps better alternatives are not explored (Arrow, 1974). In the words of Hansen (1998) the search efforts and benefits are constrained by the strong ties. The parties in established relations adopt a satisfying behaviour with respect to maintaining the relationship. Weak ties, on the other hand, increase the possibilities of linking up to a larger array of different people and networks, thus facilitating more opportunities and stimuli of ideas. Moreover, one may argue that whether close relationships are beneficial for the interaction or not, is highly dependent upon the type of knowledge to be transferred. To explore this argument further we need to apply the distinction between tacit and codified knowledge, and we shall introduce the distinction between transactional and relational transfer of knowledge. Tacit knowledge is rarely transferred by means of the market mechanism, but is rather transferred in a mutual and often repetitive exchange of knowledge. This is necessary as tacit knowledge is often inherent in individual or collective routines, which are not necessarily written down or explicit even to the members of the collective. This type of knowledge is most efficiently transferred relationally. On the contrary, standardized, codified information may be transferred by simple exchange without much interaction, sometimes through the market (Hansen, 1998).[5] However, information and knowledge are not purely either codified or tacit. Even the processing of codified knowledge may require the use of tacit knowledge, and it may even be rational to codify procedures in order to discover the tacit knowledge involved, for example in the procedures involved in a novelty search. In other words, these two dimensions of knowledge may sometimes be interdependent.

The context of transactions and the partners exchanging the knowledge are highly influential on the specific mechanisms and media for exchange of knowledge. Likewise the media and the way knowledge is transferred may differ according to the absorptive capacity of the recipient (Kristensen and Vinding, 2001). Feldman (1999) contends that the empirical literature on localized knowledge spillovers identifies some mechanisms through which they may be channelled. One branch of empirical studies has identified geographically mediated spillovers as explanations of the geography of innovation (although several studies only point out co-location of spillovers and economic activity rather than patterns of causality). Generally these types of studies do not identify the mechanisms by which spillovers are realized. Other empirical studies do, however, point to such mechanisms. First, Feldman points to 'paper trails' left by patent citations. That is, as

Jaffe, Trajtenberg and Henderson (1993) find, there is a higher frequency of patents citing another patent from the same city than citing other patents. Generally, the localized character of patent citations indicates geographic boundaries for knowledge spillovers. A second mechanism for knowledge spillovers is the skills and knowledge embodied in people. The degree to which such spillovers are geographically bounded depends on the mobility of highly skilled people, and therefore on the labour market. But empirical evidence suggests that there is some inertia in both the interfirm mobility of people as such and in geographical mobility as well. Finally, knowledge spillovers may be channelled through knowledge embodied in goods. Although this may be thought of as highly mobile, empirical studies do indicate that spillovers are primarily intranational (Branstetter, 1996).

In our case, the patent examiner may need a broad and deep technological knowledge in order to undertake efficient screening of potential infringements of other patents. In turn it benefits an efficient production of business services if the examiner is also aware of the most efficient search methods. Moreover, other firms/entrepreneurs may make use of the patent description. In order to assimilate the knowledge from such patent descriptions the entrepreneur needs abilities not only to understand the principles of the technology embodied in the patent, but also creativity, as he or she must be able to apply this technology to other fields of use not covered by the patent, or alternatively see opportunities to combine the technology with other existing technologies.

The argument above has a dual proposition: on the one hand it could be argued that knowledge spillovers are facilitated by the different, complementary competencies of the parties. On the other hand there need to be some overlapping competencies to facilitate a mutual understanding (Arrow, 1974) and an ability to discuss and absorb the knowledge of the other party (Cohen and Levinthal, 1989). These two contrasting arguments are both based on the assertion that there is a monotonic relationship between the extent of knowledge spillovers and the internal knowledge resources of the firm. However, it may be argued that the intensity of the knowledge exchange instead follows an inverted u-shaped curve. Over time the firm may have disproportionally large learning effects from the interaction until a stage when returns from additional information diminish as a result of internal build-up of internal capacity to produce this information. The interaction may prevail but may change character as it transforms into a learning-to-learn form (Stiglitz, 1987) rather than a learning-by-interaction (Lundvall, 1988). The now more knowledgeable firm may now know how to make a patent application and do a novelty search or infringement search and so on, perhaps even in a separate patent department, but will continuously need a mirror – the DKPTO – to check if the competencies that are built up are adequate compared to present and future requirements.

This proposition introduces a dynamic element in contrast to the normal theory that considers mainly a comparison between firms with high or low absorptive capacity. We may, however, also apply this theory to a static version: firms with a certain minimum of absorptive capacity may be the most inclined to interact with for example, the DKPTO, but only to a threshold, beyond which they are likely to be able to do without the competencies of the DKPTO. To be more specific, such firms could be medium-sized with only one or a few innovations and limited experience with patenting. On the other hand they may know about the IPR system (and the patenting process) as well as being perhaps able to describe adequately their technology or product.

Other studies (Kleinknecht *et al.*, 2002) have suggested that the first patent is a threshold and that patenting thereafter increases substantially. An event which will accentuate this inverted u-shaped form of interaction intensity, is if there is mobility of personnel between the parties, usually from the DKPTO to firms. In that case the interaction with the DKPTO will be upheld but as competencies regarding the patenting processes have been transferred to the firm, some of the previous interaction becomes unnecessary.

Innovation policies have largely focused upon the diffusion of knowledge (Christensen, 2003). Theories within the 'innovation systems approach' have likewise emphasized the diffusion aspects. Some even argue that what has been denoted the 'new economy' is a steep increase in what may be termed knowledge externalities. Such externalities are non-pecuniary in the sense that knowledge produced by one agent – or a set of agents – may benefit other agents without financial compensation (Foray, 2000). The externalities contribute to the build-up of the general knowledge base of the society, which is, in turn, beneficial for future innovators. In relation to the DKPTO case in this study, the knowledge spillovers from treating an application can be said to be twofold. As the interaction between the parties produces useful knowledge both within the firm and within the DKPTO as well, the spillover effect may occur. Whereas the discussion on spillovers from the patent system has previously been focused upon the transfer of knowledge through the patent descriptions *per se* (Rivera-Batiz and Romer, 1991; see Feldman, 1999 and Andersen, 2004, p. 435 for a discussion) this chapter introduces this knowledge spillover as the accumulation and subsequent diffusion of knowledge in the form of learning by patent case workers. However, one prerequisite for this spillover of knowledge to happen is that the knowledge produced is not sunk, that is, if the knowledge has a very specific character, and is not useable in other connections, then the knowledge spillover is likely to be close to nil.[6]

2.2 The Dual Nature and Transformation of Knowledge

It is obvious from the above discussion that tacit knowledge is not easily accessible to others. This tacit knowledge may therefore be the key to a competitive edge for some firms. Similarly, a patent may in some cases be essential for a firm. A paradox may arise here. On the one hand, protecting a new technology via a patent requires codification in order to specify the technology in the application. However, this process makes it much more difficult to exclude the technology from others.

It may therefore be argued that a patent description is a way of transforming knowledge into codified knowledge. This makes it possible – or at least easier – for the market to estimate the value of such assets. Such a transformation of what is sometimes tacit knowledge into codified knowledge is, however, by no means a simple process. In addition, it is often not only difficult and costly but also only possible up to a limit. One of the limitations is that the transformation has to take into account the capacity of the recipient to understand the description.

The level of interactive learning may also depend on the complexity of knowledge. Innovations based upon several different knowledge bases may for example involve collaboration with a multitude of different partners. Moreover, innovations where knowledge inputs are tacit knowledge may require more intense interaction to understand and incorporate this knowledge in the innovation process. Thus, Meeus *et al.* (2001) contend that complex innovative activities imply a higher level of interactive learning. This argument is consistent with the present discussion on transfer of tacit and codified knowledge.

2.3 The National Innovation System as a Framework for Learning Processes between Firms and the DKPTO

The discussions above have primarily referred to a non-specific context. However, the innovation process and learning processes are not only governed by inherent characteristics. They take place within external boundaries, which are of importance to the processes. As indicated above proximity in several dimensions may facilitate learning. The spatial dimension may be important to learning as close geographical proximity facilitates social networks, personal interaction and build-up of trust. In addition, proximity may stimulate mutual understanding and cultural coherence. This may in turn contribute to the development of a code of conduct or governance of interaction that may benefit spatially bounded interactions (Gertler *et al.*, 2000, Storper, 1992). A number of studies have pointed out that indeed knowledge spillovers tend to be localized (see above). It is, however, rarely specified what is meant by 'localized' – how local are spillovers? One important boundary for learning processes is the nation state. In the past 15 years there has been an increasing recognition of this fact, reflected in the amount of studies focused on and using the concept of national systems of innovation and in the use of the concept by policy makers. In the present context we shall be limited to regarding the nation state as the relevant geographical entity. In spite of generally increased internationalization, there are arguments why national borders are still a co-determinant for the scope of the innovation process.[7]

Distance is, however, not a complete argument for the nation state as a boundary for the innovation process. The argument could equally well be applied to regions or local areas. On the other hand, even if counter-examples are easily found, the general picture is that language, culture and business norms to a large extent coincide with national borders. Moreover, in the literature on localized knowledge spillovers (for example, Jaffe, Trajtenberg and Henderson, 1993, Adams, 2002) there are arguments why spillovers may be restricted in space. In the present connection one can ask if spillovers from interactions between firms and the DKPTO are confined to national borders, or if a European, centralized patent office would also produce spillovers to Denmark. At first sight one could argue that processing the patent application and informing the applicant about decisions involves limited interpersonal interaction and only codified knowledge. But a closer look shows that there are several such channels of knowledge flows that are heavily dependent upon the spatial, national context. As explained in more detail later, patent offices do many things other than processing patent applications and other IPR issues, like trademarks. For example, it is an important activity to arrange seminars, courses, increasing awareness of IPR issues generally. In addition, personnel mobility from the patent office to patent agents and patent-intensive corporate firms is likely to be most intense within national borders. Thus, the channels of localized knowledge spillovers are indeed primarily national.

In spite of an increasing share of EU legislation relative to what is decided by national parliaments, legislation, standards and other regulations are primarily national, and this is important to firms when choosing their innovation strategy. Even if liberalized, public procurement is often directed towards domestic products, and the overall government technological, industrial, and economic policy has a national focus, this also affects the innovation process. In the present context we see a case of 'pure monopoly', which is confined to the nation state – it is not feasible to have several patent granting institutions within one nation. Thus, the minimum geographical entity relevant for our study is the nation state. There is, however, a trend towards expanding this regional focus to Europe as a whole, a key question in our study.

The paths for exploration are defined through a historical process of interplay between demand patterns and the domestic production structure. The existing range and specialization of products produced in a country largely reflect this process. The area of specialization of a country will in turn impact on which types of innovation will be predominant in a nation. This path dependency of innovation may in turn have implications for the patent system in that patent engineers specialize in accordance with the volume and complexity of the applications received. This is also an issue in the debate on centralization of the patent system in Europe in case a decentralized system is upheld: will small European countries then be able to attract a sufficient critical mass of applications within a certain technological field to generate the specialist knowledge needed for processing the still more complex technologies in the applications?[8]

Some of the knowledge valuable to innovations is produced in public laboratories, universities and other parts of the education system, which is primarily national. This knowledge infrastructure has become much more important in the past decade or more (Smith, 2000). Telecommunication systems, libraries, databases, education and vocational training systems are important elements in this infrastructure. The institutional infrastructure in other areas is largely national in character. Among important institutional factors are the financial institutions, the technological service institutions and the appropriability system, as well as more traditional infrastructures.

It should also be noted that there is nothing normative in the discussion above on the role of the nation. Even if the nation state, or even the region, does facilitate learning and innovation, cross-border harmonization may in some cases be beneficial, or even a prerequisite, for utilizing the diversity of nations in a manner promoting innovation (Johnson and Gregersen, 1997). They point to the patent system as one clear illustration of this argument, as is illustrated in the quotations below:

> Compatibility between institutions at the national and the European level is a key issue in the whole integration process. The development of a European patent system is a clear illustration on this. From its origins, the registration of a patent took place within a national legal system reflecting national specific regulations on intellectual property rights. Spurred by the ongoing European economic integration and the creation of the 'Single Market' the European Patent Office (EPO) was established under the Munich Convention of 1973 in order to facilitate industrial protection based on a unified system of registration, which ensures the protection of inventions simultaneously in several European countries. (p. 55)

> A diversity of innovation systems may be a prerequisite for safeguarding innovation potentials in Europe. Every attempt to build a European system of

> innovation should take this into account. However, convergence between national innovation systems in some respects, for example in terms of intellectual property rights, communication channels, administrative routines and technical standards may be a prerequisite for utilising other aspects of the diversity. (p. 69)

Even if a firm conclusion should not be derived solely from these statements, one may learn from this that harmonization should not necessarily be an end in itself. It may be so in some areas, but it should be considered carefully which areas should be harmonized and which should not.[9]

The discussion on the nation state as a framework for innovation processes and learning thus pointed to the need to explore in more detail the pros and cons of the physical location of national institutions such as the patent offices. As was mentioned, the location could be decentralized or centralized, as patent applications are largely codified knowledge. This was also one of the main points in the strength of ties discussion: in the case of the transfer of pure codified knowledge there may be no need for strong ties. In that case, in principle the patent granting authorities could be physically located anywhere in the world. Even if it is no doubt possible to mediate some of the potential learning between the parties by way of simple transfer of codified knowledge, we need to investigate whether the tacit element in the knowledge transfer is substantial and whether possible knowledge spillovers are localized.

3 THE DKPTO IN THE DANISH INNOVATION SYSTEM

It was argued in section 2 that the environment in which the learning processes take place is important for the outcome. Earlier research has shown that the national boundaries, and how the learning processes are institutionally embedded, matter for the interaction between the parties, in this case firms and the DKPTO. Therefore, defining the role of the DKPTO in the overall innovation system is not trivial; rather it is important to the understanding of the functioning of the DKPTO.

3.1 The Functions of the DKPTO – What do Patent Offices (also) Do?

The key task of the DKPTO is to offer protection for inventions, trademarks, copyrights and design.[10] The Patent Office issues patents to individual firms, the technological institutes, technology incubators and science parks. Furthermore, the Office offers consultancy services such as information services, guidance and training within the area of industrial property rights. In addition to handling patent applications and granting patents, the DKPTO sells business services. These services consist of a number of different products; the most important include novelty searches, infringement inquiries, state of the art inquiries, and analyses of competitors or profile analyses. Educational activities, information meetings, library and information services and courses are also offered. These business services constitute the other main part of DKPTO activities.[11]

The relationship with the patent agents is particularly important as the agents constitute a major group of customers of the DKPTO and because around two-thirds of all the applications filed at the DKPTO are filed via a patent agent. The patent agents' main job is to help companies to write patent applications and specify a patent strategy. This means that most communication goes through the agents, and it means that they are the main customers for a range of the services offered by the DKPTO. At the same time the patent agents are competitors of the patent office on some of the patent-based services. They do not have the right to issue patents and trademarks but they operate within the same business service areas such as courses, market analysis, searches on prior art and so on, as the patent office. Even if the patent agents are competitors they are at the same time customers and collaborators, such as when the DKPTO cooperates with patent agents to establish different courses on technical and legal issues concerning patenting.

The DKPTO also influences the innovation system in general indirectly because patent engineers trained within the DKPTO often move to industry. The knowledge embodied in people and the mobility of skilled people is an important channel of knowledge diffusion. In the case of this study the industry may be able to enhance its capabilities within the field of IPR by way of using these mobile patent engineers. The fact that experience of employment in the DKPTO is often mentioned as an asset in job advertisements from companies advertizing for patent engineers supports the notion of the DKPTO as a supplier to the industry of these competencies.

Furthermore, the DKPTO contributes to technical / professional literature on IPR, and the DKPTO stores patent descriptions for open disclosure. This is also a direct channel through which knowledge is diffused in the innovation system in general; in the words of Feldmann (1999) they are 'paper trails'. Initiatives have also been taken to reinforce cooperation with universities in order to incorporate IPR education into existing curricula of especially technical and natural sciences education (Ministry of Industry and DKPTO, 2001).

The patent system as such may play an important role for innovation. One policy objective of the patent system is to create incentives for investments in inventions by way of IPR protection. Another policy objective is that patents are a means of establishing a market for knowledge in that patents are traded as well as used for inspiration for technological development. The knowledge from published patents and patent descriptions can for instance be used for research purposes, and other companies have the chance to use such knowledge as a foundation for new innovations. Thus the system both helps to protect knowledge (thus giving an incentive to develop new knowledge), and it may help to diffuse knowledge in the economy. The possibilities for the companies to protect new knowledge and the publishing of patents are the two main arguments why governments support the system of intellectual property rights.[12 13]

3.2 Conclusion

The role of the DKPTO in the national system of innovation thus includes the incentive system described above to develop inventions, trademarks, design and information services, guidance and training in the area of industrial property rights. Moreover, the DKPTO participates in the policy process within the field of IPR. Thus, the review above on 'what patent offices do' showed that the DKPTO might happen to fulfil a knowledge diffusing function as well, especially through delivery of services.

In addition to business services the DKPTO is engaged in a number of activities, which entail interaction with other important actors in the Danish innovation system such as patent agents, science parks, incubators and the policy system. Although the DKPTO and patent institutions generally are most often classified in the literature on innovation systems as regulatory institutions, the interactions with other institutions and the role in 'educating' staff to competency in patenting, who are subsequently being employed in industry, points to a possible diffusion role as well.

4 EMPIRICAL ASSESSMENT OF KNOWLEDGE DIFFUSION FROM THE PATENTING PROCESS

This section explores quantitatively the learning effects discussed in section 2. This research has been pursued by analysing data from a survey designed for this special purpose. Quantitative methods to reveal complex phenomena like knowledge and competencies may only take us some of the way in understanding how the DKPTO operates and its role in innovation. One complication is that IPR are many other things than patents. Firms value different measures of appropriating returns from innovation differently (Arundel, 2001); even within the firm different products may require different strategies for protection. This is supported by an earlier survey of Danish manufacturing firms and their means of appropriation (DKPTO, 2000). In that survey it was found that patenting firms are also those who use other appropriability measures to a larger degree than the average firm (ibid., p. 14). That survey also confirmed other studies on what are the most frequently used measures for protecting product innovations. Sixty-one per cent of 451 responding firms used lead time advantages, 54 per cent secrecy. Patenting ranked fifth out of eight with 38 per cent of the sample having used it.

Our own survey was conducted among all Danish firms which either applied for a patent or used business services from the DKPTO within a three-year period. The questionnaire was developed through several iterations and then tested on a patent director in one of the largest firms in Denmark. It was inspired by the theoretical considerations developed in section 2. The survey was implemented by telephone interviews. The overall response rate was 290 out of 501, which is 57.9 per cent. This is satisfactory and is sufficient to make a breakdown by various variables. Moreover, the sample encompass the actual population. In other words, there is no way of increasing the number of respondents beyond what has been obtained, for example, by using more resources on interviews.

More details about the implementation of the survey may be obtained from this note.[14]

The presentation of results from the survey is organized in three sections. Firstly, structural characteristics of the firms in the database are highlighted. This section is kept relatively short, as most of this information can be obtained from the tables and needs few comments. Secondly, knowledge flows from the DKPTO and potential effects of these knowledge flows are analysed. Thirdly, the survey showed the opinions of firms on the importance of having a nationally localized patent institution.

The tables indicate the total number of firms relevant to each variable and the percentages denote the share of each catagory of the total. Some totals do not add up precisely to 100 per cent due to rounding. It should be added that we only present here a selection of the results. A number of other issues were covered in the survey but left out here.

4.1 The Characteristics of the Realized Sample

Basic characteristics of the realized sample are presented in Tables 6.1–6.5. The realized sample is broken down by size, number of patents applied for, year of establishment, year of first contact with the DKPTO and innovations.

One of the often-used background variables of data on innovation and innovation-related issues is the size of firms. Many surveys have found substantial differences across categories of firm size.

Table 6.1 shows our realized sample in the survey by firm size.

Table 6.1 Survey realized sample by firm size in full time employees

Number of employees	Number of firms	% of firms
0	3	2
1–9	52	27
10–99	52	27
100–499	47	24
>500	38	19
Do not know	3	2
Total	195	100

The average firm size was 280 with a median of 30. This, together with the fact that 43 per cent of firms in the survey had 100 or more employees, made our realized sample relatively large-firm dominated by Danish standards.

Even if intellectual property rights are indeed many other things than patents, it is often the patent activity of firms which is in focus in the literature and empirical investigations of IPR. In our sample several of the organizations interviewed would not be expected to have patents as they are natural buyers of services from the DKPTO but are not themselves developing new products or processes. One such example is research parks, which inform their companies about intellectual property rights and therefore need information and courses from the DKPTO, but they do not necessarily (although they could) have patents themselves. In the sample, patenting is nevertheless widespread. Thirty per cent of the firms had no patent applications. The average number of patent applications was 18 with a median of three.[15]

The year of establishment is an important parameter for understanding the interaction between the firms and the DKPTO, because it may be the case that young, or even new firms or single entrepreneurs, are less aware of the opportunities of interplay with the DKPTO. In somewhat the same vein the year of first contact with the DKPTO may be important information, because for example a large, old firm which has had a long-term, frequent contact with the DKPTO may not learn much from the DKPTO any longer, whereas the same firm may have benefited substantially during the first years of contact.[16] Tables 6.3 and 6.4 show these two features.

Table 6.2 Number of patent applications through the DKPTO in the period 1997–2001

Number of patent applications	Number of firms	% of firms
0	59	30
1–2	51	26
3–5	33	17
6–20	23	12
>20	23	12
Do not know	6	3
Total	195	100

Note: Survey question: How many patents did you apply for through the DKPTO during the past 5 years?

Table 6.3 Year of establishment

	Number of firms	% of firms
1960 or before	71	36
1961–1990	64	33
1991 or later	49	25
Do not know	11	6
Total	195	100

Note: Survey question: When was your company established?

Sixty-nine per cent of firms were established before 1991, indicating a sample of relatively large, old firms. On average firms were established in the year 1963 with a median of 1978. On average firms had their first contact with DKPTO in 1987, with a median of 1995. In Table 6.4 is added 95 firms who claimed that they had no direct contact. These firms are omitted in the other analyses in this paper.

It may be worth noting in Table 6.5 that the firms in the realized sample are also relatively innovative. Thus, at least 60 per cent have introduced an innovation within the past year. It is likely that the respondents answering 'do not know' (a large proportion of responses), are highly innovative, but just do not know the exact number of new products and processes.[17]

The average number of innovations was thirteen with a median of four innovations. Innovation intensity, calculated as the number of innovations divided by number of full time employees in the firm, was 0.86 and 0.1

mean and median, respectively. On average sixteen persons in the firm were occupied with innovative activity (median four persons).

Table 6.4 Year of first contact with DKPTO

	Number of firms	% of firms
1980 or before	43	15
1981–1990	34	12
1991–1997	50	17
1998 or later	54	19
Do not know	14	5
Had no direct contact	95	33
Total	290	100

Note: Survey question: When did you get in contact with the DKPTO for the first time?

Table 6.5 Number of innovations within the past year

	Number of firms	% of firms
0	26	13
1–2	37	19
3–9	45	23
10 or more	36	18
Do not know	51	26
Total	195	100

Note: Survey question: How many innovations did your company introduce within the past year?

4.2 Potential Effects of Knowledge Flows from the DKPTO

A first step towards accessing this question is to make clear to what extent knowledge flows actually take place. Asking the firms directly on this issue, both in relation to a specific task and more generally, we find that according to the firms in our survey the assessment of this varies from not at all (6 per cent of firms in the sample and 11 per cent of firms in relation to a specific task and general knowledge on IPR respectively) to a very large extent (14 per cent of firms and 9 per cent of firms). A majority characterized the knowledge generated through the interplay with the DKPTO to be to 'some degree' or more. It is to be expected that at least some learning effects would be reflected in the responses. It is, however, uncertain what level one should expect, as we do not have any good measures for comparison. The results in Tables 6.6 and 6.7 are consequently difficult to access. It is to be expected that knowledge flows are more productive in terms of learning when it is on a specific task. This seems indeed to be the case, although the differences are not large.

There were no differences between groupings of firms, such as firms of different size, number of innovations, year of establishment or first contact. This could be said to be somewhat surprising. One should perhaps expect small, new firms to learn more. This is not the case. In fact, if anything should be concluded on this issue it would be the opposite as there is a tendency among firms which claim to have learned nothing or only little on IPR generally from the DKPTO contact to be established in 1998 or later. The discussion in section 2 pointed to the fact that absorptive capacity of the recipient may promote learning. It may be that highly innovative or large firms are more prone to learn. Later we shall investigate this issue further.

When focusing upon firms which attach importance to learning in the DKPTO interplay we can assess more precisely what is learnt in the interaction. As displayed in Tables 6.6 and 6.7, 41 per cent of the firms attach either great or very large effects to the DKPTO interplay on specific tasks, whereas 57 per cent of the firms think the impact has been some, small or none. So-called 'high scores' (a five-point Likert scale has been used in the questionnaire with 5 = Not at all and 1 = Very much). Table 6.6 shows a considerable polarization of answers and a corresponding disagreement concerning the degree of learning from interacting with the DKPTO. Nevertheless, a substantial proportion of the respondents scored 'high' on this question.

Respondents were asked to specify the most important things they had learnt. Table 6.8 lists the contributions which received the highest scores.

The results show that firms primarily see the contribution of the DKPTO as increasing their general knowledge of IPR. Secondarily, the DKPTO plays a role in the application phase. These two are by far the most important contributions. Calculating what could be patterns with respect to firm size, number of innovations and so on, we find only weak relationships.

It is evident from the results that the direct stimulation of innovative capabilities is not seen as a major contribution from the DKPTO. This is ranked low in Table 6.8, and 45 per cent of firms see the contribution in this respect as zero. Compared to previous research on information sources for innovation, such as the results from the Community Innovation Surveys, this is not very surprising. Patent disclosures and institutions are generally assessed as having a minor importance as information sources for innovation activities.

Table 6.6 The degree of learning in the firm from interacting with the DKPTO on a specific task (%)

Not at all	To a small extent	To some degree	Much	Very much	Do not know	No. of firms
6	18	33	27	14	2	195

Note: Survey question: To what degree do you think that your contact with the DKPTO has increased the knowledge of the firm in relation to a specific task?

Table 6.7 The degree of learning from interacting with the DKPTO about knowledge on IPR generally (%)

Not at all	To a small extent	To some degree	Much	Very much	Do not know	No. of firms
11	22	29	25	9	4	195

Note: Survey question: To what degree do you think that your contact with the DKPTO has increased the knowledge of the firm on IPR in general?

Table 6.8 Contributions of DKPTO interplay, high scoring categories

Contribution	% of firms
Increase knowledge of and use of IPR generally	29
Guidance about applications	24
Increase knowledge of the competitors	15
Increase the general level of competence within the firm	11
Increase the technical know-how of the firm	9
Increase the ability to develop new products or processes	8
Increase the R&D activities of the firm	7
Strategy	6
Increase knowledge of the market	6
Relations to other knowledge institutions	5
Provide contacts and networks	5
Increase collaboration with other firms	3
Other contributions (share who list one or more)	23

Notes:
1. Survey question: Please assess effects of the services from the DKPTO on (several possibilities)?
2. High scores are calculated as the share of respondents answering 'Very large effect' + 'large effect' compared to all responding.
3. Number of firms: 191.

In section 2, the transfer of knowledge was discussed. It was pointed out that tacit knowledge may be best transferred by means of what we labelled relational transfer, whereas codified knowledge may be transferred efficiently through transactional transfer. The channels of knowledge transfer are only partly indicated in the results above. One specific channel, which we have better knowledge about, is the mobility of personnel between the DKPTO and the firms interviewed. Answers to the question 'Has your enterprise, now or previously, employed people previously employed with DKPTO', showed that 12 per cent confirmed that this has been the case. In other words, every 8th firm in the sample has had one or more former DKPTO workers on the staff. This is probably a minimum figure as it is likely that some respondents are not fully aware of all the previous jobs of the staff.[18]

One of the hypotheses generated from this could be that previous DKPTO employees would stimulate the knowledge of the firm and the specific use of IPR. However, when answers of previous DKPTO employees are combined with answers to the question whether DKPTO services have resulted in more knowledge and use of IPR, there are no clear patterns. This is somewhat surprising as the implications of the theoretical considerations in section 2 are that absorptive capacity should increase.

Another plausible hypothesis is that firms which employ DKPTO staff are more patent-active. It shows that patent intensity – calculated as the number of patents per employee – is 2.01 and 0.64 respectively in firms with/without former DKPTO staff (after cleaning for two extremes). This is a significant difference. One should, though, be careful about the interpretation of these figures, as the causality is not clear. On the one hand one may presume that firms with former DKPTO staff will increase their patenting as they have the expertise in-house and as they are presumably more aware of the possibilities and necessities in patenting. On the other hand, one may think that firms are inclined to hire DKPTO staff because they have increased their patenting and therefore need, or gain cost-effectiveness from having in-house expertise.

As mentioned above, it was emphasized in section 2 that an absorptive capacity is important in order to make knowledge useful and to facilitate knowledge diffusion in the economy. Although it may only be an approximation, the innovation intensity of firms may in some respects indicate an absorptive capacity, at least in the present connection where IPR is in question. Table 6.9 shows the average innovation intensity in two groups of firms with high or some learning effects from DKPTO and firms with low or no learning effects. In the survey firms were asked to list how many innovations they had introduced. The innovation intensity is then calculated as the number of innovations per employee in the firm in 2001. Statistical tests show that the averages are not significantly different within a 5 per cent level.

Table 6.9 Mean and median of innovation intensities in 'learning' and 'non-learning' firms

	Mean	Median	Number of firms
High/some learning effect of DKPTO	1.10	0.10	60
Small/no learning effect of DKPTO	0.53	0.10	43

Note: Survey question: see Tables 6.5 and 6.7.

Similar calculations have been done on the number of patents, number of innovations, size of firm and number of personnel in innovation. However, these analyses did not render statistically significant differences, although both the number of innovations and the number of patents did show some differences in favour of firms which had large learning effects from the DKPTO.

It could be that learning effects are related to the age of the firm. It is however, not totally clear what the most appropriate hypothesis is. On the one hand, one should expect old firms to have greater absorptive capacity and to have needs that are more specific and therefore perhaps lending themselves more readily to identification of the learning effects. On the other hand, it may be that firms over time generate their own expertise and consequently will have less need for the DKPTO services. Table 6.10 indicates that none of these hypotheses is valid. In fact, the two groups are remarkably alike.

Table 6.10 Mean and median years of establishment in 'learning' and 'non-learning' firms

	Learning			No learning		
	Mean year	**Median year**	**Number of firms**	**Mean year**	**Median year**	**Number of firms**
Years of establishment	1964	1975	98	1964	1980	67

Note: Survey question: see Tables 6.2 and 6.7.

Similarly, one may propose that the DKPTO is more likely to learn from firms the more innovative they are, measured by innovation intensities and number of patents. These two innovation indicators confirm our hypothesis that firms which provide knowledge to the DKPTO are innovative. However, the number of innovation personnel does not show that pattern.

With respect to learning in the DKPTO-firm interaction it seems fair to conclude that the results are not that strong. The main contribution from the DKPTO is apparently raising IPR awareness, and analysing characteristics of firms which do learn render a somewhat blurred picture.[19]

4.3 The Importance of Being Domestically Located

In section 2 we put forward arguments from the innovation systems literature and the literature on localized knowledge spillovers as to why the innovation system prevails as a national system and why knowledge spillovers may be spatially bounded. This includes the specific, national endowment of institutions in the innovation system. With respect to national patent offices, it has been explored whether such offices should be upheld or whether harmonization should entail not only legislation but also the organization (centralization) of patenting procedures.[20]

One of the important issues in the interviews was the opinion of firms as to how important it is to have a national patent office. Table 6.11 shows the overall distribution of answers on that question. Again, the assessment of the level of the percentages is difficult since there is no 'expected level of importance' against which to compare the answers of the firms. If anything, the answers indicate considerable disagreement concerning the importance of the DKPTO being a domestic institution. Half of the respondents attach none or small importance to the national location, but one third sees it as having large or very large importance. Differences across size categories are small. Only in the very large firm segment, is there a significant tendency to attach less importance to the domestic location of the patent office.

Table 6.11 Perceived importance of use of services of the DKPTO being a domestic patent office (%)

None/negative	Small	Some	Large	Very large	Do not know	Number of firms
38	10	20	20	11	2	195

Note: Survey question: To what degree was it important to your purchase of services from the DKPTO that the DKPTO is a national authority rather than, for example, a European authority?

The share of respondents who attach any importance (even if only small) to the location, were then asked to specify the importance (if any) of the following possibilities:

- avoiding language barriers,
- higher competences in treatment of applications,
- avoiding cultural barriers,
- better possibilities for dialogue,
- speed of treatment,
- price.

More than one option was open to the respondents. As mentioned, in this question it was a precondition that the respondent attached importance to the fact that the DKPTO is located nationally, as it would not make sense to ask about specific effects if no importance is attached at all. Consequently, the number of respondents was reduced from 195 to 120. The results can be seen in Table 6.12. The respondents thought the main advantages of dealing with a domestic patent office were related to better possibilities for dialogue and direct contact in the Danish language. This corresponds with previous discussions in section 2. The competencies do not seem to be an important parameter.

Table 6.12 Advantages of being nationally located, % of firms listing a reason

Advantages	**% of firms**
Better possibilities for dialogue	84
Avoiding language barriers	73
Speedy treatment	63
Avoiding cultural barriers	56
Higher competences in treatment of applications	24
Price	21
Other contributions (share who list one or more)	29

Notes:
1. Survey question: To what degree was it important to your purchase of services from the DKPTO that the DKPTO is a national authority rather than, for example, a European authority? If confirmed – Why was this important (various options)?
2. Number of firms: 120.

An important aspect in this connection is the potential difference between small and large firms, as one could presume that especially small firms could be inclined to prefer a national office. Therefore, the 120 firms were subdivided into two groups, one with an above median number of employees, another with below the median number of employees. The share of firms within these two groups listing reasons for the advantages of being domestically located are then listed in Table 6.13. From this, we may conclude that the tendency for small firms to be more in favour of a domestic location of the patent office is only very small and statistically insignificant.

Two other indicators relating to the issue of location of the patent office should be emphasized. First, it was asked if firms had within the past five years submitted one or more patent applications directly to the European Patent Office in Munich. The responses to this question were naturally conditional on two other questions, namely if they had made a patent application within the past five years and secondly if they were aware that a European Patent Office exists (78 per cent knew this). Out of the 153 respondents which met conditions, 27 per cent answered that they did so. There is a tendency that large, old firms have submitted directly to the EPO.

Table 6.13 Advantages of being nationally located, % of firms listing a reason by two size groups

Advantages	**Large firms** %	**Small firms** %
Better possibilities for dialogue	83	88
Avoiding language barriers	72	75
Speedy treatment	60	67
Avoiding cultural barriers	57	57
Higher competences in treatment of applications	19	30
Price	26	17

Notes:
1. Survey question: See Table 6.12.
2. Number of firms: 120.

Secondly, the firms were asked if patent application was made easier in any respect because a domestic patent office exists. Again, answers were valid only if respondents had made one or more patent applications. Seventy per cent of 89 relevant firms (those which had applied for at least one patent at the DKPTO) confirmed that indeed it had been easier to apply for a patent due to the domestic location of the patent office. No significant differences across firm size appeared.

4.4 Conclusion

The results from the survey showed a broader picture of the role of the DKPTO in innovation.[21] We have found that firms disagree concerning the question of learning from interacting with the DKPTO. There are 41 per cent of firms which attach 'large' or 'very large' effects when seen in connection with a specific task, and 34 per cent see 'large' learning effects on IPR issues generally. Approximately 60 per cent of the respondents, however, perceive learning from interacting with the DKPTO to be relatively modest.

This, in combination with other results from the survey, made us conclude that the effects on innovation of the DKPTO are primarily confined to increasing general awareness of IPR. Firms did not see the role of the DKPTO either as improving directly the capability of the firms to develop new products or processes, or as improving the R&D activities of the firm.

Twelve per cent of firms stated that their organization had hired people previously employed with the DKPTO. This is a source of knowledge diffusion alongside the role of the DKPTO in arranging seminars, courses, policy formulation and so on. Thus, although the learning effects with respect to innovation at first sight seem modest, the indirect effects in terms of stimulating knowledge valuable for the innovation process should not be overlooked.

Of the firms which did learn from the DKPTO, the innovation intensity is higher. Likewise, those which transfer knowledge from the firm to the DKPTO are more innovative and more patent intensive. This is an indication that they also have more absorptive capacity with respect to learning.

A third of the companies see the domestic location of the DKPTO as having large or very large importance. In particular, firms see advantages as more easy dialogue and being able to communicate in Danish. Thus, at least the communicative processes are likely to benefit from the availability of national entries to the patent system. This is partly confirmed by the responses concerning the advantages of nationally located patent authorities (Table 6.12). There are only minor indications that small firms are more prone to prefer a domestic location for the patent office.

5 CONCLUSIONS: THE GENERAL EFFECTS OF DKPTO ON KNOWLEDGE TRANSFER AND COMPETENCE BUILDING

It was contended in section 1 that the interaction between firms or individuals applying for patents and the patent office would add to the competencies of both parties. In the end, this may have positive effects on the innovative abilities of the firms and their awareness of and actual use of the IPR system. Moreover, the competencies in the patent office may increase as a result of this interplay.

Many tend to think of patent offices as performing relatively standardized procedures ending up in a 'stamp' saying yes or no to an application for a patent. A closer examination of the question 'what do patent offices actually do?' showed that the relationships of the DKPTO with external organizations are not just confined to industrial firms and to a simple granting of a patent. A wide array of other relations and activities are important in the overall picture of the role of the DKPTO in the innovation system. Although the DKPTO has direct contact with many firms, its indirect role as a provider of information and knowledge to other organizations should not be underestimated. It also says that the traditional classification of patent offices as exclusively regulatory institutions, may be too narrow. The research reveals that the DKPTO not only grants patents, it also has a complementary role as a knowledge-diffusing organization.

The DKPTO contributes to diffusion of knowledge in the economy, primarily by way of increasing the awareness of IPR among firms, according to the survey. For example, the increase in the knowledge of firms on the awareness and use of IPR generally, was ranked at the top of possible contributions from interacting with the DKPTO. In addition, there is a transfer of knowledge through a flow of qualified patent caseworkers from the DKPTO to the patent agents and to large industrial firms.

With respect to knowledge spillover in the innovation system as a whole, we thus found that interaction with the DKPTO does not seem to render much spillover of *technological* knowledge. We have seen clearly that firms do not attach great importance to the direct help of the DKPTO in Danish firms' innovation activities. This does not rule out that the DKPTO is an important part of the innovation system in Denmark. The office's role is, however, of an indirect character. As described earlier, the DKPTO is particularly important in raising awareness on IPR.

In conclusion, the results of this analysis concerning the general role of the DKPTO in the Danish national innovation system is that the DKPTO seems to contribute to general IPR awareness and to bring together the IPR branch by constituting a central focus point for common interests. There are some indications that the DKPTO serves a role in facilitating easy access to the patent system for firms by lowering the (cultural and linguistic) barriers to IPR protection. Moreover, there are indications that the DKPTO serves a function in training patent engineers who, after a period in the DKPTO, are employed in other organizations. The role of the DKPTO in terms of stimulating innovation directly seems to be modest,[22] but knowledge spillovers may nevertheless be considerable.

5.1 Perspective: A Harmonized Patent System: The Role of the National Location for Knowledge Spillovers

As mentioned in the introduction, the debate on the future European structure of the patent system has been long and intense. In particular, the debate has evolved arguments similar to the statement below:

> If the community patent system does go ahead, it will inevitably rely on the existing EPO structure in Munich to examine and grant the new single patent. … Some governments and national patent offices fear for their small and medium-

sized enterprises, which rely on national offices for advice and support on patent issues. … Governments and national patent offices have thus argued that a centralised system would deprive them of skills and revenues for which they should be compensated. (Financial Times, 8 October 2001)

Arguments against the above perspective have claimed that the alternative approach –a decentralized system, perhaps with a subcontracting organization where European patents are granted by national patent offices on behalf of the EPO – is against the principle of simplification. Moreover, it is feared that quality standards will diverge too far and that it will not be possible to uphold them in national patent offices without a critical mass of patent cases.[23] This may distort the harmonization, as it will urge firms to 'shop around' between offices.[24]

One may question if the above-mentioned functions could effectively be taken care of by the EPO, patent agents or some other institution. After many years of negotiations, the EU countries agreed on 3 March 2003 on basic principles for an EU patent. According to the compromise reached, the EPO will in the future be the only legal institution granting EU patents. The role of national patent offices will be to disseminate information and awareness of IPR issues and provide guidelines for how to fill in application forms. Under certain conditions and quality assurance standards the national organizations may also do novelty searches after agreement with the EPO.

This issue of centralizing or decentralizing the patent system was in fact part of our questions to respondents in the survey. Drawing upon section 2 and the results from the survey our answer concerning whether it would be an appropriate policy development to centralize the system is somewhat ambiguous. Certainly many firms, especially the large ones, would not mind if the functions mentioned were fulfilled by the EPO. On the other hand, we saw in the survey that firms may feel more confident with a national patent office in the proximity, with its familiar and national language. This was discussed in section 2, where knowledge flows were seen as depending on common codes of understanding and cultural and geographical proximity. These reasons for preferring a national location of the patent office were confirmed in our survey by the firms which preferred a domestic location. This revealed that about half (48 per cent) of the respondents attached small or no importance to having a national office while, on the other hand, about one third (31 per cent of firms) saw it as being of large or very large importance.

From a general European perspective, the question of the future role of national patent offices (NPOs) is highly relevant in this connection. The empirical evidence of this analysis does provide some knowledge on this, but does not allow a general conclusion concerning the possible obsolescence or indispensability of these institutions on a European level as this may differ from country to country.[25] The role of individual NPOs should therefore be carefully considered and balanced against the benefits of a pure centralization.

If the role of national patent offices only concerned the granting of patents *per se* rather than the full processing of applications, this may pose a problem, if other activities of the national patent offices such as business services and general information and awareness raising depend on these competencies. It may thus be argued that the possibility of preserving competencies at a national level (for example, by carrying out casework as a subcontractor to the EPO) is perhaps a prerequisite if the national patent offices are to play an important role in the innovation system. If the system is fully centralized, an alternative role for national patent authorities could be to increase the awareness among firms of IPR, especially in the small firm segment, and to continue the activities already pursued such as selling business services, courses and other information services, interaction with the policy system and acting as a nodal point for the actors in the innovation system who work with IPR.[26]

A further perspective may generalize the present case to the current political interest in Europe in stimulating interplay between knowledge institutions and industry. Although the DKPTO is not a higher education institution as is often thought of when this policy issue is discussed, it may resemble that type of institution. Often the US is referred to as a role model in this connection. It should be emphasized, though, that the close university-industry interaction in the US has not come about by coincidence. On the contrary, it may better be described as a cooperative movement, which stems from long-run, deliberate policies. Adams (2002, p. 275) points to the Morill Act of 1862 and the Hatch Act of 1887 as laying the foundation for subsequent policies on this university-industry interaction that is nowadays clearly reflected in data.

Adams also finds that knowledge spillovers are localized, especially those stemming from university research. In the light of this finding one may speculate whether there is a limit to how far away patent examination can be located if such spillovers are to be preserved. The present study points to a differentiated picture of what produces knowledge spillovers within the nation state, the geographical entity described as relevant for the policy question in the introduction. It should be remembered that there are important differences between patent offices and universities in this respect. University research may be characterized as open science with elements of tacit, interpersonal knowledge,[27] whereas patent offices are characterized by codified, closed knowledge.

ACKNOWLEDGEMENTS

The author wishes to thank Benjamin Coriat, Birgitte Andersen, Lee Davis, Dominique Foray and colleagues in the Department of Business Studies, Aalborg University, for comments on earlier drafts of this chapter. Thanks to Mia B. Rasmussen for valuable research assistance. Also thanks to ESST student Joseph Stewart, Texas, for language editing. I am grateful to patent manager Dan Nissen of Sauer Danfoss for critical assessment of an earlier draft of the questionnaire used in the survey. Special thanks also to Ole Kirkelund and Steffen Rebien of the DKPTO for comments on preliminary findings and earlier drafts, as well as written notes on the content in section 3. Finally, thanks to all the people who helped with information and data during the survey and interviews in the DKPTO. Full responsibility rests with the author.

NOTES

1. Knowledge spillovers are here defined in line with Griliches (1992) as flows of ideas and/or knowledge between agents at less than original costs ('..working on similar things and hence benefiting much from each other's research').
2. Throughout the chapter the term 'patent office' is used even if activities in these offices are broader within IPR, and not just confined to patents.
3. Freeman and Perez (for example, 1988) are among the early scholars arguing that especially the ICT revolution represents a qualitative new paradigm in the production mode. Several more recent works have followed this line of argument, often with the US development as an example (see for example, Thurow, 1997, who links this development to potential reforms of the IPR system).
4. Of course, production has to some degree always been knowledge-based and the concept is not new in economics. For example, Marshall stated that 'knowledge is our most powerful engine of production' (Principles, 1920). However, the importance of knowledge has greatly increased and has regained interest in economic theory. The latter renewal of interest in knowledge in economic theory is both carried by a group of non-neoclassical economists and a revisionist wave among more traditional economists, exemplified by the work of, for example, Krugman and Romer.
5. Griliches (1992) likewise argues that pecuniary externalities flow through the market but the main body (tacit knowledge transmitted through interpersonal interaction) of spillovers is transmitted relationally.
6. In practice, however, this is likely to be a special case. Even very special cases most often generate some kind of knowledge or experience which may be used elsewhere.
7. For some time there has been a general debate on the 'death of geography' between on the one hand scholars arguing that globalization has wiped out national differences, and on the other hand those who claim that the spatial dimension is still important (see for example writings by Krugman (1991, 2001) and Morgan (1997, 2004).
8. There is currently an application under consideration in WIPO, which is 110 000 pages long.
9. The implementation of the European Currency Unit (later developed into the European Monetary Union) is probably the best known example. Not all joined every step of the ECU project. Even if this issue is well researched it is still subject to controversies.

10. In 1999 the DKPTO received 1674 Danish patent applications and 221 foreign (DKPTO, Annual Report 1999). In the same year the EPO received 34 932 patent applications applying for patents in Denmark and 592 of the applications were from Denmark (EPO, Annual Report 1999).
11. Earlier in DKPTO history business services have shown a potential for growth. Interviews in both the Sales and Marketing section and in the Patent section suggest that the DKPTO could potentially increase the revenue of business services significantly. The revenue of business services has in recent years become stagnant (EUR 511 000 for technical services in 1998, 619 000 in 1999 and 592 000 in 2000). By contrast, rapid expansion was experienced in the mid-1990s (based on interviews, no statistical data available).
12. The Danish government supports international harmonization of patent standards and procedures. It also supports the EPO and an EU patent system. However, at the same time it is believed that fully qualified national patent offices play an important role in the environment for innovation and that is why the government supports the idea of the national patent offices as sub-suppliers to the EPO. This has been a Danish policy for several years. For example it was stated in the yearly publication on Danish industrial development and policy from 1995 that a Danish patent authority would still be needed in order to ensure that Danish firms have easy access to the IPR services they need. This is particularly important for small firms, which experience geographical, cultural and language differences as major barriers to the use of the central, European patent authorities in Munich (Ministry of Industry, 1995 pp. 187, Patent- og Varemærkestyrelsen, 2000).
13. Nevertheless, there are drawbacks to a patent system as well. It may be argued that the patent system distorts the allocation of resources as certain types of production are stimulated. Other traditional arguments are that the monopoly position of the patenting firm reduces consumer welfare, and that patents block further development of a product or technology. It may be worth emphasizing that assessing pros and cons against each other is extremely difficult. In a literature review Riis (2000) concludes that since the time when Machlup in 1958 claimed that we do not know if the patent system as such is economically beneficial for society, economic theory has still not reached a conclusion to this question (see also Mazzoleni and Nelson, 1998).
14. The questionnaire was designed to produce clear answers and to keep the interview within a limited time. The average time spent on the interviews was 12 minutes. The sampling was done using two sources. Our primary interests were firms who had both applied for a patent and had experience with services from the DKPTO. From the DKPTO, we obtained two databases, one of firms which applied for a patent within the past three years, and one of customers who bought services. These bases were 1865 and 625 firms respectively. The common share made up 143 firms. As our target was 200 interviews, the 143 firms were interviewed first, then supplemented with the base of services customers. The former list was reduced to 140 after cleaning for double registration of observations, closed down firms and so on, and the latter list made up 361 firms. Re-dials were set to 25 before giving up attempting to reach the relevant respondent. Three trained and carefully instructed interviewers undertook interviews in the period 11–27 September 2001. Neither the respondents nor the interviewers had problems with any of the formulations of the questions. As the resulting sample therefore seemed realistic or even perhaps too small compared to the target of 200 interviews, it was decided during the process to attempt to contact the entire sample. This resulted in 290 interviews of which 77 stem from the group of 140, that is firms that applied for at least one patent. In this group, the response rate is thus 54%. The overall response rate was 290/501 = 57.9%, which is satisfactory, especially considering that complete abstention from participation happened in only 49 cases, and 30 interviews were terminated before completion. The remaining 132 non-responding cases proved to be either non-existent, or for other reasons could not be contacted. As mentioned, 77 interviews were performed with firms which were in the group of 140. Out of the remaining 213 firms interviewed, a surprising 95 firms claimed to have had no contact with the DKPTO. This relatively large share is surprising considering that the firms are listed in the customer base of the DKPTO Sales and Marketing Department. The interviews with these 95 firms were consequently terminated after only a few questions

(three minutes). Our realized sample thus consisted of 195 useful interviews. Non-responses were unsystematically distributed. We can therefore regard the data as reflecting the total population and no weighting of the data was necessary. There were large differences in who were the relevant respondents in the firms. In large firms there may be a special department dealing exclusively with intellectual property rights, whereas in small firms it may be the owner. There were a large number of firms that had the head of production/products handling these matters. Consequently, the interviews started with a filter process, identifying the relevant person to be interviewed. In order to make clear that the interview was not solely on patenting but rather a broader range of services from the DKPTO the subject of the interview was mentioned explicitly in the introduction, and more precise examples were given of services. Many firms use patent agents to handle matters regarding their intellectual property rights. As we were particularly interested in the effect of the DKPTO, respondents were asked to state if they used patent agents alongside the DKPTO (60% of the group of firms in the sample with previous experience of patent applications claimed to have used patent agents for services). They were subsequently asked to disregard the cases where only patent agents handled their case.

15. In a survey by the DKPTO (2000) the median of patents granted was also three. The two surveys are not directly comparable because the DKPTO survey focused upon SMEs within the manufacturing industry, whereas this survey covers all industries and all size categories. The medians will, though, tend to be fairly equal.
16. In a pilot test of the questionnaire a large Danish firm emphasized this point.
17. This was the case in the pilot test of the questionnaire. The test respondent would answer that question with ‘ many’, as he was not able to have a sense of the correct figure.
18. The estimation of the number of former DKPTO employees is likely to be underestimated for other reasons: once the employee has been working for some time in the new firm, the respondents do not think of that colleague as having benefited from external knowledge upgrading. Moreover, the need to interact with the DKPTO may be reduced when DKPTO employees are hired. The former DKPTO employees are primarily hired by large, innovative firms with a long record of DKPTO contact.
19. However, the analyses have so far assumed linear relationships between learning and our independent variables. As suggested in section 2 there might be inverted u-shaped learning effects.
20. See for example Koper (2001) for an account of the discussion seen from the perspective of the EPO.
21. In order to further verify and go deeper into the issues in the survey seven in-depth case studies were undertaken. They are reported in Christensen (2004). These case studies rendered roughly the same picture as that of the survey.
22. This is after all no big surprise considering the results of innovation research in general and the ranking of information sources for innovation, as has been displayed in numerous studies on innovation, for example studies using CIS-data.
23. It is highly uncertain, and subject to further research, to determine what more precisely is a critical mass in a world of rapidly changing technologies.
24. See in particular Koper (2001).
25. Of course this would not affect all members of the EPO equally. The role of national patent offices in national innovation systems differs from one country to another. These differences could be subject to further research through comparative analyses, which might give an overview of the effect of centralization at a cross-European level. In particular, it would be interesting to study whether it has actually been the case that patent expertise is indispensable and if it has in fact vanished in those countries which ceased to have a national examination procedure.
26. Today the DKPTO is regarded as such a ‘community creating’ organization since it arranges meetings for ‘the branch’ and its network to the other parties dealing with IPR-related issues.
27. This may explain why Adams (2002) finds that university spillovers are more significant than industry spillovers and that spillovers from consulting and so on are more localized.

BIBLIOGRAPHY

Adams, James D. (2002), 'Comparative localization of academic and industrial spillovers', *Journal of Economic Geography*, **2**, pp. 253–78.

Andersen, Birgitte (2004), 'If "intellectual property rights" is the answer, what is the question? Revisiting the patent controversies', *Economics of Innovation and New Technology*, **13**(5), pp. 417–42.

Arrow, K.J. (1974), *The Limits of Organization*, New York: W.W. Norton.

Arundel, A. (2001), 'The relative effectiveness of patents and secrecy for appropriation', *Research Policy*, **30**, pp. 611–24.

Branstetter, L. (1996), *Are Knowledge Spillovers International or Intranational in Scope? Microeconometric Evidence from the US and Japan*, NBER Working Paper 5800, Cambridge, MA: NBER.

Breschi, S. and Lissoni, F. (2003), *Mobility and Social Networks: Localised Knowledge Spillovers Revisited*, paper for DRUID winter conference, Rebild, January.

Christensen, Jesper L. (2003), 'Changes in Danish innovation policy: responses to the challenges of a dynamic business environment', in Biegelbauer, P.S. and Borras, S. (eds) *Innovation Policy in Europe*, Aldershot: Ashgate Publishers.

Christensen, Jesper L. (2004), 'Inter- and intraorganisational learning processes in the interaction between firms and patent offices', in Christensen, J.L. and Lundvall, B.-Å. (eds) *Learning, Product Innovation, and Performance*, Elsevier Publishers.

Cohen, W. and Levinthal, D. (1989), 'Innovation and learning: the two faces of R&D', *The Economic Journal*, **99**, pp. 569–96.

Coriat, B. and Orsi, F. (2001), *The Installation in the United States of a New Regime of Intellectual Property Rights – Origins, Content, Problems*, paper for DRUID conference in Aalborg, June.

DKPTO (1999), Annual report, Taastrup: DKPTO.

DKPTO (2000), 'Små og mellemstore fremstillingsvirksornheders barrierer for produktudvikling og patentering', Taastrup: IFO, Institutter for Opinionsanalyse.

Dosi, G., Freeman, C., Nelson, R., Silverberg, G. and Soete, L. (eds) (1988), *Technical Change and Economic Theory*, London: Francis Pinter and New York: Columbia University Press.

EPO (1999), Annual report, Munich: EPO.

Erhvervsfremme Styrelsen and Patent- og Varemærkestyrelsen (2001), Kompetenceudvikling og uddannelse på eneretsområdet, Copenhagen.

Feldman, M.P. (1999), 'The new economics of innovation, spillovers and agglomeration: a review of empirical studies', *Economics of Innovation and New Technologies*, **8**, pp. 5–25.

Foray, D. (1997), 'Generation and distribution of technological knowledge', in Edqvist, C. (ed.), *Systems of Innovation: Technologies, Institutions, and Organisations*, London: Pinter.

Foray, D. (2000), *Rachid and Joe: On the Essence of the Knowledge Economy*, paper for DRUID conference, Rebild, June.

Freeman, C. and Perez, C. (1988), 'Structural crises of adjustment: business cycles and investment behaviour', in Dosi, G., Freeman, C., Nelson, R., Silverberg, G. and Soete, L.(eds) *Technical Change and Economic Theory*, London: Francis Pinter and New York: Columbia University Press.

Gertler, M, Wolfe, D. and Garkut, D. (2000), 'No place like home? The embeddedness of innovation in a regional economy', *Review of International Political Economy*, **7**(4), pp. 688–718.
Granovetter, M. (1973), 'The strength of weak ties', *American Journal of Sociology*, **78**, pp. 1360–80.
Griliches, Z. (1992), 'The search for R&D spillovers', *Scandinavian Journal of Economics*, **94**, pp. 29–47.
Hansen, M. (1998), 'The search-transfer problem: The role of weak ties in sharing knowledge across organization subunits', *Administrative Science Quarterly*, **44**, pp. 82–111.
Jaffe, A.B., Trajtenberg, M. and Henderson, R. (1993), 'Geographic localisation of knowledge spillovers as evidenced by patent citations', *Quarterly Journal of Economics*, **10**, pp. 577–98.
Johnson, B. and Gregersen, B. (1997), *European Integration and National Systems of Innovation*, unpublished paper produced within the Innovation Systems and European Integration research project CTSER programme.
Kleinknecht, A., van Montfort, K. and Brouwer, E. (2002), 'The non-trivial choice between innovation indicators', *Economics of Innovation and New Technologies*, **11**(2), pp. 109–21.
Koper, Ingo (2001), *Involvement of National Offices in the European Patent Grant Procedure in Return for the Creation of a Community Patent*, Note from EPO, The Presidency, September.
Kristensen, P. and Vinding, A. (2001), 'Exchange of employees, prototypes and use of electronic media in product development collaboration: results from a Danish survey', in OECD, *Innovative Networks*, Paris: OECD.
Krugman, P. (1991), *Geography and Trade*, Cambridge, MA: MIT Press.
Krugman, P. (2001), 'The spatial economy: introduction', in Fujita, M., Krugman, P. and Venables, A.J. (eds) *The Spatial Economy*, Cambridge, MA: MIT Press.
Lundvall, B.-Å. (1988), 'Innovation as an interactive process – from user-producer interaction to the national system of innovation', in Dosi, G., Freeman, C., Nelson, R., Silverberg, G. and Soete, L. (eds) *Technical Change and Economic Theory*, London: Pinter Publishers.
Lundvall, B.-Å. (eds) (1992), *National Systems of Innovation: Towards a Theory of Innovation and Interactive Learning*, London: Pinter Publishers.
Marshall, A. (1920), *Principles of Economics*, 8th edition, London: McMillan.
Mazzoleni, R. and Nelson, R.R. (1998), 'The benefits and costs of strong patent protection: a contribution to the current debate', *Research Policy*, **27**, pp. 273–84.
Meeus, M.T.M., Oerlemans, L.A.G. and Hage, J. (2001), 'Patterns of interactive learning in a high-tech region', *Organization Studies*, **22**(1), pp. 145–72.
Ministry of Industry (1995, 1997), *Erhvervsredegørelse*, Denmark: Danish Ministry of Industry.
Ministry of Industry and DKPTO (2001), 'Kompetencepudvikling og uddannelse på eneretsområdet – en behovsanalyse', Copenhagen.
Morgan, K. (1997), 'The learning region: institutions, innovation and regional renewal', *Regional Studies*, **31**(5), pp. 491–503.
Morgan, K. (2004), 'The exaggerated death of geography: localised learning, innovation and uneven development', *Journal of Economic Geography*, **4**, 3–21.
Ordover, J. A. (1991), 'A patent system for both diffusion and exclusion', *Journal of Economic Perspectives*, **5**(1), pp. 43–60.

Patent- og Varemærkestyrelsen (2000), *Management and Evaluation of Patents and Trademarks*, Taastrup: Ernst & Young and Ementor Management Consulting.
Patent- og Varemærkestyrelsen (2001a), *Videnregnskab 2000*, Taastrup: DKPTO.
Patent- og Varemærkestyrelsen (2001b), *Partner i innovation: service til erhvervslivet*, Taastrup: DKPTO.
Podolny, J.M., Stuart, T. and Hannan, M.T. (1996), 'Networks, knowledge, and niches: competition in the worldwide semiconductor industry 1984–1991', *American Journal of Sociology*, **102**, pp. 659–89.
Riis, T. (2000), 'Patentrettens økonomiske begrundelse og function', *Samfundsøkonomen*, **3**.
Rivera-Batiz, L. and Romer, P. (1991), 'Economic integration and endogenous growth', *The Quarterly Journal of Economics*, **106**, pp. 531–55.
Shane, S. and Cable, D. (2002), 'Social relationships and the financing of new ventures', *Management Science*, **48**, pp. 364–81.
Smith, K. (2000), What is the 'Knowledge Economy'? Knowledge-Intensive Industries and Distributed Knowledge Bases, paper for DRUID summer conference, Aalborg, June.
Smith, K. (2001), Cross-country comparisons: comparing economic performance in the presence of diversity, *Science and Public Policy*, **28**(4), pp. 267–76.
Sorenson, O. and Stuart, T. (2001), 'Syndication networks and the spatial distribution of venture capital investments', *American Journal of Sociology*, **106**, pp. 1546–88.
Stiglitz, J.E. (1987), 'Learning to learn, localized learning and technological progress', in Dasgupta, P. and Stoneman, P. (eds) *Economic Policy and Technological Performance*, Cambridge: Cambridge University Press, pp 125–53.
Storper, M. (1992), 'The limits to globalisation: technology districts and international trade', *Economic Geography*, **68**(1), pp. 60–93.
Stuart, T. and Sorenson, O. (2003), 'The geography of opportunity: spatial heterogeneity in founding rates and the performance of biotechnology firms', *Research Policy*, **32**, pp. 229–53.
Thurow, L. (1997), 'Needed: a system of intellectual property rights', *Harvard Business Review*, **75**(5), pp. 95–103.

7. The determinants of patentees' use of 'continuation' patent applications in the United States Patent and Trademark Office, 1980–99

Stuart J.H. Graham

ABSTRACT

This chapter describes and examines the use of the 'continuation' patent application procedure available in the United States but not generally elsewhere in the world. The continuation procedure allows a US patent applicant to postpone the issue of a patent, affording inventors several strategic opportunities, among which are delay and secrecy. The chapter also demonstrates the perverse effects of so-called 'submarine patents', continuation patents that surface in a marketplace in which the patented technology has been widely embraced by adopters unaware that a valid patent was pending and hidden from view. In addition to examining several specific cases of submarine patents – cases in which the patentee was able to extract extraordinary economic rents – the chapter investigates through negative binomial regression the determinants of patentees' use of the continuation procedure. Continuations are shown to be significantly more likely when the resulting patent is held by an organization, is held by a domestic (US) entity, is comprised of more patent claims, or is drawn from a wider breadth of technologies. The chapter also examines how and why innovators in the semiconductor and pharmaceutical technologies have employed the continuation patent application procedure, demonstrating that in each of these important sectors the continuation procedure has been widely used, and may offer strategic benefits.

Keywords: Patents, Submarine patents, Patent continuation applications, Intellectual property strategy

> ... [The patent holder, Jerome Lemelson] has a history of using continuing patent applications in such a way that results in patents issuing several decades after the related disclosures were first included in earlier applications. Whether accidentally or purposefully, this application prosecution technique has resulted in an intricate web of applications and patents that can be traced by reference (if not by invention) back to two patent applications originally filed in the mid-1950s. Lemelson benefits from this practice by asserting the early effective filing dates of those original applications, turning all intervening systems and devices that employ such technology into infringers. (Judge Atkins, *Ford Motor Company vs. Jerome Lemelson* (16 June 1995))

1 INTRODUCTION

'Gamesmanship' has been defined as the practice of winning games by using questionable methods without actually violating the rules.[1] Difficulties associated with patent gamesmanship are legion in commercial enterprise: in the hurly-burly of head to head competition, a firm with a pending patent application may face competition from rivals reverse engineering the firm's product in order to sell competing goods that do not copy but are nevertheless intended to function similarly. Subsequently, agents of the patenting firm will often alter the pending patent application to cover the rivals' new concepts that they consider within the bounds of their original invention. This type of 'commercial gamesmanship' has been supported by the US courts as a proper use of the patent system (*State Industries, Inc. v. A.O. Smith Corp.*, 751 F.2d 1226, 1235 (Fed. Cir. 1985); *Kingsdown Medical Consultants, Ltd. v. Hollister Inc.*, 863 F.2d 867, 874 (Fed. Cir. 1985)).

A less welcomed, but nevertheless practised, form of patent 'gamesmanship' occurs when patentees use a 'submarine patent application'. The archetypical 'submarine patent', characterized by an unusually long period of pre-issue secrecy and delay, is granted into a marketplace in which the patented technology has been widely adopted, thus making these prior uses now infringing the recently issued patent. The patent is thus like the naval submarine: it surfaces from a secret place to menace the lanes of commerce. The phenomenon of 'pre-issue' secrecy in patenting is unique to the United States among the industrialized countries, and is described in section 2 of this chapter below. Circumstances surrounding a number of Jerome Lemelson's patents covering 'bar coding' and 'machine vision' have become exemplars of the submarine patent strategy. Originally filed in the 1950s, several of Lemelson's patent applications were kept secret inside the US Patent and Trademark Office (USPTO or 'Patent Office') while Lemelson and his patent attorney altered the claims of the original patents to cover later-created products and adoptions of the technologies. When Lemelson finally allowed his patents to issue, some had been secreted for almost 40 years. For instance, his US patent 5 283 641, 'Apparatus and methods for automated analysis' was granted on 1 February 1994, but its original filing date was 24 December 1954. The method used by Lemelson to 'submarine' these patents was the 'continuation' application available at the USPTO: in the case of US patent 5283641, Lemelson had used no fewer than eleven continuation applications during the 39 years that the application languished in the Patent Office.

The continuation is a procedure available under the US patent laws that gives a patent applicant the right to extend the period of pre-issue pendency before the patent examiner's final patentability decision can take effect. This procedure gives an applicant effective control over the timing of the patent's grant. The first in what may become a long string of applications wins for the applicant a 'priority date', this date being subsequently applied to all later continuation applications. Thus the applicant captures with the first filing a presumption of having been 'in the Patent Office door' early. Furthermore, during the period of extended continuation delay, the applicant has the opportunity to file amendments to the original application, preserving for an applicant the opportunity to engage in patent 'gamesmanship'. Because prior to 1999 all applications enjoyed secrecy until grant in the United States – and even after 1999 a subset of patent applications enjoy this benefit – the benefits to gamesmanship are magnified.

The potential economic consequences of the most notorious type of gamesmanship, submarine patenting, are illustrated by the actions taken by Lemelson and his attorney as regards the 'bar coding' patents: they practised economic hold-up on large firms in major industries that had adopted these technologies. Armed with these late-emerging patent rights, and with the threat of court action and possible injunction, Lemelson and his attorney demanded licensing fees first from Japanese, and then US automakers, firms that by the 1990s were using the technology extensively throughout the value chain. By practising just such economic hold-up, using threatening costly infringement litigation, large damage award demands and injunctions used to shutter operations, Lemelson and his attorney are estimated to have collected $1 billion in fees and settlements from firms in many industries (Albright, 2004).

Because the 'continuation' procedure is unavailable in the other major industrialized nations (Europe and Japan), it comes as a surprise to many observers that Lemelson was allowed to use the US patent laws to practise such a hold-up strategy. This strategy, permitted by the courts and by Congress, appears to run afoul of the basic *quid pro quo* that is often used to justify the patent regime: the public will offer to inventors limited monopolies over their inventions, creating incentives to encourage investment in research, while inventors will in turn give to the public a timely disclosure of these ideas so that follow-on innovation will not be unduly retarded, and the invention itself will ultimately be made available for public use after the limited monopoly expires. To an economist, it is no surprise that Lemelson engaged in a submarine strategy – he appears to have been rationally maximizing the expected returns from the patent right. When general adoption of a technology is comparatively slow, and firms may be expected to deploy substantial complementary assets alongside the adopted technology thus 'locking-in' to the technical regime, the type of delay and hold-up strategy practised by Lemelson can be quite beneficial to the patent holder, as evidenced by the enormous rents he captured from industry. More confounding to observers, however, is the recognition that the courts and Congress created the 'continuation' procedure at all, and allowed it to operate for well over a century, unimpeded by meaningful equitable limits on its use by applicants.

Despite the fact that the continuation procedure is only available in the United States, innovators and researchers around the world should be familiar with its ramifications. First, the United States is a large and important market for many goods, particularly in technology products, and innovations from outside the US are often embodied in products sold in the US, thus opening non-US innovators to infringement liability under the US patent laws. Second, the US is also an important intellectual property market, with a substantial share of US patents now issuing to non-US firms. This demand for US patents opens foreign entities to the operations of the US patent laws, and thus the continuation procedure is both a strategic opportunity and a strategic risk to any firm that either sells, or patents, in the US.

The continuation could historically be used to hide the original application and all subsequent amendments for extended periods of time, and it was the method used by Lemelson and others to keep applications secreted. In 1995, however, Congress changed the Patent Act in ways that appear to have removed some of the patentees' incentives for engaging in continuation practice. By changing the patent term from 17 years from date of grant to 20 years from date of application filing, the Congress intended to force those patentees using the continuation to choose between *ex ante* grant delay and *ex post* property rights (see section 2.1 below). While the new legislation reduced the incentives motivating patentees, it did not completely eliminate incentives to use, or the actual use by, patent applicants of continuation practice.

This practice by patentees, both before and after the 1995 regime change, raises a number of questions. First, what are the determinants of continuation practice by patentees? Second, what effect has the 1995 legislation had on the use by patentees of the continuation procedure? Third, are there significant differences in the incidence of continuation practice by industry or technology sector and if so, have these differences persisted since the incentive changes brought about by the 1995 regime change? I employ data on the use by patent applications of 'continuation' practice in the USPTO from 1980–99 to shed light on these questions.

To that end, this chapter analyses the continuation's use by applicants in several important industrial sectors, and empirically examines the determinants of the incidence of the continuation application's use in US patenting. The chapter is organized as follows. Part two describes continuation practice and the 1995 policy changes meant to reduce the incentives for its use. Part three examines the available data on continuation application use in several important sectors, notably pharmaceutical and semiconductor technologies. Part four conducts regression analysis to shed light upon the determinants of patentees' use of the continuation application. Part five offers observations and conclusions.

2 CONTINUATION APPLICATION PRACTICE UNDER THE US PATENT LAW

In the United States, inventors enter into a complex application process when seeking a patent. Inventors may claim a utility patent[2] on processes, machines, manufactures, or compositions of matter by making application to the United States Patent and Trademark Office (USPTO or 'Patent Office'). Procedurally, the application must be filed within one year of the invention's public use or publication[3] and must contain an adequate description with one or more claims.[4] Before the patent issues, the Patent Office ensures that the invention covers patentable subject matter,[5] is useful,[6] novel,[7] and not obvious.[8] The patent examiner, a Patent Office employee with specialized technical knowledge, is the initial arbiter of these requirements.[9] Prosecution of the patent has been characterized as a 'give-and-take-affair', with negotiation and re-negotiation between the patentee and the patent examiner that ordinarily continues for an average of 2–3 years (Merges, *et al.*, 1997).[10]

There is a wide variance in the elapsed time between application date and issue, however, and Patent Office processes can be 'gamed' to use time to advantage. Data show that applications pend, in reality, for as little as several months to as much as several decades and, while technological complexity and examiner expertise are certainly major determinants, applicants exert substantial control over their applications' pendency periods. Such control would be advantageous in the light of the absolute secrecy that applications historically enjoyed (prior to 1999) before issue. While the 'give and take' of negotiation with the Patent Office provides an applicant with a limited opportunity to delay the examiner's decision, patent applicants may be using the 'continuation' mechanism to achieve longer pendency for their applications – and thus longer periods of secrecy. The continuation, an institutional mechanism, allows the patentee to keep the invention under a cloak of secrecy for longer than the 2–3 year average for first applications, and provides a means for the applicant to exert considerably more control over pre-issue secrecy than simple negotiation with the examiner.

The 'continuation' patent regime in the United States appears to be a result more of historical path dependence than of sound economic and social policy making. Continuation applications have been available to patentees in the United States at least since 1863. In *Godfrey v. Eames*, 68 US 317 (1863), the US Supreme Court interpreted the Patent Act of 1836 to allow continuation applications; in that case when the original application was abandoned on the same day that the new continued application was filed. The court appeared to be offering the patentee an opportunity to keep an application alive in a situation that, otherwise, would have led to injustice. It is a feature of the form of common law used in the United States, with its adherence to precedent, that singular cases – even if correctly decided – can produce general rules that are inappropriate for judging the broader class of phenomena to which the rule applies. Thus, the continuation procedure in US patenting became a feature of the law, being upheld decades later by the Supreme Court in *Crown Cork & Seal Co. v. Gutmann Co.*, 304 US 159 (1938) and *General Talking Pictures Corp. v. Western Electric Co.*, 304 US 175 (1938). The continuation remained judge-made law for over a century, but the procedure was finally codified in statute by the US Congress in the Patent Act of 1952. It appears that Congress made relatively few judgements about the propriety or welfare consequences of its actions in passing the 1952 Patent Act: it is clear from legislative histories that the Congress simply intended to codify the existing state of judge-made law into federal law.[11]

Continuations are currently authorized under the patent statute[12] and allow an applicant under certain conditions[13] to adopt the date of an earlier application still pending within the patent office. The essential condition for the filing of a continuation is that both the first and the new applications must disclose the same invention. An application may remain hidden for extended periods of time if the original application is abandoned by the patentee. Since there are no limits to the number of times this abandonment may occur, chains of continuations may develop, as evidenced by Lemelson's bar-coding patent with its string of eleven continuations and abandonments. A strategic applicant can, in this manner, keep inventions secret for an extended period of time.

Without other benefits, however, a rational strategic applicant would have no incentive to seek a period of added secrecy through continuation.

On its face, the continuation appears to offer no advantage over extended and exclusive trade secret protection, while imposing costs through early payment of fees, expenditures for prosecution, and added risks of valuable information 'leaking' from the Patent Office to competitors.[14] But the patent applicant does receive a significant benefit from a chain of continuations – an early 'filing date'. In the US 'first to invent' patent system, the filing date is a government-sanctioned recognition that the applicant had reduced an invention to practice by that date. A competitor claiming an earlier invention date must show why it was not diligent in reducing the invention to practice or had otherwise delayed the filing.[15] Additional benefit is offered to the applicant through a legally recognized protection of the common law rights to trade secret protection during pendency of the application.[16] Thus, the patent applicant historically retained secrecy of invention throughout the application period.

The patent regime in place prior to 1995, moreover, enabled the applicant to extend this period of secrecy virtually without limit. Because the patent term was 17 years after issue and there were no requirements that applications be published prior to issue, patentees could protect their priority dates based upon filing for many years before beginning their patents' monopoly protections. Continuation allowed the strategic applicant to manage this process, both in terms of timing and technological change.

2.1 Changes in the US Patent Law, 1995

As part of a series of statutory modifications meant to harmonize US law with its international trading partners, Congress altered the patent regime's seventeen-year term in 1995. Measuring the patent term from issue rather than application date had put US law out of step with most of the world while also creating incentives for 'submarine' patenting (Lemley, 1994). The 1995 legislative changes which followed the GATT trade talks[17] altered the US patent laws that had supported the submarine practices. By increasing the patent term from seventeen to twenty years, the new legislation offered patentees some additional *de jure* length, but began measuring the patent term from the application date instead of the issue date. The Act's legislative history demonstrates that this change was intended to eliminate some of the incentives to engage in 'submarine' patenting by forcing the patentee to 'trade off' *ex ante* secrecy for *ex post* protection. Users of the continuation, and particularly submarine patenters, would henceforth have a maximum of 20 years to delay the patent's grant, and each extra day of delay would come at the cost of one day of protection (see Table 7.1).

Table 7.1 Comparison of the benefits to patentees of using the continuation application, pre- and post-1995 regime change

Time Period	Patent Protection	Application Secrecy	Trade-off
Pre-1995	17 years from date of patent grant	No time limits in the law	None (apart from delaying the beginning of patent protection)
Post-1995	20 years from date of application filing	20 years maximum, after which the application sunsets	Each additional day of secrecy chosen results in one lost day of patent protection

While the 1995 legislation reduced a strategic applicant's incentives to engage in continuation practice, it nevertheless did not entirely eliminate these incentives. The statute was engineered to reduce 'submarine' incentives while also offering a longer patent term, by granting each patentee a maximum twenty-year window in which to both prosecute his application and enjoy the benefits of patent protection. So long as patent prosecution lasted less than three years, a patentee could enjoy an added benefit – a longer patent term than had been available under the 17-year term provided by the previous law. For inventors considering a continuation strategy, the legislation required that the applicant weigh the present value of early priority, coupled with extended *ex ante* non-disclosure, against added patent protection at the end of the patent term. Patentees whose value in early priority and a period of relatively lengthy pre-issue secrecy outweighed that of late term patent protection retained an incentive under the new statutory scheme to resort to continuation practice.

Because the continuation process is expensive and the rational applicant would avoid the investments in monetary fees and time that it entails, a non-strategic continuation is probably the result of information asymmetries between applicants and examiners concerning the technology (that the applicant may understand better) or the application process (that the examiner may understand better). These asymmetries are more likely in the presence of technological newness. When the subject matter of the patent is a new technology, applicants and their agents – as well as the examiners – have had limited time in which to learn the technology, and all parties face increased uncertainty about its patentability. Information asymmetries can also be expected to increase with technological complexity.

2.2 Data Analysis: Continuation Patents

To shed light upon patentees' uses of the continuation, as well as its importance as an economic phenomenon, the overall trend in the use by patentees of continuations from 1980–1999 is presented in graphic form in Figure 7.1. This plots the fraction of patents issued in each of the listed years that had at least one continuation[18] in application lineage. The data thus represent only the terminal patent, the patent that emerges at the end of the chain of continuations. Because some applications may have been abandoned, this terminal patent may be the only evidence of a continuation chain. The data in Figure 7.1 are based upon issue date, and not upon application date because, under continuation practice, the recorded application date for what is essentially the final application in a chain of continuations is a somewhat artificial measure. Issue dates are a more meaningful metric of the use by patentees of the procedure because the issue date is one over which the applicant exercises a greater deal of control than in the 'normal' single-application patent case, and gives an indication of when, within a certain distribution, the patentee intends the period of secrecy to end.[19]

These numbers suggest that the continuation remains an important economic phenomenon, accounting for at least 17 per cent and as much as 31

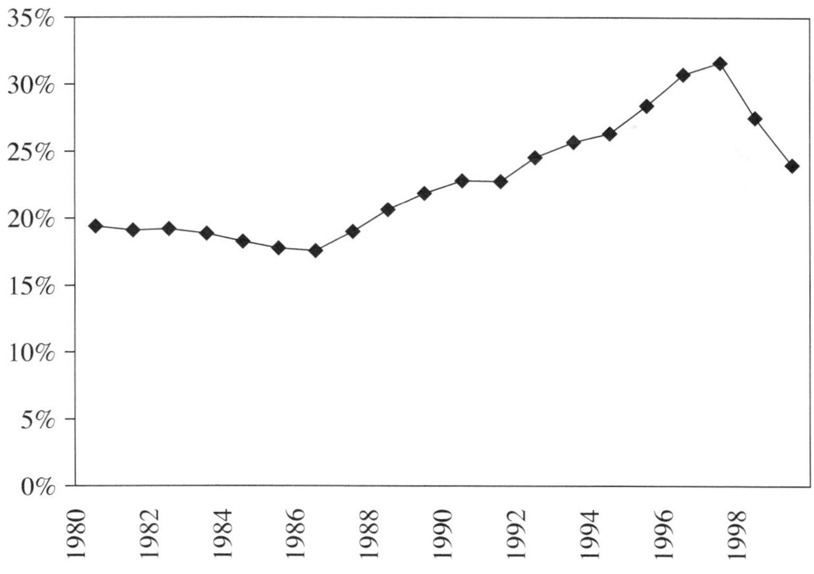

Figure 7.1 Patents issued after a continuation application, as a share of annual issued patents, 1980–1999

per cent of annual issued patents during the 1980–99 period. Continuation practice was commonly used by patentees before 1995 and such use remains significant after the Congressional changes to the patent law. The downward trend after 1997 may be an indication that the disincentives intended in the 1995 regime change have had an impact on behaviour, when one corrects for some identifiable lag in the prosecution of patents already in the system. For these overall data, continuation practice has fallen from a high of 31 per cent in 1997 to 24 per cent in 1999.

It is important here to note that the growth in the use of the continuation procedure beginning in 1986 reflects continuation applications that were filed several years earlier – certainly prior to the 2–3 year mean delay for non-continuation applications. The increased use of continuations by patentees began well before the data reflects an upturn in their issuance, and may well correspond with the pro-patent legal regime that attended the founding of the Court of Appeals for the Federal Circuit in 1983 (Kortum and Lerner, 1997). Nonetheless, fully 24 per cent of the patents issuing in 1999 involved continuations, and, as will be discussed below, these 'post-reform' shares are much higher in specific patent classes.

3 CONTINUATIONS: DESCRIPTIVE STATISTICS WITHIN SECTORS

The trend presented in Figure 7.1 demonstrated that the use of continuation is widespread across all patenting through the period 1980–99, and thus of economic interest. To answer the questions posed in section 2 above, however, it is necessary to supplement this aggregate trend with data from individual technology classes, thus providing a window into the patterns of use across different technologies and sectors. As a benchmark, I used a reasonably mature technology – combustion engines.

3.1 Combustion Engines

Combustion engine technologies were chosen as a benchmark on two grounds. First, the technology is mature – Daimler and Benz produced the first working gasoline combustion engines in the mid-1880s.[20] Because the technology has been progressing incrementally for over a century and underpins a large, mature industry (automotive), the technology has been more insulated from rapid, discontinuous change and greater uncertainty than have newer technologies.[21] Second, the technology sector into which this technology falls, motor-generator, appears to be one in which secrecy is not an important consideration. In fact, the technology group is characterized in Cohen *et al.* (2000) as having effectiveness ratings for both secrecy and patenting below the mean of all sectors, for both products and processes.

Using the International Patent Class identifier for 'Combustion Engine' technologies (F02-: Combustion engines and Hot-gas or Combustion-product engine plants), Figure 7.2 (left axis) plots the share of combustion engine patents within all utility patents issued in the years 1980–99, demonstrating that over time this technology has become increasingly marginalized in the post-1980s surge in patenting, one indicator that it is not a rapidly changing technology area. Figure 7.2 (right axis) shows that the use of continuations by combustion engine patentees over time lacks the dynamics shown in the aggregate of all technologies summarized in Figure 7.1. The share of all F02- patents showing a continuation application lineage after 1980 appears to be a random walk between 12 per cent and 17 per cent, and does not exhibit the sharp downturn after 1997 characterized by the trend of all patents.

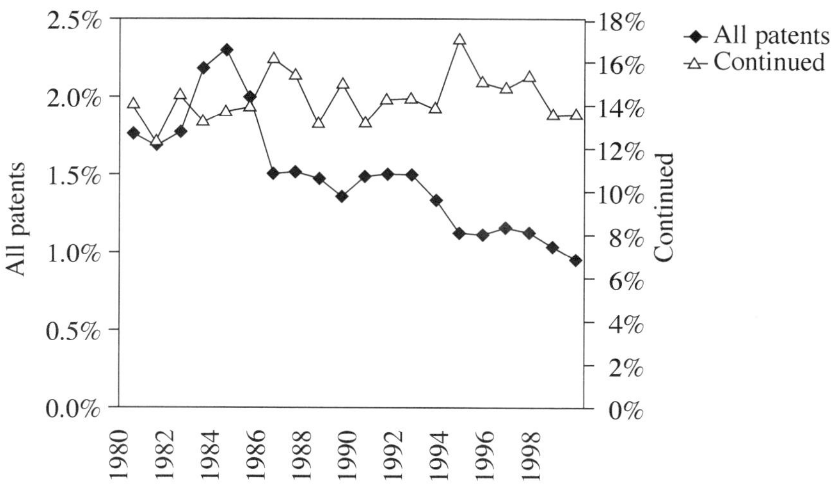

Figure 7.2 Motor-generator technologies, share of all patenting and 'continuations' share, 1980–99

3.2 Pharmaceuticals

Because of the vital role that patents play, and the regulatory hurdles imposed by the US government, the pharmaceutical industry is demonstrably different from other industries in terms of its innovation characteristics – and therefore meaningful comparisons with other industries are difficult, if not impossible. This observation is also true in terms of continuation practice, because the pharmaceutical industry has historically used the continuation application to aid in solving the thorny problems of patenting within the regulatory regime surrounding new drug applications (NDAs). Thus the pharmaceutical industry, unlike other sectors, enjoyed an added and potentially dominant motivation for using the continuation strategy: it allowed firms to 'fit' the beginning of a product's patent protection to the timing of a drug's exit from the extended regulatory approval process, thus allowing maximum patent protection during the time when the drug is actually marketable.[22] Thus regulatory demands may have been the primary motivator for the use of the continuation application in this industry.

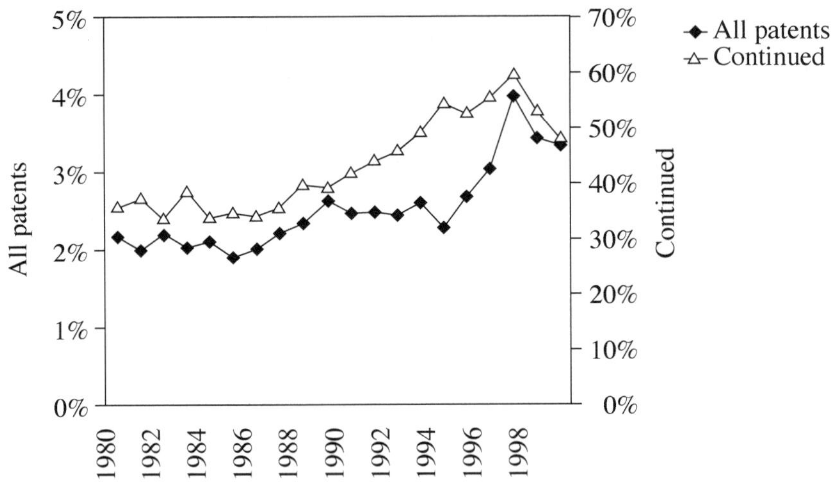

Figure 7.3 Pharmaceutical technologies, share of all patenting and 'continuations' share, 1980–99

The drugs industry is characterized by scholars as one in which patents are economically valuable and important in appropriating returns to innovation (Henderson and Cockburn, 1996; Cohen *et al.*, 2000). The characteristics of the industry and pharmaceutical products make a long patent term particularly valuable: because the products emerge from regulatory procedures quite late, and because a large portion of industry revenues is generated from drugs that generate massive sales and have long lives, longer patent terms are more valuable than in industries with reasonably quick invention-to-manufacture intervals and short product life cycles (Comanor, 1986).[23] The 1962 Kefauver amendments requiring stronger proof of the 'efficacy' of new pharmaceutical products shortened the patent term for pharmaceuticals by extending the period of clinical trials and regulatory approval (Grabowski, 1976). Partly in response to lobbying from the pharmaceuticals industry and the desire of pro-consumer law makers to facilitate the entry by producers of generic drugs following the expiration of pharmaceutical patents, the 1984 Drug Price Competition and Patent Term Restoration Act extended the patent term for pharmaceuticals by up to 5 years.[24] While there was some empirical support for this argument leading up to the passage of the Act (Schwartzman, 1976; Grabowski and Vernon, 1983), the effects of continuation practice in extending the effective patent term were underplayed in the literature (Comanor, 1986). Under the pre-1995 patent regime, pharmaceutical companies were using continuation practice to engage in 'serial prosecution'. This allowed the pharmaceutical company to patent different components of the invention – often beginning first with the molecule – over a long period of time, thus extending the *de facto* patent term to much longer than the 17 years permitted under the then-existing law (Burchfiel, 1995). Firms may have also used the continuation to coincide with their extended regulatory approval periods, maximizing the patent term by launching the patent close in time to their drugs emerging from the regulatory approval process.

In order to gain some insight into the use of continuations in the pharmaceutical industry, I examined trends in the share of continuations within international patent classification (IPC) A61K (Preparations for Medical, Dental, or Toilet purposes; excluding A617–7 'cosmetics or similar toilet preparations', following Harhoff and Reitzig (2000)), a patent class shown in Figure 7.3 (left axis) to have grown from 2.1 per cent to 3.9 per cent of overall US patenting 1980–99. IPC A61K has been used to define pharmaceutical and biotechnology patents in several studies (Lanjouw and Schankerman, 1997; Harhoff and Reitzig, 2000).

The share of pharmaceutical patents that are the terminal patent in a chain of continuation applications are plotted from 1980–99 in Figure 7.3 (right axis). A large percentage of pharmaceutical and biotechnology patents are the product of continuation practices, ranging from an annual low of 34 per cent to a high of 60 per cent, well above the 12–17 per cent exhibited by a mature technology like combustion engines. As with the broader population of patents, some downward trending is exhibited after 1997, with continuations in this sector falling by 12 percentage points through year 1999 from the 1997 high of 51 per cent. Continuations, however, still accounted for about 48 per cent of issued drugs patents by 1999, several years after the disincentives of the 1995 Act had been introduced.

Unlike some other sectors, the comparatively high level of continuation practice exhibited in this industry in the late 1980s continued after the 1995 Act. Because this Act forced a 20 year term inclusive of prosecution, it eliminated the alternative and potentially dominant motivation for pharmaceutical firms' use outlined above – maximizing the drug patent term. The figures thus lend evidence to support a role for other strategic motives, such as protecting technology secrecy for example, in addition to maximizing the patent term, as a motivating factor for continuation practice in this sector.

3.3 Semiconductor Products

I identified semiconductor technology classes by referring to the patenting from 1983–1994 of five major semiconductor firms – Texas Instruments, Intel, Advanced Micro Devices, Micron Technology, and National Semiconductor.[52] Analysis of patenting for these five firms allowed me to identify two international patent classes, H01L (Semiconductor Devices; Electric Solid State Devices not Otherwise Provided for) and H03K (Pulse Technique) which constitute a large percentage of overall patenting by these firms (23.4 per cent and 10.0 per cent, respectively) while at the same time covering product (for example, circuit) process technology. The trend in Figure 7.4 (left axis) shows that these electronic technologies have captured a steadily increasing share of patenting through 1980–99, growing from 2 per cent to 5 per cent of all patenting during this period. This growth suggests that these technologies are more dynamic and fast-changing – and thus more uncertain – than mature technologies like combustion engines.

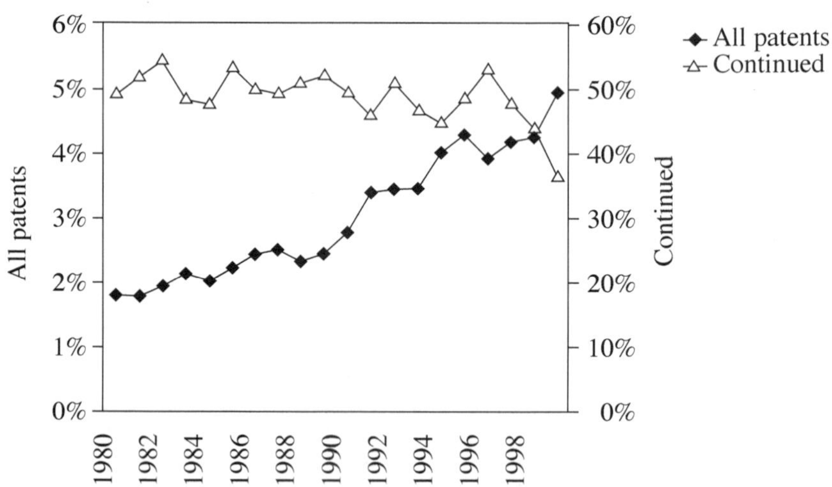

Figure 7.4 Semiconductor technologies, share of all patenting and 'continuations' share, 1980–99

Figure 7.4 (right axis) plots the share of patents in these patent classes that were the terminal patent in a continuation chain, 1980–99. In these semiconductor technologies, the use of the continuation in patenting has been common since 1980, with shares of patents issued with some continuation use fluctuating between 45–53 per cent through 1996. Unlike pharmaceutical patenting, there does not appear to be any discernible pattern in the change of use by applicants of the continuation during the pre-1995 era: use has been fairly strong and constant.

The trend for continuation use in semiconductor patenting, like pharmaceuticals and the broader sample of patents, does show a marked downturn after 1997. In this sector, it is of a similar magnitude, dropping 16 percentage points through year 1999 from a high of 53 per cent in 1996. Furthermore, by year 1999, continuations in these technologies account for only slightly more than 36 per cent of issued patents, the minimum demonstrated throughout the 1980–99 period. This industry embraced continuation practice in the years prior to enactment of the 1995 changes, but the disincentives wrought by the new law appear to have brought a behavioural change in patenting.

My discussions with patent counsel at several large semiconductor firms give me some insight into these continuation patterns. It is common practice in the industry to carve out claims that the examiner deems as objectively patentable, and for the patent agents to leave the less-certain claims behind as continuing applications. Some share of these 'secondhand' applications is then later issued as patents. What is unanswered by such a behaviour is the quality of these 'secondhand' applications. While some of the patent attorneys I interviewed saw the claims associated with these continued applications as 'junkier' (less deserving of patent protection), it is possible that some of these 'secondhand' applications embody high quality patents, the patentability of which was not, or not capable of being, taught to the patent examiners in a timely manner.

In both pharmaceutical and semiconductor technologies, however, the use of continuations appears to have been negatively impacted by the disincentives envisioned and implemented in the 1995 Act. This pattern in these two technologies is consistent with the dramatic decline in continuation usage that Graham and Mowery (2004) demonstrate in US software patenting after 1995. Graham and Mowery, however, also show that in the software industry, characterized like semiconductors by short product life cycles, patentees continued to use the continuation mechanism relatively intensively as of 2000, despite the fact that the marginal value of a 21st year of protection is surely low. This pattern is unlike that shown above for semiconductor technologies, which exhibits continuation practice falling to levels not unlike those found in 'static' mature technologies like combustion engines. This limited evidence suggests that patenting behaviour in these two technology sectors differs, and that the returns to patenting vary, and begs further research and comparative studies.

4 THE DETERMINANTS OF CONTINUATION APPLICATION PRACTICE

The heterogeneity displayed in the innovators' differing uses of the continuation application across these different technologies begs a more systematic analysis. Accordingly, Table 7.2 displays the results of a negative binomial regression that relates the probability that a patent is continued – and continued an increasing number of times – to several standard characteristics of the patent. The data includes a total of $n = 1\,026\,595$ observations, of which 22 per cent (= 227 438) are patents showing at least one continuation application filed. The dependent variable in the regression is the count of the number of continuations filed by an applicant prior to the patent issuing (minimum 0 and maximum 34; the mean continuations statistic is 0.68 continuations with a standard deviation of 1.10; the mean continuations statistic conditional on at least one continuation being filed is 1.50, with a standard deviation of 1.07; the share of patents showing exactly one continuation of all patents exhibiting at least one continuation is 70.6 per cent). Several of the right-hand variables used in the regression are dummies, the estimates for which show the change in the probability of continuation if the dummy changes from 0 to 1.

The number of continuations for which a patentee applies on any given patent is inherently a discrete, non-negative integer. This count is often a small number – in fact, in the data analysed in this chapter, the cumulative share of patents with either no or one continuation is 86.2 per cent – thus revealing a skewed distribution in which only a few patents show relatively many continuations (to a maximum of 34 continuations in these data). While a Poisson model is generally appropriate for count data of this sort, the Poisson model's assumption that the variance of the count is equal to mean may be violated, thus resulting in an overdispersion of the data. The negative binomial regression (Hausman, Hall and Griliches, 1984) is an appropriate means to correct for overdispersion in the count data.

I employ the negative binomial regression because the dependent variable exhibits overdispersion in the variation of its counts. Overdispersion is suggested in these data because the variance of the dependent variable is greater than its mean (in this sample, variance = 1.21 as compared with a mean of 0.68). The regression equation thus used relates the number of

Table 7.2 Negative binomial regression results (as incident rate ratios)

Variable	Coefficient	Std. Err.	Z-stat	Significant
FIRM OWN	1.8812	0.0382	31.12	*
US	1.3516	0.0063	64.55	*
BACKCITE	1.0219	0.0003	86.94	*
FORCITE	0.9996	0.0003	–1.38	
Claims: (compared to 1–6)				
7–20	0.7555	0.0039	–54.85	*
21–40	0.8571	0.0061	–21.62	*
41–60	1.1089	0.0163	7.02	*
61–99	1.3437	0.0341	11.64	*
100+	1.7567	0.0960	10.31	*
GENERALITY	1.0390	0.0090	4.41	*
ORIGINALITY	1.4449	0.0125	42.49	*
RATIO SELF	1.6564	0.0139	60.26	*
Technology: (compared to 'constructions')				
Drugs	2.0023	0.0325	42.74	*
Process	1.3470	0.0215	18.69	*
Chemical	2.2980	0.0368	51.97	*
Textiles	1.5332	0.0359	18.27	*
Mechanical	0.9332	0.0161	–4.01	*
Physics	1.2583	0.0201	14.38	*
Electrical	1.1249	0.0182	7.28	*

continuations Y_i filed on patent *j* with a set of *n* interaction parameters X_{i1}, X_{i2}, ... X_{in} as follows:

$$\text{Function}(Y_i) = \beta_0 + \beta_1 X_{i1} + \beta_2 X_{i2} + \ldots + \beta_n X_{in}$$

where β_0, β_1, ... β_n are the regression coefficients. I assume that the continuation count Y_i exhibits a negative binomial distribution following Hausman, Hall and Griliches (1984).

The incident rate ratio is reported in Table 7.2 as 'Ratio' for ease of determining the effect of changes in these right-hand side variables on the likelihood of a patent showing an increasing count of continuation applications in its lineage. The incident rate ratio is a transformation of the left-hand-side coefficient *b*, calculated as e^b, and represents the rate of increase in the count of the dependent variable (here, continuation application counts) produced by an increase in the relevant independent variable. It thus offers a readily interpretable coefficient statistic.

Table 7.2 relates the change in the number of continuations filed to various characteristics of the patent and its holder. The variables in the regression, and interpretations of the results, are as follows:

1. A dummy variable FIRM OWN that takes the value 1 if the patent was assigned to a firm or corporate entity (as determined by the USPTO coding system, codes '2' or '3'), 0 otherwise. The incident rate ratio suggests that firm-assigned patents are 1.88 times more likely to have been issued after some continuation procedure than patents not assigned to firms. Patents not assigned to firms include patents assigned to individuals, to governments, and 'unassigned' patents.
2. A dummy variable US that takes the value 1 if the patent was invented by or assigned to an individual or entity domiciled in the United States, 0 otherwise. US-domiciled persons and entities are 1.35 times more likely to have a patent issued after some continuation process.
3. A variable BACKCITE for the number of US patents cited in the focal patent. US patent law requires that a patent applicant must reference or 'cite' prior patents, a process which serves to limit the scope of the property right awarded to the instant, or focal, patent. The choice of which 'citations' are included on the written patent document, however, is ultimately the province of the government patent examiner, an expert versed in the technology. The results of the regression show that one additional backward citation raises the likelihood of the patent having been continued by 2 per cent. This result is made ambiguous by the realization that the give-and-take of the application negotiation process may make the adding of additional backward citations more likely.
4. A variable FORCITES for the number of US patent citations made by later-issuing patents to the focal patent, between the issue of the focal patent and 1999 (forward citations). Results for this variable are not significant, and the confidence interval does not permit a reasonable determination of the direction of the effect of a patent collecting one more forward citation.
5. A set of dummies for the number of claims (1–6, 7–20, 21–40, 41–60, 61–99, >100). The US patent law requires that a patent be described in a number of claims, essentially descriptive elements of the technical characteristics of the invention. Because the base case in this regression is a patent having between 1–6 claims, the effect of adding claims to a patent on the probability of the patent having been continued appears to be U-shaped. Having more claims raises the probability of continuation, over the base case, but only if the number of claims exceeds 40. Adding claims between 7 and 40 actually lowers the likelihood of the patent having been continued compared to the base case. Patents showing

between 61 and 99 claims are 1.34 more likely to have been continued than the base case, while those with 100+ claims are 1.76 more likely to have issued after some continuation practice. The meaning of this result is ambiguous, because the number of claims in a patent is itself subject to multiple interpretations. On the one hand, patents with a large number of claims may represent a narrowly tailored invention. In other words, these patents are occupying a space in a relatively 'crowded' field populated by many similar inventions, raising the likelihood of continuation practice. On the other hand, patents with large numbers of claims may be broader. An alternative explanation is that, due to the ongoing negotiations between inventors, examiners and lawyers that the continuation triggers, more claims are necessarily written.

6. A variable ORIGINALITY, which is the Herfendahl-Hirschman concentration index describing the breadth of technology classes to which the patent cites (backward citations). This variable has been used to proxy for the 'basicness', in terms of the overall technology, of the patent in terms of prior innovators (Trajtenberg, Jaffe and Henderson, 1997), on the theory that a patent citing a wide body of different technological antecedents is likely to be more original (that is, the technology is not limited to a narrow technology area, nor is it sufficiently well-developed to have invited its own technological classification in the patent office). An increase in the originality of a patent has a positive and substantial impact on the likelihood of continuation.
7. A variable GENERALITY, which is the Herfendahl-Hirschman concentration index describing the breadth of technology classes of later-issued patents that cite the focal patent (forward citations). This variable has been used to proxy for the generality, in terms of the overall technology, of the patented technology's use by later innovators. Trajtenberg, Jaffe and Henderson (1997) propose the measure as an indicator of an invention's 'basicness', constructing it to demonstrate the extent to which an invention's follow-on technological impact is spread across many fields, rather than being concentrated in a few. An increase in the generality of a patent has a positive, but not substantial, impact on the probability of the patent having been continued.
8. A variable RATIO SELF, which is the ratio of self-citations to total backward citations (see 3) above). A self-citation is a backward citation listed on patent *i* that is assigned to the same entity to which patent *i* is assigned. This measure has been used to proxy for the extent to which a firm controls the technology trajectory in which patent *i* lies (Hall, Jaffe and Trajtenberg, 2000). An increase in the self-citation ratio of a patent has a positive and substantial impact on the likelihood of continuation.

9. Technology class dummies that conform to broad, international-patent-class defined technology groupings established by the World Intellectual Property Organization (A – health, drugs; B – processes; C – chemicals; D – textiles, paper; E – fixed constructions; F – mechanical engineering; G – physics, software; H – electronics). In comparison to the patents in the base case technology ('fixed construction'), drugs patents are 2.0 times more likely, process patents are 1.34 times more likely and chemical patents are 2.30 times more likely to show a continuation in their lineage than base-case patents. Textiles, physics and electrical patents are also more likely to have been continued than base-case patents (1.53 times, 1.25 times and 1.12 times respectively). Only mechanical engineering patents are less likely (–0.07 times)[26] to have been continued than the base case.

In general, the results from the negative binomial regression demonstrates that changes in several standard patent characteristics have substantial impacts upon the probability that patents undergo some continuation procedure in their application lineage, and show the determinants of 'more' (as measured by the number filed) continuation application activity.

5 CONCLUSION

In his use of the continuation application to engage in 'submarine' patenting, Jerome Lemelson employed a potent strategic mechanism. Because the continuation allowed an applicant to protect an early priority, and coupled this protected priority with secrecy, the pending patent right could be engineered to maximize the applicant's rent transfers from other 'users' of the patented technology. The use that Lemelson made of the continuation application was unlikely to have been isolated: this chapter demonstrates that overall usage of the continuation was reasonably high, and in several important technology sectors, notably pharmaceuticals and semiconductors, a majority of patents issued in many of the years 1980–1995 were granted after some continuation practice. While I lack conclusive evidence that submarine tactics were used by a large share of other applicants during these years, several patent attorneys and corporate patent counsels active during these years have reported to me that it was common practice for applicants to take advantage of priority and secrecy to ensure maximum value from their patent rights.

Such practice runs afoul of the social contract between innovator and the public, however, and this failure was used as a justification for Congress to limit the incentives for engaging in continuation practice in the GATT legislative changes that took effect in 1995. The United States Constitution directs the Congress to create an intellectual property system in order to support the 'progress of the useful arts', and the policy arguments supporting the patent system have consistently referenced the limited monopoly granted to patentees in return for disclosure, and the opportunity on the part of the public to use the disclosure to 'progress the useful arts'. From the standpoint of economics too, the manner in which 'submarine' tactics reward an innovator for keeping an innovation purposefully hidden, for many years after the inventive spark, from which the public had no chance to benefit and which was, in reality, independently invented and adopted by others prior to the patent's issue, has little to suggest that an offer of a patent monopoly is an appropriate incentive.

In addition to raising questions about the appropriateness and the economic necessity of having a 'continuation application' system, this chapter demonstrates that the practice has been and continues to be used extensively in several important technology sectors in the economy, notably pharmaceuticals and semiconductors. While continuation practice may be instrumental in maximizing the returns from patenting in drugs technologies – by allowing patentees to manage the new drug approval regulatory process in the US – different motives appear to be at work in semiconductor technologies. In fact, the use of the continuation in semiconductor patenting may be driven by the desire to maximize the firms' total patents. Such a strategy would be consistent with the suggestion by practitioners that, in the semiconductor industry, firms seek quick patents from the 'stronger' disclosures made in an application, but leave 'ambiguous' claims behind as continuation applications pending in the Patent Office. To the extent that some share of these 'ambiguous' claims finally issue as patents, firms are able to increase the sheer number of company patents, a story consistent with the defensive patent strategies suggested by Hall and Ziedonis (2001) in their study of the semiconductor industry. A more thorough study of the use of continuation applications in the patenting of semiconductor technology is needed, however, to determine the full portrait of strategic drivers and choices by firms in that industry.

Looking away from these sector-specific cases, this chapter also takes a more general look at the characteristics of patentees' uses of the continuation application, allowing a window into the broader effects of the procedure's availability. To open this window, I use regression analysis to uncover the determinants of patentee's use of the continuation application in US patenting. While the regression results reported in this chapter demonstrate that domestic US applicants and firms are more likely to use the continuation in patenting, the results associated with these determinants raise as many questions as they answer. So, while the results show that more 'basic' inventions (in terms of the generality and originality score) are correlated with a greater use of the continuation application, I cannot say whether this finding may be an artifact of the manner in which longer-pending patents collect citations, or that the underlying technologies indeed show a higher level of 'basicness'. More thorough study of differences in continuation use, as well as patenting strategy more generally, is clearly needed across technologies and industries.

In 1999, the American Inventors Protection Act (AIPA) included a provision to require the publication of patent applications after 18 months of filing. Largely enacted to harmonize US patent practices with the rest of the industrialized world, it was argued that such a requirement would have the added benefit of removing substantial incentives to engage in 'submarine' patenting. Because technology disclosures could no longer be kept secret from technology adopters for extended periods, adopters could not be 'surprised' by the late-surfacing patent right.

In practice, however, the provisions of the AIPA do not appear to have effectively removed incentives to use the continuation application to engage in 'submarine' patenting. A major loophole was allowed in the Act: patent applicants making a positive declaration to the Patent Office that they do not intend to seek patent protection outside the US in a nation that also requires 18-month publication are exempted from the disclosure requirement. So, for instance, a US patent applicant declaring to the USPTO that no patent application is intended to Europe or Japan, would be automatically entitled to an exemption from the publication requirements.

The opportunity for patentees to gain advantage from the use of the continuation thus remains open for a large share of US patent applicants, even after the AIPA has become effective. Indeed, estimates of the number of patent applications seeking exemptions under the 'no foreign application' loophole range from USPTO estimates of 10 per cent to as high as 20 per cent (Graham, 2004a). While an applicant contemplating a submarine continuation patenting strategy would face disincentives if unable to collect rents for adopters' uses in some countries outside the US, it is not clear that the disincentive is any more powerful now under the AIPA-created regime than it was previously, under the operations of the Patent Cooperation Treaty (PCT) to which the United States and many important industrialized nations were signatories prior to 1999. The PCT demands the effective loss of patenting rights to applicants in the event that their patents were not pursued in a nation after public international disclosure, such as a publication. This pre-1999 reality thus renders an oft-cited element of the AIPA regulations simply a reiteration of the previous patent regime, uncovering the AIPA as a much more toothless regulation of the innovation system than is often demonstrated.

NOTES

1. Merriam-Webster Collegiate Dictionary (2002).
2. While the vast majority of US patents – and the focus in this chapter – are the so-called Utility patents authorized by 35 USC §101, patents are also available on Plants (35 USC §161) and Designs (35 USC §171).
3. 35 USC §102(b).
4. 35 USC §112, 113, 114. The 'written description' requirement is intended to allow any person skilled in the art to either make or use the invention.
5. 35 USC §101. See *Diamond v. Chakrabarty*, 447 US 303 (1980) (determining that man-made living micro-organisms are patentable subject matter).
6. 35 USC §101. See *Brenner v. Manson*, 383 US 519 (1966) (upholding the examiner's determination that the output of a chemical process was not useful if merely similar to a useful compound).
7. 35 USC §101, 102. See *Jamesbury v. Litton Industrial*, 756 F.2d 1556 (CAFC 1985) (finding that an invention was 'novel' when no prior art was precisely equivalent).
8. 35 USC §103. See *Graham v. John Deere Co.*, 383 US 1 (1966) (finding an invention invalid on grounds that the improvement would have been obvious to a person of ordinary skill in the art).
9. While courts are given the opportunity to decide on the legitimacy of these determinations by the examiners, so few patents are litigated in practice that these initial findings by examiners are often the final determinations on these questions of patentability.
10. Lemley (1994) found an average length of 864 days (2.37 years) for 2081 patents issued on 27 December 1994.
11. Patent law is not apparently immune from Otto von Bismarck's remonstrance regarding legislation and sausages – that none of us should like to see either being made.
12. 35 USC § 120 (1991). Benefit of earlier filing date in the United States.
13. Under 35 USC § 120, a patent application is entitled to adopt the filing date of a 'parent' application when (1) both applications disclose the same invention; (2) both applications are filed by the same inventor; (3) both applications are simultaneously co-pending; (4) the earlier application meets the disclosure requirements of 35 USC § 112; and (5) the later application contains a specific reference to the earlier application. *Sampson v. Ampex Corp.* (1971, DC NY), 333 F. Supp. 59, aff'd. (2nd Cir. NY) 463 F2d 1042.
14. While formally the contents, and even the existence, of the patent application were historically kept secret, any revelation of corporate information outside the confines of the firm raises the risk that the information will 'leak' to competitors.
15. 'Public policy favors the early disclosure of inventions. This underlies the requirement for "reasonable diligence" in reducing an invention to practice...' *Naber v. Cricchi*, 567 F.2d 382 (CCPA, 1977), quoted in *Griffith v. Kanamaru*, 816 F.2d 624 (CAFC, 1987).
16. The applicant is 'promised that merely by soliciting, before the Patent Office, [patent protection for his secret invention] he is not giving up his common-law rights. Though the Patent Office may refuse to issue a patent, it must do nothing to jeopardize even an unsuccessful applicant's common-law rights'. *Irons & Steel v. Dann*, 606 F.2d 1215 (D.C. Cir. 1979).
17. The legislation was offered and passed in 1994 as part of the fast-track vote on the Uruguay Round of the General Agreement on Tariffs and Trade (GATT). The law's provisions did not take effect until 1995 so it will be termed the '1995 Act'.
18. My definition of the term 'continuation' includes also the 'continuation-in-part' and 'division' processes by which particular claims or groups of claims can be continued as opposed to an entire application and all disclosures therein.
19. There will always be a certain amount of uncertainty about the date of issue, although the patentee can minimize this uncertainty through the negotiation process with the USPTO examiner and the deft use of the continuation process itself.
20. Coal gas models predated these improvements, with Lenoir and Otto early pioneers.
21. Although the patterns of radical (versus incremental) change in technologies can create discontinuities in even the most mature technologies.

22. In the United States, the Federal Food and Drug Administration (FDA) requires that all pharmaceuticals be tested for efficacy and safety in a lengthy drug approval process. So, for instance, if a company's patent on a new drug's molecular make-up were to issue prior to the drug completing this government approval process, then patent protection would be 'wasted'. Because of the long life of drug products in the marketplace, and to the extent that patent protection suppresses competition from 'generic' drug producers, it is a benefit to the innovator to extend patent protection as long as possible.
23. Lemley (1994) suggests that pharmaceutical and biotechnology patents may be more valuable at the end of their patent terms than are software patents.
24. The Act also reduced entry barriers to generic drug providers.
25. I thank Rosemarie Ziedonis for allowing me to use her semiconductor patent data to complete this analysis.
26. As an incident rate ratio, a 1.0 would be no change in the odds of an event. A 2.0 is a doubling, or +100%. A 1.05 is thus +5%, and a 0.9332 would be a 1/0.9332 = 1.07% less odds, or –7%.

REFERENCES

Albright, B. (2004), 'Bar Code Industry Wins Case against Lemelson Foundation', *Frontline Solutions*, January 27, p. 1.

Burchfiel, K. (1995), 'US GATT Legislation Changes Patent Term', *Journal of the Patent and Trademark Office Society*, **77**, pp. 222–52.

Cohen, W., R. Nelson and J. Walsh (2000), *Protecting their Intellectual Assets: Appropriability Conditions and Why US Manufacturing Firms Patent (or Not)*, NBER Working Paper No. 7552, Cambridge MA: NBER.

Comanor, W.S. (1986), 'The Political Economy of the Pharmaceutical Industry', *Journal of Economic Literature*, **24**, pp. 1178–217.

Grabowski, H. (1976), *Drug Regulation and Innovation*, Washington, D.C.: American Enterprise Institute.

Grabowski, H. and J. Vernon (1983), *The Regulation of Pharmaceuticals: Balancing the Benefits and Risks*, Washington, D.C.: American Enterprise Institute.

Graham, S.J.H. (2004a), 'Patenting in the Shadow of Secrecy: Innovators' Uses of US Patent Office Continuation Practice, 1975–2002', in *Continuation, Complementarity, and Capturing Value: Three Studies Exploring Firms' Complementary Uses of Appropriability Mechanisms in Technological Innovation*, doctoral dissertation, University of California, Berkeley.

Graham, S.J.H. (2004b), 'Hiding in the Patent's Shadow: Firms' Uses of Secrecy to Capture Value from New Discoveries', in *Continuation, Complementarity, and Capturing Value: Three Studies Exploring Firms' Complementary Uses of Appropriability Mechanisms in Technological Innovation*, doctoral dissertation, University of California, Berkeley.

Graham, S.J.H. and D.C. Mowery (2004), 'Submarines in Software? Continuations in US Software Patenting in the 1980s and 1990s', *Economics of Innovation and New Technology*, **13**(5), pp. 443–56.

Hall, B., A. Jaffe and M. Trajtenberg (2000), *Market Value and Patent Citations: A First Look*, NBER Working Paper No. 7741, Cambridge MA: NBER.

Hall, B.H. and R.H. Ziedonis (2001), 'The Patent Paradox Revisited: An Empirical Study of Patenting in the US Semiconductor Industry, 1979–95', *RAND Journal of Economics*, **32**(1), pp. 101–28.

Harhoff, D. and M. Reitzig (2000). *Determinants of Opposition against EPO Patent Grants – The Case of Biotechnology and Pharmaceuticals*, CEPR/ESRC Workshop paper, March.

Hausman, J., B. Hall and Z. Griliches (1984), 'Econometric Models for Count Data and with Application to the Patents-R&D Relationship', *Econometrica*, **52**(4), pp. 909–38.

Henderson, R. and I. Cockburn (1996), 'Scale Scope and Spillovers: The Determinants of Research Productivity in Drug Discovery', *RAND Journal of Economics*, **27**, pp. 32–59.

Kortum, S. and J. Lerner (1997), *Stronger Patent Protection or Technological Revolution: What is behind the Recent Surge in Patenting?*, NBER Working paper No. 6204, Cambridge MA: NBER.

Lanjouw, J. and M. Schankerman (1997), *Stylized Facts of Patent Litigation: Value, Scope and Ownership*, NBER Working Paper No. 6297, Cambridge MA: NBER.

Lemley, M. (1994), 'The Implications of GATT on US Intellectual Property Laws: An Empirical Study of the 20-year Patent Term', *AIPLA Quarterly Journal*, **22**, pp. 369–88.

Merges, R.P. (1997), *Patent Law and Policy*, Charlottesville, VA: Michie Publishing.

Merges, R., P. Menell, M. Lemley and T. Jorde (1997), *Intellectual Property in the New Technological Age*, New York: Aspen Press.

Schwartzman, D. (1976), *Innovation in the Pharmaceutical Industry*, Baltimore, MD: Johns Hopkins University Press.

Trajtenberg, M., A. Jaffe and R. Henderson (1997), 'University versus Corporate Patents: A Window on the Basicness of Invention', *Economics of Innovation and New Technology*, **5**, pp. 19–50.

PART IV

Coordinating institutions of intellectual property rights governance

8. Public and private institutions in the governance of intellectual property rights

Eric Brousseau and Christian Bessy

ABSTRACT

Based upon a comparative institutional analysis of the institutional frameworks involved in the governance of intellectual property rights (IPR) systems in France and in the US, both in the domain of patents and copyrights, we demonstrate that the differences of performances among contrasted systems of property rights do not only depend upon the wording of the law, but also result from the governance mechanisms that implement and complete the law. In particular we show that there are essential complementarities between public and private institutions designed by the owners of IPRs. Institutions allow agents to reduce the costs of settling and defending exclusive rights of use over intangible goods by collectivizing the related operation. Collectivization can however generate maladaptation costs since the management of these rights cannot be customized. We then show that the optimal 'division of labour' between public institutions, private institutions and individuals varies according to the type of IPR infringement and according to the diffusion strategy used by the owner(s) of the IPRs. We conclude by pointing out that the design of the organization of the institutional framework should be more carefully taken into account when dealing with the optimal design of IPR systems to solve the protection/diffusion dilemma.

Keywords: Patent, Copyright, Institutional design, Protection/diffusion dilemma

1 INTRODUCTION

The governance of intellectual property rights (IPRs) is becoming a crucial question for economic policies because activities related to intangible resources represent a growing share of our GDPs and a major source of growth. This has led several scholars to describe our economies as becoming knowledge-based economies (Foray and Lundvall 1996). Indeed, the vast majority of scholars involved in the intellectual property field (for example, Besen and Raskind 1991, Scotchmer 1991, Ordover 1991, Gallini 2002, Lerner 2002) agree on the idea that the IPR regime strongly impacts on the dynamics of industries that produce or rely on intangible resources because it affects both the remuneration of creative and inventive activities, and the costs of using and transferring the results of these activities. Today, most discussions are concerned with the determination of the most appropriate IPR regime in various situations (for example, the efficiency of the *Droit d'Auteur*[1] regime as compared to copyright in the multimedia industry, optimal scope and duration of patents in contrasted technical fields, respective virtues and vices of 'open' regimes as compared to closed ones, optimal scope of the public domain and so on).

Our contribution comes within the scope of this literature questioning the relative efficiency of alternative IPR systems. However, it focuses on a different question and is based on a different methodology from most contributions (for example, Nordhaus 1969, Gilbert and Shapiro 1990, Klemperer 1990, Gallini 1992, Chang 1995). Indeed, rather than restricting our investigation to the rules implemented by the law, we point out the importance of the devices that govern – that is, design and implement – these rules. Taking into account the institutional bodies that are hidden by the wording of the law becomes increasingly important because the legal protection of the work of invention and authorship is tending towards standardization at the international level through the many international conventions: the Bern Convention for the Protection of Literacy and Artistic Works, the Universal Copyright Convention, the Paris Convention for the Protection of Industrial Property, the Technological and Cultural section of GATT and WTO, TRIPS and so on. Despite this standardization of the wording of laws (when conventions are actually ratified), the diverse national IPR systems remain differentiated because laws are implemented differently from country to country. These differences are also found across industries.

According to North (1990), one of the essential roles of the institutional framework is to set up property rights (PRs). A necessary condition for the efficient use of resources is the definition of exclusive rights of uses over them – aimed at avoiding conflicts and at providing incentives to create and use them efficiently – and enabling agents to transfer these rights at a low cost to allow efficient reallocation (see also Coase 1992). The general institutions of the society play an essential role in settling these rights. However economic agents must always dedicate resources and efforts to set the boundaries of their rights of use and to exclude unauthorized parties from access to 'their' resources (which correspond respectively to the 'measurement' and 'enforcement' costs defined by Barzel (1989)). This leads them to build devices aimed at governing their rights of access and of use so as to minimize costs.

In this paper, we shall follow the New Institutional Economics (NIE) approach by studying the 'division of labour' among various types of institutions. One of our objectives is to point out how the governance of PRs is carried out by the association of public institutions emanating from public authorities, private institutions that are formed by agents that try to collectivize efforts (Brousseau and Fares 2000, Brousseau 2000, Brousseau and Raynaud 2004), and by the direct intervention of agents.[2] In our view it is important to establish such a distinction between private and public institutions since they are not built according to the same logic (the former are imposed by the State, whereas the latter are freely constituted by agents) and cannot be considered as equivalent from a public policy point of view. Moreover, private institutions can strongly impact on the properties of public ones. This chapter will therefore focus on the role of private bodies and on the complementarities between private and public institutions.

From a methodological point of view, we perform comparative institutional analysis because, when it is question of governance, it is difficult to refer to an ideal world populated by rational decision makers and without radical uncertainty. This is in line with the methodological statement of NIE (Coase 1992, North 1990, Williamson 1996), which is particularly relevant when one deals with creative and innovative activities. This paper is thus based upon the comparison of various systems of governance of IPRs. Dealing with the institutions that govern the patent system and the copyright system both in France and in the US, we try to point out that the differences between the diverse systems do not only depend upon the wording of the law, but also pertain to the governance devices that manage and complete the law. As a result, there are also unexpected similarities among these various systems, and legal backgrounds.

We illustrate our arguments by comparing:

- the US and the French institutional frameworks because both systems are archetypal of the two dominant legal regimes in the world – the common law and the civil code (or statutory legislation) – which rely on a number of contrasted principles. There are in addition key differences that are specific to intellectual property. It is especially the case for property regimes over works of art and creations of mind where the French *Droit d'Auteur* contrasts with the US copyright (see note 1).[3]

- two categories of intangible goods: technological inventions (protected by patents) and works of authorship (protected by copyright) because they correspond to different types of intangible goods ('ideas' and 'expression of ideas') that are often characterized by contrasted diffusion policies (from pure exclusivity of use to unrestricted diffusion) and because the logic of IPR infringement can differ (as developed later).

Taking into account these contrasting IPR regimes allows us to compare a broad set of situations for which (private) institutions matter.

Before focusing on the role of private institutions, we present the theoretical framework (section 2) and explain what 'governing' an intellectual property rights system means (section 3). This will lead us to point out why public institutions set 'incomplete' property rights, that force agents to bear high costs to settle rights of use over intangible goods (section 4). Agents are therefore encouraged to minimize these costs, by collectivizing the governance of their exclusive rights of use to benefit from economies of scale and scope, and of learning effects (section 5.1). However, collective management of rights has disadvantages (section 5.2), which limit the ability to collectivize the governance of their IPRs. This ability depends in particular upon the nature of the resources they want to protect and of their strategy in making the most of these resources (section 5.3). In addition, they can also play on the scope of specialization (section 6). Our concluding remarks will be dedicated to the identification of different IPR regimes; given their implementation by diverse configurations of governance devices rather than through the wording of the Law (section 7).

2 ANALYTICAL FRAMEWORK: PUBLIC AND PRIVATE INSTITUTIONS

This chapter is dedicated to the assessment of the relative efficiency of the various types of governance devices that play a role in IPR settlements. We will focus essentially on formal institutions as defined by North. However we will not reduce institutions to a set of rules as North (1990) does. We agree with the idea that institutions are those devices that constrain agents' behaviour, and thus decide the 'rules of the game' in which individuals develop their strategies. However these constraints result from a combination of 'rules' and of 'decisions' made by 'Institutional organizations' (Brousseau 2000). These institutional organizations play three roles. They make these rules enforceable. Put another way, they perform various operations to transform these rules into the behaviour which agents adopt. Enforcement does not only mean constraining the agents. It also means observing behaviours so as to compare them with the rules, making the rules known to the players and so on. Secondly, institutional organizations design the (formal) rules, either by providing means of interpretation when the rule is vague and ambiguous, or by designing additional rules. The set of existing formal rules is to a large extent the activity of previous institutional organizations. Thirdly, institutional organizations make decisions and state the required behaviour by parties when rules do not apply. In our opinion, institutions are therefore made of a combination of rules and institutional organizations that impose constraints on agents so as to frame their behaviours; the main goal of these constraints is to enable them to coordinate.

When they need to coordinate, agents can rely on three (constitutional) types of coordination device (Brousseau 2000). First of all, they can rely on public and general institutions instituted by the State as the law, the patent office and the judicial system. These 'public and general' devices rely on the State's power of last resort, and therefore impose their order on all agents acting under the relevant State's sovereignty. Secondly, agents can rely on 'private and specialized' institutions voluntarily created by agents who want to share the costs and the efforts of governing their interactions.[4] This is the case, for instance, when professional associations set common rules of interactions among the members of a community. These common rules make it unnecessary for agents to write complex contracts. The resulting private collective order relies on voluntary adhesion and the related 'institutional organizations' – like mutual societies of authors – derive their 'power' from the fact that their members delegate them authority. Acceptance of the private order draws from the fact that members make savings when coordinating with others, despite the cost of the constraints. Thirdly, since public and private bodies do not always solve all the coordination difficulties, economic agents can implement interindividual contracts aimed at settling a governance structure in the sense of Williamson (1996). We will refer to these as 'interindividual governance structures'.

When they need to coordinate, agents have to decide to resort to a central solution provided by 'public and general institutions' (PGI) or to a decentralized one based on 'interindividual governance structures' (IGS), or to an intermediary one. Their choice depends upon a trade-off that can be summed up in terms of the degree of (de)centralization. Relying on PGI allows them to benefit from low costs of governance of their transactions for two reasons (Brousseau and Fares 2000). First, by avoiding redundant efforts to settle coordination rules, these general institutions benefit from economies of scale and scope. Second, agents usually do not bear directly the cost of resorting to these solutions. On the contrary when they use IGS, agents bear directly the costs of governance. However these economies have a cost: a lack of flexibility and of adaptation to their specific coordination needs. These costs correspond to the notion of 'maladaptation costs' as defined by Williamson (1985). The solutions that are designed to solve the most common cases (or which correspond to the lowest common denominator) of contrasted coordination problems do little to solve these problems and result in losses (for example, disputes, low performance and so on), while customized solutions minimize maladaptation costs. General and public institutions result therefore in low governance costs and high maladaptation costs, while contracts result in high governance costs and low maladaptation costs. Private and specialized institutions that take from both logics of coordination devices – they are voluntary (as contracts) and collective (as general institutions) – result in medium costs for both categories since specialization reduces economies of scale (as compared to general institutions) but mitigates maladaptation.

At a specific moment of time – in the strategic space of economic agents – public and general institutions of society are given in the sense that agents can hardly impact on their features. They therefore try to reduce coordination costs by establishing contractual agreements that reduce the level of maladaptation costs resulting from the design of the public and general institutional framework. However, this can lead them to face excessive governance costs. They therefore pool coordination efforts, by building private and specific institutions, so that they can benefit from economies of centralization.

Consequently, coordination always results from the combination of the recourse to two contrasted types of institutions – the publics and general ones, on the one hand; the private and specialized ones on the other hand – and of (bilateral) contractual agreements. Agents try to maximize efficiency (or minimize transaction costs) by designing private institutions and establishing contracts so as to benefit from the most efficient possible ones; and by adequately combining these various coordination devices.

3 SETTLING INTELLECTUAL PROPERTY RIGHTS

According to Barzel (1989) and North (1990) a PR system is a set of rules and mechanisms that delimits rights of use over economic resources and allocates them to decisions makers so as to enable them to take economic actions. It is based, first, on a delimitation of these rights – consisting in setting the frontiers among different ways of using resources and among regimes for appropriating the output of these uses – and on a process of allocation of these rights, that are granted to individuals or groups. These operations are qualified as 'measurement' by Barzel and they generate measurement costs. Second 'enforcement' mechanisms implement these rights of use by excluding every untitled agent from access to the protected resources, or from capturing the output of its use. This refers to controlling access, supervising use, granting authorization for use and punishing unauthorized use (either to get damages or to dissuade potential infringers) and it generates 'enforcement' costs.

The 'measurement' and the 'enforcement' of property rights can be performed by either the public and general institutions of the society, or by private and specialized institutions, or by the agents themselves. In fact, they are performed jointly by the three types of agent given the optimal mix of advantages and costs of centralization (as pointed out in section 2). Indeed, if property rights were measured and enforced by the agents on a decentralized basis only, the community would be deprived of economies of centralization. In addition, negative externalities would occur because a decentralized claim of exclusive rights of use would result in conflicts and in excessive private capture of public goods (Brousseau 2004). On the contrary, if the measurement and enforcement of property rights was performed centrally by the public and general institutions only, it would result in inefficiencies, because of excessive maladaptation costs. In addition it would lead to an excessive protection of property rights since the costs of securing exclusive rights of use would not be balanced by the evaluation of the marginal utility to protect (while when individuals bear protection costs, they inevitably compare costs with benefits).

Public institutions are therefore essential in participating in the measurement and enforcement of property rights, but they necessarily set up 'incomplete' property rights, since the agents are left with the responsibility to bear (partially) the costs of establishing and defending their exclusive rights of use. They have therefore incentives to do so only when it is of economic value. This contributes to an 'optimal' level of protection (which is therefore incomplete). Then economic agents can decide to minimize the costs associated with measurement and enforcement by collectivizing their efforts in creating private institutions aimed at contributing to settling property rights.

To be more precise, it seems necessary to establish a distinction between the diverse underlying operations under the measurement and enforcement terms distinguished by North (1990):

- PR measurement implies two essential operations: the delineation of rights of use (so as to avoid, in particular, overlaps among them), and the identification of the owners of intangible goods (that should be clearly established so as to minimize *ex-post* conflicts over the use of resources). The delineation of the scope of PRs impacts on transaction costs: too narrow rights of use multiply transactions, but rights of use which are too wide lead to under-exploitation of resources;[5] it also affects the alignment of private incentives with the collective interest.[6]

- According to French law, which derives from Roman Law, property rights are composed of three sub-categories of rights: 'Usus' is the right to (exclusively) use a resource; 'Fructus' is the right to benefit from the goods and services that are produced thanks to this resource; 'Abusus' is the right to waive the use of resource. One can be inspired by these three categories to point out the diverse operations required to enforce property rights.

  - First, by referring to the 'Usus' notion, it is necessary to perform operations to implement one's right to exclude any third party from the use of the protected resources. This implies two types of operation. First, a supervision effort has to be made to detect unauthorized uses. Second, infringers have to be obliged to stop (and possibly to compensate for the losses borne by the owner of intangible goods).
  - Second, by referring to the 'Abusus' notion, it is necessary to perform operations to enable third parties to use the protected intangible resource when its owner wishes them to do so. This implies granting authorizations of uses.[7] It consists of designing arrangements with users that precisely delineate their rights and duties.
  - Third, by referring to the 'Fructus' notion, IPR enforcement implies the transfer of revenues from the users to the owners of intangible goods when third parties are authorized to use a protected intangible resource. This requires a control of the actual uses of the resource and fee collection operations.

To go further in the analysis of the optimal design of the institutional framework that governs IPRs, we need to analyse how these various tasks are performed by public institutions, private ones and agents (thanks to bilateral contracting).

4 THE INCOMPLETE SETTING OF IPR BY PUBLIC INSTITUTIONS

'Because with any property rights structure transaction costs are positive, rights are never perfectly specified and enforced; some valued attributes are in the public domain' (North 1990, p. 33). North developed these ideas with reference to PRs over tangible resources. We think that this incompleteness is even greater for IPRs, because it is harder to define rights to use, exclude or benefit from the fruits of intangible resources.

In a related paper (Bessy and Brousseau 1997), we analysed why the formal patent system implements incomplete PRs:

- The delimitation of IPR is incomplete for three reasons. First, the description of the invention in the wording of the patent – the codification – is necessarily incomplete. This is due to the boundaries of the human language that cannot completely grasp the very nature of knowledge that is partly embodied in human skills, organizational routines and equipment. It is also due to the strategic behaviour of inventors who often do not disclose all the details of their inventions to protect them through secrecy (because they anticipate imperfect legal protection). Second, the claimed protection – the patent scope – is irremediably unclear. Since technology is constantly evolving, it is difficult to anticipate with certainty all the actual materialization and implementation of a technical principle.[8] Third, the universe of technologies is so complex that it would be prohibitively costly to gather in the patent office the required skills and information to perform an efficient *ex ante* control guaranteeing that no overlap exists between a given claim and a pre-existing (patented or not) invention. An *ex post* control based on contradictory debates in courts is resource saving, since it enables public institutions to control only a minute part of the registered patents, and courts get free access to the expertise of the prosecutor and of the defender (see section 6).
- Public institutions also incompletely enforce IPR. This requires a complex evaluation of technical realizations in order to detect patent infringement. It would be prohibitively costly to require from a central administrative body the systematic evaluation of all technical devices. This body would also come up against the difficulty of gathering together the needed cognitive capacities to cover efficiently all the technical fields. That is why the supervision of patent infringement is delegated to patentees that have to detect infringers and to bring cases before the courts by themselves. As pointed out above, courts, moreover, rely on the expertise capacities of economic agents to settle infringement disputes.

For works of authorship, the measurement and enforcement difficulties are similar to those associated with patents if one establishes comparisons with PRs over tangible resources.[9] Interpretation problems are however weaker, since it is the form of expression that is protected, not the 'parent idea'.

Property rights on the works of authorship are not, however, systematically and completely measured and enforced by public institutions.

- There is first a measurement boundary that is related to the management of a central registration system for title deeds. Such a system is essential to the working of an IPR system. Without it, it would be prohibitively costly for a producer to check if he or she has not recreated an already protected work. Users would not be able to know easily if the resources they use are in the public domain. Moreover, the identification of the owners of protected works would be prohibitively costly. However, works of authorship are so numerous that it would be excessively expensive to systematically and freely register all of them. In the copyright system, copyright holders have to register their works voluntarily at the copyright office (otherwise their title deeds cannot be legally defended). *Droits d'Auteur* are incompatible with a registration process because no one can be obliged to claim 'natural rights'. There is therefore no systematic registration process.[10] Thus, both in the US and in France, public institutions do not ensure a complete 'measurement' of property rights over works of authorship.
- There is a second measurement problem that is linked to the 'fair use doctrine' (*droit de courte citation* in *Droit d'Auteur* law). For practical reasons, but also to preserve freedom of expression and creation, the reproduction without explicit authorization of a part or of an entire work of authorship is permitted in certain conditions. A writer can quote another writer, a musician can be inspired by a theme created by another composer, the user of a record or software can duplicate it for safety reasons and for private use and so on. These various minor infringements to the wording of the law create many ambiguous situations where it is difficult to judge the fraudulent character of a quotation or copy or public performance of a protected work. Thus copyrights are property rights whose boundaries are ambiguous.
- Third, enforcement problems arise. As in the case of patents, the cost of a centralized and systematic detection of IPR infringements would be prohibitive given the tremendous number of daily uses of protected works of authorship. Moreover, central detection would generate problems of interpretation because of the ambiguities mentioned above.

In addition to these arguments, the non-rival nature of information has to be taken into account. In order to motivate inventors to innovate, authors to create and entrepreneurs to finance their activities, public authorities have to create the framework of an IPR system. However, they have to favour *ex post* the diffusion of inventions and works of authorship since they are non-rival goods. Moreover, it is not in the collective interest to favour the constitution of monopolies and dominant positions. In that context, it can be considered as efficient to create a minimal framework that sets up IPR principles, and to let potential owners of intangible goods pay for making their rights of use effectively exclusive. This favours diffusion, everything remaining equal, since authors and inventors will not exercise their exclusion rights for those creations that do not have a high economic value. It eases also the diffusion of works that are not created according to a rent seeking logic. At the same time, it creates high incentives for authors, inventors and entrepreneurs to dedicate means to produce radical inventions and major creations. Moreover, the fact that they bear the costs of measuring and enforcing their IPRs leads them to limit their efforts to prevent leakages and encourages them to create efficient structures to govern IPRs.

With regard to IPRs, a minimal level of public intervention is therefore necessary. It consists, first, in creating a minimal framework. This leads to the promulgation of an IP law that establishes the principle of IPRs and enables the general judicial system to settle conflicts. The second necessary intervention is the management of a registration system. A unique and free database centralizing all the claims for exclusiveness is essential to avoid overlapping among claims and unintentional infringement. At the same time, public authorities could be led to check the costs and benefits of claims for exclusivity on non-rival resources to solve optimally the protection diffusion dilemma. In particular, when expected positive effects of diffusion are strong, public authorities are likely to avoid the emergence of monopolies too wide in scope. This is typically the risk with technological monopolies that can slow down innovation. That is why public institutions are more strongly involved in the measurement of patents than of copyright. While patent offices do not control the validity of claims perfectly,[11] their role is to restrict their scope. The copyright office does not perform that task, which is eventually done *ex-post* by courts when conflicts occur.

5 THE PRIVATE INSTITUTIONS TRADE-OFF

Public institutions do not set complete IPRs because it would be prohibitively costly, while at the same time economies of scale, scope and learning seem to occur in the performing of certain tasks related to the enforcement of rights (section 5.1). Agents are therefore encouraged to create private institutions responsible for making these economies in settling their property rights over intangible goods. One can however wonder why the whole governance of IPRs is not fully taken charge of by these private institutions. In our view, this is due to two causes. First, collective governance mitigates IPRs (section 5.2). Second, the trade-off between collective and individual governance is not in all circumstances in favour of private institutions (section 5.3).

5.1 The Benefits from Collectivization

Since public institutions do not set up a complete IPR system, owners of intangible goods must perform an important part of measurement and enforcement operations. However, many redundant operations are required to govern different intellectual title deeds, and since these operations require common expertise and means, there are potential economies of scale, economies of scope and learning effects in collectivizing the performing of these operations:[12]

- Economies of scale arise because the supervision of users and detection of potential IPR infringements are largely independent of the specific features of each protected piece. Moreover, there are potentially large transaction cost economies when transactions are performed over a title deed portfolio rather than piece by piece.
- Economies of scope: when a set of agents decides to coordinate their efforts in governing their property rights, they can reach the critical mass in the performance of each operation that is needed to actually measure and enforce rights. They can also specialize resources. This allows them to dedicate the saved resources to perform additional operations in order to extend their scope. In concrete terms, when a collective governance device manages a title deed portfolio, it can extend defence efforts to markets and uses that otherwise would not be targeted by individual owners of intangible goods.
- Learning effects draw from learning by doing occurring when investigation, negotiation and fee collection operations are repeated. Learning benefits are also linked to the division of labour that allows specialization. Therefore, the wider portfolio of title deeds to be governed and the larger the organization in charge, the stronger the learning curve.

These diverse potentialities encourage the emergence of private collective governance devices that manage portfolios of title deeds by detecting IPR infringements and negotiating authorizations of use and remuneration principles. They can also fix general terms of contracts (and even norms of interactions among agents) to reduce negotiation costs.

5.2 The Mitigating Effect

By reducing individual measurement and enforcement costs, these private institutions make IPRs stronger. At the same time collectivization leads to the mitigation of the actual properties of the property rights as they are designed by the wording of the law (section 5.2.1). Information costs are to a large extent the cause of this mitigation (section 5.2.2).

5.2.1 Collective management and IPR mitigation

To actually benefit from economies of scale and scope, the collective management of IPRs, and especially of enforcement, requires a common policy by the owners of intangible goods. Indeed, if owners were to grant diverse users with customized rights of use at customized prices, many of the economies generated by the collectivization would be lost. In fact, collectivization really leads to a mitigation of the sovereignty of IPR owners since it often makes it impossible for them to discriminate between the various users when there is a large number of them.

For instance, collectivization often leads to the implementation of statutory licence regimes (*licence légale* in France). Thanks to statutory licences, any potential user can use the protected work without requesting authorization from the owner. In turn the user has to pay a statutory licensing fee. This saves the costs of managing authorizations for each specific use of each protected piece. In the case of music, statutory licences draw on the impossibility of actually applying the rights granted to authors to authorize or forbid the uses of their recorded/published works because of the tremendous number of possible uses by a vast amount of users (private users, but also broadcasters, discos, managers of public facilities and so on).[13]

Such general authorization regimes prevent owners of intangible goods from exercising their exclusion rights. In addition, they do not benefit from the actual revenues of their asset. The collective governance device in charge of gathering revenues does not negotiate fees for use work by work. This would annihilate most economies of scale in bargaining. It claims a general fee for the use of its portfolio without checking how each piece is actually used. Irrespective of distribution rules, the collected fees do not therefore correspond to the actual revenues generated by each individual invention or work of authorship. As a result, inventors and authors do not get revenues in relation to the actual use and value of their creation when they rely on collective governance.

This second effect can, however, be alleviated by the management of a 'per use' fee system. Such a system is highly preferable for owners of the most successful creations because they can benefit from the revenues actually generated by their work,[14] without any deduction being made by the other members of the pool. This ability is, however, linked to information costs that are themselves influenced by technology.

5.2.2 IPR mitigation and information costs

The mitigation of IPRs, which becomes apparent when they are managed by collective bodies, is strongly linked to information costs. This is well illustrated by the potential impact of information and communication technologies (ICTs) on the management of patented and copyrighted works of the mind. By enabling a fine tracking at a low cost of any use of intangible assets, these technologies potentially enable the restoration of a customized management of at least royalties collection and authorization granting.

Digital information dissemination systems, like the Internet, do not only provide patent and copyright holders with new opportunities to diffuse their resources, they also enable them to obtain better control of the uses of their material. *Ex ante*, they can encrypt data files to prevent unauthorized use and copies. *Ex post*, it is also possible to keep track of every use of a protected asset and to identify who (at least what computer) processed it. This 'revolution' in the ability to control rights of use thanks to ICTs is now analysed in many papers, among which Lessig (1999), Lemley (1998) and Brousseau (2004) can be quoted since they point out how the principle of IPRs *per se* is questioned. ICTs can be used to strengthen or bypass the current IPR system, and challenge the economics of the system.[15] This leads to the possibility of developing new types of broadcasting and diffusion systems that enable a more customized management of IPRs (often qualified as Digital Rights Management (DRM) systems). For instance, in the music industry, several companies are currently implementing 'pay per downloading' systems (which might even discriminate between 'pay per listening' and 'pay per copying'). These systems allow users to download digital files. There are also digital radio channels that, when they are not free, may charge the listeners according to what they actually listened to. In these types of systems, it is very easy to know exactly the intensity of 'use' of each copyrighted work. This leads to the possible diversification of licensing agreements, since statutory licences are no longer the sole workable solution. As in the case of 'source licences' in music, on-line broadcasters can directly negotiate licences with copyright holders both to by-pass collective societies and to avoid enforcing collective agreements about the level of licence fees.

They can also negotiate voluntary collective licensing (Working Group on Intellectual Property Rights 1995).

In fact, all these technological solutions enable the easy identification at a relatively low cost of pieces of protected works, their users and owners. It potentially facilitates the remuneration of authors, inventors or copyright holders according to the actual exploitation of their pieces of work. The major effect is, however, to enable the unbundling of the various operations associated with transactions over intangible goods: 'control of actual uses of authorized uses', 'authorization management', 'money gathering' and so on. In particular, the former ('control of actual uses of authorized uses') can remain centrally managed by specialized bodies since there are strong economies of scale, scope and learning, while the latter ('authorization management') can be more decentrally managed by owners of intangible goods (who could continue to prefer collectivization in some cases) to reduce the mitigating effect described in this section. This is confirmed by the analysis made by Paris (1998) on the evolution of the devices of collective governance of IPRs in France.

5.2.3 Pooling means, managing risks

So far we have not dealt with the way commercial risk can be managed by collective bodies. There are several ways of paying authors or inventors when their IPRs are collectively valued. Two extreme cases illustrate this in the case of works of authorship.

- On the one hand, the collective body can act as if it was a 'transparent medium' between the users and the owners. This means that it tries to collect all the revenues generated by each intangible asset and transfer them back to each owner (its cost deducted). This requires a huge supervision effort since the collective body has to identify every use of each protected work. SACEM, in France, is a good example of this way of operating. Its different investigation means concentrate on the estimation of the uses of each type of work of authorship and collected revenues are shared according to the observed uses of each piece of the repertoire.[16]
- On the other hand, the collective body takes charge not only of the gathering of generated revenues but also of the enforcement of the risks associated with the valorization of the intangible assets and of the collection process. This happens when the collective body pays the owners of intangible goods through an *ex ante* lump sum payment (*ex ante* meaning before revenue collection) and is the residual claimant for all the generated revenues. To a large extent, major companies correspond to this case. By employing authors or by acquiring works

of authorship from freelance authors for a lump sum, they typically bear the risk of valorization of the work of authorship.[17]

Obviously, the latter case is an extreme case of 'collectivization', since the collective body becomes the property rights holder. But there are similar cases in which there is no actual property right transfer (and therefore a lower level of risk bearing by the collective body). The US royalty collection societies in music are examples of such an intermediate case. These societies neither pay *ex ante* lump sum payments to copyright holders, nor pay according to the generated revenues. Instead, they pay fees that are linked to some measure of the success of pieces (essentially based on charts) but that are statutory and independent of the collected fees. They thus do not share the collected fees among owners of intangible goods. They are the residual claimants of all the collected revenues, but pay the authors according to their relative contribution to those fees. This incentive mechanism encourages owners to join the society (or to continue membership of it) instead of valorizing their works by themselves, and to produce valuable works.

It must be pointed out that the two extreme logics of managing risks and authors' remuneration do not provide the collective bodies with the same incentives to collect fees. The 'transparent medium' shares the collection costs with the authors. Its marginal costs of collection are therefore lower than those of the 'risk bearer' since the latter bears the whole collection cost. It therefore leads to smaller revenues than the 'transparent medium'. This is probably one of the reasons why the scope of SACEM's collection effort is wider than that of the US collection fee societies.[18] Although it is difficult to obtain accurate data, one can imagine that the 'transparent medium' solution provides authors (who have to be risk lovers) with higher revenues than the 'risk bearer' system. However, the latter should ensure a better allocation of collective resources than the former because it prevents too intensive collection effort and favours diffusion (since many marginal uses of intangible assets are free).

5.3 Factors Favouring the Recourse to Private Institutions

Before analysing how various tasks associated with the management of IPRs are taken charge of by diverse governance devices, it is useful to point out the diverse factors that favour a collective management of these rights. Indeed, measurement and enforcement operations do not require the same type of capabilities. Moreover, there are various types of property right infringements that do not require the same level of expertise to be countered.

In this section, we will therefore point out three categories of factors that influence the ability to collectivize IPR enforcement efforts and means:

- The first is related to the behaviour of users that can infringe IPRs in different ways (section 5.3.1).
- The second is connected to the very nature of the assets that are protected (section 5.3.2).
- The third is correlated to the behaviour of intellectual property owners (owners of intangible goods) whose diffusion policies also influence the ability of collective bodies to take charge of the defence of IPRs (section 5.3.3).

This will help us clarify the type of task that can be collectivized and establish a link between the obviousness of IPR infringements and the ability to collectivize their defence.[19]

5.3.1 Users' influence: the various modes of IPR infringements

There are at least two ways of infringing IPRs and collective governance devices are not necessarily equally efficient in dealing with both of them.

- The 'servile copy' (to use the French law categories) consists in duplicating or using an unauthorized copy of a protected intellectual work. It can also consist in displaying it to the public without authorization. This work can be either a technical realization or a work of authorship, and the copy can be made either by the user or by a third party. Since it is a question here of a 'line for line' duplication (or display) of the protected material, it is quite easy to note and certify the rights violation in order to claim either for the payment of royalties (and possibly damages), or for the suspension of the use (and possibly the destruction of the copy).
- 'Plagiarism' consists in drawing one's inspiration from an existing work to produce a new and original one. In this case there is only a partial duplication of the protected initial work. This partial copy is, moreover, incorporated into a new and different work that can incorporate actual innovations and original creations. IPR infringement is therefore much harder to collectivize because it requires specific knowledge of each of the features of each protected work. In fact, it is essentially the authors or the innovators who know their creation well enough to detect plagiarism efficiently (Bessy and Chateauraynaud 1995).

As a consequence, defence against plagiarism is much more complex to carry out at a collective level since it requires a close knowledge of what is plagiarized, which is not the case for servile copies that requires a way to recognize salient features of the copied material only.

Servile copying and plagiarism can be performed on technical realizations as well as on works of authorship. There are thus potentialities for and obstacles to the collective management of both patents and copyrights. However, the potential of both forms of IPR modes of infringement is not equal for technical realization and for works of authorship. Since it is the form of the latter that is protected, they are relatively more intensively vulnerable to servile copies. For instance, in the music industry most copyright infringements are performed through the public display or through the duplication of a particular recorded performance of a piece of music. The cost of reproduction is very low and there is little difference, for the user, between the value of the copy and the value of the original (Besen and Kirby 1989). This is basically why collective bodies play an important role in the enforcement of IPRs. It must be pointed out, however, that the various authors' rights management societies that exist either in the US or in France do not take charge of the detection and combat of plagiarism. Therefore they do not arbitrate in conflicts between authors. It is the same for the associations – like the Business Software Alliance or the Software Publishing Association – that have been created at the international level to detect illicit copies of software but that do not take charge of the management of plagiarism conflicts between software publishers.

5.3.2 The nature of intangible assets

Whatever the type of IPR infringement, two essential features of the protected material influence the ability of the owners of intangible goods to collectivize the management of their rights: the ambiguity with which their rights are defined (section 5.3.2.1), and the public display of the uses of the protected material (section 5.3.2.2). Whereas the first feature corresponds to the ease with which competitors can invent around or the capacity with which misappropriation of IPR can be specified, the second feature is linked to the ease with which misappropriation of IPR can be detected.

5.3.2.1 The ambiguity of measurements As pointed out above, the (use, exclusion, remuneration and so on) rights granted by public institutions to an author or an inventor can be either precise or quite vague. If one compares patents to copyrights, the former provides the patentee with exclusive rights that are more difficult to interpret than the latter. Indeed, there are many gaps between actual technical realizations and the wording of the patent because of the incomplete description of the invention, and because of the 'equivalence doctrine'. It is therefore difficult to decipher an actual technical realization sufficiently to reveal and evaluate overlapping between it and the title deed. Moreover, it is quite impossible to forecast such overlapping before the achievement of the technical realization both because any development process is uncertain and because the scope of a patent is partially *ex post* clarified by the courts (when prosecutions occur). On the other hand, in the case of copyright it is the codification of an expression that is protected. The title deed is therefore composed of the protected work itself. Moreover, the law states precisely how the codification has to be performed to delineate IPR. It also anticipates, in the case of collective production, what the rights of the diverse participants in the production process are (for example, composers, lyricists, arrangers, singers, musicians, in the case of recorded music). As pointed out above, copyright can therefore be considered as less ambiguously delimited (measured) by public institutions.

As a result, it is easier to create collective bodies to manage the latter category of property rights than the former. Indeed, when delineation is clear, any third party, including the one to whom their governance is delegated, can more easily identify protected works. Moreover, it is easier to specify and to detect the uses of a protected material (because interpretation margins are small) and to track their actual uses. Lastly, clear delineation facilitates the design of standardized and codified methods of identification of works – word sequences for written materials, note sequences for music and so on. This facilitates the comparison between the copy of the displayed material and the original and does not call for value judgments to certify similarities. The decoding of a realization (performance) can also be performed by less specialized individuals than in the case of patents. For instance, in France, SACEM's inspectors are not specialized in any kind of music. They visit any type of public place where music is played and record, thanks to special codification methods, the main characteristics of the pieces played. This enables the organization to check if the fees have been paid and to detect infringements.

5.3.2.2 Public display The ability to collectivize the combat against IPR infringement also depends upon the public character of the use of the protected material. Indeed, when by nature the use of the intangible resources cannot be kept secret, actual uses of it are easier to observe. Supervision efforts are potentially more fruitful. IPR owners are therefore encouraged to collectivize these efforts, essentially to benefit from economies of scope. On the contrary, when potential infringements are not made public, collective supervision is less profitable.

This is basically why there is at first sight a difference between the copyright regime and that of patents. Works of authorship are, to a large extent, products or components of products that will be transmitted to some third party either for private use or for public performance or broadcast. Technological ideas can, however, be incorporated into equipment that is privately used. It is therefore much more complex to organize a collective verification system of patent infringements than to design a mechanism to supervise copyright use.

This statement, however, needs qualifying. Indeed, technological ideas are often incorporated into products sold to the public. In that case, it is possible to collectivize the means of performing a costless systematic supervision system. This is, for instance, the case in the pharmaceutical industry, where specialized consultant firms produce very precise and accurate data on the actual sales of the different patented molecules. This enables patentees to benefit from precise information about the actual uses of their patents by licensees.

In the same spirit, collective institutions cannot easily combat some types of copyright infringement because they are fundamentally private. The private copying of records, for instance, is quite impossible to actually prohibit. On-line exchange of music pieces is easier to prohibit, especially if the defenders can implement technologies that enable them to analyse the details of exchanges among members of P2P communities, or even to analyse the content of hard disks on computers in networks. Obviously, privacy legislation and technologies enable users to fake their private exchanges. It is thus the public display and more generally the visibility of uses, and not the legal nature of the rights, that influence the ability to collectivize their enforcement.

5.3.3 Owners' influence: the diverse diffusion policies

The ability to collectivize supervision is also strongly dependent upon the diffusion policies of owners of intangible goods. They can either favour the widest possible spread and use of their intellectual production in order to be remunerated by high royalty fees, or prefer to forbid any use in order to benefit from their exclusive rights of use. An intermediate policy consists of discriminating among the various potential users by providing authorization to exploit only to specific categories of complementary users.

The first policy is dominant in the case of works of authorship because these works are consumer products rather than production means. The consumption of a work by a final user or by an intermediary that performs or broadcasts it does not reduce the potential revenues of the author or of the copyright owners. On the contrary, it can increase its reputation and therefore the propensity of the public to consume its production. A patentee can also follow this type of policy. Indeed, in some industries technological interdependencies are so high that patentees are either encouraged or obliged to licence their patents to any demander. Technological spillovers, increasing returns of adoption or regulation and standardization constraints can indeed lead all the players in an industry to use the same technology. The resulting widespread policy leads to the adoption of a regime of general authorization of duplication and use in exchange for royalty fee collection, and favours recourse to collective governance.

On the other hand, when it is a question of prohibiting uses, the implementation of a collective mechanism is much more difficult. There are two reasons for this. First, most of the time the prohibition is not absolute. Many situations in which some types of uses are authorized exist. For instance, a patentee whose policy is to exploit directly its patented inventions can nevertheless grant licences (at least restrictive ones) to partners that control assets which are essential to exploit the patent in a specific national or niche market, or to developers that can invent around the initial technology. In such cases, a central supervision body would be obliged to deal with a tremendous number of dispensations to a general principle of forbidden use, which would be quite impossible to manage. The second reason why collective mechanisms are less efficient in case of discriminatory and use-forbidding policy is linked to the difficulty of enforcing the prohibition of uses. In the last resort, banning can only depend upon public authorities that are the sole agent granted with the ability to use violence to enforce a decision. As a result, actual exclusion can occur only if IPR infringement is verifiable and duly certified by a court. Moreover, the court has to estimate that an actual exclusion is legitimate because damages would not suffice to atone for actual losses. Given the long delays and the high cost of lawsuits (see Williamson 1985) especially in the case of patents (Lanjouw 1998, Lanjouw and Schankerman 2001), the difficulty in actually enforcing exclusion rights often leads owners of intangible goods (especially patentees) to negotiate with infringers.[20] The actual management of exclusion rights requires a high level of customization, and it is difficult to collectivize.

5.3.4 The public versus private governance of IPRs trade-off

Owners of intangible goods face a trade-off when they have to decide how to organize the defence of their property rights. On the one hand, there are economies in collectivizing it, which call for the establishment of private institutions, and even for the performance by public institutions of certain tasks. On the other hand, the collective defence of IPRs generates inefficiencies, especially when infringements consist of plagiarism rather than servile copy; when formal institutions ambiguously delineate IPRs; when the uses of intangible resources can be kept private; or when owners of intangible goods seek to discriminate the users of their creations. Table 8.1 sums up these diverse elements according to the different types of operation required in managing IPR systems, given the various possible governance needs.

Table 8.1 IPR governance tasks and the division of labour among governance devices

Operations	Device Likely to Perform the Operation (and conditions)		
	Public Institution	**Private Institution**	**Owners (competitors)**
Measure:			
Delineation of IPR scope	+	Possible support	Possible support
Identification of owners	+	If no public institution	Possible support
Enforcement			
Usus: Exclusion enforcement			
Detection of illegal use	SC CD PD DP	SC CD PD DP	Pl AD SU PP
Exclusion	+ +		
Abusus: Waivement enforcement			
Authorization management		DP	PP
Fructus: Revenue collection enforcement			
Control of actual usage of authorized uses		PD	SU
Money collecting		DP	PP

Note: SC: Servile copies; Pl: Plagiarism; CD: Clear delineation of IPRs; AD: Ambiguous delineation; PD: Public display; SU: Uses kept secret; DP: Diffusion policies; PP: Prohibition and discrimination policies.

In matter of measurement there are strong advantages in relying on public and general institutions, both because there are strong economies of 'collectivization' and because general and unspecialized solutions do not generate too high costs of maladaptation.

- Property right delineation is likely to be taken charge of by public institutions (i) because public authorities are really able to implement mandatory registering, ensuring that the delineation of exclusive rights of use is really public and clear, for most of the potential stakeholders

(other owners of intangible goods, potential users, future creators and so on); (ii) because they are able to cover wide communities; and (iii) because they benefit from a power of last resort. Public institutions can, however, as shown in section 6, rely on private efforts and expertise to decrease the cost of PR delineation.
- The identification of owners should also be centralized to benefit from a more efficient IPR system (see section 4). Moreover, it should be performed by public institutions to enable intangible resource users to identify owners easily.

In matter of enforcement, collectivization is also useful. The ability to collectivize is however strongly dependent upon the owners' policy:

- 'Usus'
    - There are many obstacles to the collectivization of illegal use detection. Collectivization is feasible for private copies, when IPR delineation is clear, when there is public display or when diffusion policies are performed.
    - To maintain civil peace, public institutions have to maintain the monopoly of legitimate violence. As a result, last resort exclusion operations have to be performed by public institutions.
- 'Abusus': the ability to collectivize the management of the granting of authorization for use greatly depends upon the chosen diffusion policy.
- 'Fructus':
    - The control of the actual (intensity of) uses of the resources is likely to be centralized because there are economies of scale, scope and learning, if the type of use of the diverse works of mind is at least partially standardized and made public.
    - Money collecting operations can be a source of major economies of scale and scope if the users are numerous and using a wide range of protected intangible resources, because centralization will enable the limitation of the number of bilateral transfers and associated transaction costs (negotiation, payment securization and so on).

Table 8.1 indicates, for instance, that the detection of illegal uses is efficiently performed by public institutions in case of servile copies (SC in the 'Public institution' column on the 'Illegal use detection' line).

6 SPECIALIZED AND GENERIC INSTITUTIONS

When it focuses on the performing of some specific task in a specific field, an institution benefits from economies of learning. Moreover, while they are collective, institutions generate less maladaptation costs when they are focused since the specificities of the domain can be taken into account. On the other hand, more general and less specialized institutions benefit from potentially larger economies of scale and scope.

A good example of the positive effects of specialization is given by SACEM. This French collective governance structure has developed specialized investigation methods that are tailored to the specificities of works of authorship in music. It has also developed specific codification methods and databases to keep track of protected pieces. SACEM's investigators systematically track the uses of the various music pieces and the organization systematizes the collection of royalty fees from every kind of user. Its focus on music enables the organization to be aware of what is happening in every aspect of the music world. This maximizes its ability to gather royalties, and also to finely tune the rate of royalties to the users' actual willingness to pay (which depends both on the added value of music and its profitability). SACEM's specialization also enables it to share the collected funds efficiently among its members.

While there are exceptions to the principle, the more focused the institution (on a specific field and a specific task), the more likely it is to manage IPR governance efficiently. Since private institutions are constitutionally built to exercise a specific set of tasks in a specific field, they tend to be more specialized than public institutions, which are designed to deal with general situations. For example, the judicial system was created to solve all kinds of problems. As argued by Williamson (1985), this leads courts to be relatively inefficient conflict resolution mechanisms when they deal with complex and idiosyncratic cases.

However, this general principle can be countered by proactive specialization policies. Indeed, public institutions involved in the governance of property rights are sometimes tailored to specific tasks or to specific fields. This is, for instance, typically the case of patent offices that are public, but that are specialized in the task of measuring property rights. Although they are not specialized in every sub-field of each technique, they employ engineers that are used to dealing with the legal, economic and technical issues, which enable them to exercise some control over claims and to arbitrate debates among claimants and their potential competitors. This leads to more efficient control than that which is performed over copyrighted material. Another example is given by the comparison between the US and French courts in charge of patent infringements. In France, courts that are not entirely dedicated to IPR related problems determine suits. Judges manage a small number of such cases in their careers. They are often reproached with judging technico-economic conflicts according to a purely legal logic that leads to inefficiencies. This is not the case in the US, where the Federal court created a specialized court in 1982. Intellectual property specialists consider that this specialized court considerably reinforces the strength of IPRs because they can efficiently manage complex technological cases.

Focusing an institution on the performing of a specific set of tasks in a specific field is a good way to generate learning effects. But other factors come into play. In particular the way the organization relies on individual players' expertise matters, since the latter know the details of the technological and economic problems they have to deal with.

- Such a use of expertise can be performed, first, by implementing litigation processes based on a conflictual debate between economic agents – that is, an accusatory process arbitrated by a judge between a prosecutor and a defendant – rather than processes based on investigations performed by the judge or a police system – that is, an inquisitory process where the judicial system manages the investigations itself. This is fundamentally the difference between US courts and French ones and it prevents the latter from dealing efficiently with highly complex technical cases,[21] whether they are related to technology or not, because information asymmetries and costs of access to the relevant knowledge are always higher for a third party than for the parties involved in the dispute.
- It can also be performed by linking the institution to the informal conventions and information networks that often structure communities. Both the US Patent Office's examiner and US specialized judges maintain close relationships with the professional milieu they are in charge of. They can be members of expert societies, attend conferences, consult experts and so on. All these means are used to learn the informal interpretation rules, fair practice rules, technical knowledge and so on that are specific to any scientific and industrial field (for example, Nelson 1993). This enables them to take more accurate decisions than French examiners and judges who are more cut off from the industrial milieu (Bessy and Brousseau 1997). Cooper (1993) explains these strong interactions between experts and judges in the US by the fact that, in its origins, the US patent system was partially managed by industrial unions.

These elements explain why the US patent system seems to guarantee IPRs better than the French one,[22] even if in both systems a wide degree of measurement and enforcement operations have to be performed by owners of intangible goods.

7 CONCLUDING REMARKS

By referring to the organization of governance of patents and copyrights both in the US and in France, Table 8.2 indicates the entity that is responsible for the various tasks involved in the settlement of intellectual property rights.

Table 8.2 The governance of patents and copyrights in France and in the US

	Patents		Copyrights/DAs	
Operations	**US**	**France**	**US**	**France**
Measure:				
Delineation of scope of IPRs	Spec Pub Inst	Spec Pub Inst	Owner	Owners
Identification of owners of intangibles	Spec Pub Inst	Spec Pub Inst	Spec Pub Inst	Owners/ Priv Inst
Enforcement				
Usus: Exclusion enforcement				
Illegal uses detection	Owners	Owners	Owners/ Priv Inst	Owners/ Priv Inst
Exclusion	Spec Pub Inst	Pub Inst	Pub Inst	Pub Inst
Abusus: Waivement enforcement				
Authorization management	Owners	Owners	Pub & Priv Inst	Priv Inst
Fructus: Revenues collection enforcement				
Control of actual usage of authorized uses	Owners	Owners	Priv Inst	Priv Inst
Money gathering	Owners	Owners	Priv Inst	Priv Inst

Note: Pub Inst: Public Institution; Priv Inst: Private Institution; Spec: Specialized.

There are two major differences between the patent and copyright systems. First, public institutions are more involved in the measurement of IPRs in the former case than in the latter. This is largely due to the potentially high negative externalities of a bad governance of property rights on technological inventions. Second, the enforcement of IPRs and management of their valorization is more collectivized in the copyright system than in the patent one. The former system is well suited to combating servile copies and to the management of large-scale diffusion policies, while the latter is more efficient against plagiarism and when customized diffusion policies are carried out. One can, however, point out that, to an extent, this situation could evolve. Indeed, in industries where many standardized technological licence agreements are set up because innovators have diffusion policies (Bessy and Brousseau 1998), the implementation of private collective governance means would be efficient to supervise use and collect fees. Institutions comparable to SACEM could emerge. This is probably a major issue in the software industry, especially with the development of digital networks. This highlights the fact, at least, that the debate around the protection of software by patents rather than by copyright misses two important points: the type of diffusion policy chosen by owners of intangible goods; and the efficiency of the institutional framework to actually enforce IPRs. If such collective private institutions existed, producers of works of the mind would be less reluctant to authorize their use widely because they would benefit from higher revenues at not significantly higher costs. Favouring the emergence of such institutions in the software or pharmaceutical industries would therefore probably favour a wider diffusion of patented material.

There are obviously other arguments to consider. Indeed, software developers can be interested in benefits other than financial returns. In particular, they can seek to benefit from spillovers provided by the other developers. In this case, open source licences are an efficient way to organize the diffusion of source code (see the arguments developed by Bessen and Maskin (2000) and Saint Paul (2003)). At the same time, as pointed out in Bessy and Brousseau (1998), private institutions can be useful to facilitate the transmission and sharing of knowledge among partners involved in the development of a common technology. Put another way, private institutions are not only used to support and facilitate commercial transactions – for example, by taking charge of the management of payments – they are also useful to coordinate economic agents. This is exactly the role played by communities in open source software. Communities establish and enforce rules to ensure an efficient management of knowledge; efficient being interpreted in various ways across different communities. The same might happen within patent pools (see Merges, 1996, 2001 and Shapiro, 2000).

When one compares the US and the French patent systems, one can point out that the main difference is the greater specialization of US institutions. This greater specialization is largely due to the dedication of some courts to patent infringement cases and to the intensive relationship between patent office examiners and judges with the professional and technical communities. Since the French and US patent laws are very similar, this huge governance difference is probably one of the major reasons why technological IPRs are stronger in the US than in France. The comparison between the US and the French concerning works of authorship indicates two things. First, since public institutions do not participate in the measurement operations, especially because there is no *Droits d'Auteur* registration system, there is a source of inefficiency because involuntary *Droit d'Auteur* infringement is more likely to occur. Second, the US system enables a greater flexibility in finely tailoring the governance structure according to authors' preferences and to the specific economics of each type of work of authorship. Put another way, the US public institutional framework allows a greater flexibility in the way individual owners can manage their rights. It is partly linked to the fact that public institutions try to provide an efficient infrastructure to measure IPRs *ex ante* and solve conflicts *ex post*; while in France public institutions do not provide such an efficient infrastructure to IPR owners, leading them either to trade less on technology or to collectivize (and thus mitigate) the management of their property title deeds.

This paper therefore illustrates the potentiality of New Institutional Economics to provide useful insights into economic policy. It especially enables us to point out the important complementarities between public and private institutions. It also shows how the devices that govern laws are essential to their actual implementation because they affect their actual properties. This suggests that research in IP economics but also in law and economics in general, especially when it has to deal with competition policies, should take into account the implementation problems more carefully. This would lead to recommendations being made about the organization of public institutions as well as about the support for private ones.

ACKNOWLEDGEMENTS

This paper draws from a research project supported by the French Commissariat Général du Plan's programme *L'entreprise et l'économie de l'immatériel* (The Firm and the Economics of Intangible Resources). It is also extracted from a study funded by the French Department of Culture on the economics of property rights in the music industry. Earlier versions of the paper, entitled *The Governance of Intellectual Property Rights: Patents and Copyrights in France and in the US* were presented and discussed in various conferences and workshops; especially the Inaugural Conference for The International Society for New Institutional Economics (ISNIE) *The*

Present and Future of the New Institutional Economics (19–21 September 1997, Washington University, St. Louis, Missouri, USA) and the DRUID Summer Conference 2003 *Creating, Sharing and Transferring Knowledge, The Role of Geography, Institutions and Organizations*, Copenhagen 12–14 June 2003. We thank the institutions that supported the research programme financially, the organizers that allowed us to have this paper discussed and the participants to those conferences for useful comments. Usual caveats apply.

NOTES

1. As David (1993) reminds us, modern statutory protection of author's copyright arose in early 18th century England with the Act of Anne (1709). Its aim was to implement a workable regulation since the old perpetual monopoly of printers and publishers was no longer actually enforced. Temporary exclusive copyrights were therefore instituted and were no longer reserved to guild members. Thus since its origin copyright holding is not limited to authors and has little to do with the protection of authorship works. This explains why copyright law is a 'regular' property right whose transferability is not submitted to any specific constraint.

   The *Droit d'Auteur* derives from the 18th century philosophy of the Enlightenment. The author, as a human being, is protected because his work reflects his personality and he shall therefore have rights to control how third parties use his work. The 'moral right' (to authorize or forbid any specific use of the protected works) is therefore non-waiveable and the author can license the right to use or reproduce his works. Even if a licence is granted, the author maintains the option of forbidding any specific use of his work.
2. Palmer (1989) or Shapiro and Varian (1998) highlight the available methods that substitute IPRs to protect and valorize innovation, either through contracts (leasing contracts, professional agreements, and so on), protection methods (entry fees, technological protections, bundling…) or commercial strategies (first to market, price discrimination, alliances, exclusion pre-contracts based upon the revelation *ex ante* of consumers' demand).
3. At the same time our analysis will lead us to point out that, while the wording of the law is contrasted under the two legal regimes, the actual practices of producers and users of intangible goods can be made similar, in particular because private institutions complete the incompleteness of the public ones and allow orders to be implemented which are adapted to the transactional constraints that derive from the types of traded intangible goods, from the inventor's strategy to valorize their creation and so on.
4. Throughout this chapter we will contrast public and general institutions with private and specialized ones. Of course we recognize that public institutions could be specialized and that private institutions could be involved in the solving of very heterogeneous coordination problems. However in the first instance it seems relevant to consider that public institutions are, all things being equal, less specialized than private ones, since their scope is intrinsically wider. They apply to all coordination problems to be solved in a given jurisdiction; while private institutions result from the desire of agents who face common coordination problems to solve them jointly (so as to reduce coordination costs). Private institutions tend to be more focused and therefore more specialized (see also section 6).

   The analysis could however be refined by contrasting along an axis on which focus and voluntary joining would increase: public and general institutions (for example, contract law), then public and specialized institutions (IPR system), then private general institutions (for example, trade associations), then private and specific institutions (patent pool).

5. For two reasons. A resource would not be used in the many ways it can be simultaneously used, if no specific rights are associated to each of these uses, since multiple users would mean multiple ownership and negotiated use of a common resource that can be costly and inefficient. Second if rights of use are bundled, transferring property rights to a third party can result in too high a price for the buyer (who is interested only in a sub-set of possible uses), and might be too risky for the seller (who would eventually prefer to control how the asset will be used *ex-post* by the buyer), resulting in non-occurrence of trade.
6. First, externalities are directly dependent upon the scope of PRs. Second, non-rival resources can be inefficiently captured by private interests if exclusive rights of use are bundled.
7. One can consider that the 'illegal uses detection' mentioned above to guarantee the exclusiveness of use is also dedicated to the supervision of authorized users. Indeed to detect illegal uses and to check that the authorized users do not infringe their rights, the same type of investigations are required. This is however different from the supervision of the intensity of use (see below).
8. That is why the 'equivalence doctrine' is central in the patent infringement jurisprudence. This states that the patent covers not only the precise realization that it describes, but also the technical realization that differs from it only by the substitution of technical components that can be considered as equivalents (Haas 1975). As a result, a patent claim is complex to interpret.

   The incompleteness of PRs is reinforced because the knowledge incorporated in a parent idea can generate the production of new (patentable) knowledge. The resulting tangle of PRs generates much fuzziness in 'usus' and 'abusus' rights. Moreover, the patent claim often covers applications that have not already been developed or tested. There are often gaps between the claimed protection and the actual realization. A parallel between these and North's observations (1990) must be established. Indeed North points out that the more uncertain (both quantitatively and qualitatively) the flows generated by an asset, the more difficult the delimitation and allocation of PRs.
9. 'Copyright Laws tend to be rather vague and, once enacted, become subject to a wide range of interpretation by the courts where oversimplification and a misunderstanding of even the most basic elements of a musical structure are common. And finally, in order for the legal framework of copyright to become the basis for a realized economic right, it must be implemented by various institutions – including government agencies (copyright tribunals), collective bodies (performing and mechanical rights societies) and others – where the day-to-day business of negotiating the monetary value of musical works and their use actually takes place' (Théberge 1993, p. 41).
10. When there is no centralized public registration system, private registration emerges. The SACEM does that in France for music pieces. Arruñada (2003) shows that private registration emerges also for tangible property, while private and decentralized solutions can be less efficient than centralized ones.
11. It must be pointed out, however, that patent offices might have biased incentives to control efficiently the validity and scope of claims, since they can be considered as profit making entities. Indeed the revenues from patent offices directly draw from the registration fees paid by the innovators registering patents. It might influence the willingness to reject claims and to proceed to a tough examination process. At the same time, in the long run, a patent office might also consider the reputation effect. If it grants patents after a serious examination process, the patents issued will be considered to be of high quality because they will be hard to contest in courts. Intellectual title deeds owners will therefore compare the cost born *ex ante* (positively correlated to the length and the complexity of the process) with the quality of the protection (and therefore the cost to be born *ex post* in case of judicial conflict, including the cost of uncertainty).
12. Although it is quite difficult to evaluate this type of economy, one can point out that in France the SACEM, which manages authors' and editors' rights, is also a subcontractor for the other rights management and fee collection societies that represent producers, performing artists and musicians. Indeed, while the SACEM was created in the 19th

century, the other societies were created in 1985. The former developed its own supervision capabilities. Since there are economies of scale, scope and learning, the latter have preferred to subcontract their supervision and investigation efforts to the SACEM. In the US, copyright owners also recognize the existence of such economies since they rely on fee collection societies to gather the revenues generated by their IPRs, especially in the case of public performance of them.

Let us remind the readers that:

- In France the Société des Auteurs, Compositeurs et Editeurs de Musique (SACEM) is the only collective society responsible for the collection and distribution of revenues associated with the works of authorship in music. There are also societies involved in the management of the 'neighbouring rights' of performing artists: the ADAMI is in charge of those of the singers and musicians (whose names are printed on the record label); the SPEDIPAM manages the rights of the 'anonymous' orchestra musicians.
- In the US there are three authors' societies: The American Society of Composers, Authors and Publishers (ASCAP), is the most important; Broadcast Music Inc. (BMI) and The Society of European Stage Authors and Composers (SESAC), are smaller.

13. In fact, in the music industry externalities as well as transaction costs led to the implementation of compulsory general licences by public authorities. Parliaments, and therefore the wording of the law, have defined a principle of general statutory licence for the use of recorded material. Any record is therefore considered by the law as licensed to any user or broadcaster (under certain conditions) who has to pay a fee to copy it ('fair remuneration of private copies' in France) or to broadcast it according to rates that have been decided either by the Parliament or by negotiations among organizations representing, on the one hand the users, and on the other hand the owners of intangible goods (unions, collecting societies and so on).
14. From the origin of the broadcasting network until 1941, such a system of flat rate licences – blanket licences – was used to limit transaction costs. Such a licence authorizes the licensee to display any work of the licensor's repertoire in exchange for a fee (generally indexed on licensee's sales) that does not depend upon the type and the quantity of music actually played (Bloch *et al.* 1997). Since such practices have been considered as anticompetitive since 1941, broadcasters have benefited from programme licences (1941 for radio broadcasting, 1950 for TV broadcasting). These licences provide the licensee with a general authorization to use any work of their repertoire, but fees are calculated only on the licensee's revenues affected by the licensor's repertoire.

    That said, most licences remain blanket licences today because they are less expensive to manage. There is however an increasing number of programme licences. Broadcasters seek to make their relationship with collective bodies that represent copyright owners more balanced. They even try to conclude 'source licences' directly with copyright owners. Specialized companies (such as Music Report) developed investigation and information systems that enable them to count precisely each playing of a work and calculate the generated revenues. These systems considerably reduce the cost of such bilateral agreements. Obviously the tracking capabilities provided by ICTs are modifying the traditional trade-off behind the choice of a licensing regime.
15. ICTs can by-pass the IPR-based system to share music as it is done in P2P communities where gift/counter-gift is the basis of exchange. Such principles raise however a problem of long term viability since the incentives to create might be low in a system where the 'consumers' do not make any transfer to the creators. The remuneration of the latter category could however be based on the sales of derived products, on the selling of the attention of 'audience' to a third party, on voluntary transfers by the community of 'consumers' that might agree to fund the provision of a public good, and so on. Moreover, intrinsic motivations (for example, the search for fame or the simple desire to create) could also be strong enough to motivate creators. On the economics of P2P see Krishnan *et al.* (2004).

16. However, the SACEM is not a pure medium since it does not estimate the revenue actually generated by each work of authorship. For instance, when SACEM collects royalty fees in discos, restaurants and other public places, it cannot estimate how each piece of its repertoire impacts on the sales. It therefore collects a fee for the use of music in general and then shares the collected sums among the authors according to the relative intensity of their uses. This is indeed a way to approximate the revenues generated by each piece, but it is not a perfect way.
17. Major companies collect by themselves the copyright fees generated by their repertoire through licences set up with users like broadcast channels. However, they can quasi subcontract some aspects of fee collection to collective copyright management companies. This is for instance what they usually do to collect fees generated by public performances of works of authorship. This makes the simple framework described above more complex, because the two types of institution play a role in the collection of fees. However, it is clear that authors do not only collectivize the gathering of their revenues, they also pool (and waive) their risks.
18. In the French music industry SACEM has developed means of investigation that enable it to perform a quasi systematic investigation into the actual uses of protected works on each broadcasting network, in each music theatre, disco and so on. It has also developed means of assessing the private reproduction of records on tapes. These means of evaluation are dedicated to the gathering of licence fees that otherwise could not be systematically collected.

    Although this type of comparison must be carefully manipulated one can compare the revenues collected by the US copyright fee collection societies with those collected by the French ones. As compared to its US counterparts, the SACEM collects copy or display rights in many 'niches' (such as discos, restaurants, stores, where music is played). It allows SACEM to collect fees that are above 80 per cent of the fees collected in the US, even though its population is four times larger than the French and the GDP more than six times larger. This huge 'productivity' gap cannot be entirely due to the fact that the French DA Law is more favourable to authors than the US copyright law. Moreover, it is difficult to relate it to the SACEM's market power. Indeed in each market, the SACEM does not collect higher fees than its foreign 'sister' companies. The originality of the French collection system lies in its ability to collect royalties from almost every category of music users. In the US, copyright collection societies target the less costly users to identify, supervise and tax.
19. Most of the literature generally considers that the PR regimes governing the works of authorship enable a wide collectivization of IPR governance, while the patent system does not. It is generally argued that this is because it is easier to protect forms collectively than ideas because interpretation margins are less strong in the former case than in the latter. While we agree that there are strong differences between the two domains, it seems to us that the demarcation line is much more subtle. The ability to collectivize the governance of IPRs does not depend upon the nature of the legal rights only. It also depends on the various governance tasks and on the type of protection that is sought by the owner of intangible goods.
20. The latter are also interested in negotiating out-of-court settlements. Indeed, the cost of a prohibition of use can be extremely high because the infringer can be forced to discard industrial and commercial investments and pay damages to its own clients (who can be involuntary infringers or who would no longer have access to specific inputs provided by the infringer). Following a paretian logic, patentees and infringers often negotiate bilateral agreements that enable them to reduce the potential costs of actually enforcing prohibition of use. This is documented, for instance, in the case of the semiconductor industry by Hall and Zeidonis (2001).
21. Obviously experts can help judges, but in that case it is the expert who makes the judge's decision. This is because such experts are supposed to state the 'truth' and because the opinion is not submitted to contradiction (since they are not supposed to defend any parties' interests).

22. There are however weaknesses in the US system, especially when it addresses new technological domains. As pointed out by Lerner (2002), the insufficient knowledge of 'prior art' by the PTO examiner explains why standards of patentability have been excessively low in new technological domains such as software, biotechnologies and business methods. As had happened in the chemical industry by the end of the 19th century, institutions need time to learn (see Arora and Fosfuri 2002).

BIBLIOGRAPHY

Arora, A. and Fosfuri, A. (2002), 'Licensing in the Chemical Industry', in E. Brousseau and J.-M. Glachant (eds), *The Economics of Contracts: Theories and Applications*, Cambridge: Cambridge University Press, pp. 373–93.

Arruñada, B. (2003), 'Property Enforcement as Organized Consent', *Journal of Law, Economics, and Organization*, **19**(2), 401–44.

Barzel, Y. (1989), *Economic Analysis of Property Rights*, Cambridge: Cambridge University Press.

Besen, S.M. and Kirby, S.N. (1989), 'Private Copying, Appropriability, and Optimal Royalties', *Journal of Law and Economics*, **32**, 255–80.

Besen, S. and Raskind, L. (1991), 'An Introduction to the Law and Economics of Intellectual Property', *Journal of Economic Perspectives*, **5**, pp. 3–27.

Bessen, J. and Maskin, E. (2000), 'Sequential innovation, Patents and Imitation', MIT Working Paper No. 00–01, Cambridge MA: MIT.

Bessy, C. and Chateauraynaud, F. (1995), *Experts et Faussaires: Pour une Sociologie de la Perception*, Paris: Métailié.

Bessy, C. and Brousseau, E. (1997), 'Brevet, Protection et Diffusion des Connaissances: Une Relecture Néo-institutionnelle des Propriétés de la Règle de Droit', *Revue d'Economie Industrielle*, Numéro spécial: Economie Industrielle de la Science, 1er semestre, pp. 233–54.

Bessy, C. and Brousseau, E. (1998), 'Technology Licensing Contracts: Features and Diversity', *International Review of Law and Economics*, **18**, December, pp. 451–89.

Bloch, R.E., Perlman, S.P. and Byron, H.T. (1997), 'US Antitrust Law and its Effect on Copyright Protections for the Music Industry', in E. Lauvaux and J. Turton (eds), *The Impact of Competition Law on the Music Industry*, Reports presented at the meeting of the International Association of Entertainment Lawyers, Midem, Cannes, Apeldoorn: MAKLU Publisher.

Brousseau, E. (2000), 'What Institutions to Organize Electronic Commerce: Private Institutions and the Organization of Markets', *Economics of Innovation and New Technology*, **9**(3), July–September, pp. 245–73.

Brousseau, E. (2004), 'Property Rights in the Digital Space', in E. Colombatto (ed.), *Companion to Economics of Property Rights*, Cheltenham, UK and Northampton, MA, USA: Edward Elgar.

Brousseau, E. and Fares, M. (2000), 'The Incomplete Contract Theory and the New Institutional Economics Approaches to Contracts: Substitutes or Complements?', in C. Ménard (ed.), *Institutions, Contracts, Organizations: Perspectives from New-Institutional Economics*, Cheltenham, UK and Northampton, MA, USA: Edward Elgar.

Brousseau, E. and Raynaud E. (2004), 'The economics of private institutions', paper presented at the 8th Conference of the New Institutional Economics, *Institutions and Economic and Political Behavior*, Tucson, USA, September 2004.

Brousseau, E. and Foray, D. (1997), 'Les Enjeux Economiques des Droits de Propriété Industrielle', Rapport IMRI pour le Ministère de l'Industrie, Direction Générale des Stratégies Industrielles, Contribution à la 'Mission Lombard', Juin.

Brousseau, E. and Moati, P. (1997), 'L'Economie du Droit D'auteur et des Droits Voisins; Le Cas de la Filière Musicale', Rapport CREDOC pour le Ministère de la Culture et de la Francophonie, Direction des Etudes et de la Prospective, 09/97.

Chang, H.F. (1995), 'Patent Scope, Antitrust Policy and Cumulative Innovation', *Rand Journal of Economics*, **26**, pp. 34–57.

Coase, R.H. (1992), 'The Institutional Structure of Production', *American Economic Review*, **82**(4), pp. 713–19.

Cooper, C. (1993), 'Nineteenth-Century American Patent Management as an Invisible College of Technology', in R. Thomson (ed.), *Learning and Technical Change*, St. Martin's Press.

David, P.A. (1993), 'Intellectual Property Institution and the Panda's Thumb: Patents, Copyrights and Trade Secrets in Economic Theory and History', in M.B. Wallerstein (ed.), *Global Dimensions of Intellectual Property Rights in Science and Technology*, Washington DC: National Academy Press, pp. 19–61.

Edelman, B. (1993), *Droits d'Auteur Droits Voisins: Droit d'Auteur et Marché*, Paris: Dalloz.

Foray, D. and Lundvall, B.A. (eds), (1996), *Employment and Growth in the Knowledge-based Economy*, Paris: OECD.

Gallini, N.T. (1992), 'Patent Policy and Costly Imitation', *Rand Journal of Economics*, **23**, pp. 52–63.

Gallini, N. (2002), 'The Economics of Patents: Lessons from Recent U.S. Patent Reform', *Journal of Economic Perspectives*, **16**(2), Spring, pp. 131–54.

Gilbert, R. and Shapiro, K. (1990), 'Optimal Patent Length and Breadth', *Rand Journal of Economics*, **21**, pp. 106–12.

Griliches, Z. (1990), 'Patent Statistics as Economic Indicators: A Survey', *Journal of Economic Literature*, **28**, pp. 1661–707.

Haas (de), M. (1975), 'La Théorie des Equivalents', in *Aspects Actuels de la Contrefaçon*: 3ème rencontre de propriété industrielle, Paris: Librairies Techniques.

Hall, B. and Zeidonis, R. (2001), 'The Patent Paradox Revisited: An Empirical Study of Patenting in the U.S. Semi-conductor Industry, 1979–1995', *Rand Journal of Economics*, **32**(1), pp. 101–28.

Jaffe, A. (2000), 'The U.S. Patent System in Transition: Policy Innovation and the Innovation Process', *Research Policy*, **29**(4–5), pp. 531–57.

Klemperer, P. (1990), 'How Broad Should the Scope of Patent Protection Be?', *Rand Journal of Economics*, **21**, pp. 113–30.

Krishnan, R., Smith, M.D. and Telang, R. (2004), 'The Economics of Peer-to-Peer Networks', Working Paper, Carnegie Mellon University, H. John Heinz III School of Public Policy and Management.

Lanjouw, J. (1998), 'Patent Protection in the Shadow of Infringement: Simulation Estimations of Patent Value', *Review of Economic Studies*, **65**(4), pp. 671–710.

Lanjouw, J. and Schankerman, M. (2001), 'Characteristics of Patent Litigation: A Window on Competition', *RAND Journal of Economics*, **32**(1), pp. 129–51.

Lemley, M.A. (1998), 'The Law and Economics of the Internet Norms', *Chicago-Kent Law Review*, **73**, p. 1257.
Lerner, J. (1995), 'Patenting in the Shadow of Competitors', *Journal of Law and Economics*, **28**, pp. 463–95.
Lerner, J. (2002), 'Where does State Street Lead? A First Look at Finance Patents, 1971–2000', *Review of Finance*, **57**(2), pp. 901–30.
Lessig, L. (1999), *Code and other Laws of Cyberspace*, New York: Basic Books.
Merges, R.P. (1996), 'Contracting into Liability Rules: Intellectual Property Rights and Collective Rights Organizations', *California Law Review*, **84**(5), pp. 1293–393.
Merges, R. (2001), 'Institutions for Intellectual Property Exchange: The Case of Patent Pools', in R. Dreyfuss (ed.), *Intellectual Products: Novel Claims to Protection and Their Boundaries*, Oxford: Oxford University Press.
Nelson, R. (1993), 'Technical Change as Cultural Evolution, in Learning and Technical Change', in R. Thomson (ed.), *Learning and Technical Change*, St. Martin's Press.
Nordhaus, W. (1969), *Invention Growth and Welfare*, Cambridge, MA: MIT Press.
North, D. (1990), *Institutions, Institutional Change and Economic Performance*, Cambridge: Cambridge University Press.
Ordover, J.A. (1991), 'A Patent System for Both Diffusion and Exclusion', *Journal of Economic Perspectives*, **5**(1), pp. 43–60.
Palmer, T.G. (1989), 'Intellectual Property: a Non-Posnerian Law and Economics Approach', *Hamline Law Review*, **12**, pp. 261–320.
Paris, T. (1998), 'L'Organisation de la Gestion Collective des Droits d'Auteur: Entre Rationalisation et Logique D'institution', *Revue Réseaux*, no. 88/89.
Saint Paul, G. (2003), *Information Sharing and Cumulative Innovation in Business Network*, CEPR Discussion paper no. 4116, Centre for Economic Policy Research (CEPR).
Scotchmer, S. (1991), 'Standing on the Shoulders of Giants: Cumulative Research and the Patent Law', *Journal of Economic Perspectives*, **5**(1), pp. 29–41.
Scotchmer, S. and Green, J. (1990), 'Novelty and Disclosure in Patent Law', *RAND Journal of Economics*, **21**, pp. 131–46.
Shapiro, C. (2000), *Navigating the Patent Thicket: Cross Licenses, Patent Pools and Standard-Setting*, Working Paper, Berkeley: University of California.
Shapiro, C. and Varian, H. (1998), *Information Rules: a Strategic Guide to the Network Economy*, Cambridge MA: Harvard Business School Press.
Théberge, P. (1993), 'Technology, Economy and Copyright Reform in Canada', in S. Frith (ed.), *Music and Copyright*, Edinburgh: Edinburgh University Press, pp. 40–66.
Warren-Bulton, F.R., Baseman, K.C. and Woroch, G.A. (1995), *The Economics of Intellectual Property Protection for Software: the Proper Role for Copyright*, Working Paper, Berkeley: University of California Berkeley, April.
Williamson, O. E. (1985), *The Economic Institutions of Capitalism*, The Free Press.
Williamson, O. E. (1996), *The Mechanism of Governance*, Oxford: Oxford University Press.
Working Group on Intellectual Property Right (1995), Report: Intellectual Property and the National Information Infrastructure, Bruce A. Lehman, Chair, Library of Congress.

9. The exploration of knowledge networks through patent citations

Stefano Breschi, Lorenzo Cassi and Franco Malerba

ABSTRACT

The aim of this chapter is to discuss the methodological issues arising from the use of patent citation data as relational data and to provide an example of empirical analysis. In particular, we propose to use patent citation data to explore knowledge networks at the level of organizations, that is, companies and other institutions. We focus our analysis on two different types of network: citation and co-citation networks. We argue that the former type of network could map knowledge diffusion networks; the latter could map the technological space. Using this perspective, this chapter examines the main structural properties of the knowledge networks in semiconductor and computer industries. In order to capture the organization's position in both co-citation and direct patent citation networks, we calculate, for each sector, two different measures: the crowdedness of a company's position in the technological space and a measure of its status. These two measures allow us to map the position of any organization and to define a taxonomy of four different kinds of organizations: technological leaders, technological followers, brokers of new technologies and isolated organizations. The results of our analysis show differences between the semiconductor and computer sectors and the difference between European and non-European companies in terms of technological niches.

Keywords: Innovation, Networks of knowledge, Technological positioning, Network analysis, Patents data

1 INTRODUCTION

Saying that 'networks' matter for technological innovation is nowadays almost to state the obvious. It is in fact widely recognized that both the creation and the diffusion of new ideas are processes which imply the integration and recombination of existing knowledge coming from different sources, locations and organizational positions. Yet, as fashionable as it has now become to speak of knowledge and social networks, quantitative research on this topic is still in its infancy. In contrast with the abundance of case studies and narrative evidence, there are only a few papers, all of them quite recent, which attempt openly to detect knowledge networks on a large scale.

On the empirical side, some consensus has emerged on the unique role that patent data can play once again, in their newly discovered capacity as relational data, namely citations. Several types of networks of relations can be built and examined using patent data. Such networks differ according to the nature of the nodes[1] and to the nature of the relations linking those nodes. In the context of this study the term 'nodes' represents organizations.

One of our aims is to discuss the methodological issues arising from the use of patent citation data as relational data. In particular, we propose to use patent citation data to explore knowledge networks at the level of organizations, that is, companies and other institutions. We focus our analysis on two different types of network: citation and co-citation networks (section 2.1). We argue that the former type of network could map knowledge diffusion networks; the latter could map the technological space.

Using this perspective, this chapter examines the main structural properties of the knowledge networks in the semiconductor and computer industries. In order to capture the organizations' position in both co-citation and direct patent citation networks we calculate, for each sector, two different measures. In relation to the co-citation network, we calculate a measure that captures the crowdedness of a company's position in the technological space; in relation to the direct patent citation network, we calculate a measure of status. These two measures allow us to classify any organization and, via a combination of crowding and status measures, to define the taxonomy of four different kinds of organizations: technological leaders, technological followers, brokers of new technologies and isolated organizations.

The rest of the chapter is organized as follows: in section 2 we analyse to what extent and how patent citation data can be used as 'relational' data in order to map the overall network of linkages among innovating agents. In section 3, we analyse the knowledge networks of the semiconductor and computer industries; in particular we explore the position occupied by individual companies in the networks, by developing appropriate firm-level indicators. Finally, section 4 concludes.

2 USING PATENT CITATIONS TO EXPLORE KNOWLEDGE NETWORKS

The new perspective on innovation as a multi-node, multi-channel network process has offered an attractively flexible and very powerful heuristic framework, which has largely inspired 'system'-oriented approaches to technical change. Yet, as fashionable as it has now become to speak of 'networks of innovation', there is a surprising lack of systematic studies on the processes of network formation and evolution, on the differences between different types of networks (for example, personal networks versus networks of organizations), and on the structural properties of networks and their impact upon firms' innovative performance.

The problem is both conceptual and empirical. On the one hand, systematic efforts to model networks have started only recently, most often outside the disciplinary field of economics. On the other hand, the work necessary to undertake empirical analysis of networks requires the collection of large masses of 'relational' data, something that is either not affordable by or not attuned to economists' attitudes towards data collection. This explains why, for example, most of the recent economic research on innovation networks has focused its attention on formal connections between organizations, that is, relationships involving some kind of contractually specified agreement, like joint ventures, joint R&D, R&D contracts, technology exchange agreements, manufacturing, marketing or service agreements. Indeed, these are the only connections which are recorded frequently, if not by official sources, at least by consultants and business magazines. It ends up that almost all of the empirical studies on 'innovation networks' refer to formal ties among organizations, particularly strategic alliances.[2]

It should also be noted that the process of data collection itself is somehow impaired by a certain conceptual and methodological confusion. In the first place, there is a sort of theory gap in innovation network studies. Roughly speaking, it is as if economists are conscious of the potential of a network perspective and glimpse the opportunity to exploit a set of tools, (chiefly social network analysis and graph theory) to answer interesting problems and questions, but fail to develop a set of falsifiable theories and predictions. The most evident outcome is a sort of borrowing by economists of theories and testable propositions from the sociological literature (see the debate on social capital versus structural holes, for example, in Burt, 2001). A further source of conceptual uncertainty has to do with the notion of knowledge flows. Whereas the very attractiveness of the network concept boils down to the fact that it captures the essence of innovation as an interactive process, not much attention has been devoted so far to discussing through what channels knowledge actually diffuses. The overall discussion has instead centered around the *vexata quaestio* of the relative importance of tacit versus codified knowledge, whereas little attention has been paid to examining the specific patterns through which knowledge diffuses (labour mobility, informal conversations, papers...) and what that implies for measuring network properties.

As already mentioned above, a novel approach for analysing knowledge flows has been proposed recently by a group of US scholars (Jaffe and Trajtenberg, 2002). Broadly speaking, they argue that a more creative use of a traditional innovation indicator, like patent statistics, may contribute a lot to our understanding of several important questions, like measuring the 'value' of innovations, tracking the flows of knowledge, and assessing the importance of academic research on industrial technology. In particular, patent citations, that is, references contained in a patent document to previous patent documents, provide trails of the 'knowledge link' between inventions and this allows us to track knowledge linkages between scientists, inventors, firms, regions and so on.[3]

The aim of this section is to discuss the methodological issues arising from the use of patent citation data as relational data, that is, data that provide information on knowledge relations and that can be analysed through network-analytic methodologies. It must be said that the use of patent data in general, and of patent citations in particular, as relational data is still at its very beginning. The literature approaching these data in this way is still quite limited and scattered around different perspectives and methodologies.

Once we look at the relational contents provided by patent data, the first point to note is that several types of networks of relations can be built and examined. Such networks differ according to the nature of nodes and to the nature of relations linking those nodes. Table 9.1 is a (non-exhaustive) attempt to summarize the various kinds of networks that one could build from patent data.

The next section, 2.1, will focus on the first three rows of the table; the following one will explain some recent works on networks of inventors; finally, section 2.3 will consider the networks of organizations.

2.1 Networks of Patents

A first type of network is a graph where entities (that is, nodes) are patents. The linkage (edge) between them may be of three broad types, resulting in different types of graphs: citation, co-citation and bibliographic coupling.

A citation link refers to a relation where a patent cites (or is cited by) another patent. The citation relation may be of a direct or indirect type.[4]

Table 9.1 Types of networks from patent data

Nodes	**Relations**	**Type of graph**	**Objective**	**References**
Patents	Citation	Binary directed acyclic	Detect key patents and key paths in the cumulative evolution of technological fields	Batagelj (2003)
Patents	Co-citation	Valued (undirected or directed)	Detect coherent technological niches within broad technological fields	Pier *et al.* (2003)
Patents	Bibliographic coupling	Valued (undirected or directed)	Detect technological foundations of subsequent inventions	Pier *et al.* (2003)
Inventors	Co-authorship	Valued undirected	Detect social networks of inventors	Breschi and Lissoni (2004, 2005); Singh (2003)
Organizations	Co-patenting	Valued undirected	Detect networks of organizations collaborating in R&D	Hagedoorn (2003)
Organizations	Citation	Valued directed	Detect knowledge spillovers among companies	Verspagen (2006)
Organizations	Co-citation (bibliographic coupling)	Valued (undirected or directed)	Detect coherent clusters of organizations pursuing similar research activities	Podolny, Stuart, Hannan (1996)

For example, in Figure 9.1, the link 'patent A cites patent B' is a direct citation link between patent A and patent B, while the link 'patent A cites patent B, patent B cites patent C' is an indirect citation link between patent A and patent C. The resulting graph will be a binary (a citation link is either present or absent), directed (the arrow indicates some kind of information flow from the cited to the citing patent) and acyclic (no patent is reachable from itself by a nontrivial path) graph. The analysis of such a graph may provide insights into the cumulative evolution of technological fields and into the role played by some key patents. It should be pointed out that most of the traditional literature on patent citations focuses the analysis upon direct citation links, disregarding indirect ones.

A bibliographical coupling link refers to the fact that two patents cite the same patent or the same patents, for example, patent A and patent B both cite patent D. The frequency with which any pair of patents cite the same prior patents is therefore a measure of the extent to which they build

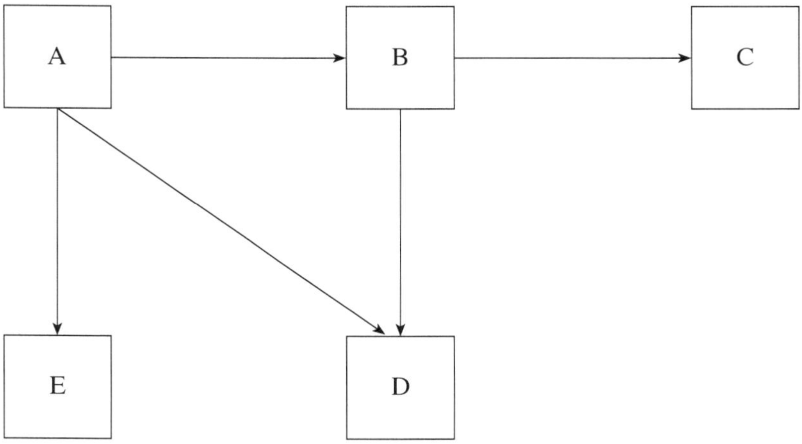

Figure 9.1 *Network of patents*

upon the same technological antecedents. The resulting network will be a valued (directed or undirected) graph where the value attached to the lines is the frequency of co-citation between two patents. This type of network is therefore useful for detecting clusters of patents sharing a common knowledge base, that is, technological niches within broader technological fields.

Finally, a co-citation link occurs when two patents are cited by the same patent, thus representing building blocks for subsequent inventions, for example, patent D and patent E are both cited by patent A. The frequency with which any pair of patents are cited by the same subsequent patents is therefore a measure of the extent to which they represent a common technological foundation for subsequent inventions.

2.2 Networks of Inventors

Co-authorship data from scientific papers have always been a powerful tool for empirical analysis in the sociology of science, and have more recently proved useful to test 'small world' theories on the positive relationship between the size of social networks and the closeness of individuals therein.

The main reason for this success is that it is widely acknowledged that scientists form quite a close community, whose distinctive codes of practice set them apart from the rest of society: expressions such as 'ivory tower' are still widely used to underline the scientific community's self-referential attitudes with respect to its own core activities, namely research and teaching. As long as scientific ideas originate, circulate and are improved mainly within a set of connected cliques sharing some inaccessible jargon and a very odd reward system, social scientists feel safe to assume that most of the knowledge diffusion takes place within the community, so that they can concentrate on social links therein, and set aside links towards society at large.[5]

Co-authorship of scientific papers requires mutual understanding or at least knowledge complementarity between the scientists. We may presume that co-authors know each other so well that they can effectively exchange important knowledge assets, especially if directly relevant to the contents of their publications. Each time two scientists work on a joint paper, we can safely treat them as two nodes of a social network connected by a bi-directional link (which can also be weighted by considering if other joint papers exist, and their scientific relevance). By considering all scientists within a given discipline, we can build the entire social network for that discipline, and proceed to explore its structural properties (very much along the lines of Newman, 2000 and 2001).[6]

The same basic methodology can be extended to co-authorship of patents, in particular to co-invention. If we assume that inventors listed on the same patent know each other, and have possibly exchanged key technical information, classifying patents by inventor becomes a crucial scientific exercise. To our knowledge, extensive efforts in that direction have just started, and only a handful of studies are available.[7]

The following hypothetical example, taken from Balconi, Breschi and Lissoni (2004), illustrates the main idea (see Figure 9.2). Let us suppose we face five patent applications (1 to 5), coming from four different applicants α, β, γ and δ. Applicant α is responsible for two applications (1, 2), and applicants β, γ and δ one each. Patents have been produced by thirteen distinct inventors (A to M). We can reasonably assume that, due to their collaboration in a common research project, the five inventors are 'linked' to each other by some kind of knowledge relation. The existence of such a linkage can be graphically represented by drawing an undirected line between each pair of inventors, as in the bottom part of Figure 9.2. Repeating the same exercise for each team of inventors, we end up with a map representing the network of linkages among all inventors.[8] Using the graph just described, one can derive various measures of social distance among inventors (for example, connectedness, geodesic distance)[9] and measure of centralities[10] (for example, degree, betweenness).[11]

2.3 Networks of Organizations

There are two basic ways in which patent data can be exploited to build and examine knowledge networks among organizations (private companies as

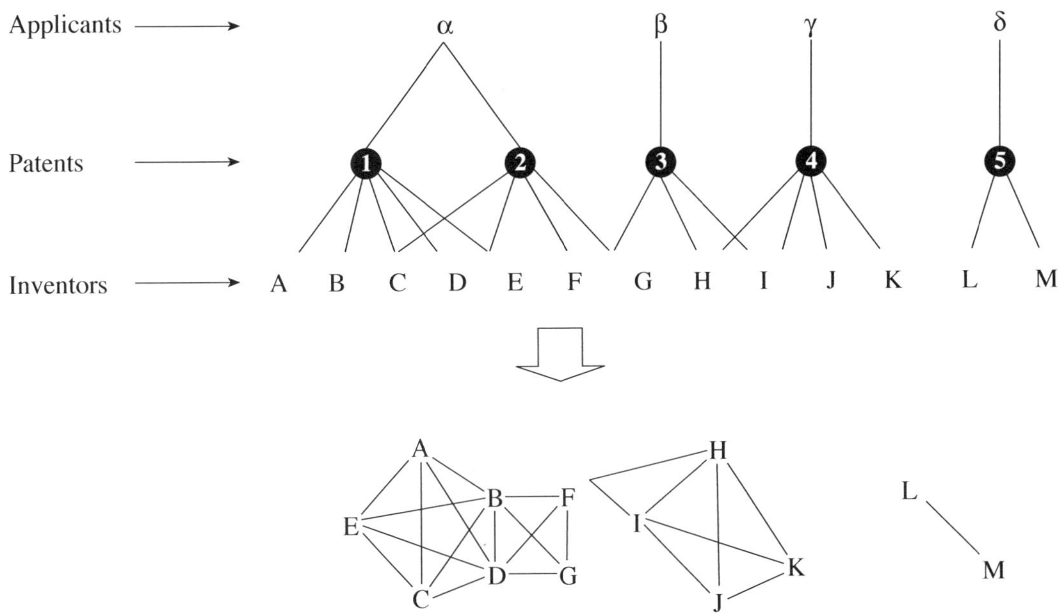

Top: Tripartite graph of applicants (α, β, γ, δ), patents (1 to 5) and inventors (A to M), with lines linking each patent to the respective inventors and applicants.
Bottom: The one-mode projection of the same network on to just inventors.

Figure 9.2 Networks of inventors

well as public institutions), that is, networks where nodes are organizations and linkages (edges) are relations among them (see Figure 9.2).

In the first place, one can look at joint patenting or co-patenting, that is, the co-application for a patent or the joint ownership of a granted patent by two or more companies. Any pair of patenting organizations is linked by a line to the extent that they co-apply for or co-own at least one patent. The resulting network is therefore a valued (directed or undirected) graph, where the value attached to the lines is the frequency of co-applications or co-owned patents. One of the main explanations for the existence of co-owned patents sees them as the result of small-scale inter-firm R&D collaborations where companies are unable to divide the inventions among partners (Hagedoorn, 2004). However, the fact that joint patents still represent a very tiny fraction of all patents, coupled with the fact that most of these co-owned patents often involve parent-subsidiary relations, limit their usefulness as a relational indicator for the purpose of analysing inter-organizational networks of knowledge.[12]

A second possible approach to the investigation of inter-organizational knowledge networks is through exploiting the relational nature of patent citation data. In turn, this can be accomplished in two different ways.

The first way is looking at patent citations as indicators of a knowledge flow (spillover) from the cited to the citing company. Patenting organizations represent the nodes in this network, while a directed arc from the cited to the citing organization indicates the presence of a spillover of knowledge emanating from the former to the latter. The resulting network is therefore a valued directed graph, where the value attached to the arcs represents the frequency of citations from the cited to the citing nodes. This graph may be easily represented and analysed as an adjacency valued matrix, in which rows represent cited applicants (spillover generators) and the columns correspond to citing applicants (spillover receivers). The generic cell (c_{ij}) corresponds to the number of citations (spillovers) from applicant j to applicant i. Obviously, the matrix is likely to be asymmetrical, that is, in general (c_{ij}) ≠ (c_{ji}). To the best of our knowledge, there has been only one attempt so far to analyse knowledge networks adopting this approach (Verspagen, 2006).

There are several methodological problems in approaching the study of knowledge networks by looking at the direct citation link between pairs of companies. In our view, a major problem has to do with the way one deals with the size of the citing and cited organizations. Because the number of citations a company receives or generates is obviously highly correlated with the number of its patent applications (citations may occur only as a result of patent applications!), companies exhibiting, for example, the highest in-degree and out-degree centrality values are the ones with a higher number of patent applications. In addition, the fact that one observes a high number of citations from company *i* to company *j* may simply depend on the fact that both companies have a large number of patent applications, that is, potentially citeable and citing patents. To put it differently, the probability that a company cites another company increases (perhaps in a non-monotone way) with the number of patent applications of the two companies. Thus, unless one finds a suitable way to account for size effects, the position of nodes in the knowledge network may provide information on their size, rather than any information on their role as knowledge brokers or providers.[14]

More generally, even assuming that some of these methodological problems can be solved, it is not clear how to interpret the resulting network when one moves from the dyadic level to relations involving three or more organizations. Figure 9.3 illustrates two observationally equivalent citation networks of organizations. In the example, boxes correspond to patent applications, letters identify applicants, letter subscripts denote specific patents and arrows correspond to citations. In both cases, organizations A and B cite patents of organization C twice, and the resulting citation network is therefore the same. However, in case 1 the two companies cite completely different subsets of firm C's patents, while in case 2 they cite exactly the same patents. When one considers companies A and B and the relation one would expect to exist between them, it is quite evident that cases 1 and 2 point to quite different conclusions. In other words, looking only at the resulting citation network (that is, the bottom part of Figure 9.3) misses crucial information for interpreting correctly the relations among sets of companies, that is, the identity of patents upon which relations are established. This is not to say that examining direct citation links among companies is useless or leads to misleading results. Our point is rather that such an analysis should be complemented by an analysis that is able to capture the technological contents of the relations linking companies.

What has been said above leads us to discuss the second alternative way in which patent citation data can be used to identify and examine inter-organizational knowledge networks. The basic methodology has been developed in a series of papers by Joel Podolny, Toby Stuart and Michael Hannan (Podolny *et al.*, 1996; Podolny, 1993; Podolny and Stuart, 1995, 1996; Stuart, 1999) and it is based upon the concept of bibliographic coupling (or co-citation).

Roughly speaking, the idea is to detect relations among patenting organizations by inspecting the (backward) citations to previous inventions. To the extent that two companies build upon (that is, cite) the same technological antecedents, their research profile is likely to be very similar, that is, their products or development directions are very similar, indicating

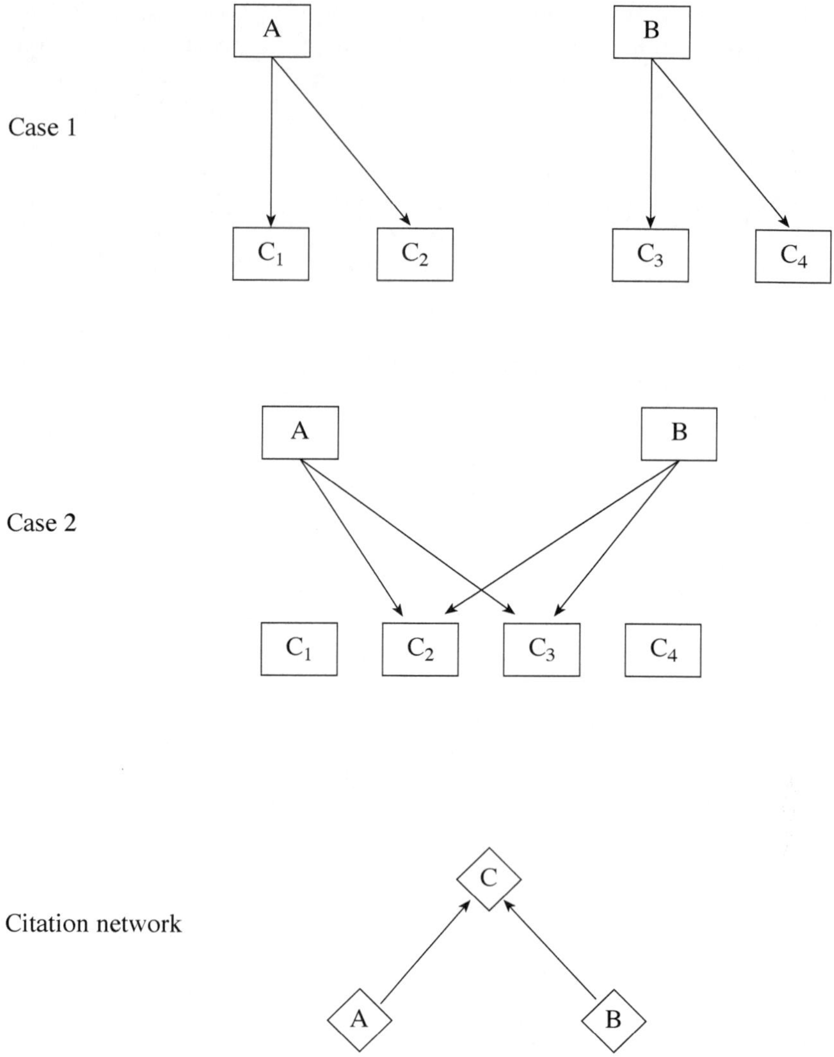

Figure 9.3 Citation network of organizations

opportunities for a cooperative alliance or the existence of a potential competitive relation.

Formally, let

$$C_{ipt} = 1 \tag{9.1}$$

be a citation at time t from a company i's patent to a previous patent p, with $p = 1....z$. The technological link (or overlap) between company i and j is defined as:

$$\alpha_{ijt} = \frac{\sum_{p=1}^{z} C_{ipt} C_{jpt}}{\sum_{p=1}^{z} C_{ipt}} \tag{9.2}$$

The numerator equals 1 whenever company i and company j cite the same antecedent patent p and 0 otherwise. The α_{ijt} coefficient is therefore the proportion of all citations made by company i at time t that overlap with citations made by company j, that is, the proportion of firm i's technological niche that is occupied by another firm j. Therefore, α_{ijt} is bounded between zero and one: at zero two firms are completely differentiated (their citations have no overlap); at one firm j fully occupies firm i's niche (all of firm i's citations overlap with firm j's citations). It should be noted that in general $\alpha_{ijt} \neq \alpha_{jit}$, that is, the citation overlap is not symmetric. In fact, while the numerator is identical, the denominator is likely to be different.

Given N patenting organizations, it is possible to define a co-citation network of organizations as a graph $G = \{N,E,A\}$, where $N[=1...n]$ is the set of organizations, E is the set of arcs linking organizations, and A is the set of values attached to the arcs. The graph may also be represented by an adjacency matrix A_t. This matrix is an asymmetric matrix of order $N \times N$, whose ijth cell is simply the α_{ijt} coefficient. As described above, each pair of organizations (i,j) sharing at least one common citation is linked by two arcs with values α_{ij} and α_{ji}.

Figure 9.4 provides a graphical illustration for the hypothetical case of a three firms network.[15] In the figure, the numbered boxes represent existing inventions (that is, technological antecedents), while the arcs emanating from firms represent citations from firm i's current patents. In the example, firm A's current inventions build upon previous inventions 1, 2, 3 and 5, while firm B's current inventions build upon previous inventions 3 and 5. In this example, α_{AB} takes value 0.5, given that B shares with A two common citations, out of a total of four citations made by firm A. Similarly, α_{BA} takes value 1 given that A shares with B two common citations out of a total of two citations made by firm B.

Figure 9.4 also reports the corresponding adjacency matrix for the three firms. The first row of the matrix reports the degree to which each firm's pattern of patent citations overlaps with firm A's pattern. The first column indicates the extent to which firm A's pattern of patent citations overlaps

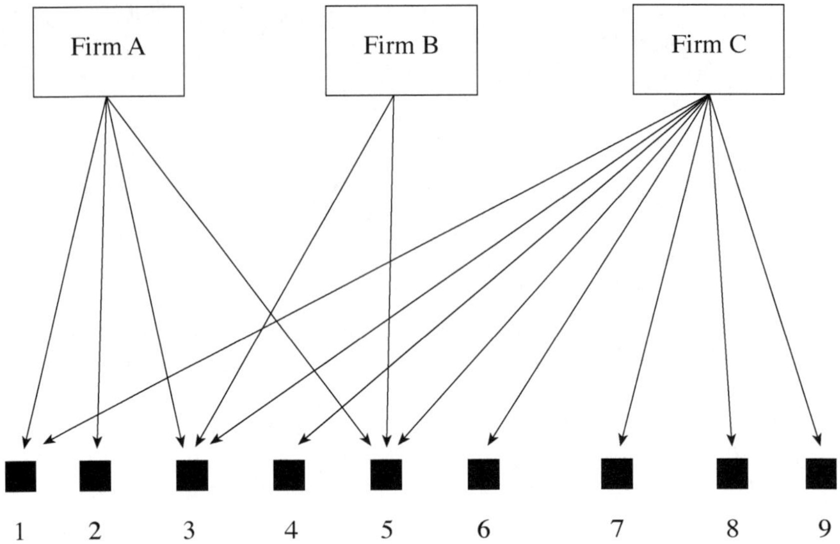

	A	B	C
A	0	0.50	0.75
B	1	0	1
C	0.375	0.25	0

Figure 9.4 Co-citation network of organizations

with the pattern of all other members of the network. In this context, the main diagonal of the matrix has no special significance and can be ignored. As made clear by Podolny and Stuart (1996), taken together row *i* and column *j* define the technological position of a focal firm with respect to all other firms at a particular time *t*. More specifically, the entries in row *i* and column *j* define a global position for firm *i* in a $2N - 2$ dimensional space, where *N* is the number of firms in the network.[16]

It has to be pointed out once again that the two approaches to the analysis of knowledge networks based upon patent citations capture quite different aspects and phenomena. The approach that looks at direct patent citations between companies captures the idea that R&D activities generate knowledge spillovers, but misses the technological contents of such spillovers. On the other hand, the approach based on patterns of co-citations does not provide any information on knowledge flows among companies, but is able to capture the technological similarity in the research profile and competencies of different organizations.[17] For these reasons, the two approaches have to be considered as complementary rather than alternative, and we will adopt both of them in the analysis that follows.

3 AN ANALYSIS OF KNOWLEDGE NETWORKS OF SEMICONDUCTOR AND COMPUTER INDUSTRIES

3.1 The Sources of Data and our Sample

The data set on patents and patent citations used in our analysis is a subset of a larger data set constructed and maintained by the Centre for Research on Innovation and Internationalization (CESPRI). This data set includes all patent applications to the European Patent Office (EPO), from 1 June 1978 to 18 June 2001.[18] The European patent dataset maintained by CESPRI (from now on the EP-CESPRI data set) includes the full set of bibliographic variables concerning each patent application.

Our sample is defined using two classifications: industrial (SIC code 4 digits) and technological classification (30 classes based on IPC code).[19] Table 9.A1 shows the correspondences adopted between the two classifications. In the following analysis we make a clear overlap between technological sector (defined by patent class) and industry, so that, for example, we only consider semiconductor technologies in relation to the semiconductor industry (and vice versa).

For each industry, the sample analysed has been defined by including:

1. All companies whose primary business activity is in industry *m* (for example, semiconductors) and that register patents in industry *m*'s related technologies (for example, semiconductor-related patents) in the period 1994–98;
2. All other organizations that register patents in industry *m*'s related technologies (for example, semiconductor-related patents) in the period

1994–98 whose total number of patents is above the average number of patents per organization in the field examined.

The first criterion allows us to include the main organizations belonging to the two industrial sectors. The second criterion permits us to consider some key actors patenting in the corresponding technological field, independent of their industrial sector. These actors could be relevant in a network of citations, however it is built up.

Table 9.A2 shows the sample breakdown by the two selection criteria. For any sector, the second criterion permits us to add a lot of information, above all in terms of number of patents. Table 9.A3 reports the coverage of our sample within the corresponding technological fields.

We turn to a consideration of the coverage of our sample in terms of patent citations made and received. Tables 9.A4 and 9.A5 report information on that, distinguishing citations to other companies from self-citations. In both these tables, citations made refer to citations by the sampled patents (that is, in the period 1994–98) to all patents registered from 1977 to 1998,

Table 9.2 Structural properties of the co-citation network

	Semiconductors	**Computers**
Number of organizations (that is, nodes)	270	408
Number of nodes not isolated (V) (*)	188	309
Number of arcs (E)	2250	4174
Average (Std dev) (α)	0.077 (0.137)	0.076 (0.138)
Min (α)	0.0018	0.0013
Max (α)	1	1
% of arcs with $\alpha \leq 1\%$	22.3	26.8
% of arcs with $\alpha \leq 5\%$	64.0	62.5
Density (valued**)	0.0049	0.0033
Density (binary)	0.0640	0.0438
Average degree	11.9	13.5
Average distance	2.43	2.48
Diameter	5	5
Clustering coefficient	0.336	0.283

Notes:

* A node is isolated if it does not make any citations at all or if it does not cite patents cited by some other sampled firms.

** The density of a valued graph returns the average value attached to the edges. The difference between the average value of α (4th row of the table) and the density of the valued graph is that in the calculation of the former only $\alpha > 0$ have been included.

and citations received refer to those received by sampled firms in the period 1977–1998 from sampled patents (period 1994–1998).

We use patent citations to build up networks among firms. It is possible to define two different kinds of networks of firms: a directed graph based on citations or an undirected one based on co-citations. The former uses citations between patents in order to define a direct link between two assignees (for example, if firm A registers a patent X that cites a patent Y whose assignee is firm B, there will be an arc from node A to node B). The latter has been built up on co-citations: two patents are linked by citations to a common third patent (for example, if firm A registers a patent X that cites a patent Z, and firm B registers a patent X citing patent Z, there will be a line between node A and node B).

3.2 Positioning Companies in the Knowledge Networks

In this section, we aim to explore the position occupied by individual companies in the network, by developing appropriate firm-level indicators. Moreover, we will also exploit information from the direct citation relations linking firms.

Stuart (1999) has proposed two measures that allow us to summarize the position of individual companies within the overall network. The first measure, which he calls technological crowding, is defined as:

$$A_{it} = \sum_{j \neq i} \alpha_{ijt} \tag{9.3}$$

where α_{ij} are the niche overlap coefficients defined above (section 2.3). The technological crowding index is meant to measure the extent to which company *i* makes research in crowded technological areas, that is, areas where the research efforts of firm *i* overlap with those of other companies, resulting in redundancy.

The second measure aims to capture instead the technological scope of a firm. In an industry with N companies, there are N–1 potential alternatives, such that $\alpha_{ij} > 0$. A company may be defined as a generalist if its pattern of patent citations overlaps with many of the N–1 alternatives. On the other hand, it may be defined as a specialist to the extent that its research activities directly overlap with a few (or even none) of the N-1 alternatives. A suitable index for capturing this basic idea is the entropy index defined as:

$$C_{it} = -\sum_{j \neq i} P_{ijt} \log\left(P_{ijt}\right) \tag{9.4}$$

where

$$P_{ijt} = \frac{\alpha_{ijt}}{\sum_j \alpha_{ijt}} \tag{9.5}$$

and α_{ij}, α_{ji} are the niche overlap coefficients defined above (section 2.3).

The C_{ij} index is bounded between 0 and log(N–1). It tends to zero for firms with no overlap across all other firms, as well as for firms that overlap with only one alternative. The C_{ij} index reaches a theoretical maximum of log(N–1) for a company whose pattern of patent citations overlap, in the same proportion, with all other companies in the network.

3.2.1 Prestige status and crowding

Podolny *et al.* (1996) draw an important distinction between the concept of niche overlap deriving from a similar dependence on technological antecedents and the notion of status deriving from the direct (possibly asymmetric) technological ties between actors, that is, direct patent citations.

While an indirect connection based on common technological antecedents signals the existence of potential competitive relations and perhaps opportunities for collaboration between companies, the significance of a direct technological relation is less clear cut. In the sociological jargon used by Podolny *et al.* (1996), a patent citation from one organization to another suggests a certain deference, that is, it shows that the former regards the activity of the latter as a more suitable foundation for its inventive activities than other alternatives. This act of deference confers to the firm cited legitimacy and status, thus improving its prospect for profitability and growth.

An economist would probably use a different jargon and look at this problem from a different perspective. He would probably say that a direct technological relation, that is, a patent citation, indicates a knowledge spillover flowing from the citing firm to the firm cited. To the extent that a patent citation signals a spillover and restricts the scope of the cited invention, a direct relation would also indicate the existence of a potentially competitive relation between the two organizations.

According to Podolny *et al.* (1996) the status enhancing effect of a citation tie prevails when the cited organization occupies a relatively uncrowded region of the technological space, that is, it develops relatively novel and uncertain technologies. In these circumstances, the act of citation enhances the perceived quality of the inventions produced by the cited organization. On the other hand, the competitive effect is likely to prevail when the cited organization is positioned in a relatively crowded region of the technological space, that is, it develops quite standardized and mature technologies. In other words, the meaning and the impact of a direct citation tie cannot be separated from an evaluation of the position that the cited and the citing organization have in the technological space.

Formalizing these ideas requires measuring the position of each company in the technological space as well as its status in the direct patent citations network. Concerning the first problem, the technological crowding coefficient A_{it} is the measure that captures the crowdedness of a company's position in the technological space. The notion of status in a direct patent citations network can be instead captured by some index of network centrality.

Among the many possible indexes of centrality, we follow once again Podolny *et al.* (1996) and adopt the so-called Bonacich power centrality index (Bonacich, 1987). The index for company i is formally defined as:

$$c_{it}(\alpha,\beta) = \sum_j (\alpha + \beta c_{jt}) R_{ijt} \tag{9.6}$$

where R_{ijt} is the number of patent citations from organization j to organization i within the five-year time window ending at t (1994–98). Mathematically, we have a system of N equations with N unknowns (the c_{it} coefficients). Using matrix notation, the system can be written as follows (Bonacich, 1987):

$$c_{it}(\alpha,\beta) = \alpha(I - \beta R)^{-1} R1 \tag{9.7}$$

where 1 is a column vector of ones and I is an identity matrix of order $N \times N$. R is the matrix of order $N \times N$, whose ijth cell is the count of patent citations from organization j to organization i. The crucial parameter here is the parameter β: the magnitude of this parameter reflects an actor's status relative to the status of the actors that cite it.

In our context, a positive value of β indicates that the status of a company is higher the higher the status of the companies that cite it.[20] To put it in a different way, the magnitude of the β parameter reflects the degree to which $c(\alpha,\beta)$ is a local or global measure of status (Bonacich, 1987). Specifically, if one set $\beta = 0$ the above expression reduces to:

$$c_{it}(\alpha,\beta) = \alpha \sum_j R_{ijt} \tag{9.8}$$

namely, the status of a company in the direct citations network is proportional to its degree, that is, only the local ties from j to i matter. On the contrary, when $\beta > 0$, indirect (global) connections also enter into the definition of the status of company i. More generally, the higher the value of β the more the $c(\alpha, \beta)$ index reflects the status of a company in the network as a whole.

A crucial issue concerns the value of the parameter β that one should use in the actual calculation of the status index. Following a diffused practice, we have chosen to set the parameter β as equal to ¾ of the reciprocal of the largest eigenvalue λ of matrix R that solves:

$$\lambda e = Re \tag{9.9}$$

where e is an eigenvector and λ is its associated eigenvalue.[21]

Finally, the parameter α is simply a normalization factor, which is introduced to take into account differences in size across networks. The parameter α is chosen so that

$$\sum_i c_{it}(\alpha, \beta)^2 = N \tag{9.10}$$

namely, the sum of squared centralities equals the number of actors in the network. In this way, the company that has $c_{it}(\alpha, \beta)=1$ has a status that is neither high nor low.

We have calculated for each of the two industries and for each of the companies included in them, both the technological crowding coefficient A_{it} and the status index $c_{it}(\alpha, \beta)$. For each industry, we have then reported the values of the two coefficients on a scatterplot (Figures 9.5 and 9.6), also indicating the mean value of the crowding and of the prestige status coefficients. This identifies four major quadrants (that is, combinations of crowding and prestige status) that partition all companies in the industry according to their position in the technological space and to their centrality in the direct patent citations network. Companies positioned in the upper-left portion of the plots have a high centrality in the direct citations graph (that is, they are cited by many other organizations), but occupy a relatively uncrowded region of the technological space (that is, their technological antecedents overlap with relatively few other companies). Podolny *et al.* (1996) define these organizations as brokers of new technologies, to convey the idea that they are the sources of knowledge in relatively new and unexplored fields. Such companies are likely to be the ones experiencing the fastest rates of growth.

Companies positioned in the upper-right part of the graphs in Figures 9.5 and 9.6 can be instead defined as technological and market leaders. They represent a key source of knowledge spillovers for many other organizations in the industry, but the focus of their research activity is geared towards

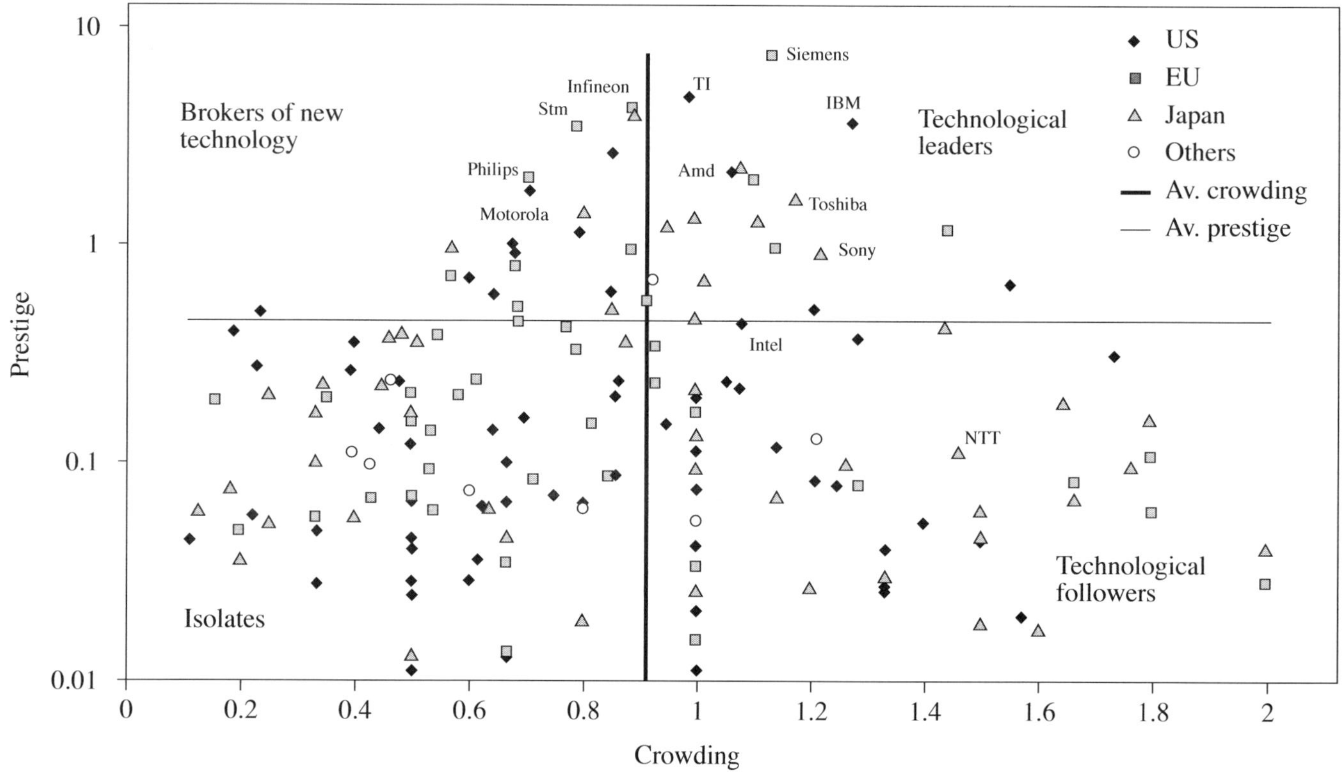

Figure 9.5 Prestige and crowding, semiconductors industry

the exploitation of opportunities in relatively mature and therefore highly crowded fields. This combination of high status (that is, direct ties) and high crowding (that is, common antecedents) suggests the existence of clique structure around these organizations' position.

Companies in the lower-right part of the graphs, on the other hand, engage in relatively mature and crowded technological subfields without producing significant spillovers for other organizations. These companies are likely to occupy a peripheral position around the technological leaders. For this reason, one might term them technological followers.

Finally, the group of companies positioned in the lower-left part of the graphs is made up of firms that are exploring relatively untapped technological subfields, but that do not receive direct citations from many other organizations. These are isolated companies. It is possible that a few of them shift over time to the upper-left quadrant (that is, brokers of new technologies). However, it is also likely that most of them are good candidates for exiting the industry. One may expect in fact that high rates of entry and exit from the industry (and/or from the technology) take place exactly in this group of firms. This intuition seems to be indirectly confirmed by the fact that this is the most numerous region of the graphs.

The graphs reveal some differences between the two industries examined. Concerning the semiconductor industry (Figure 9.5), the plot shows a quite clear partition between Japanese companies, on the one hand, and US and European companies, on the other hand. While Japanese companies are mostly located in the upper-right part of the graph (that is, they are technological leaders in this area) EU and US firms are mostly located in the upper-left quadrant (that is, they tend to explore relatively untapped technologies). EU companies are also mainly located in the lower-left quadrant, that is, they are small isolated companies, while Japanese companies are also present in the lower-right quadrant, that is, technological followers.

Concerning the computer industry, Figure 9.6 shows that US companies, and to some extent also Japanese companies, are the most important brokers of new technologies, while EU companies, with few exceptions, are either isolated or technological followers.

The previous analysis categorizes companies according to their position in the overall networks of co-citations and direct citations respectively. However, it does not tell us anything about the relations between companies belonging to different categories. For example, we do not know whether followers (that is, firms positioned in crowded technological niches) overlap mainly with other followers or with other types of companies. Similarly, we do not know whether firms with high prestige (that is, highly cited companies) are mainly cited by other high prestige companies or by other types of firms. To answer these questions, one needs to investigate directly

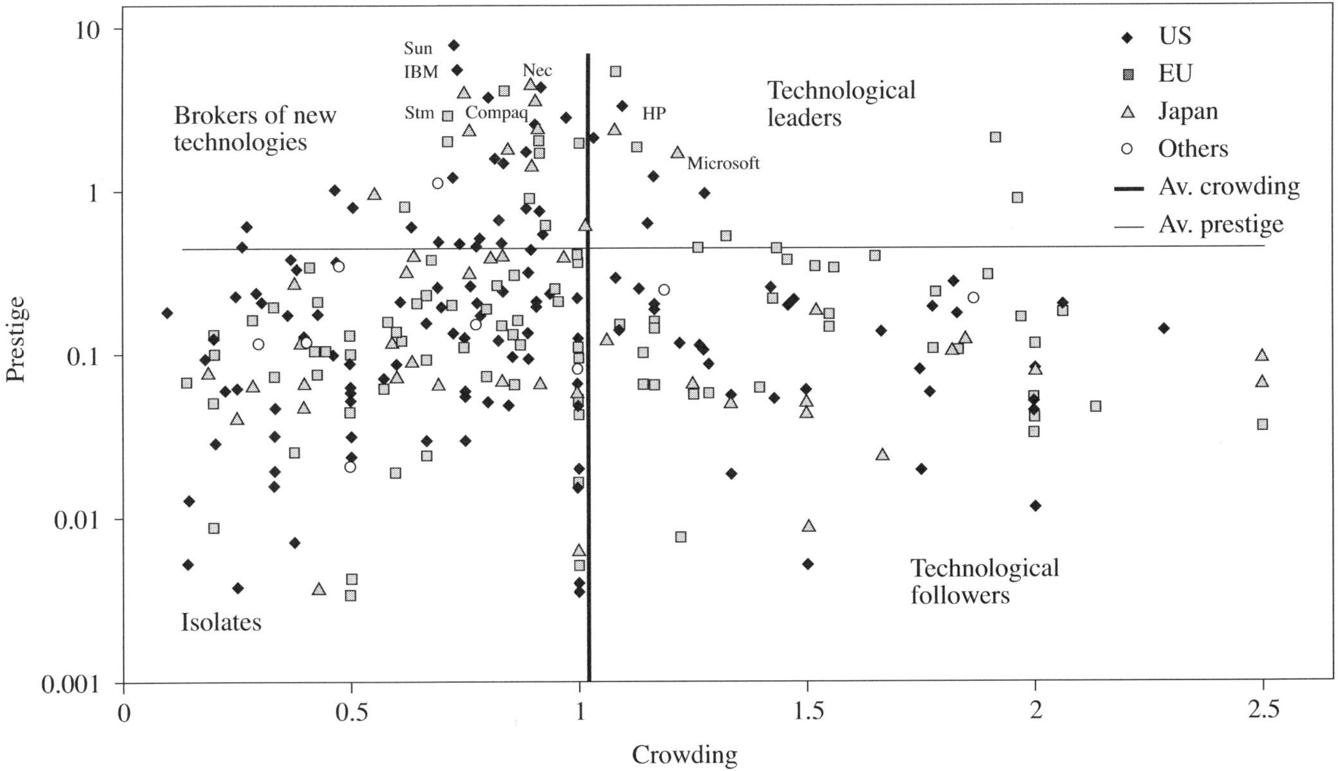

Figure 9.6 Prestige and crowding, computer industry

the relations between pairs of companies. To this purpose, we have first labelled each company according to the four categories defined above (that is, brokers, isolates, followers and leaders). For each pair of companies we have then calculated the technological niche overlap coefficients α_{ijt}. In addition, for each pair of companies we have also calculated the patent citations intensity rate defined by the following equation:

$$I_{ijt} = \frac{C_{ijt}}{P_i \cdot \sum_{\tau=0}^{t} P_{j\tau}} \tag{9.11}$$

where C_{ijt} is the total number of patent citations made by company *i*'s patents to patents of company *j* over the period *t*, P_{it} is the total number of patents (that is, *potentially citing*) of company *i* over the same period and ΣP_{jt} is the cumulated number of patents (that is, potentially citeable) of company *j* over the period from 1978 to 1998. Given that the denominator of the ratio is typically much larger than the numerator, we multiplied the citation rate by 10^5. The above ratio can be therefore interpreted as the expected number of citations from patents of firm *i* to patents of firm *j*. Finally for each combination of firm types (isolate-isolate, isolate-follower and so on), we have reported in Table 9.3 the average values of the technological niche overlap coefficients and of the direct patent citations intensity rates.

Results suggest quite clearly the existence of strong asymmetric relations between types of companies. In general, followers tend to overlap to a large extent among themselves, namely they are not only positioned in crowded technological regions, but they are also positioned in regions occupied by other followers. Moreover, the inter-company patent citations rates are also very high, signalling the existence of strong competitive relations. Followers do not only overlap to a large extent among themselves, but also with all other types of companies. This kind of overlap, however, is not reciprocal. For example, while followers tend to rely to a great extent on the same technological antecedents of brokers, the reverse is not true. An interesting pattern emerges by comparing leaders and followers. In both the industries examined, the amount of niche overlap between followers and leaders is generally much higher than the amount of niche overlap between leaders and followers, that is, the amount of competition from followers to leaders is smaller than the amount of competition from leaders to followers. At the same time, however, the intensity rate of patent citations from leaders to followers is not significantly different (sometimes higher) than the intensity rate of patent citations from followers to leaders.

Table 9.3 Technological niche overlap and patent citations intensity across categories of firms

		Semiconductors		Computers	
		Overlap	**Citations**	**Overlap**	**Citations**
Broker	**Broker**	0.020	7.5	0.019	4.3
	Follower	0.009	22.7	0.009	18.5
	Isolate	0.007	34.5	0.006	17.2
	Leader	0.025	12.1	0.021	5.6
Follower	**Broker**	0.129	53.9	0.142	21.2
	Follower	0.192	301.6	0.148	253.1
	Isolate	0.137	347.9	0.113	158.6
	Leader	0.157	33.0	0.184	25.3
Isolate	**Broker**	0.063	33.0	0.069	18.0
	Follower	0.065	219.7	0.059	358.7
	Isolate	0.044	143.3	0.072	194.8
	Leader	0.048	33.5	0.057	24.1
Leader	**Broker**	0.029	8.9	0.029	4.6
	Follower	0.014	29.5	0.015	32.5
	Isolate	0.006	33.4	0.006	17.3
	Leader	0.041	11.8	0.044	7.9

4 CONCLUSIONS

This chapter has provided an exploratory analysis of inter-organizational networks of technology based upon patent citations data. Although one should be aware of possible abuses of these data, we also argued that they represent a rich source of information for mapping networks of knowledge.

Patent data in general, and patent citations data specifically, can be exploited as 'relational' data, that is, data that provide information about the existence of some kind of relation among two or more agents, to build and examine 'knowledge networks'. In this chapter, we have argued that there are several ways in which this can be done, and that one should be careful about interpreting the significance of the resulting network of relations.

In our analysis, we have proposed using patent citations data to explore knowledge networks at the level of organizations, that is, companies and other institutions. Specifically, we claimed that a meaningful analysis of such networks should be conducted from two complementary (rather than mutually exclusive) perspectives. On the one hand, the examination of the patterns of patent co-citations, that is, citations to common patents between pairs of organizations in an industry allows us to position them in the technological space and to derive hypotheses about the degree of technological and product market competition as opposed to complementarity between them. On the other hand, the analysis of direct patent citations provides information on the quality and the type of innovations developed by each organization. The important point to stress here is that the (competitive) significance of a patent citation cannot be separated by the consideration of the technological relations linking two companies and the position they occupy in the overall technological space.

Using this methodological apparatus, this chapter has examined the main structural properties of the knowledge networks in two industries: semiconductors and computers. We calculated for each of the two industries and for each of the companies included in them, both a technological crowding coefficient and a status index. These two measures allowed us to classify any organization and, via a combination of crowding and status measure, to define a taxonomy of four different kinds of organizations: technological leaders, technological followers, brokers of new technologies and isolated organizations.

We have observed some differences between the two industries. Concerning the semiconductor industry, our analysis shows a quite clear partition between Japanese companies, on the one hand, and US and European companies, on the other hand. While Japanese companies are mostly technological leaders in this area, EU and US firms mostly tend to explore relatively untapped technologies. Many of the EU companies are small isolated companies, while some Japanese companies are technological followers. Concerning the computer industry, we show that US companies, and to some extent also Japanese companies, are the most important brokers of new technologies, while EU companies, with a few exceptions, are either isolates or technological followers.

APPENDIX 9

Table 9.A1 Sectors, SIC codes, technological classes, and corresponding IPC codes

Sector	SIC code	Technological Class	IPC code
Computers	3571 – Electronic Computer 3572 – Computer storage 3575 – Computer Terminals	4 – Information technology	G11C: static stores G10L: speech analysis or synthesis; speech recognition G06: computing; calculating; counting
Semiconductors	3674 – Semiconductors	5 – Semiconductors	H01L: semiconductor devices; electric solid state devices not otherwise provided for

Table 9.A2 Breakdown of sample coverage by selecting criteria

		Computers	Semiconductors
First criterion (a)	**Number of firms**	96	120
	% of firms patenting in the corresponding classes	2.94%	10.07%
	Number of patents	4227	1616
	% of patents in the corresponding classes	23.48%	18.63%
Second criterion (b)	**Number of firms**	312	150
	% of firms patenting in the corresponding classes	9.54%	12.58%
	Number of patents	9390	5490
	% of patents in the corresponding classes	52.15%	63.31%
Our sample (a+b)	**Number of firms**	408	270
	% of firms patenting in the corresponding classes	12.48%	22.65%
	Number of patents	13617	7106
	% of patents in the corresponding classes	75.63%	81.94%

Table 9.A3 Coverage of the sample in terms of number of patents

	Computers	Semiconductors
Number of patenting firms included in the sample	408	270
% of firms on total of the corresponding classes	12.48%	22.65%
Number of patents	13 617	7106
% of patents on total of the corresponding classes	75.63%	81.94%
% of patents on total of the firms	14.02%	8.44%
Average number of patents for firms included in the sample	33 375	26 319
Average number of patents for firms excluded from the sample	1 534	1 698

Table 9.A4 Coverage of the sample in terms of citations made and received

			Computers	Semiconductors
	Number of firms		408	270
	Citing firms	**Number**	348	218
		% of total	85.29%	80.74%
	Citing firms (*)	**Number**	344	216
Citations made		**% of total**	84.31%	80.00%
	Number of citations made to patents of the corresponding classes		10439	6771
	Number of citations made to patents of the corresponding classes (*)		9004	5499
	% of citations on total made by included firms (*)		71.07%	74.30%
	Average number of citations made by patents included in the sample (*)		0.661	0.774
	Average number of citations made by patents excluded from the sample (*)		0.479	0.602

Table 9.A4 continued

Citations received	**Cited firms**	**Number**	328	193
		% of total	80.39%	71.48%
	Cited firms (*)	**Number**	318	186
		% of total	77.94%	68.89%
	Number of citations received by patents of the corresponding classes		11 504	7221
	Number of citations received by patents of the corresponding classes (*)		10 069	5949
	% of citations on total received by included firms (*)		80.86%	82.88%
	Average number of citations received by patents included in the sample (*)		0.739	0.837
	Average number of citations received by patents excluded from the sample (*)		0.237	0.315

Note: (*) excluding self citations.

Table 9.A5 Citation flows across firms included/excluded from the sample

		Cited			
		Firms included in the sample	**Firms excluded from the sample**	**Total**	**Total Citations**
Computers					
Citing	**Firms included in the sample**	92.54%	7.46%	100.00%	9004
	Firms excluded from the sample	82.56%	17.44%	100.00%	2104
Semiconductors					
Citing	**Firms included in the sample**	93.62%	6.38%	100.00%	5499
	Firms excluded from the sample	84.94%	15.06%	100.00%	943

NOTES

1. Many terms and concepts used in social network analysis are taken from graph theory or matrix algebra. In a graph, nodes represent actors (that is, entities) and lines represent ties between actors. In graph theory, the nodes are also referred to as vertices or points, and the lines are also known as edges or arcs.
2. Surveying the whole (and fast growing) empirical literature on networks of strategic alliances is a daunting task, which goes beyond the scope of this chapter. For papers and surveys, see: *Academy of Management Journal* (vol. 40, 1997, edited by R. Osborn and J. Hagedoorn), *Organization Science* (vol. 9 n. 3, 1998, edited by M. Koza and A.Y. Lewin), *Organization Studies* (vol. 19 n. 4, 1998, edited by A. Grandori), *International Studies of Management and Organizations* (vol. 27 n. 4, 1998, edited by M. Ebers and C.J. Jarillo), *Strategic Management Journal* (vol. 21, 2000, edited by R. Gulati *et al.*), and *Journal of Technology Transfer* (vol. 26 n.1–2, 2001, edited by D.S. Siegel *et al.*). See also Gulati (1998, 1999), Oliver and Ebers (1998), Hagedoorn, Link, and Vonortas N.S. (2000), Nohria and Eccles (1992) and Nooteboom (1999).
3. The use of patent and patent citations data has quite a well-established tradition in the economics of innovation. Econometric studies of technological change have traditionally relied heavily on patents as indicators of innovation activity. As well explained by Griliches' (1990) classic survey, patent data are easily available, cover many countries, and are rich in technical information, thanks to their fine classification. The US Patent & Trademark Office (USPTO) and, from the 1980s, the European Patent Office (EPO) are the most heavily exploited sources.
4. In general, a relation can be binary or valued, and directed or undirected. A network could be labelled according to the kind of relation, for example, direct network.
5. When pointing at jargon as inaccessible we mainly refer to our own practical experience, both in making clear our own jargon to scientists from different disciplines, and even more to non-scientists. As for the reward system, we clearly refer to Merton's definition of science as being driven by an 'institutionalized system of open-communication-and-correlative-reward' (Merton, 1977, p. 48).
6. For a long time, citations to and from scientific papers have been exploited as a useful source of relational data. Scientists cite each other for a number of reasons, all of them pointing at some social bonds: they acknowledge the help they received from colleagues, or simply try to please them (so that we can use citations to track mutual bonds); or they may cite early authors to acknowledge their priority or authority (in which case we can compare two scientists' citation set, and uncover some common roots). Patent citations serve the same purpose much less effectively, for all the reasons we outlined above. Notice also that patent citations show statistical patterns which are very different from those of scientific citations, first and foremost by not displaying any sign of being affected by the so-called 'Matthew effect' (see data reported by Karki, 1997). This is understandable, since no reward system (either for the inventors, or for the applicants) is attached to patent citations, certainly not one as sophisticated and decisive for invidividuals' careers as the one attached to citations of scientific papers (Merton, 1988).
7. Fairness requires us to point to Sirilli (1987) as the true pioneer study using an extensive inventor-based patent dataset. However, Sirilli's dataset was never regarded, even by its author, as a source of relational data, nor was it ever coupled to citation data.
8. In the language of graph theory, the top part of the figure reports the affiliation network of patents, applicants and inventors. An affiliation network is a network in which actors (for example, inventors) are joined together by common membership to groups of some kind (for example, patents). Affiliation networks can be represented as a graph consisting of two kinds of vertices, one representing the actors (for example, inventors) and the other the groups (for example, patents). In order to analyse the patterns of relations among actors, however, affiliation networks are often represented simply as unipartite (or one-mode) graphs of actors joined by undirected edges – two inventors who participated in the same patent, in our case, being connected by an edge (see bottom part of Figure 9.2).

9. Connectedness considers if inventors belong to the same component (that is, subgraph) or they may be located in disconnected components. The geodesic distance is defined as the minimum number of steps (or, more formally, lines) that separate two distinct inventors in the network.
10. Degree centrality is defined as the number of lines' incident with a node. In the context of this study where nodes represent organizations, degree centrality is therefore defined as the number of other organizations with which the focal organizations have a relation tie.

    Betweenness centrality is a measure of the influence a node has over the spread of information and knowledge through the network. The basic idea is that a node, which lies on the information path linking other nodes, is able to exercise a control over the flow of knowledge within the network.
11. For instance, it is possible to consider all pairs of patents with different application dates in order to check whether a citation link exists, and try to explain the probability of its existence with social distance between the inventors, or their connectedness. Breschi and Lissoni (2004) have employed our social distance measures to test the robustness of Jaffe *et al.* (1993) findings on the role of geographical distance in knowledge diffusion. Other recent studies using a similar methodology include Agrawal, Cockburn and McHale (2003), Singh (2003), Stolpe (2002).
12. Joint patent applications represent roughly 1.5 per cent of all patent applications to the European Patent Office.
13. The in-degree of a node is the number of arcs (or arrows) terminating to the node itself. The out-degree of a node is the number of arcs (or arrows) originating with the node itself.
14. For a thorough discussion of the methodological problems involved in analysing an inter-organization citation network, see Breschi *et al.* (2003).
15. The example is adapted from Podolny and Stuart (1996).
16. The dimensionality of the technological space can be reduced by means of appropriate techniques, like multidimensional scaling (see Podolny and Stuart, 1996).
17. This approach shares many similarities with the approach proposed by Jaffe (1986).
18. The European Patent Office (EPO) grants European patents for the contracting states to the European Patent Convention (EPC), which was signed in Munich on 5 October 1973 and entered into force on 7 October 1977.
19. The IPC is an internationally agreed, non-overlapping and comprehensive patent classification system. For the purposes of this paper, we adopted a technology-oriented classification, jointly elaborated by Fraunhofer Gesellschaft ISI (Karlsruhe), Institut National de la Propriété Industrielle (INPI, Paris) and Observatoire des Sciences et des Techniques (OST, Paris).
20. In other contexts, the parameter β can assume negative values. This is for example the case in bargaining situations or power relations, where being connected to high status actors may have a negative effect.
21. Note that as β approaches the reciprocal of the largest eigenvalue λ of R, the $c(\alpha, \beta)$ index converges to the so-called eigenvector centrality e.

BIBLIOGRAPHY

Agrawal, A.K., Cockburn, I.M., McHale, J. (2003), 'Gone but not forgotten: labor flows, knowledge spillovers, and enduring social capital', NBER Working Paper 9950, Cambridge MA: NBER.

Akers, N. (1999), 'The European Patent System: an introduction for patent searchers', *World Patent Information*, **21**, pp. 135–63.

Akers, N. (2000), 'The referencing of prior art documents in European patents and applications', *World Patent Information*, **22**, pp. 309–15.

Almeida, P., Kogut, B. (1999), 'The localization of knowledge and the mobility of engineers in regional networks', *Management Science*, **45**, pp. 905–17.

Andrews, S., Knoke, D. (eds) (2001), *Networks In and Around Organizations*, Greenwich CT: JAI Press.

Balconi, M., Breschi, S., Lissoni, F. (2004), 'Networks of inventors and the role of academia: an exploration of Italian patent data', *Research Policy*, **33**, pp. 127–45.

Batagelj, V. (2003), 'Efficient algorithms for citation network analysis', mimeo, University of Ljubljana, http://www.ijp.si/ffp/pub/preprints/ps/2003/pp897.pdf.

Bonacich, P (1987), 'Power and centrality: a family of measure', *The American Journal of Sociology*, **92**(5), pp. 1170–82.

Breschi, S., Lissoni, F. (2001a), 'Knowledge spillovers and local innovation systems: a critical survey', *Industrial and Corporate Change*, **10**(4), pp. 975–1005.

Breschi, S., Lissoni, F. (2001b) 'Localised Knowledge Spillovers vs. Innovative Milieux: Knowledge "Tacitness" Reconsidered', *Papers in Regional Science*, **80**(3), pp. 255–74.

Breschi, S., Lissoni, F. (2004), 'Knowledge networks from patent data: methodological issues and research targets', in W. Glänzel, H. Moed and V. Schmoch (eds), *Handbook of Quantative S&T Research*, Kluwer Academic Publishers.

Breschi, S., Lissoni, F. (2005), 'Mobility and social networks: localised knowledge spillovers revisited', *Annales d'Economie et de Statistique*, (forthcoming).

Breschi, S., Lissoni, F., Malerba, F. (2003), *STI-NET Patent and Patent Citations Database: Methodology and Preliminary Analyses*, mimeo.

Burt, R.S. (2001), 'Structural holes versus network closure as social capital', in N. Lin, K.S. Cook, R.S. Burt, A. de Gruyter (eds) *Social Capital: Theory and Research*, Aldine de Gruyter.

Burt, R.S. (2003), 'Social Origins Of Good Ideas', mimeo, web.mit.edu/sorensen/www/SOGI.pdf.

Cowan, R., David P.A., Foray, D. (2000), 'The explicit economics of knowledge codification and tacitness', *Industrial and Corporate Change*, **9**, pp. 211–53.

Duguet, E., MacGarvie, M. (2003), 'How well do patent citations measure flows of technology? Evidence from French innovation surveys', mimeo, http://people.bu.edu/mmacgarv/papers.html.

Griliches, Z. (1990), 'Patent statistics as economic indicators: a survey', *Journal of Economic Literature*, **28**, pp. 1661–707.

Gulati, Ranjay (1998), 'Alliances and networks', *Strategic Management Journal*, **19**, pp. 293–317.

Gulati, Ranjay (1999), 'Network location and learning: the influence of network resources and firm capabilities on alliance formation', *Strategic Management Journal*, **20**, pp. 397–420.

Hagedoorn, J. (2003), 'Sharing intellectual property rights – an exploratory study of joint patenting amongst companies', *Industrial and Corporate Change*, **12**, pp. 1035–50.

Hagedoorn, J., Link, A.N. and Vonortas, N.S., (2000), 'Research partnerships', *Research Policy*, **29**, pp. 567–86.

Hall, B.H., Jaffe, A., Trajtenberg, M. (2000), 'Market value and patent citations: a first look', NBER Working Paper 7441.

Hall, B.H., Jaffe, A., Trajtenberg, M. (2001), 'The NBER patent citations data file: lessons, insights and methodological tools', NBER Working Paper 8498, Cambridge MA: NBER republished in Jaffe and Trajtenberg (2002).

Jaffe, A.B. (1986), 'Technological opportunity and spillovers of R&D: evidence from firms' patents, profits and market value', *American Economic Review*, American Economic Association, **76**(5), pp. 984–1001.

Jaffe, A.B., Trajtenberg, M. (2002), *Patents, Citations, and Innovations: A Window on the Knowledge Economy*, Cambidge MA: MIT Press.

Jaffe, A.B., Trajtenberg M., Fogarty M.S. (2000a), 'The meaning of patent citations: Report on the NBER/Case-Western Reserve Survey of Patentees', NBER Working Paper 7631, Cambidge MA: NBER.

Jaffe, A.B., Trajtenberg, M., Fogarty, M.S. (2000b), 'Knowledge spillovers and patent citations: Evidence from a survey of inventors', *American Economic Review*, **90**(2), pp. 215–18.

Jaffe, A.B., Trajtenberg, M., Henderson, R. (1993), 'Geographic localisation of knowledge spillovers as evidenced by patent citations', *Quarterly Journal of Economics*, **108**, pp. 577–98.

Karki, M.M.S. (1997), 'Patent citation analysis: a policy analysis tool', *World Patent Information*, **19**, pp. 269–72.

King, G., Zeng, L. (2001), 'Explaining rare events in international relations', *International Organization*, **55**(3), pp. 693–715.

Kortum, S., Lerner, J. (1998), 'Stronger protection or technological revolution: what is behind the recent surge in patenting?', *Carnegie-Rochester Conference Series on Public Policy*, **48**, pp. 247–304.

Merton, R.K. (1961), 'Singletons and multiples in scientific discovery', *Proceedings of the American Philosophical Society*, **105**, pp. 470–86.

Merton, R.K. (1977), *The Sociology of Science: An Episodic Memoir*, Southern Illinois University Press.

Merton, R.K. (1988), 'The Matthew effect in science, II: cumulative advantage and the symbolism of intellectual property', *ISIS* 79, pp. 606–23.

Meyer, M., Siniläinen, T., Utecht, J.T. (2003), 'Towards hybrid triple helix indicators: a study of university-related patents and a survey of academic inventors', *Scientometrics*, **58**, pp. 321–50.

Møen, J. (2000), 'Is mobility of technical personnel a source of R&D spillovers?', NBER Working Paper 7834, Cambridge MA: NBER.

Murray, F. (2002), 'Innovation as co-evolution of scientific and technological networks: exploring tissue engineering', *Research Policy*, **31**, pp. 1389–403.

Newman, M.E.J. (2000), 'Who are the best connected scientists? A study of scientific co-authorship networks', SFI Working Paper 00–12–64, Santa Fe: SFI.

Newman, M.E.J. (2001), 'The structure of scientific collaboration networks', *Proceedings of the National Academy of Science USA*, **98**, pp. 404–9.

Nohria, N. and Eccles, R. (1992), *Networks and Organizations: Structure, Form and Action*, Boston MA: Harvard Business School Press.

Nooteboom, B. (1999) *Inter-Firm Alliances: Analysis and Design*, London: Routledge.

Ogburn, W.F., Thomas, D. (1922), 'Are inventions inevitable? A note on social evolution', *Political Science Quarterly*, **3**, pp. 83–98.

Oliver, A.L. and Ebers, M. (1998), 'Networking network studies – an analysis of conceptual configurations in the study of inter-organizational relations', *Organization Studies*, 19(4), 549–83.

Pier, H., Rost, K., Teichert, T., von Wartburg, I. (2003), '"HO4Q–007" – Deconstructing the technological blob of mobile telecommuncation. An application of social network analysis for categorizing technological fields', ZEW Workshop 'Empirical innovation and patenting' March 14–15 2003, Mannheim, Germany.

Pilkington, A., Dyerson, R., Tissier, O. (2002), 'The electric vehicle: patent data as indicators of technological development', *World Patent Information*, **24**, pp. 5–12.
Podolny, Joel M. (1993), 'A status-based model of market competition', *American Journal of Sociology*, **98**(4) January, pp. 829–72.
Podolny, Joel M. (1994), 'Market uncertainty and the social character of economic exchange', *Administrative Science Quarterly*, **39**(3), pp. 458–83.
Podolny, J.M. and Stuart, T.E. (1996), 'Local search and the evolution of technological capabilities', *Strategic Management Journal*, **17**, pp. 21–38.
Podolny, Joel M., Stuart, Toby E., Hannan, Michael T. (1996), 'Networks, knowledge, and niches: competition in the worldwide semiconductor industry, 1984–1991', *American Journal of Sociology*, **102**(3) November, pp. 659–89.
Podolny, Joel M. (2001), 'Networks as the pipes and prisms of the market', *American Journal of Sociology*, **107**(1) July, pp. 33–60.
Podolny, Joel M., Page, Karen L. (1998), 'Network Forms of Organisation', *Annual Review of Sociology*, **24**, pp. 57–76.
Podolny, Joel M., Stuart, Toby E. (1995), 'A role-based ecology of technological change', *American Journal of Sociology*, **100**(5) March, pp. 1224–60.
Sampat, B.N., Ziedonis, A. (2002), 'Cite-Seeing: patent citations and economic value', mimeo.
Saragossi, S., van Pottelsberghe de la Potterie, B. (2003), 'What patent data reveal about universities: the case of Belgium', *Journal of Technology Transfer*, **28**, pp. 9–15.
Singh, J. (2003), 'Inventor mobility and social networks as drivers of knowledge diffusion', mimeo, Harvard Business School.
Sirilli, G. (1987), 'Patents and inventors: an empirical study', *Research Policy*, **16**, pp. 157–74.
Song, J., Almeida, P., Wu, G. (2003), 'Learning-by-hiring: when is mobility more likely to facilitate knowledge transfer?', *Management Science*, **49**, pp. 351–65.
Sorenson, O. (2003), 'Social networks, informational complexity and industry concentration', mimeo, Los Angeles: UCLA.
Sorenson, O., Fleming, L. (2001), 'Science and the diffusion of knowledge', mimeo, Boston MA: Harvard University.
Stolpe, M. (2002), 'Determinants of knowledge diffusion as evidenced in patent debates: the case of Liquid Crystal Display technology', *Research Policy*, **31**, pp. 1181–98.
Stuart, T.E. (1999), 'A structural perspective on organizational innovation', *Industrial and Corporate Change*, **8**(4), pp. 745–75.
Thompson, P. (2003), 'Patent citations and the geography of knowledge spillovers: what do patent examiners know?', mimeo, Carnegie Mellon University.
Thompson, P., Fox-Kean, M.(2003), 'Patent citations and the geography of knowledge spillovers: a reassessment', mimeo, Carnegie Mellon University.
Verspagen, B. (2006), 'Small worlds and technology networks: the case of European research collaboration', in Y. Caloghirou, N. Constantelon and N.S. Vonortas (eds), *Knowledge Flows in European Industry*, Routledge.
Wasserman, S., Faust, C. (1994), *Social Network Analysis: Methods and Applications*, Cambridge: Cambridge University Press.
Watts, D.J. (2003), *Six Degrees: The Science of a Connected Age,* W.W. Norton & Company.
Zucker, L.G., Darby, M.R., Armstrong, J. (1998), 'Geographically localized knowledge: spillovers or markets?', *Economic Inquiry*, **36**, pp. 65–86.

10. Intellectual property rights for governance in and of innovation systems

Ove Granstrand

ABSTRACT

This chapter attempts to look at the role of IPRs in different innovation systems – national, sectoral, corporate, university and military systems – in a governance perspective. The rapid advent of the pro-IP era from the 1980s on, embedded in the gradual emergence of a new type of economy dominated by intellectual capital, has generally transformed and strengthened various IP regimes in these innovation systems, with an increasing use of patent and licensing oriented regimes.

The availability of enforceable and valuable IPRs together with more large-scale R&D and complex new technologies, calling for more inter-firm technology collaborations and various forms of technology trade (through licences, small firms, services and so on) have fostered quasi-integrated corporate innovation systems. Seen in a governance perspective the IPR approach creates governance tools but also governance problems, but so do other approaches to incentivizing and coordinating innovative activities as well. A re-evaluation of various approaches is needed, focusing on both incentivizing and coordinating functions, for sustaining efficient and effective innovation systems.

Keywords: Technology, Governance, Intellectual Property, Innovation system, Licensing

For a list of key concepts, see Appendix 10A and a list of abbreviations, see Appendix 10B.

1 INTRODUCTION

1.1 Background

Sustained progress almost by definition requires a sustainable flow of innovations, that is, new and useful information and things. All currently known economic systems have difficulties in inducing and governing such a flow efficiently and alleged signs of their dysfunctioning are likely, for example, in terms of over- and under-investments in R&D and innovation. As innovations moreover become larger in both scale of production and scale of use and interdependencies among them proliferate, coordination problems within and across different flows of innovations grow in addition to incentive problems. This is particularly true for technological innovations due to the cumulative and interactive nature of new technologies. In this context, the innovation systems approach has emerged, as described below.

Innovators, being early movers, have to perceive sufficient advantages accruing from their innovative efforts and may deploy various means or strategies towards that end, such as creating lead times in exploration and exploitation or creating strong user ties or other barriers to imitation. Societies and organizations urging for progress in turn have various institutional means or policies to help foster innovations and innovators, such as creating incentive schemes and motivation structures through for example, recognition, prizes, subsidies, contracts and limited rights.

The use of various rights to induce innovations of various kinds is an old institutional arrangement although the by now customary recognition of these rights as intellectual property rights (IPRs) is of more recent origin. The (growing) family of IPRs comprises old types of rights such as patents for inventions, trade secrets, copyrights, trademarks and design rights, together with newer ones such as breeding rights, maskwork rights and database rights. These rights – although subsumed under the label IPRs, suggesting some coherence – in fact comprise a very heterogeneous set of rights hardly (yet) constituting what could be called an IPR system. The various IPRs usually have long running and fairly separate histories of legal and economic developments and concomitant controversies, surrounded by relative neglect on average among the public at large, including policy makers, managers and the economics and law professions in general. Nevertheless, the underlying criteria for granting these rights have a surprising number of similarities in emphasizing novelty, usefulness and distinctive originality (or inventiveness).

1.2 Purpose and Outline

The purpose of this chapter is to make a first attempt to elaborate on the role of IPRs in various innovation systems and then to view them in a governance perspective. In so doing not only national and sectoral innovation systems but also corporate, university and military systems will be dealt with. These latter three types of innovation systems are usually not dealt with in the innovation systems literature. As will be seen, different innovation systems at national, sectoral and corporate levels have employed different IP regimes. The regimes have also changed over time, and in recent decades in particular, in connection with the emergence of a strong IP regime globally, commonly referred to as the pro-IP era, linked to the emergence of a new type of economy in which intangible assets or intellectual capital in some sense have come to dominate. In this context IPRs have increasingly become viewed not only from an incentive point of view but also in a wider governance perspective, that is, how different modes of governance of innovation and diffusion (through management, markets or hybrid forms) are helped or hindered by the use of the IPR approach. In this perspective, various forms of technology trade and inter-organizational technology collaboration contracts become important. The chapter describes the property approach to governance with the intellectual property approach as a particular but increasingly important special case. First a historical account of IPRs and innovation systems is given, followed by an account of theories and rationales of the patent system as a special but most important case. Finally an empirical part follows, dealing with the role of IPRs in the five types of innovation systems mentioned.

2 EVOLUTION OF THE IPR SYSTEM AND SYSTEMS OF INNOVATION

2.1 Early Patent History

Notions of intellectual property have evolved from the dawn of history, especially oriented around secrets.[1] Identity-related symbols are also of early origin.[2] IP for gaining trade-related advantages was less important in prehistoric times, but secrets and symbols as means to build and preserve power and governance structures were important, especially in political, military and religious settings.

IP notions developed as trade and technology developed in the Middle Ages and a need to finance increasingly large-scale innovations arose. Remunerating the disclosure of secrets, an ancient practice in itself, became increasingly important as technical know-how and its cumulation gained importance. Various types of compensations – prizes, grants, patent privileges and so on – were considered. What probably made a patent-like privilege particularly attractive to a ruler or a governing body was its financial feature. Privileges that protected privilege holders from competition allowed them to charge higher prices. To the extent that competitive trade developed, the privilege holder was remunerated by the privilege granter, that is, the governor, in such a way that the privilege granter did not have to risk any finance.[3] A patent privilege also carried the advantage that the remuneration was tied to the actual useful working of a device, that is, to its innovative nature, and the expressed demand for that device, that is, its diffusion or market penetration. This advantage could be achieved by a prize system as well, but then the governing body had to finance the prize. From the patent holder's point of view, a patent privilege implied a risky remuneration *ex post*, that is, in connection with commercial success, based in turn on technical success, and it financed neither any necessary investments *ex ante* nor any failures *ex post*. This disadvantage could be mitigated by a grant or a loan in combination with the patent, however, but then at the discretion of the governing body. Thus, the emergence of the patent system can be seen partly as a reaction against secrecy in a context of the rising importance of technology and trade, and as a scheme for jointly promoting inventions, innovations and their diffusion, a scheme that provided an attractive mode of financing for the privilege granter.

As mining became a more technically complex operation, for example, going deeper into the ground, more technical devices were needed, for example, for removing water. Patent-like privileges were then granted in Europe to originators and financiers of these devices by extending mining law principles (Kaufer 1989). Often remuneration took the form of rights to a certain share of the mine's output, again an attractive mode of financing, similar to licensing on a barter basis.

In the 14th and 15th centuries the Republic of Venice was engaged in mining and 'water arts' as well. At this time Venice had two types of privileges, invention privileges and trade privileges. An invention privilege gave protection from unlicensed imitation of an invention, while a trade privilege gave protection from competition in general.[4] In 1474 Venice promulgated a formal patent code, the first one known in history. The code incorporated various ideas practised in preceding cases. Inventions shown to be workable and useful received ten years of protection subject to compulsory licensing provisions. The 1474 patent code and its preceding practices were a way for Venice to attract engineers from the outside and stimulate orderly technical progress, although it was not the only way.

2.2 Emergence of Innovation Systems, the Pro-IP era and a New Type of Economy

Since the 20th century, industrial and military science-based R&D has emerged on a substantially larger scale as well as research universities, entailing very different modes and settings for innovations. The individual inventor, who was the original target for patent laws, has gradually become relatively less important. Innovations increasingly require large resources, and industrial firms and the military establishment have become the prime owners and movers of technology in inter-organizational settings that could be described as innovation systems, both in terms of technical (artifact) systems and actor (organizational) systems. Similarly, cultural arts and innovations (movies, concerts, books and so on) have become big business, with more professional artists and organizations than ever. Differences between countries have increased, industries have grown and diversified, science and technology have progressed and accumulated, globalization has increased and so on. Still the IPR system and its essential ideas have survived and continued to diffuse internationally, not least after the downfall of the Soviet Union and the corresponding planned-economy systems. This resilience of ideas and persistent adoption of a fairly well-preserved and long-standing institution is indeed surprising as its current context has changed radically since its distant origins, such as 15th-century Venice in the case of patent legislation. For example, an anti-patent movement in the 19th century Europe more or less ended in the 1870s (see Machlup and Penrose 1950). Political and economic forces largely defeated the anti-patent movement. These forces were under the surface not directly linked to the patent system so they did not produce a marked reversal into a pro-patent era. Patent legislation continued to carry weight, and the patent system was internationally adopted and harmonized to some extent, but patent issues were by and large circling in the backwaters of business, economics and policy making and continued to do so for a good century. In the USA a revival of certain anti-patent sentiments appeared in the interwar years, as large corporations with strong in-house R&D emerged, some of them blatantly using the patent system to build up dominant market positions (see for example, Folk 1942 and Scherer 1980, p. 451).

However, a pro-patent era was set in motion in the USA in the 1980s and then gained ground internationally for various reasons, also evolving into a broader pro-IP era (see further Granstrand 1999, Jaffe 2000 and Coriat and Orsi 2002). Since the 1990s, criticism of 'overshoot' has grown but with no signs of a significant reversal of the pro-IP era; quite the contrary. This may be seen as a reflection of the growing strength of more fundamental forces in the international economy. The rapid emergence of a much stronger IP regime since the 1980s, has by and large been concomitant with a much grander and more gradual emergence of a new type of economy, the roots and trends of which stretch much further back in history. This economy is essentially characterized by a confluence of old capitalist institutions, more dominant than ever after the downfall of the Soviet empire and the demise of planned economies, and a new kind of dominance of intellectual capital, comprising intangible assets (knowledge, IPRs and so on) valued or weighted by various means and methods. Hence this type of economy, being new in the sense that knowledge and intellectual capital has come to dominate, has been referred to as the knowledge (learning, information) based economy or intellectual (knowledge) capitalism or simply the 'new economy'.[5] However, the newness derives from the new role of dominance of intellectual capital that has gradually emerged, while the old, basic capitalist institutions remain (that is, firms, markets, property rights and profit seeking). Thus, the notions that the new economy is entirely new and is resulting from a rapid change have to be dismissed (rapidly and entirely).

2.3 IPRs in the Emergence of Intellectual Capitalism

What role has the IPR system played then in the emergence of intellectual capitalism? This must be left largely as an open question here, but a few observations may be made. First, the IPR system has historically been neither necessary nor sufficient for technical or economic progress, such as in the first industrial revolutions (Granstrand, 1999). This is hardly a surprising statement but is nevertheless important to keep in mind, especially since technical progress is increasingly seen as necessary for economic progress.[6]

Second, although information and communication technologies (ICTs) have contributed significantly to the emergence of intellectual capitalism, IPRs do not appear to have contributed significantly to the emergence of ICTs, at least not until the 1980s. In fact it may even be argued that lax IPR regimes were instrumental for the early emergence of several ICT industries.[7] A few examples will illustrate this. The transistor was patented at Bell Labs but licensed out generously and the subsequent emergence of the semiconductor industry was significantly spurred by public procurement and a lax IP regime (Mowery 1996). The same could be said about the emergence of the Internet under the Defense Advanced Research Projects Agency (DARPA). The software industry also emerged under a lax IPR regime (Samuelson 1993). The telecom industry was largely nationally monopolized till the 1980s and 1990s, with little interest in IPR. Mobile telephony also emerged until the late 1980s under a lax IPR regime (Granstrand 1999). In other words, the absence rather than presence of strong IPRs was arguably important in the early stages of various sectoral innovation systems based on ICTs.[8]

Third, the relatively rapid emergence of a much stronger IP regime since the 1980s has been embedded in the much grander and more gradual emergence of intellectual capitalism as mentioned above. The strengthening of the IP regime may very well have strengthened some features of intellectual capitalism, for example, through the appreciation of IPR values, and speeded up the development of some of its components in the recent decade or so. But with our limited knowledge at present about the feedback structure involved it is only safe to say that the pro-IP era appears to be more a consequence of intellectual capitalism than a cause of it.[9] In any case a strong IP regime is a feature of the new type of economy with a concomitant expansion of IPRs by volume, type, value and strategic attention paid to them. The rapid strengthening of the old IPR institutions in the slow, gradual emergence of a new type of economy has in turn strengthened old misfits plus created new ones for the IPR institutions, for example, misfits between the patent system on the one hand and nations at different stages of development or industries with different innovation characteristics (see further Granstrand 2004b). Nevertheless, despite mounting criticism there are no signs of a significant reversal of the pro-IP era, but rather that IP reforms of various kinds will appear, as IP policies will be increasingly attended to in the national and international innovation systems.

3 ECONOMIC RATIONALES FOR A PATENT SYSTEM

3.1 Overview

The long history of the IPR system as an economic and also social institution has naturally produced much debate and rationalizations over the years. Only a brief summary can be given here and then with a focus on patents as an IPR of prime importance with a focus on rationales of an economic nature.[10]

For a classic qualitative review of theories of the pros and cons of patents, see Machlup (1958) and for a current review (with similar classification of theories) from an economic perspective, see Mazzoleni and Nelson (1998), and from a legal perspective Gutterman (1997). The received theories build on old notions that in the absence of patents under-investment in R&D and innovation would occur and/or that too much secrecy would occur. Thus an extra incentive to invent, disclose and innovate would be needed and a patent right would help fill this need.[11]

However, a strong patent right tailored as a reward to an inventor who is first in some sense with an invention may also lead to excessive competitive races with over-investment and uncoordinated exploitation of new technologies as a result. Then it has been argued that a patent right should be tailored as a prospect right giving an exclusive right to the rights holder to further exploration in a wider area, handed out at an early stage of the exploitation process as in mineral extraction. In this way further exploitation of new technological areas could presumably be better coordinated or governed by a firm.[12]

The received theories focus on different parts or stages of the compound invention, innovation and diffusion process and on the different but related roles of IPRs as incentivizing and coordinating mechanisms. Thus the received theories altogether contain the elements in what could be said to constitute two newer integrated perspectives. One views patents as joint incentives to both exploration and exploitation through integrated innovation and diffusion processes. The other perspective views patents (and more generally IPRs) as a mode of coordination or governance similar (but not equivalent) to the role of property rights in tangibles.

Table 10.1 gives a summary of both the received economic rationales for a patent system and the newer economic perspectives on patents. Viewing patents as a joint innovation/diffusion incentive integrates received incentive-oriented rationales (treating disclosure as diffusion of information) and in doing so also focuses on the interdependence and dynamics over time of the processes involved. Hereby dynamic (Schumpeterian) competition is more clearly articulated and contrasted against static (price) competition.

3.2 The Property Approach Viewed in a Governance Perspective

A general controversy (or set of controversies) concerns the use of a property approach with its pros and con not only for incentivizing innovators compared to alternative approaches (tax-based subsidies, procurement contracts and so on) but also for handling coordination or governance problems in innovation and diffusion. The property approach has been criticized for creating rather than solving coordination problems, for example, in the common context of sequential or cumulative innovation or in the contexts of 'open science' and complex technologies, thus creating anti-commons problems or problems with assembling different necessary IPRs for productive use of resources.

However, information and knowledge are uncertain and highly heterogeneous entities and so are the conditions under which they are produced and diffused, justifying a combined variety of approaches to foster suitable conditions. Thus, using the property approach means decentralizing decision making about scarce resources to agents with unique

Table 10.1 Economic rationales for a patent system

Received economic theories	**Newer economic perspectives on patents**
Incentive-to-Invent theory *Focus:* Impact on invention and R&D *Concerns:* • Distortion of R&D (for example, too many substitutes/too few complements, too little basic/too much applied, too much patentable/too little unpatentable) • Barriers to competition • Heterogeneity of industries/firms/inventors	**Patents as a joint incentive to innovate and diffuse** *Focus:* Impact on dynamic competition through 'continuous' and entangled (interdependent) innovation and diffusion processes *Concerns:* • As for incentive-to-innovate • Efficiency/distortion of diffusion • Interdependence of inventions and innovations over time (for example, in sequential innovation) • Dynamic interaction between innovation and diffusion processes
Incentive-to-Disclose theory *Focus:* Impact on secrecy *Concerns:* • Quality/quantity of disclosure • Impact on R&D (for example, stimulation, coordination) • Impact on diffusion (for example, on technology markets)	**Patent rights and patent information as a governance mechanism** *Focus:* Property rights allocation and disclosure as a mode of incentivizing and organizing for decentralized governance through management hierarchies and markets and hybrids of these two governance modes. *Concerns:* • Allocation and transfer of rights • Cumulation and dispersion of rights • Interdependence of rights • Scope and duration of rights • Enforcement of rights • Governance efficiencies, for example in terms of coordination and communication costs, such as market efficiencies, for example in terms of transaction costs • Optimal decentralized 'tariffs' or 'taxation' (through prices or damages) • Role of governance bodies and institutions (legislators, courts, patent offices, patent management, patent pools, clearing houses, anti-trust authorities and so on) • Alternative governance mechanisms
Incentive-to-Innovate theory *Focus:* Impact on innovation and competition *Concerns:* • Incentives *ex ante* and *ex post* invention • Impact on complementary investments • Transaction costs • Invention/innovation distinction • Patent scope and duration	
Prospect theory *Focus:* Resource exploitation efficiency *Concerns:* • Coordination and duplication of R&D • Exploration • Improvement • Firm strategies	

access to localized information for proper decisions, and incentivizing them to exercise their capabilities by providing them with access to a share of the extra surpluses they then generate. The latter is done by allowing the property holder to charge prices higher than marginal cost in order to help cover fixed investment costs.

Such monopolistic pricing is a drawback of the property approach, as it incurs a certain loss of consumer surplus apart from a shift of some surplus from consumers to the producer. However, in order to assess the property approach, this drawback (cost) has to be compared with corresponding drawbacks of other approaches. If the right to exercise certain monopolistic pricing is seen as a decentralized right to tax consumers, it corresponds to the right to impose a targeted sales tax administered by private agents. The administrative cost could then be fairly low in comparison with public forms of taxation, be they targeted (selective) or general.[13] Of course, taxes could be more than minimally distorting and over-taxation could occur, as it could with any form of tax. (Few people seem to disagree on this.) One real virtue as well as a drawback of the property approach is its amenability to flexible decentralization which could then easily lead to over-decentralization in the sense that too many and costly agent interdependencies would arise, resulting in too high transaction costs, eventually high enough to outweigh incentive effects and other efficiency gains. In addition, recentralization is usually more difficult (costly) than decentralization.

This view of the property approach is actually a governance view comparable to an organization theory view, in which the handing out of private property rights is comparable to handing out or decentralizing responsibilities and accountabilities (liabilities) in an organization, applying management by objectives, dealing with principal-agent and information asymmetry problems, intervening for conflict resolution and so on.[14] There are many organizational principles, some of which are that decentralization should be aligned to the information structure, incentive structure and structure of interdependencies, and should not be carried so far that the management cost of coordination outweighs benefits, for example, from entrepreneurial motivation and economies of scale from division of labour. To illustrate, the adoption of the so-called M-form of organization (that is, a form of organization of a firm being decentralized into product divisions) is a recognition of stronger interdependencies within product-related activities than for example, within functionally related activities (that is, activities within R&D, production and marketing functions). Handing out patent rights to product inventions is then comparable (but not equivalent) to adopting an M-form of decentralization. If, however, inter-product interdependencies become more costly to coordinate than intra-product ones, the M-form has been carried too far, with too many small interdependent divisions with internal transfer pricing problems (transaction costs), conflicts and costly higher management intervention (the organization's internal court system). Thus, using a property approach is largely a matter of how far decentralization should go along what organizational principles, in order not to let transaction costs and administrative expenses outweigh innovative and efficiency gains by handing out too many small interdependent or overlapping property rights.

This does not imply that a proper trade-off along the centralization-decentralization continuum makes the property approach the single best solution. For this all costs and benefits of a property approach relative to other approaches have to be weighed up, and in particular for an intellectual property approach these costs and benefits are far from well understood. An IPR system is likely to be more costly to run than a physical property right (PPR) system, although its benefits may have increased as technological innovations have become more highly valued (see Landes and Posner 2003).

3.3 Patents as a Governance Mechanism

Viewing patents as a governance mechanism incorporates coordination aspects besides incentive aspects (and thereby has a focus related to the prospect theory). To some extent the governance perspective on patents and IPRs is more generally similar to a governance perspective on physical property rights (PPRs). However in a fundamental way, IPRs differ from PPRs, and the difference actually strengthens the justification of viewing IPRs in a governance perspective. The difference refers to the simple (but important) fact that, in contrast to an exchange of a physical object (resource, artifact) between two agents, an economically motivated exchange of proprietary information new to one of the agents (for example, through a market transaction), leaves both agents in possession of the information. As dispossession of human embodied information is impossible and information does not wear out through usage, a long-term need arises for coordinating or controlling the agents as to their use of the symmetrically possessed but asymmetrically owned information. This could be done (more or less imperfectly) through explicit or implicit contracting, for example, through a licence contract or an employment contract with a non-disclosure agreement. Thus, exploiting IPRs tends to create longer post-exchange contractual relations than for PPRs (for which exhaustion of the seller's rights occurs when selling a physical object – warranties, product liabilities and so on apart).

Different forms of licensing (in a broad sense) and other forms of contracting on markets for IPRs then become essential for the transfer and assembly of resources via markets in the economy. In the aftermath of the pro-IP era licensing has also grown considerably and one may even expect a 'pro-licensing era' to emerge (see Granstrand 2004). Other growing phenomena are the trading of small hi-tech projects and start-up firms, which are essentially IP-based; the organizing of large inter-firm technology collaborations which are employing various complex schemes for managing IPRs; employing some form of open source or creative commons licensing in development communities; clearing houses for IPRs and digital rights management schemes in creative industries and so on. These are all phenomena that not only illustrate how IPRs are managed in different settings but also how they are used to manage or govern the underlying productive operations. An example of the latter in an intra-firm setting is the use of IPRs and intellectual capital concepts to boost the asset value of a firm. Going one step further one could use a kind of distributed intellectual capital management to vitalize the entire organization of the firm to make it more efficient and innovative, just as total quality management has been used (see Granstrand 1999).

Not only patent rights but also patent information (disclosures) could provide a basis for governance. This will be dealt with next.

3.4 Role of Patent Information Disclosure for Governance

A strong motive historically for handing out patent-like privileges was to disclose and diffuse secrets, for example, held by skilled artisans and guilds.[15] The disclosure would thereby stimulate and coordinate the R&D of others, speed up differentiation and cumulation of results, speed up exploration of new, promising areas, help to avoid duplication, and provide for more efficient technology markets.[16]

The idea of disclosure as the inventor's payment (apart from fees) for patent rights has thus been central to the patent system from early on. Despite this apparently important role of patents, there is not much systematic evidence of its functioning and value. Recent studies have pointed to the value of patent information for companies in managing their R&D as well as for countries in disseminating new technologies, for example, in Japan (Ordover 1991, Granstrand 1999, Cohen *et al.* 2003).

A whole set of methods and services (some even patented) around patent information has also developed, spurring a whole industry of patent information analysts, especially in connection with the computerization of patent information and patent processing. The turnover of this industry is still small but growing. In addition a considerable amount of R&D and patent-related work in firms in general is devoted to technology intelligence (monitoring, scanning), using patent information.[17]

There is also a growing number of estimates showing that the amount of unused technologies and patents is considerable, together with a growing number of initiatives by patent offices, firms, licence brokers, universities and so on to increase the utilization ratio, for example, by start-ups, (tax-deductable) donations or licensing. Accurate, cheap and timely patent information is then of course crucial.

Moreover, the amount of R&D duplication is formidable. For example, the EU has estimated it to be US$20 billion per year just in Europe (Arora *et al.* 2001). Part of this is inherent in a competitive market economy but part is also due to reducible inefficiencies in technology markets and division of R&D labour. The governing function of patent disclosures has been comparatively weak in the past, before the current pro-patent era, and before the advent of new infocom technologies for processing patent information as described above. However, despite the growth of patent information and its cheap and fast dissemination, which will increasingly help coordinate complex and expensive R&D, there are nevertheless limitations. Positive research results signalling that something is found to work are more efficiently disseminated through patent information as well as through other publications than negative research results signalling that some approach does not work, which is a result that is not patentable and frequently not published.[18] Although such negative results are often disseminated in informal communications within professional communities (von Hippel 1988), this type of selective, *ad hoc* communication is probably not reducing duplication of negative R&D results very much. Neither would patents work in coordinating duplicative failures across firms in their collective trial-and-error R&D process. To achieve this, some special incentive system would be needed for publishing (disclosing) negative R&D results, being perhaps novel and non-obvious but lacking the inventive step.

4 IPRS IN INNOVATION SYSTEMS

4.1 The Innovation Systems Approach and its Rationales

Over the centuries technological innovations have become more systemic in two aspects – first their provision on average requires increasingly large scale, complex R&D, manufacturing and marketing operations and then their use and usefulness depend on an increasing number of other innovations, new as well as old, technological as well as non-technological (indicated for example, by the increasing number of standards). Using a systems approach then becomes natural, not only as in systems engineering but in the studies of innovation as a social phenomenon.

A new and important strand of economics literature in the 1990s also adopted an explicit systems approach to the studies of innovations.[19] As a result, a number of concepts of innovation-related systems were introduced, such as national, sectoral and regional innovation systems. However, although mentioned in the literature, there has been no focus so far specifically on corporate innovation systems. This is a gap in the literature on innovation systems, especially in the light of the indication that companies, and large ones in particular, control a major share of the world's technology (Patel and Pavitt 1995).[20] A focus on corporate innovation systems may also offer a new approach towards understanding the nature and evolution of large, technology-based corporations, which increasingly have to develop structures and processes to generate and exploit innovations of all kinds, not only technological innovations, but also managerial, financial and so on.

Universities and the military sector are two highly important sources of innovations as well. Pursuing the systems approach in innovation studies then leads to the identification of university innovation systems and military innovation systems.[21] In general, the IP regimes in these two innovation systems have shifted in the last decades for different sets of reasons, with increased attention paid to patenting and licensing, in addition to the traditional emphasis on secrecy and copyright in military and university innovation systems respectively.

A 'corporate innovation system' is then defined as 'the set of actors, activities, resources and institutions and the causal interrelations that are in some sense important for the innovative performance of a corporation or a group of collaborating companies, including universities and other organizations'.[22] Some comments are in order. Different types of components are specified (actors, activities, resources and institutions) to indicate important subsystems like the actor system within and around the corporation involved in innovation, including R&D labs, R&D cooperative partners and so on; the R&D, production, marketing and outsourcing systems, where R&D, production and so on are activities; and the resource structure, with the system of technologies (seen as intellectual resources) in particular and the institutional structure (or system or infrastructure). The system of technologies or, in other words, the technological system is then taken in the literal sense in line with Freeman *et al.* (1982), that is, as a set of interrelated bodies of technical knowledge, for example, a set of complementary or substituting product and process technologies. The technologies may be interrelated conceptually or causally, and in the latter case they are then interdependent. A technological system in this sense is then distinguished from a technical system, which is essentially a set of physical parts of products or artifacts, that is, a 'hard' system.

By corporation, is meant any company (firm, enterprise), not necessarily a large one. A corporate innovation system extends beyond the boundaries of a specific corporation and are moreover not necessarily sub-systems of national innovation systems or sectoral innovation systems, since there are multinational corporations as well as multi-product corporations active in many sectors. The significance of such corporations in innovation is part of the motivation for introducing the concept of corporate innovation system.

4.2 IPRs in National Innovation Systems

Codified IPRs have historically emerged in a national context for promoting innovations in the interests of the nation. Thus, the role of IPRs, and patents in particular, in national innovation systems has a long track record, which can only briefly be described here. Given the long existence of IPRs one can expect that they have played some kind of a functional role over the years. However, the only point of consensus regarding the role of the IPR system in economic history is that its role is intrinsically difficult to assess and that there is no persuasive evidence that the IPR system has ever played a major role.[23] At the same time there is widespread consensus today that technological innovativeness, the promotion of which is the direct purpose of the patent system, has probably been the major determinant behind economic progress.[24] Innovations have flourished in several periods and places in history without a patent system, for example, in ancient Greece and in medieval China. Also the most important factor during all periods, as persuasively emphasized by North (1981), is the military sector, which has a quite different incentive system for innovations than the commercial and cultural sectors. Moreover, some countries industrialized before they had a patent system (for example, Germany, Holland and Switzerland)[25] while most countries, including Japan, did so after they had installed a patent system, and then with greatly varying lags.

The size and growth of a domestic market most likely matters to technological innovativeness, and perhaps more so in the absence of patents. In connection with industrialization, North (1981, p. 165) has argued that 'In the absence of property rights over innovation, the pace of technological change was most fundamentally influenced by the size of the markets', because large and growing markets would increase the private return upon innovation, other things being equal. Large markets would also allow for specialization, in turn favouring creativity. Small, industrializing countries could then look for foreign markets. If these markets in turn had a patent system, the small countries would be more likely to have to adopt a patent system themselves sooner or later, which Holland and Switzerland eventually did.

There is some consensus that the patent system has played a positive role for the rate, if not the general direction, of technical progress, but only a role secondary and complementary to other developments, particularly other institutional developments, including a general property rights system (see North 1981). A patent system, awarding temporary monopolies, was initially designed and implemented in countries mainly for their importation of new technologies and technological catch-up in various sectors, for which it proved functional (David 1993). This was true for, among others, Italy, England, the USA, Japan and Switzerland.[26] From this alone, one cannot infer that a patent system would be functional for the catch-up of the less developed countries in the contemporary world, with an immensely more internationalized economic system having MNCs, FDIs, TRIPs and other international trade and agreement interdependencies and so on.[27] One could even argue that it would be unlikely or highly costly in the pro-IP era on the grounds that most instances of nations catching up have taken place in the absence of a strong international IP regime. Neither can one infer that a patent system initially designed for catch-up would be dysfunctional for sustaining a technological lead gained thereby. On the contrary, a patent system might even function better for the latter purpose in a world with increasingly globalizing companies and markets and a relative weakening of the nation state.[28] The advent of the pro-patent and pro-IP era fostered by the US and later supported by other developed countries as described above is a strong case in point. Several countries have also changed from a weak to a strong IP regime once they have reached a certain stage on the 'development ladder'.

4.3 IPRs in Sectoral Innovation Systems

Industrial sectors in market economies without monopolies do not have some form of centralized governance in the same way as nations and companies have (although industry associations in some countries are strong). This would have an impact on the governing role of IPRs in sectoral innovation systems, especially regarding seller diffusion of new technologies through licensing, cross-licensing and other forms of technological transfer and imitation, including patent information disclosure. The governing role of the IPR system for a given industry or sector moreover differs widely across different types of IPRs, just as the role of a given IPR type differs across industries.[29] Some industries rely heavily on certain IPR types as witnessed by references to them as copyright industries or design industries or witnessed by valuations of their IPR capital stock (for example, with very high trademark values). The large industry differences have moreover led to misfits between industries and the patent system in particular, which is fairly much the same across industries (and across most nations as well regarding patentability criteria). Thus, demands on industrial tailoring of patent rights have grown, although without much impact in sight.

The large differences in the role of patents, licences and trade secrets across sectors have been widely studied and documented (see for example Scherer 1980, Levin *et al.* 1987, Mansfield 1986, Granstrand 1999, Arora *et al.* 2001, Cohen *et al.* 2003). Less attention has been paid to the longitudinal role of IPRs for a sector, which will be briefly touched upon here.[30]

The role of a strong IP regime in emerging industries is unclear. There is some evidence that several leading edge industries based on ICT have developed after the Second World War under a fairly lax IP regime[31] (see Section 2.3). There seems moreover to be few cases where a strong IP regime has not only co-existed but clearly fostered the emergence of new leading edge industries and their rates of innovation.[32] One could expect to find such examples in areas with particularly low ratios of imitation to innovation costs and times in the absence of strong patent systems (as would be the case in chemistry). Such low ratios are likely in large-scale R&D areas with high costs of innovation (for example in aerospace or telecom). However, emerging industries often operate on smaller R&D scales. They also tend to have good growth prospects and their incentive structures then tend to be less sensitive to free-rider problems and waiting games. Moreover, if emerging industries operate on large R&D scales, other institutional means for incentivizing and coordination than a strong patent system have often been used, for example procurement or natural monopolies.

It is rather in later stages of industry evolution with subsequent innovations on a growing R&D scale (for example, in the form of new product generations) that a strong IP regime might be particularly conducive to further developments. At the same time barriers to entry can be built up by incumbents, especially against small firms. The use of various patent portfolio strategies by large firms (both incumbents and diversifying entrants) serves this purpose. This may in turn result in a changed division of R&D labour, where small R&D firms increasingly resort to licensing and acquisitions rather than aiming for stand-alone growth. The emergence and functioning of technology markets and markets for corporate control are in turn facilitated by strong IPRs, which therefore contribute to vertical specialization and other forms of intra-sectoral division of labour.

4.4 IPRs in Corporate Innovation Systems

Quite naturally companies are and have been embedded in various innovation systems and IP regimes pertaining to their relevant sectors and nations. As in-house R&D became institutionalized since the 19th century and the need for companies to constantly generate innovations – minor as well as major, product as well as process – became more pronounced, innovative activities became mainly internalized although with a fair amount of interaction across company boundaries with inventors, investors, institutes, users, competitors and so on.

The internal IP regime was, and still is, mainly oriented around trade secrets and also around trademarks, while patents (as well as copyrights and designs) have been of minor importance traditionally.[33] Company governance through management has simply not paid much attention to these latter IPRs as a rule. While private property rights in general have arguably been of decisive importance for well-functioning interaction between markets and companies, IPRs have not by and large. Even for trade secrets, their legal protection through property rights has had, and still has, a minor role compared to other means to protect them.

Internal company management moreover rather resembles a liability approach than a property approach and internal innovative activities resemble a kind of localized open source approach with layers of internal openness and external closure. A company also by design has a rapid feedback structure on several levels responding to performance signalling through external accounting as well as through managerial accounting. This has often created tension with the relatively slow and uncertain feedbacks involved in R&D and innovation, calling for institutions complementary to companies such as research universities and institutes and government procurement (for example by the military).

The rapid rise of the pro-patent era and the rapid recognition in industry of IP as being of economic and strategic importance has created a number of significant changes, however, in line with changes in general linked to the emergence of a new type of economy. IPRs are now increasingly used as a managerial or governance tool for influencing the pattern of trade, competition and cooperation in a larger context than just for protecting product and process innovations from price competition, as well as a tool for formation and exploitation of intellectual capital (IC). New types of (pure or hybrid) IC-based firms and markets also emerge. Large IPR portfolios are built up through various IPR strategies in order to create action space (in R&D, design, commercialization and so on), power in various forms of bargaining (for acquisition, financing, standard-setting, cooperation and so on) and market value (for IPOs, M&As, shareholders and so on). Strategic licensing and cross-licensing are used for standard-setting, sustaining technological leadership, oligopolistic clubbing, outsourcing, franchising and so on.[34] Licensing and servicing are also increasingly becoming a primary business compared to product sales and a 'pro-licensing era' might very well follow as a consequence of the pro-IP era as mentioned above. Licensing also offers a flexible contractual form for governing future transactions and customer relations, compared to spot transactions of tangibles with their exhaustion of rights.[35] This also applies to inter-organizational collaborations, although a great deal of managerial or organizational learning has to take place in this arena. Nevertheless there are various examples of how collaborating companies create different IP regimes as an important part of the governance structure.[36] The open source movement (OSM) is also a good example of a particular governance structure in and of a community of collaborators, an innovation system which is in fact very much IP-based and as such could be considered an organizational innovation (see for example McKelvey 2001).

All in all one can observe an increase in the use of a range of various other strategies for technology sourcing and technology exploitation than the traditional ones with in-house R&D and in-house production and marketing, corresponding to vertical integration. These other technology strategies correspond through their contractual nature to various degrees of organizational integration or market mediation. Thus one can argue that corporate innovation systems increasingly employ a quasi-integrated mode of governance, intermediate to governance through management and markets. The advent of the pro-IP era has contributed to this development in that the availability of enforceable and valuable IPRs has fostered the use of various technology market mechanisms.

4.5 IPRs in University Innovation Systems

The continuous 'roll-over' of human knowledge from older to younger generations constitutes a large investment for mankind.[37] This knowledge investment has traditionally been affected by IP considerations but only to a minor extent, mainly in the form of secrecy (in families, churches, guilds and so on), copyrights and branding (trademarks, names and so on). The generation of knowledge new to mankind in the form of scientific endeavours also constitutes a major investment, traditionally affected by IP considerations only to a minor extent, again in the form of secrecy, copyrights and branding. Universities of the Humboldt type,[38] integrating higher education, research and science, play a major role in these two endeavours. For various reasons universities now undergo major transformations into economic institutions, leaving some of their functions as cultural institutions in jeopardy. One could even venture to say that a major industrialization of universities is taking place. In the course of this process universities gradually behave more like knowledge-based corporations (as well as the latter becoming somewhat more university-like in their R&D and education). What is behind this institutional process of university-industry convergence and whether it is to the better or worse for society is an open question. However, scholars and policy makers worldwide are beginning to have a closer look at this process, its causes and consequences, and especially in the US, which has the leading and most competitive and market-oriented universities.[39]

In this transformation process university innovation systems are being built up or redesigned, especially involving science, engineering, business and medical faculties. These systems are provided with seed capital, venture development units, special facilities for financing and commercialization, science parks, incubators for start-ups, technology licensing and liaison offices, support units for services (accounting, legal and so on), innovation and entrepreneurial management training and so on.

In this context more active and industry-like IPR policies become adopted by university management, often with initial over-expectations of economic returns and underestimations of negative consequences. A major event fostering these developments in the US and later elsewhere in the world was the Bayh-Dole Act of 1980, enabling US universities to patent inventions from federally funded research. However, the Bayh-Dole Act was not a decisive or triggering event but rather reinforced developments already underway (see Nelson 2003). Nevertheless, the pro-IP era in industry has extended into university life. Not surprisingly this has led to clashes with the traditional IP regime in universities being oriented around science and eventually open scientific publications and licence-free use of results, while recognizing copyrights and the role of trademarks for reputation building. This is quite distinct from the IP regime in industry and its sectoral and corporate innovation systems, being more oriented around technology, secrecy, patents and other registered IPRs. Table 10.2 illustrates some of these differences.

The scientific society or community has, over the centuries, developed IP notions quite different from those in the industrial-technology community. Priority for new creations is important in both scientific publishing and patenting but is decidedly more vague in science on the basis of the 'first to publish' principle, rather than on the 'first to file' (a patent application that is) or the 'first to invent' principle as is the case with technical inventions. A publisher's decision to 'grant' a publication is based on some criteria of newness, non-obviousness and usefulness of the publication, similar to but not exactly the same as the criteria used in granting patent rights for an invention. The newness criteria and priority ground moreover foster secretive behaviour prior to publication and patenting in both regimes. Scientists then use each other's works, and in so doing, are expected to cite them as a basis for recognition and further career, funding and award possibilities (although a fair amount of 'publishing around' someone else's

Table 10.2 Comparison of IP regimes in universities and industry

Regime feature	University publishing	Industry patenting
Priority	First to publish (First to discover/write)	First to file (First to invent)
Criteria	Newness to the field Non-obviousness Scientific applicability	Newness to the world Non-obviousness Industrial applicability
Examination system	Publishers Journal editors and referees	Patent offices Patent examiners
Opposition system	Informal	Formal
Sanction system	Informal	Formal
Legal basis	Copyright matters codified in law, otherwise weak Professional norms	Codified in patent law
International coordination	Strong in some disciplines. No unifying framework or treaties	International treaties and cooperation
Licensing provision	General permission to use 'publication pool'	Usually subject to patent holders' discretion
Remuneration system	Citations Reputation Community prizes and job offers Research grants Promotion Non-contract-based	Royalty or lump sum payments or barter Product or licence sales Contract-based

work takes place in science just as inventing around takes place in technology, the latter being in fact encouraged by the patent system). Certainly citing fulfils other functions in academic work as well, but in this respect, citing is thus analogous to paying a royalty for using the results of someone else's work (compare Trajtenberg 1990). However, the 'payment' is made 'liquid' in quite a different manner. Peer recognition for contributions that are scientifically innovative is perhaps the biggest 'payment' to academics, albeit a non-monetary reward. The monetary rewards in science are partly oriented around prizes, grants and salaries. These forms of rewards are in fact alternatives to patent rights as means to promote scientific as well as technological progress.[40]

Thus, science may be called open but only in a specific sense and certainly open science is not synonymous with IP-free science. Moreover, the differences between universities and industry go beyond IP regimes. There is a complementary division of labour between universities and industry to which the IP regimes and other means for provision of innovations have adapted. For example, it can be argued that universities and industry provide differently adapted incentives for creative individuals and thereby utilize heterogeneous creative resources in the overall innovation system more efficiently. It can also be argued that publicly financed production of highly uncertain but generic knowledge (innovation) with transaction-free diffusion is more efficient than using patents, which would then generate high transaction costs. These complementarities would be reinforced by the cumulative nature of the knowledge produced and long lead times to its economic fruition, for which the short-term feedback structure of corporate innovation systems is ill-suited.

University patenting and the Bayh-Dole Act have also been subjected to considerable concern and research in recent years in the US. There is a fair amount of scepticism growing in the US about the overall economic benefits involved (not only benefits for leading universities) as clear evidence of them fails to show up, while negative side-effects do.[41]

4.6 IPRs in Military Innovation Systems

For a long time roughly half of the world's science and technology (S&T) and R&D activities have been defence-related with R&D activities performed in mostly national military-industrial complexes, led by superpowers in distinctive alliance structures. These military-industrial 'complexes', as they have usually been referred to, could be seen as embracing a military innovation system, in turn with similarities to a sectoral innovation system as dealt with by Malerba (2004), but with special strong links to a national innovation system. The 'appropriation' and control of military S&T has formed a special military IP regime based on secrecy and various types of controls and sanctions, quite separate from the civilian IPR systems (regardless of type of economic system – market or planned). The performance criteria and the feedbacks from performance to resource allocation and so on have also been quite different and generally much slower and more uncertain compared to civilian innovation systems. The system boundaries have also been more well defined. Military and civilian technology, R&D, industrial activities, IP regimes and other governance structures, as well as dedicated ICT systems, have been quite separate from each other (even within firms). For various reasons (the downfall of the

Soviet Union, multi-polarization of power, US hegemony, the growing importance of China, terrorism, rising capital intensity in conventional warfare, rising R&D costs, new technologies, waning geographic borders and distances and so on) this situation is now subjected to far-reaching changes and trends (without completely changing the nature of military affairs, of course).

What is increasing, and already visible in the USA, are: integration of military and civilian technologies (through dual use, lead/lag reversals, scientification and so on); outsourcing of defence R&D, production and services to firms (for example so-called PMCs – Private Military Corporations), nations and even cross-national alliances; internationalization and globalization of defence R&D, defence services and defence industries; limited military/police international 'ventures'; cross-national trade of military technology; R&D and production collaborations.

The likely implications of this is increasing R&D collaboration across nations, sectors, companies and civilian-military borders; industrial restructuring (divestments, joint ventures, M&As) and global concentration. Defence R&D as well as defence services (based on surveillance, command and control, robots, unmanned vehicles, electronic warfare, network defence and so on) will increasingly be ICT-based, but possibly with closer integration of military and civilian ICT systems. This is especially likely in the area of security and surveillance with its vast possibilities for using ICTs for development, production and exploitation of databases. (Note the military role in developing for example the Internet, GPS and Echelon[42]). Awareness and use of IPRs beyond trade secrets are also increasing and likely to continue to increase in military industry.

The implications of changes like these are of course many and important, for instance for a Europe lagging in civilian and military technology, but wanting to avoid technological over-dependence on the USA. A major objective is to foster integration of European defence-related R&D, industry and services and in that connection to consider integrating defence-related R&D in European framework programmes – some military, some hybrid military/civilian ones, some closed, some open to non-Europeans. Military R&D then becomes more integrated into the build-up of the European Research Area (ERA), a concept launched for a more integrated and cooperative R&D system in the EU in connection with the proclaimed objective of investing at least 3 per cent of GDP in R&D and innovation by 2010. (Compare the notion of a European innovation system.) Awareness and use of IPRs are then perceived as crucial, necessitating the nurturing of an IP culture and IPR investments in the traditional military industry.

5 SUMMARY AND CONCLUSIONS

This chapter has made a first attempt to look at the role of IPRs in different innovation systems and moreover to look at IPRs in a governance perspective. This provides a fairly new view of the effects of IPRs both upon incentives and coordination. Although IPRs and their associated licensing and sales provide opportunities to govern innovative activities in markets as well as in firms and in the increasingly important intermediate quasi-integrated forms of organized innovative activities, for example interfirm technology collaborations, the proliferation of IPRs also creates governance problems. This is particularly so after the rapid emergence of a pro-IP era embedded in the slow emergence of a new type of economy. This in and of itself calls for more attempts and research on IPRs with a governance lens.

In comparing innovation systems a number of differences and some similarities stand out. National, sectoral, corporate, university and military innovation systems are all vested systems with different and changing boundaries, but they also differ in a number of other ways, for example regarding performance criteria (ranging over welfare, equity, survival, growth, profits, knowledge and security); feedback structure (for example type, speed and uncertainty of performance signalling); hierarchical connectedness (ranging from centralized management hierarchies to decentralized markets); and dominant IP regimes (ranging over trade secrets, patents, trademarks and copyrights).

At the same time there is a certain convergence, for example between corporate and university innovation systems and between military and civilian sectoral innovation systems. The advent of the pro-IP era has not only strengthened the various IP regimes but also led to shifts between them with a certain degree of convergence on patents. Various types of IP-related contracts – licensing and collaborative agreements in particular – are also increasingly used. Changes like these could be interpreted as an emerging shift to an increasingly common use of IPRs for governance in and of the innovation systems. This magnifies the need for further research.

ACKNOWLEDGEMENTS

I gratefully acknowledge the financial support from Lars Erik Lundberg's Foundation for Research and Education. Valuable comments and suggestions by Birgitte Andersen are also gratefully acknowledged.

APPENDIX 10A: LIST OF KEY CONCEPTS

Key concepts in this chapter are used in the following way (with approximate synonyms within parentheses):[43]

Governance: An umbrella term for rule-based institutions incentivizing and coordinating economic and social activities, with management hierarchies and markets as two main polar types of institutions.
Innovation: Anything new and useful, where new is new to the world, that is, new to everyone and useful is useful to someone.
Innovation system: A system that involves innovations. These systems usually comprise actors, activities, artifacts, knowledge and institutions, usually with economic functions and performance criteria. They can be defined at various levels – national, regional, sectoral, corporate etc., and can be hierarchical or non-hierarchical (as in some nations and commonly at sector level). See further a special section in this chapter.
IP (intellectual property) denotes the underlying intangible (intellectual, immaterial) resource (or asset or capitalized entity) with which an IPR is associated. The distinction between IP and an IPR is often important.
IP regime: A type of IP-based governance, oriented around particular IPR types and their associated legislation and enforcement. Thus one talks about strong and weak IP regimes (referring to strength of legislation and enforcement) and patent versus trade secret regimes (referring to the particular dominant IPR type). The concept is somewhat vague or elastic but commonly used (perhaps due to its vagueness, since what is vague could not be clearly wrong).
IPRs, that is, intellectual property rights, include patents, copyright, designs, trademarks, trade secrets, databases, animal/plant breeding and some other rights in intangible creations.
R&D will include any creative or inventive research and development activity, not only confined to what is formally accounted for or organized as R&D.
System: A set of components, related (connected) to each other in some ways. Usually a system is functional in some sense with respect to some associated performance criteria. Moreover a system has boundaries across which it interacts with its environment through inputs and outputs; it has internal structures and processes, with feedbacks as an especially important type; it could be hierarchical or not and is decomposable into sub-systems. The components of systems could be almost anything – ideas, artifacts, humans, organizations.
Technology is a body of knowledge about techniques and is used here in the commonly restricted sense of natural science-related engineering techniques.

APPENDIX 10B: LIST OF ABBREVIATIONS

DARPA	Defense Advanced Research Projects Agency
EPO	European Patent Office
ERA	European Research Area
EU	European Union
FDI	Foreign direct investment
GATT	General agreement on tariffs and trade
GDP	Gross domestic product
GPS	Global positioning system
IC	Intellectual capital
ICT	Information and communication (Infocom) technology
IP	Intellectual property
IPO	Initial public offering
IPR	Intellectual property right
LDC	Less developed country
M&A	Merger and acquisition
MNC	Multinational corporation
MNU	Multinational university
OSM	Open source movement
PCT	Patent cooperation treaty
PMC	Private military corporation
PPR	Physical property right
R&D	Research and development
S&T	Science and technology
TRIPs	Trade-Related Intellectual Property Section (of GATT)
WIPO	World Intellectual Property Organization

NOTES

1. One may in fact argue that some fundamental IP notions are not part of a culture-specific institution but more deeply biologically rooted in features of human identity formation, information processing, incentive structure and propensity to trade common to all cultures (such as the protection possibility of individual secrets and the dispossession impossibility of an individual's know-how). See Granstrand (1999).
2. These symbols correspond to trademarks, but could also be seen as related to designs and copyrights since they involved visual expressions.
3. Thus, a patent privilege, in a way, functioned as a decentralized scheme to tax consumers for a period of time. Also in modern times a strong patent system is attractive to a government in an advanced country as a policy measure since it is easy to finance. The government does not have to pay subsidies and the patent offices and court system can be largely self-financed. There need not be any losses to the government through business tax money, either. On the contrary, tax revenues might increase due to monopolistic pricing.

4. These two privileges could overlap, but not necessarily. This parallels the contemporary fact that a patent right does not convey a right to trade a product based on the patent, for example, in pharmaceuticals where government approvals are needed.
5. The concept of intellectual capital has often been defined as a residual once tangible assets are defined, just as the notion of technology once was in the decomposition of inputs in a production function. However, several efforts have been made and are underway to give more precision to the concept, not least for accounting purposes.
6. Of course, it is difficult to infer very much from history by relating the absence or presence of an institution such as the patent system to a lower or higher rate of technical, industrial or economic progress in different periods and places. There is some consensus, however, that the patent system has played a positive role for the rate, if not the direction at large, of technical progress, but only a role secondary and complementary to other developments.
7. History in general has plenty of examples of how pockets of open S&T have been instrumental for progress, at least temporarily. These pockets or pools of open S&T may be open also to the general public by design (as with open standards or the current open source movement) or by default. Commonly, they are closed or semi-closed with some kind of entry commitment (for example, granting back of improvements or agreeing not to take certain actions).
8. The role of strong patents in other sectoral innovation systems is also not clear, not even in those sectors where patents have traditionally been most important, that is pharmaceuticals and chemicals (see for example, Scherer and Weisberg 1995). The new database protection directive in Europe has also not clearly spurred a European database industry, at least not yet (see Maurer *et al.* 2001).
9. North (2005) focuses on three main interacting factors in the process of economic change – demography, growth of knowledge and institutions. The emergence of intellectual capitalism then mainly appears to be spurred by growth of knowledge and to a lesser extent by the IPR institutions, with a possible minor influence by the World War II baby boom on the growth of knowledge.
10. Rationales or justifications of IPRs are categorized more generally in legal philosophy into deontological and consequentialist. The former category includes moral rights and rules that are largely exogenous to the economic and legal systems – they are 'natural rights'. The latter category includes economic rationales, which in turn are often classified as teleological (fulfilling proper ends of human life) and utilitarian (fulfilling consumer utilities). Utilitarian rationales for IPRs dominate contemporary society and are focused on here. See further Granstrand (1999) and Andersen (2004).
11. Although the notion about under-investment is old it was not formalized until the 1960s by Arrow (1962) as a truly seminal work. Arrow discussed generic reasons behind under-investment and alternative remedies, including patents. Later works have shown that over-investment may occur also, even without patents.
12. This so-called prospect theory was introduced by Kitch (1977) building partly on Barzel (1968) and earlier works by Scherer and has been highly cited but also subjected to severe critique.
13. Just to mention one comparable alternative, consider the popular use of R&D tax credits or tax deductions for stimulating innovation, based on the idea of subsidizing R&D inputs through targeted cuts in general taxes. This tax arrangement has significant limitations and hardly qualifies as a minimally distorting tax arrangement (see Mansfield 1982). It could be modified of course, for example, to cover commercial activities as well, not just R&D, but it will still be inherently limited (see Granstrand 1998).
14. Compare the discussion of the property approach and the liability approach in Calabresi and Melamed (1972).
15. Note that the dual functions of patents as incentives and disclosures do not need to be integrated, that is, a patent system could in principle be designed to offer incentives without requiring disclosure and disclosure could be achieved in other ways.
16. There is also a growing dilemma when R&D information protected by patents becomes used by others in their R&D in a way being considered as infringement.

17. Regular conferences and exhibitions are held (for example, arranged by patent offices such as the Epidos conferences) around a flurry of databases and tools being developed. With more intelligent agents, AI tools for full-text analysis and joint analysis of patent and other publications, this industry could be expected to grow in commercial conditions, thereby probably reinforcing technical information asymmetries between firms and nations.
18. The demonstration effect of showing that something works (rather than how it may work) may have a strong impact on contenders (as shown by the detonation of the A-bomb). Patent applicants are required to reveal how an invention supposedly works through so-called enabling disclosure but evidence that it works properly is not always necessary.
19. If one can speak of some kind of a breakthrough for the systems approach in innovation studies occurring in the 1990s, it might be due to the surge of studies of innovations in general, the quest for meso-level concepts (like industrial clusters, development blocks, regional complexes), the general appeal of the systems approach as used in engineering and the adoption of the systems approach by key opinion leaders in economics and policy analysis.
20. Some large corporations moreover have R&D budgets comparable in size with total industrial R&D in some small countries.
21. As there are many diverse sources and contexts of innovations, several types of innovation systems could be identified. One could then ask what the systems approach could contribute to innovation studies beyond merely adding the empirically ambiguous term 'system' to the term 'innovation'. Available space here just allows us to refer to the standard virtues of the systems approach such as providing a generic language with a number of key concepts (system boundaries, structure, processes and performance, input/output relations, feedback, sub-systems and so on), providing a systematic method of analysis and a dynamic perspective with feedback analysis as a key element, and providing (mostly) some kind of governance or control function for a purpose. These are all virtues which are difficult to illustrate in the brief expositions presented here.
22. This definition is syntactically and semantically aligned to the common definitions of national and sectoral innovation systems as surveyed in Edqvist (1997). See further Granstrand (2000).
23. It may be argued that the collection of IPRs, as we know it, is not, and never has been, legally connected enough to be called a 'system' and to be studied as an entity with causal relations.
24. Note that a patent is granted to a technical invention primarily on the merits of its technical features, not on its economic merits (apart from a general and weak requirement of industrial applicability or usefulness of the invention), although the underlying assumption is that by so doing, economic progress will be stimulated.
25. Schiff (1971), studying Holland and Switzerland, found no evidence that industrialization in these countries was hampered by the absence of a patent system.
26. Japan is a particularly interesting case which shows how the IPR system (patents in particular) could be designed and used together with various licensing schemes and technology policies to foster not only catching up but also forging ahead (see for example Granstrand 1999).
27. Mansfield (1994, 1995) and Lee and Mansfield (1996) have shown that strong patent protection is functional for attracting FDI. However, FDI is not necessarily functional for catch-up. Scherer and Weisberg (1995) are also sceptical about whether a switch from weak to strong patent protection alone can induce a catch-up, based on a study of the adoption of patent protection for pharmaceuticals in Italy in 1978.
28. The patent system is likened to a panda's thumb by David (1993) in describing its evolution into something quasi-functional from strange origins.
29. Industries differ widely and so do their associated innovation systems. For an excellent recent treatise on sectoral innovation systems in general, see Malerba (2004). For instance, sectoral innovation systems differ regarding the dynamics behind the changes in system boundaries (for example through technological convergence), feedback structure between R&D, innovation, growth and structural change, appropriation mechanisms, industry

life cycle characteristics and the nature of their technology base. Differences like these naturally reflect in differences in corporate innovation systems.

30. For a good example of a longitudinal study of patenting behaviour in an industry, see Hall and Ziedonis (2001).
31. There are in addition many examples historically of how lax IP regimes (regarding patents in particular) have fostered the emergence of industries in countries trying to catch up with leading edge countries.
32. The standard examples being within pharmaceuticals, chemicals and biotech. Other examples may be found in copyright and design industries. A counter-example might be the database industry where the (fairly) new database protection directive in Europe has not yet clearly spurred a European database industry (see Maurer *et al.* 2001). New *sui generis* IPRs and IPRs tailored for a specific industry or sector offer interesting natural experiments in this respect, of course.
33. There are many accounts in business history indicating the importance of IPRs for the economic progress of companies in various places and periods or stages of their development. Still, there are as many examples of companies that have succeeded without any significant IPRs as there are companies with strong patents that have failed. There are also examples of companies, mostly small, that have been forced out of business because of the IPR and litigation power of large competitors. The importance varies with country, period, industry, company and type of IPR. The overall, long-run impact of the IPR system upon a stream of company formations and developments cannot be assessed across industries in our present stage of knowledge. There has also been a patenting paradox in the sense that firms take out patents even if they see them as fairly unimportant (Mansfield 1986). Nevertheless some studies have established that patents do play a role as intended for R&D investments (Taylor and Silbertson 1973 and Granstrand 1999). The role of trademarks and trade secrets is conspicuous, however, even decisive for the formation and growth of a firm (see Wilkins 1992 for trademarks).
34. A classic case is the 'systems battle' between JVC and its VHS system and Sony and its Betamax system, in which JVC pioneered in using an IP licensing scheme to build a corporate innovation system around VHS with collaborating competitors, thus outcompeting Sony and its Betamax system.
35. Note the range of types of licensing contracts (exclusive, sole, simple, sub, cross, block, grant-back, compulsory and so on). Moreover, patent licensing could be performed on-line, leading to what could be dubbed 'e-licensing', which in turn could be linked to 'e-research'.
36. For examples see for example, Gawer and Cusumano (2002) and Granstrand and Lindmark (2002). Companies could and do use licensing also for some form of intra-firm governance (for example, of foreign subsidiaries) as well but historically this has mainly been for profit transfer purposes. (For an example, see Granstrand and Fernlund 1978). Needless to say efficient internal transfer pricing is difficult to achieve for intangibles.
37. The investment aspect is a narrow economic one. The roll-over also involves consumption. Moreover, economic aspects are far from the only relevant ones. In fact, the roll-over could be seen as a defining characteristic of culture, as described in North (2005), thereby implying that universities are cultural institutions.
38. A university that integrates research and education, that is, a 'research university', is often generically labelled after the reformer of the Prussian education system in the early 19th century, Wilhelm von Humboldt.
39. See for example, Rosenberg and Nelson (1994), Rosenberg (2000), Rosenberg (2003), Nelson (2003) and Mowery and Sampat (2004).
40. Much can be said and debated about the differences and relations between science and technology. See especially the works by D. de Solla Price and N. Rosenberg, two leading scholars on this topic, for example, de Solla Price (1973) and Rosenberg (1982). For a discussion of the traditional IP regime in science, see for example, Nelkin (1984), Merton (1988) and Long (1991) and Stephan (1996), Eisenberg (1987), Rosenberg (2003), Mowery and Sampat (2004) and David (2004) for how it may clash with the IP regime in technology and industry. The distinction between science and technology and the division

of intellectual labour between universities and companies is also becoming less clear as companies do more basic research and universities take out more patents.
41. For further reading, see Nelson (2003), Rosenberg (2003) and Fagerberg *et al.* (2004).
42. GPS is a (technical) system for determining the geographical positions of radio transmitters based on satellite communications. Echelon is an alleged US system for global surveillance of radio communications (not confirmed by US authorities for a long time).
43. More concise definitions could be given, but emphasis here is on brief and sufficiently clear descriptions.

BIBLIOGRAPHY

Andersen, B. (2004), 'If "intellectual property rights" is the answer, what is the question?', *Economics of Innovation and New Technology*, **13**(5), pp. 417–42.

Arora, A., Fosfuri, A. and Gambardella, A. (2001), *Markets for Technology: The Economics of Innovation and Corporate Strategy*, Cambridge, Mass: The MIT Press.

Arrow, K.J. (1962), 'Economic welfare and the allocation of resources for invention', in *The Rate and Direction of Inventive Activity: Economic and Social Factors*, Princeton NJ: National Bureau of Economic Research, pp. 609–25.

Barzel, Y. (1968), 'Optimal timing of innovations', *Review of Economics and Statistics*, Aug. pp. 348–55.

Calabresi, G. and Melamed, A.D. (1972), 'Property rules, liability rules, and inalienability: one view of the cathedral', *Harvard Law Review*, April, **85**(6), pp. 1089–128.

Cohen, W.M., Goto, A., Nagata, A., Nelson, R.R. and Walsh, J.P. (2003), 'R&D spillovers, patents and the incentives to innovate in Japan and the United States', in Granstrand O. (ed.) *Economics, Law and Intellectual Property*, Dordrecht: Kluwer Academic Publishers, chapter 6, pp. 123–54.

Coriat, B. and Orsi, F. (2002), 'Establishing a new intellectual property rights regime in the United States: origins, content and problems', *Research Policy*, **31**, pp. 1491–507.

David, P.A. (1993), 'Intellectual property institutions and the panda's thumb: patents, copyrights, and trade secrets in economic theory and history', in Wallerstein, M.B., Mogee, M.E. and Schoen, R.A. (eds) *Global Dimensions of Intellectual Property Rights in Science and Technology*, Washington DC: National Academy Press, chapter 2. pp. 19–61.

David, P.A. (2004), 'Can 'Open Science' be protected from the evolving regime of IPR protections?', *Journal of Institutional and Theoretical Economics*, **160**(1), pp. 9–34.

de Solla Price, D. (1973), 'The relations between science and technology and their implications for policy formation', in Simons, E.M. and Strasser, G. (eds): *Science and Technology Politics*. Cambridge, MA: Ballinger.

Edqvist, C. (ed.) (1997), *Systems of Innovation: Technologies, Institutions and Organizations*, London: Pinter.

Eisenberg, R.S. (1987), 'Proprietary rights and the norms of science in biotechnology research', *Yale Law Journal*, **97**(2), pp. 177–231.

Fagerberg, J., Mowery, D. and Nelson, R. (eds) (2004), *Oxford Handbook of Innovation*, Oxford: Oxford University Press.

Folk, G.E. (1942), *Patents and Industrial Progress. A Summary, Analysis and Evaluation of the Record on Patents of the Temporary National Economic Committee*, New York, NY: Harper & Brothers.
Freeman, C., Clark, J. and Soete, L. (1982), *Unemployment and Technical Innovation*, London: Pinter.
Gawer, A. and Cusumano, M. (2002), *Platform Leadership: How Intel, Microsoft and Cisco Drive Innovation in Industry*, Boston, MA: Harvard Business School Press.
Granstrand, O. (1982), *Technology, Management and Markets: An Investigation of R&D and Innovation in Industrial Organizations*, London: Pinter.
Granstrand, O. (1998), 'Towards a Theory of the Technology-Based Firm', *Research Policy*, **27**(6), pp. 465–89.
Granstrand, O. (1999), *The Economics and Management of Intellectual Property*, Cheltenham, UK and Northampton, MA, USA: Edward Elgar.
Granstrand, O. (2000), *Corporate Innovation Systems: Final Report Submitted to the EU Dynacom Project*, (CIM Report 2000:01). Department of Industrial Management and Economics, Chalmers University of Technology.
Granstrand, O. (ed.) (2003), *Economics, Law and Intellectual Property*, Dordrecht: Kluwer Academic Publishers.
Granstrand, O. (2004), 'Innovation and intellectual property rights', in Fagerberg, J., Mowery, D. and Nelson, R. (eds), *Oxford Handbook of Innovation*, Oxford: Oxford University Press. pp. 266–90.
Granstrand, O and Fernlund, I. (1978), 'Coordination of Multinational R&D', *R&D Management*, **9**(1), pp. 1–7.
Granstrand, O and Lindmark, S. (2002), *Technology Collaborations in Corporate Innovation Systems: Final Report Submitted to Vinnova*, December, 2002, (CIM Report 2002:01), Department of Industrial Management and Economics, Chalmers University of Technology.
Gutterman, A. (1997), *Innovation and Competition Policy*, London: Kluwer Law International.
Hall, B.H. and Ziedonis, R.H. (2001), 'The determinants of patenting in the U.S. semiconductor industry, 1980–1994', *Rand Journal of Economics*, **32**, pp. 101–28.
Hart, D.M. (ed.) (2003), *The Emergence of Entrepreneurship Policy: Governance, Start-ups and Growth in the U.S. Knowledge Economy*, Cambridge: Cambridge University Press.
Harvey, C. and Jones, G. (eds) (1992), *Organizational Capability and Competitive Advantage*, London: Frank Cass & Co. Ltd.
Jaffe, A.B. (2000), 'The U.S. patent system in transition: policy innovation and the innovation process', *Research Policy*, **29**, pp. 531–57.
Kaufer, E. (1989), *The Economics of the Patent System*, New York, NY: Harwood Academic Publishers.
Kitch, E. (1977), 'The nature and function of the patent system', *Journal of Law and Economics*, **30**(1), pp. 265–90.
Landes, W.M. and Posner, R.A. (2003), *The Economic Structure of Intellectual Property Law*, Cambridge, MA: Belknap Press.
Lee, J.-Y. and Mansfield, E. (1996), 'Intellectual property protection and U.S. foreign direct investment', *Review of Economics and Statistics*, **78**(2), pp. 181–6.
Levin, R.C., Klevorick, A.K., Nelson, R.R. and Winter, S.G. (1987), 'Appropriating the returns from industrial research and development', *Brookings Papers on Economic Activity*, **3**, pp. 783–831.

Long, P. (1991), 'The openness of knowledge: an ideal and its context in 16th century writings on mining and metallurgy', *Technology and Culture*, **32**, pp. 318–55.
Machlup, F. (1958), *An Economic Review of the Patent System*. Study no 15 of the Subcommittee on Patents, Trademarks, and Copyrights of the Committee on the Judiciary, US Senate: Washington, DC: US Government Printing Office.
Machlup, F. and Penrose, E. (1950), 'The patent controversy in the nineteenth century', *Journal of Economic History*, **10**(1), pp. 1–29.
Malerba, F. (ed.) (2004), *Sectoral Systems of Innovation: Concepts, Issues and Analyses of Six Major Sectors in Europe*, Cambridge: Cambridge University Press.
Mansfield, E. (1982), 'Tax policy and innovation', *Science*, **215**(12), pp. 1365–71.
Mansfield, E. (1986), 'Patents and innovation: an empirical study', *Management Science*, **32**(2), pp. 173–81.
Mansfield, E. (1994), *Intellectual Property Protection, Foreign Direct Investment, and Technology Transfer*. Discussion Paper 19. Washington, DC: International Finance Corporation (IFC).
Mansfield, E. (1995), *Intellectual Property Protection, Direct Investment, and Technology Transfer: Germany, Japan, and the United States*. Discussion Paper 27. Washington DC: International Finance Corporation (IFC).
Maurer, S.M., Hugenholt, P.B. and Onsrud, H.J. (2001), 'Intellectual property: Europe's database experiment', *Science*, **294**(5543), pp. 789–90.
Mazzoleni, R. and Nelson, R.R. (1998), 'The benefits and costs of strong patent protection: a contribution to the current debate', *Research Policy*, **27**(3), pp. 273–84.
McKelvey, M. (2001), 'The economic dynamics of software: three competing business models exemplified though Microsoft, Netscape and Linux', *Economics of Innovation and New Technology*, **11**, pp. 127–64.
Merton, R.K. (1988), 'The Matthew effect in science, II: cumulative advantage and the symbolism of intellectual property', *ISIS*, **79**, pp. 606–23.
Mowery, D. (ed.) (1996), *The International Computer Software Industry: A Comparative Study of Industry Evolution and Structure*, Oxford: Oxford University Press.
Mowery, D. and Sampat, B.N. (2004), 'Universities in national innovation systems', in Fagerberg, J., Mowery, D. and Nelson, R. (eds), *Oxford Handbook of Innovation*, Oxford: Oxford University Press.
Narin, F. and Noma, E. (1985), 'Is technology becoming science?' *Scientometrics*, **7**(3–6), pp. 369–81.
Nelkin, D. (1984), *Science as Intellectual Property: Who Controls Research?* New York, NY: Macmillan.
Nelson, R. (2003), 'Is university patenting necessary or sufficient to make university research valuable economically?' Chapter 15 in Granstrand O. (ed.) *Economics, Law and Intellectual Property*. Dordrecht: Kluwer Academic Publishers, pp. 347–61.
North, D.C. (1981), *Structure and Change in Economic History*. New York, NY: W.W. Norton & Company.
North, D.C. (2005), *Understanding the Process of Economic Change*. Princeton: Princeton University Press.
Ordover, J.A. (1991), 'A patent system for both diffusion and exclusion', *Journal of Economic Perspectives*, **5**(1), pp. 43–60.

Patel, P. and Pavitt, K. (1995), *Technological Competencies in the World's Largest Firms: Characteristics, Constraints and Scope for Managerial Choice*, Working Paper 95–66. Laxenburg, Austria: International Institute for Applied Systems Analysis.
Rosenberg, N. (1982), *Inside the Black Box: Technology and Economics*, Cambridge: Cambridge University Press.
Rosenberg, N. (2000), 'American universities as endogenous institutions', in Rosenberg, N., *Schumpeter and the Endogeneity of Technology*, London: Routledge, chapter 3, pp. 36–57.
Rosenberg, N. (2003), 'America's entrepreneurial universities', in Hart (2003), chapter 6, pp. 113–37.
Rosenberg, N. and Nelson, R.R. (1994), 'American Universities and Technical Advance in Industry', *Research Policy*, **23**, pp. 328–38.
Samuelson, P. (1993), 'A case study on computer programs', in Wallerstein, M.B., Mogee, M.E. and Schoen, R.A. (eds) *Global Dimensions of Intellectual Property Rights in Science and Technology*. Washington DC: National Academy Press, chapter 12, pp. 284–318.
Scherer, F.M. (1980), *Industrial Market Structure and Economic Performance*. Chicago, IL: Rand McNally.
Scherer, F.M. and Weisberg, S. (1995), 'Economic effects of strengthening pharmaceutical patent protection in Italy', *International Review of Industrial Property and Copyright Law* (IIC), **26**(6), pp. 1009–24.
Schiff, E. (1971), *Industrialization without Patents*, Princeton, NJ: Princeton University Press.
Simons, E.M. and Strasser, G. (eds) (1973), *Science and Technology Politics*. Cambridge, MA: Ballinger.
Stephan, P.E. (1996), 'The economics of science', *Journal of Economic Literature*, **34**, September, pp. 1199–235.
Taylor, C.T. and Silberston, Z.A. (1973), *The Economic Impact of the Patent System: A Study of the British Experience*, Cambridge: Cambridge University Press.
Trajtenberg, M. (1990), 'A penny for your quotes: patent citations and the value of innovations', *RAND Journal of Economics*, **21**(1), pp. 172–87.
von Hippel, E. (1988), *The Sources of Innovation*, New York, NY: Oxford University Press.
Wilkins, M. (1992), 'The Neglected Intangible Asset: The Influence of the Trade Mark on the Rise of the Modern Corporation', in Harvey, C. and Jones, G. (eds), *Organizational Capability and Competitive Advantage*, London: Frank Cass & Co. Ltd., pp. 66–95.

Index

Abel, R. 57
'abusus' rights 250, 264, 265, 268
Accelerating Access Initiative (AAI) 86, 90–91
Adams, J.D. 208
aeronautical engineering 34, 38
Africa Group of the TRIPS Council 76
Agrawal, A. 25
agricultural technology 38, 40
AIDS/HIV 4–5, 70–105
  generic producers and supply-side competition in reduced-cost ARVs 98–9
  scale of pandemic in Sub-Saharan Africa 84–6
  supply of anti-retroviral drugs in Sub-Saharan Africa 84–98
Air Pirates comic books 58
Albright, B. 217
ambiguity
  of measurements 260–61
  of patent claims 229, 235
Andersen, B. 112, 114, 117, 129, 132
antibodies 33–4, 35, 41
anti-competition costs 122–3
antigen 33–4
anti-patent movement 315
anti-retroviral drugs (ARVs) 71, 74–5, 84–101
  key role of generic producers and supply-side competition in reduced-cost ARVs 98–9
  supply in Sub-Saharan Africa 84–98
    AAI 86, 90–91
    ARVS patented in OAPI zone 97–8
    current situation and future prospects 94–8
    Indian generic supply 86–7, 91–3, 98, 100
    supply of patented drugs 87–90, 92, 93
AOL 50
applied sciences 23–4
appropriability
  problem of 118–20
  reasons to not patent 154, 156, 166–7, 168
arbitrary technological trajectories 122
Arora, A. 32–3, 323
Arrow, K.J. 72, 118–19, 120, 127, 128, 134, 182–3, 184, 185
Arthur, B. 126, 129
Arundel, A. 120, 150–51, 192
Ashdown v. Telegraph Group 64
assignability of copyright interest 48, 60–61
Atkinson, R. 40
Atomic Energy Commission (UK) 27
Attaran, A. 98
Audretsch, D.B. 151
Aurobindo 93
Australia 63
  contemporary music industry 50–51, 55–6
authorization management 264, 265, 268
authors' rights management societies 260
awareness of IPR 197, 199, 204, 206

backward citations 231, 232
Bacon, F. 26
Balconi, M. 284
Bangui Agreement 4, 78–84
  Revised 78, 82–4, 100
Bansee, L. 91
bar coding patents 217, 220
Bar-Shalom, A. 33–4, 41

bargaining 121
complexity of bargain agreements 135–6
Barzel, Y. 248
'basicness' of inventions/technology 233, 235–6
Bayh-Dole Act 1980 (US) 2–3, 110, 332
reforming 40–42
universities and patenting 29, 37, 39, 121, 137, 330
Bell Laboratories 23, 316
Bentham, J. 113, 117, 131
Bently, L. 60, 62
Bernal, J.D. 26, 27
Berne Convention for the Protection of Literacy and Artistic Works 61, 244
Bertin, G.Y. 152, 153, 154, 159
Bessen, J. 269
Bessy, C. 251, 259, 267, 269
Bettig, R. 49–50, 51
bibliographic coupling 282–3
bio-piracy 132
biotechnology 39
small high-tech firms and patenting 150, 157–70, 170–71, 172
Blakeney, M. 47, 61
blanket licences 273
blocking patents 122–3, 128–9
small high-tech firms 152, 159, 162, 163
BMG 50
Bok, D. 37, 40
Bonacich, P. 295
Brazil 74, 86, 87, 90
Breschi, S. 183, 284
Bristol-Myers 88, 89
brokers of new technology 296–301, 302
Brousseau, E. 246, 247, 249, 251, 256, 267, 269
Burchfiel, K. 227
Burkina Faso 88, 91
Burundi 88
Bush, V. 18, 26–7, 28
business services 191
Business Software Alliance 260

Campbell, D. 24
Campbell v. Acuff-Rose Music, Inc. 62
capital, attracting from external investors 153–4, 161–2, 163
capitalism 17, 21–2
intellectual capitalism 315–17
Capling, A. 50, 55, 55–6
catch-up 326
CBS 50
CBS/Fox 51
cell biology 20
Centre for Research on Innovation and Internationalization (CESPRI) 291
Chateauraynaud, F. 259
Chayes, A. 55
chemical engineering 23, 38
chemical patents 231, 234
Cheung, S. 116, 130
China 325
Christensen, J.L. 136, 181, 186
CIC Video 51
Cipla 93, 94, 100
citation networks 279
networks of organizations 282, 286–7, 288, 291
networks of patents 281–2
semiconductor and computer industries 293–301
citations of published works 330–31
civil engineering 23
Clark, J.B. 117
clearing house, international 64, 322
co-authorship 282, 283–4, 285
co-citation networks 279
networks of organizations 282, 287–91
networks of patents 282, 283
semiconductor and computer industries 292, 293–301
codified knowledge 184, 187, 199
Cohen, W. 25, 32–3, 38, 116, 120, 129, 155, 162, 185, 225
Cohen-Boyer gene-splitting process 39
collective governance *see* private institutions
Columbia Pictures Entertainment 50
Columbia Tri-Star Home Video 51
Colyvas, J. 39
Comanor, W.S. 226, 227
combustion engines 224–5
Comcast Inc. 50, 65

commodification of creativity 46–9
  limiting 60–61
'common procedure' 82, 100
commons
  global 2–5
  loss of and copyright 57–9
  scientific 2–3, 17–45
    protecting 32–42
communication 182–3
communitarianism 30
comparative institutional analysis 243–77
competence building 205–8
competition 22
  innovation-enhanced 127–30, 141
  publicly supported research and private research 31
  supply-side 98–9
competition law 64
complex industries 150
compulsory licensing 75–6, 77, 124, 128–9, 255
  Bangui Agreement 81
    Revised Agreement 83–4
Computer and Communication Industry Association (CCIA) 7
computer industry 291–301, 302, 303–5
computer science 24, 34
concentration 49–51
Conference on Patent Policy Making 7
contextual patent strategies 171–2
continuation patents 8–9, 12, 215–39
  descriptive statistics within sectors 224–30
  determinants of continuation application practice 230–34
  practice under US patent law 219–23
    changes in patent law 221–2
    patentees' use of procedure 222–3
contracts and contracting 12, 248, 321
control of actual uses of authorized uses 264, 265, 268
Cook-Deegan, R. 33–4, 41
Coombe, R. 58–9
Cooper, C. 267
cooperation, legal basis for 152–3, 160, 163
coordinating institutions 9–11
coordination 321–2
coordination devices 247–8
co-patenting 282, 286
Copyleft 52
copyright 3–4, 46–69
  acquisition of private power 49–55
  commodification of creativity 46–9
    limiting 60–61
  compared with patents 260–61, 268–9
  counterbalancing rights 61–2
  current debates 14
  and development 59–60
  fair use/fair dealing rights 53, 59, 62–3
  holistic thinking 64
  public and private institutions 9, 243–77
  public interest right 63–4
  significance of private power 55–60
  traditional cultural expressions 132
Coriat, B. 74, 120
Corley, Eric 52–3
corporate dominance 3–4, 46–69
  acquisition of private power 49–55
  significance of private power 55–60
corporate innovation systems 324–5, 327–9
corporate law 64
corporate strategies 128–30
costs
  administration 122
  costs of applying and maintaining patent too high 155, 164
  enforcement 122, 154, 155–6
  governance and maladaptation 247–8
  information costs 256–7
  monopoly costs 122–3
  transaction costs *see* transaction costs
counterbalancing rights 61–2
courts in charge of patent infringements 266–7
creativity
  commodification of 46–9, 60–61
  economic rationale of organizing 133–9, 141
  incentives to be creative 117–24
Crixivan 88, 89
cross-licensing 123

crowding, technological 279, 293, 294–301
Crown Cork & Seal Co. v. Gutmann Co. 220
culture 2, 3–4
filtering and homogenization 55–7
fundamental approach 59–60
symbols and dialogue 58–9
traditional cultural expressions 132

Danish Patent and Trademark Office (DKPTO) 7–8, 179–214
in Danish innovation system 190–92
functions 190–92
general effects on knowledge transfer and competence building 205–8
knowledge diffusion from patenting process 192–205
importance of domestic location 201–4
potential effects of knowledge flows from DKPTO 196–201
David, P. 125–6, 127, 129, 135, 326
Davis, L. 115
decentralization 318–21
DeCSS (Decrypted Content Scrambling System) source code 52–3
Defense Advanced Research Projects Agency (DARPA) 316
delay 219–20
Demaine, L. 35
Denmark 172–3
small high-tech firms and patenting 151, 157–70
Department of Defense (US) 27
design of IPR system 11–12, 142
detection of infringements 7, 154, 156, 165, 168, 264, 265, 268
developing countries 4–5, 70–105
development
copyright and 59–60
level of and access to drugs before TRIPS 74
patent system and catch-up 326
development rights 10, 130
diffusion 136, 253, 280–81
diverse policies 259, 262–3
from patenting process 192–205
digital rights management (DRM) systems 256–7, 322
direct citation links 281–2
disclosure
incentives to disclose 133–8, 317, 319
problem 119
role of patent information disclosure for governance 322–3
discrete industries 150
disinterestedness 30
Disney Corporation 50, 51, 58, 65
distributed innovation processes 114–15
distributed intellectual capital management 322
distribution rights 48, 49–55, 60–61
diversion of activity 122
Doha Declaration (2001) 76–8, 100–101
dot.com bubble 121
Dreyfuss, R. 36, 42
Droit d'Auteur 244, 245, 252, 270, 271
drugs *see* pharmaceuticals/drugs
Dumoulin, J. 87, 88
duration
copyright protection 48, 59, 60–61
patents 81–2, 83
DVDs 52–3
dynamic efficiency argument 125

economic hold-up 217
economies of scale 254
economies of scope 254
efficiency 125–7
Eisenberg, R. 29, 31, 32, 41
Eldred v. Ashcroft 61, 63
electrical engineering 24, 38
electrical patents 231, 234
electronic self-publishing 57, 67
emerging industries 316–17, 327
EMI 50
enforcement
problems and patenting 154, 155–6, 165–6, 168
public and private institutions 246–7, 248–50, 268, 269
incomplete IPRs 251, 252
prohibition of use 263
public vs private governance trade-off 264, 265
see also infringements

enforcement costs 122, 154, 155–6
engineering 23–4, 38
entrepreneurial talent, market protection of 130–33
entropy index 293–4
Epivir 88, 89
European Patent Convention (EPC) 180
European Patent Office (EPO) 180, 189, 203–4, 206–8, 291
European Research Area (ERA) 333
European Union (formerly European Community) (EU) 61, 110
  EU companies and knowledge networks 297, 298, 299, 302
  harmonized patent system 189–90, 206–8
  military innovation system 333
evolution of IPR system 313–17
evolutionary processes 21–5
ex officio licences 81, 83–4
exclusion 263, 264, 265, 268
expertise 267
externalities 28

fair use/fair dealing rights 53, 59, 62–3
Fares, M. 247
fees *see* licensing; revenue collection; royalties
Feldman, M.P. 184–5, 191
Fellmeth, A. 35
Festival 50
filing date 221
Film Council (UK) Digital Screen Network 56–7
film sharing software 53–4
films and filmed entertainment 51–2, 52–4
  cultural filtering 56–7
  performers' rights 61–2
filtering, cultural 55–7
firm
  age 194–5, 201
  size 194, 203, 204
first-line treatments 94, 97
fixed-dose bitherapies 94, 96
fixed-dose tritherapies 92, 94, 96, 99
followers, technological 297, 298–301, 302
Foray, D. 186, 244
Ford Motor Company v. Jerome Lemelson 215–16
formal rules 247
forward citations 231, 232
Foundation for a Free Information Infrastructure (FFII) 7
Fourth Estate 57
FoxVideo 51
France 245, 252
  IPR system compared with US's 266–70
  SACEM 257, 258, 261, 266, 272–3, 274
free speech 53
free trade 131–2
Freeman, C. 324
French Union 79
'fructus' rights 250, 264, 265, 268

Gaines, J. 59, 60
gamesmanship, patent 216–18
General Agreement on Tariffs and Trade (GATT) 47, 221, 244
General Talking Pictures Corp. v. Western Electric Co. 220
generality of a patent 231, 233
generic drugs 74, 100
  Bangui Agreement 80–81
    Revised Agreement 82–3, 84
  supply of ARVs in Sub-Saharan Africa 86–7
    current situation and future prospects 94–8
    Indian generic supply 86–7, 91–3, 98, 100
    key role of generic producers in reduced-cost ARVs 98–9
    pharmaceutical companies and TRIPS 89
generic institutions 266–8
geographically mediated spillovers 184–5
germ theory of disease 23
Gillespie-White, L. 98
Glaxo 88, 89
Glazier, S. 162
global commons 2–5
global dominance 49–55
global rights 49–55
Godfrey v. Eames 220

governance 335
  coordinating institutions 9–11
  economic rationales for a patent system 318–23
    patents as a governance mechanism 321–2
    property approach in a governance perspective 318–21
    role of patent information disclosure for governance 322–3
  governing institutions 11–14
  innovation systems *see* innovation systems
  public and private institutions 9, 243–77
    analytical framework 246–8
    incomplete setting of IPRs by public institutions 249, 250–53
    private institutions trade-off 253–65
    public vs private governance trade-off 263–5
    settling IPRs 248–50
    specialized and generic institutions 266–8
  of public science 20–21, 26–32
GPO 93
Grabowski, H. 227
Graham, S.J.H. 229, 236
Granstrand, O. 129, 316, 322
Greece 325
Gregersen, B. 189–90
Griliches, Z. 230, 231
Guennif, S. 89
Guinea 88
Guston, D. 26
Gutterman, A. 317

Hagedoorn, J. 286
Hall, B. 230, 231, 233, 235
Hannan, M. 287
Hansen, M. 184
Harabi, N. 155
Harhoff, D. 227
harmonized patent system 189–90, 206–8
HarperCollins (UK) 57
Hart, D. 26
Hasenzahl, C. 75
Hausman, J. 230, 231
Hayakawa 57
head-start profit 116–17
healthcare 2, 4–5, 26–7
  see also AIDS/HIV
Heller, M. 32
Henderson, R. 25, 183, 233
Herfindahl-Hirschman concentration index 231, 233
Hetero 93, 94, 100
Highly Active Anti-retroviral Combination Therapies (HAART) 74–5, 87, 94
Hobbes T. 113
Holland 325
homogenization, cultural 55–7
human genome 31
hybrid seed revolution 38
Hyde Park v. Yelland 63

IBM 153
IFO 151, 155, 164
imitation
  high barriers to 136
  problems relating to preventing 154, 155, 164–5, 168
  protection against 151–2, 159, 163
inborn inventive activity 118
incentives
  to disclose 133–8, 317, 319
  economic incentive rationales 117–27, 141
  efficient resource allocation and use 125–7
  to innovate 117–24, 317, 319
  to invent 117–24, 317, 319
incomplete IPRs 249, 250–53
Indian generic ARV drugs 86–7, 91–3, 98, 100
indicators of value 152, 153–4, 161–2, 163
indirect citation links 281–2
indivisibility 118–20
industrial development from patents 127–33, 141
industrialization 325
information
  asymmetries 222

rationale of increased information 138–9
revealing too much in patent application 155, 165
spillovers *see* spillovers
suitability of patents and 154, 156, 166, 168
information and communication technologies (ICTs) 256–7
integration of military and civilian ICT systems 333
IPRs and emergence of 316–17
information costs 256–7
information disclosure *see* disclosure
infringements
courts in charge of 266–7
detecting 7, 154, 156, 165, 168, 264, 265, 268
problems relating to patent infringement 154, 155–6, 165–6, 168, 172
various modes of 259–60
see also enforcement
innovation 11–14, 335
incentives to innovate 117–24, 317, 319
innovation-enhanced competition 127–30, 141
innovation intensity 195–6, 200, 205
innovation systems 10–11, 186, 311–43
corporate 324–5, 327–9
emergence of 315–16
evolution of IPR system and 313–17
innovation systems approach and its rationales 323–5
IPRs in 323–33
military 324, 332–3
national *see* national innovation systems
sectoral 324, 326–7
university 324, 329–32
innovator's head-start profit 116–17
Institut National Français de la Propriété Industrielle (INPI) 79
institutional environment 11–14
institutional infrastructure 189
institutional organizations 246–7
intangible assets, nature of 259, 260–62
integrated innovation and diffusion processes 318, 319
intellectual capitalism 315–17
intellectual property (IP) regimes 313, 335
intellectual capitalism and 315–16, 317
interindividual governance structures (IGS) 247–8
international agreements, hierarchy of 99–100
international clearing house 64, 322
International Intellectual Property Alliance 47
Internet 316
inter-organizational collaborations 322, 329
'inventing around' patents by competitors 155, 164, 170
invention
accidental 118
diffusion 136
incentives to invent 117–24, 317, 319
social origin of inventions 114–15
invention privileges 314
inventors, networks of 282, 283–4, 285
isolated organizations 297, 298–301, 302
issue date 223
Ivory Coast 88

Jaffe, A.B. 138, 183, 233, 281
Japan 325, 326
companies and knowledge networks 297, 298, 299, 302
Jobard, J.-B.-A.-M. 112
Johnson, B. 189–90
joint innovation/diffusion incentive 318, 319
joint patenting (co-patenting) 282, 286
joint ventures 120–21
Judson, H. 30–31

Kaufer, E. 111, 314
Kelley, D.J. 151
Kilgore, H. 27
Kingston, W. 124
Kitch, E. 131
Kitcher, P. 24
Kleinknecht, A. 186
Klevorick, A. 25
Kline, D. 122, 123, 129, 153, 154

knowledge 181–2
diffusion/flows *see* diffusion
dual nature and transformation of 187
traditional 132
transmission of 182–6, 199, 205–8
knowledge based economy 316–17
knowledge externalities 186
knowledge institutions
interaction with firms and potential learning processes 181–90
see also universities
knowledge networks 9–10, 278–310
semiconductor and computer industries 291–301
data sources 291–2
positioning companies in the knowledge networks 293–301
sample coverage 292–3, 303–5
using patent citations to explore 280–91
networks of inventors 282, 283–4, 285
networks of organizations 282, 284–91
networks of patents 281–3
knowledge spillovers *see* spillovers
Kortum, S. 224
Kristensen, P. 184

Lamivudine 89, 94, 95, 96, 97
Lanjouw, J. 155, 172
lead time advantages 193
leaders, technological 296–301, 302
leading edge industries 316–17, 327
learning
benefits from collectivization 254
from interaction with DKPTO 196–201
learning processes from interaction between knowledge institutions and firms 181–90
Lefebvre, E. 151
Lefebvre, L.A. 151
legal basis for cooperation 152–3, 160, 163
Lemelson, Jerome 215–16, 216–18, 234
Lemley, M. 221, 256
Lerner, J. 224
less developed countries (LDCs) 4–5, 70–105
Lessig, L. 256
Levin, R. 25, 116, 120
Levin, T.C. 150, 155
Levinthal, D. 185
libraries 134
Libreville Agreement 79–80
licensing 12, 321–2
compulsory *see* compulsory licensing
corporate innovation systems 328–9
DRM systems 256–7, 322
economic hold-up 217
open source 269, 322, 329
patents as legal basis for cooperation 152–3, 160, 163
universities and licensing widely 39–42
see also revenue collection
Lissoni, F. 183, 284
location of patent office 201–4, 205
lock in 129–30
Locke, J. 112
Lopinavir 97
Lucchini, S. 90, 91
Lundvall, B.Å. 185, 244

M-form of organization 320–21
Machlup, F. 111, 114, 121, 135–6, 315, 317
Macmillan, F. 46, 48, 49, 52, 63
Macmillan Patfield, F. 55
Madey v. Duke 36
maladaptation costs 248
Malerba, F. 332
Mali 88
Mansfield, E. 116, 120
'market protection of entrepreneurial talent' rationale 130–33, 141
Maskin, E. 269
Matsushita Electric Industrial Company 50
Maville, G. 87, 88
Maxwell's theory of electromagnetism 23
May, C. 114
Mazzoleni, R. 111, 112, 137, 317
MCA 50
MCA/Universal Home Video 51

measurement 248–50, 268–9
ambiguity of 260–61
public institutions and incomplete 251, 252
public vs private governance trade-off 264–5
mechanical engineering 231, 234
media law 64
medical schools 38
Meeus, M.T.M. 187
Merck 88, 89
mergers and acquisitions 49–50
Merges, R. 114, 124, 128–9, 219
Merton, R. 18, 30
metallurgy 23
Metro-Goldwyn-Mayer Studios Inc. v. Grokster Ltd 53–4
M'Fuka, C. 89
military innovation systems 324, 332–3
military research 137–8
Mill, J.S. 117
mining 314
mission-oriented agencies 27
mobile telephony 316
Mogee, M.E. 151
Molas-Gallart, J. 138
molecular biology 39
monautopoly 112–13
monoclonal antibodies 33–4
monopolistic pricing 320
monopoly costs 122–3
monopoly profits, pre-invention 126–7
moral rationales 112–17, 141
moral rights 61–2
Morkel, A. 151
Morpheus software 53–4
motor-generator technologies 224–5
Mowery, D. 38, 229, 316
MP3 files 52
Murdoch, R. 57
music 52, 256
Australian music industry 50–51, 55–6
infringements 260, 262
US royalty collection societies 258

Nasdaq 110, 120
national emergency 77
national innovation systems 324, 325–6
Danish innovation system
DKPTO in 190–92
as a framework for learning processes 187–90
National Institutes of Health (NIH) (US) 27, 41
National Research Council (US) 32
National Science Foundation (US) 27
national security 26–7
natural phenomena 33, 35
natural rights 112–17, 141
'nature of ideas' argument 127–30
negative binomial regression 230–34
negative R&D results 323
negotiating position, strengthening 153, 161
Nelfinavir 97
Nelson, R. 25, 31, 111, 112, 114, 124, 128–9, 137, 317
Netanel, N.W. 63
networks, knowledge *see* knowledge networks
Nevirapine 94, 95, 96, 97
new institutional economics (NIE) 11, 243–77
News Corporation Ltd 50
niche overlap 289, 293–4, 300–301
Niger 88
'no foreign application' loophole 236
nongovernmental organisations 78
'non-rivalrous in use' 28–9
North, D. 118, 244, 246, 248, 249, 250, 325, 326
novel technological ideas 115–16

OECD 110
Office Africain et Malgache de Propriété Industrielle (OAMPI) 79
Olsen, T. 126, 127, 135
open science 18–19, 25, 30–32
public support of 20–21, 26–32
open source licensing 269, 322, 329
Oppenländer, K.H. 152, 159
opportunity costs
of depriving inventors of what they had before 123
in depriving others from using most efficient solution 123
of investment in arbitrary technological trajectories 122

Orbital Engine Corporation 151
order 138–9
Organisation Africaine de la Propriété Intellectuelle (OAPI) 78–84, 99–100
organizing science, technology and creativity 133–9, 141
organization theory 320–21
organizations, networks of 282, 284–91
organized scepticism 30
originality of a patent 231, 233
Orsi, F. 74, 120
overdispersion 230
owner behaviour 259, 262–3

parallel imports 50–51
Paramount 51
Paris, T. 257
Paris Convention for the Protection of Industrial Property 73, 79, 244
Parke-Davis & Co. v. H. K. Mulford & Co. 33
Pasteur's quadrant 20, 24
Patel, P. 324
patent agents 191
patent application process 172–3
  guidance 198, 199
  problems associated with 154, 155, 162–4, 168
patent blocking *see* blocking patents
patent citations 9–10, 278–310
  using to explore knowledge networks 280–91
patent code of 1474 314
Patent Cooperation Treaty (PCT) 236
patent demotivations 154–6, 162–7, 168, 172
  nature of information 154, 156, 166, 168
  other strategies of approbriability 154, 156, 166–7, 168
  problems associated with application process 154, 155, 162–4, 168
  problems relating to patent infringement 154, 155–6, 165–6, 168, 172
  problems relating to preventing imitation 154, 155, 164–5, 168
patent engineers 191
patent examiners 219, 267
patent information analysts 322
patent intelligence 172
patent intensity 200
patent litigation insurance 172
patent motivations 151–4, 159–62, 163, 167–70, 170–72
  indicators of value 152, 153–4, 161–2, 163
  legal basis for cooperation 152–3, 160, 163
  protection against imitation 151–2, 159, 163
  strategic signals 152, 153, 160–61, 163, 171
patent offices 136–7, 180, 188, 266
  functions 190–92
  harmonized patent system 207–8
  importance of national patent offices 201–4, 205
  knowledge spillover 136–7
    from Danish office 7–8, 12, 179–214
  US 8–9, 208, 215–39
patent panic, cost of 124
patent scope 33–4, 35
  problem of 128–30
  welfare cost of broad patent scope 124
patent term 218, 221, 222
  pharmaceuticals and 226–7
patent walls 122–3
patentability 155, 162–4, 168, 172
patents and patenting 315
  Bangui Agreement 78–82
  comparison with copyright 260–61, 268–9
  comparison with publishing 330–31
  current issues 13–14
  drug patenting 72–3
  early history 313–14
  economic rationales for a patent system 317–23
    patents as a governance mechanism 321–2
    role of patent information disclosure for governance 322–3
  incentive rationale 119–20
  industrial development from 127–33, 141

networks of 281–3
patent system and losses to inventors 115
performance of patenting process 7–9
public and private institutions 9, 243–77
science and patenting 2–3, 29–30, 31, 32–3
protection of scientific commons by patent law 33–7
small high-tech firms *see* small high-tech firms
social benefits from 117–27, 141
universities and 29, 38–9, 330, 332
Patten, C. 57
Pavitt, K. 324
Penn, M. 66
Penrose, E. 111, 114, 121, 135–6, 315
'per use' fee system 256
performers' rights 61–2
personnel mobility, between DKPTO and firms 191, 199–200, 205
Pharmaceutical Industry Association 76
pharmaceuticals/drugs 38, 150, 262
anti-retroviral drugs *see* anti-retroviral drugs
continuation patents 225–8, 231, 234, 235
impact of TRIPS Agreement 70–105
changes in international legal system 71–84
patenting drugs 72–3
see also biotechnology
physical property rights (PPRs) 320–21
physics 231, 234
Pigou, A.C. 118
plagiarism 259–60
Plant, A. 114, 119–20, 122, 125, 128
Podolny, J. 287, 290, 294, 296
Poisson model 230
Polanyi, M. 18, 26, 27
policy goals *see* rationales for IPRs
political expediency 117, 127, 133, 141
Polygram 50
Popper, K. 24
Porter, R. 31
positive theory of the social contract 113, 139
Posner, R. 125
power
corporate domination and private power 49–60
acquisition of private power 49–55
significance of private power 55–60
exponentiality of 54–5
power centrality index 295
practical payoffs 18, 19, 19–20
practice, understanding and 21–5
pre-issue secrecy 216, 219–21, 221–2
pre-qualification of ARVs 94, 95–6
prestige status 279, 294–301
Price, D. 26
prices of ARVs 87, 88, 91, 92, 93, 98–9
private institutions 9, 243–77
analytical framework 246–8
benefits from collectivization 254–5
factors favouring recourse to 258–65
mitigating effect 255–8
public vs private governance trade-off 263–5
specialized and generic institutions 266–8
private power *see* power
private sector
interdependence with public sector 55
role of public institutions in knowledge spillover to/within 136–8
privatization of scientific commons 3, 17–18, 21, 31
privileges
patent 314
rights vs 113–14
process innovations 156
process patents 231, 234
production rights 10, 130
prohibition of use 262–3
pro-IP era 313, 315–16, 317
propeller design 34, 38
property approach 318–21
prospect theory 318, 319
protection diffusion dilemma 253
prototype technologies 25
public display 261–2
public domain 137
copyright and loss of the commons 57–9
protecting 60–64

public goods 28–9
public health *see* AIDS/HIV
public institutions 9, 243–77
analytical framework 246–8
incomplete setting of IPRs 249, 250–53
public vs private governance trade-off 263–5
role in knowledge spillover to/within private sector 136–8
specialized and generic institutions 266–8
public interest right 63–4
public laboratories 37–42
public sector/private sector interdependence 55
'Public Sector Intellectual Property Resource for Agriculture' 40
public support for science 20–21, 26–32
publication 156, 166
university innovation system 330–31
publishing industry 57
'pure ideas' 129
purified natural substances 33, 35

Rai, A. 41
Ranbaxy 93, 94, 100
rationales for IPRs 5–6, 109–47
economic rationales for a patent system 317–23
increased information spillover 133–9, 141
industrial development from patents 127–33, 141
social benefits from patents 117–27, 141
social contract theory 112–17, 141
typology of rationales 139–42
RCA/Columbia 51
regional IPR agreements *see* Bangui Agreement
Reichman, J. 75
Reitzig, M. 227
relational transfer of knowledge 184–5, 199
'Republic of Science' 18, 26
research, scientific *see* science
research and development (R&D) 315, 335
duplication 323
measuring results of R&D staff 154, 162
military innovation systems 332–3
and patenting 117
research exemptions 35–7, 42
research organizations 36–7
research tools 32–3, 39–40
resource allocation
incentives and efficient 125–7
science 18, 19, 27
resource constraints 171
Retrovir 88, 89
revenue collection 255–6, 257–8, 264, 265, 268
see also licensing
Revised Bangui Agreement 1999 78, 82–4, 100
rewards 114–16
Rice, M.P. 151
rights
natural 112–17, 141
vs privileges 113–14
'risk bearer' system 257–8
risk management 257–8
Rivera-Batiz, L. 131, 134–5
Rivette, K.G. 122, 123, 129, 153, 154
Rogers v. Koons 62
Romer, P. 131, 134–5
Rosenberg, N. 23
Ross, D. 117
royalties 152–3, 160, 163, 170, 262–3
as social costs 124
royalty collection societies 258

SACEM 257, 258, 261, 266, 272–3, 274
Saint Paul, G. 269
sales tax 320
Samuelson, P. 316
Saquinavir 97
Say, J.-B. 117
scarcity, creation of 125–6
Schankerman, M. 155, 172
Scherer, F.M. 72, 74, 116, 117, 120, 124
Schumpeter, J. 21–2
Schumpeterian theory of the innovator's head-start profit 116–17
science 2–3, 17–45
co-evolution of practice and understanding 21–5

economic rationale of organizing 133–9, 141
governance of public science 20–21, 26–32
importance of protecting the scientific commons 32–42
patent law 33–7
universities 37–42
scientific controversies 30
scientific papers 284
second-line treatments 94, 97
'secondhand' patent applications 229, 235
secrecy 156, 166–7, 193
continuation procedure 216, 219–21, 221–2
sectoral innovation systems 324, 326–7
Sell, S. 47, 55, 113–14
self-citation ratio 231, 233
semiconductors 23, 316
continuation patents 228–30, 234, 235
knowledge networks 291–301, 302, 303–5
Sened, I. 113
Senegal 88
serendipity 18
serial prosecution 227
servile copies 259–60
Shockley, W.B. 23
signals, strategic 152, 153, 160–61, 163, 171
Simon and Schuster 57
small high-tech firms 6–7, 148–76
empirical data 157–9
literature review 149–56
patent demotivations 154–6, 162–7, 168, 172
patent motivations 151–4, 159–62, 163, 167–70, 170–72
results of empirical study 159–67
small high-tech projects 322
Smiers, J. 49, 62
Smith, A. 117, 131
social benefits from patents 117–27, 141
social contract theory 112–17, 134, 135–6, 141
IPR system rewards all novel technological ideas equally 115–16
reward and value created by inventor 115
rights vs privileges 113–14
Schumpeterian theory of innovator's head-start profit 116–17
social origin of inventions 114–15
social costs
of broad patent scope 124
royalties as 124
social network theory 183–4
social origin of inventions 114–15
software 316
continuation patenting 229
open source 269, 322, 329
small high-tech firms and patenting 150, 157–70, 170, 171–2
Software Publishing Association 260
Sony Corporation 50
Sorenson, O. 183
South Africa 76
Spain 51
Special 301 watch list 47
specialization
institutions 247–8, 266–8, 269–70
nations and products produced 189
spillovers
from industrial R&D 28
knowledge spillovers from patenting process 7–8, 12, 136–7, 179–214
rationale for IPR 133–9, 141
stakeholders in IPR system 13
Stanford University 34, 38
start-up firms 322
static efficiency argument 125
statutory licences *see* compulsory licensing
Stavudine 89, 94, 95, 96
Steinmueller, E. 150–51
stem cell patents 41
Stiglitz, J.E. 185
Stokes, D. 20
strategic alliances 280
strategic signals 152, 153, 160–61, 163, 171
streptomycin 38
strong patent portfolio 153, 160
strong ties 184
Stuart, T. 183, 287, 290, 293
submarine patenting 8–9, 12, 216–18, 221, 234–5, 236

Sub-Saharan Africa 4–5, 70–105
  scale of AIDS/HIV pandemic 84–6
  supply of anti-retroviral drugs 84–98
supply-side competition 98–9
Switzerland 325, 326

tacit knowledge 184, 187, 199
Tankoano, A. 78
tariff protection analogy debate 131–3
Taussig, F.W. 118
technical system 324
technological crowding 279, 293, 294–301
technological followers 297, 298–301, 302
technological interdependence 114–15
technological leaders 296–301, 302
technological niche overlap 289, 293–4, 300–301
technological region occupied by a patent holder, avoiding 126
technological system 324
technological trajectories, arbitrary 122
technology 2–3, 335
  brokers of new technology 296–301, 302
  copyright and private power 52–4
  development too rapid for patenting 156, 166, 168
  economic rationale of organizing 133–9, 141
  new and continuation process 222
  science and 18, 19, 19–20, 21–5
technology transfer 39
Teece, D. 120, 150
telecommunications 316
  small high-tech firms and patenting 150, 157–70, 170, 172
Texas Instruments 153
textiles 231, 234
Thailand 86
t'Hoen, E. 89
'Three by Five' (3x5) Initiative 94
Time Warner Entertainments Company LP v. Channel 4 Television Corporation plc 62
Time Warner Inc. 50
Towse, R. 48, 49, 51
trade
  free trade 131–2
  incentive to disclose ideas in 134–5
trade privileges 314
Trade Related Aspects of Intellectual Property Rights (TRIPS) Agreement 2, 55, 61, 110, 133, 244
  commodification of creativity 47–8
  and hierarchy of international agreements 99–100
  impact on healthcare in developing countries 4–5, 70–105
    changes in international legal situation 71–84
    impact of TRIPS on Bangui Agreement 78–84
    public health conflict 73–6
    supply of ARVs in Sub-Saharan Africa 84–98
trade rights 10, 130
trade secrets 328
trademarks 14, 167, 328
traditional cultural expressions 132
traditional knowledge 132
Trajtenberg, M. 138, 183, 233, 281
transaction costs 119, 120
  rationale for IPR system 139
transactional transfer of knowledge 184–5, 199
transformation of knowledge 187
transmission of knowledge 182–6, 199, 205–8
'transparent medium' system 257–8
Traoré, V. 91
'TRIPS plus' 4, 78, 82–4, 100
typology of IPR rationales 139–42

UNAIDS 90
uncertainty 118–20
understanding, practice and 21–5
uniformity 138–9
United Kingdom (UK) 51, 56–7, 326
  governance of public science 26–7
  public interest right 63–4
United Nations 89
United States (US) 315, 326, 332
  American Inventors Protection Act 1999 (AIPA) 236
  Bayh-Dole Act *see* Bayh-Dole Act
  companies and knowledge networks 297, 298, 299, 302
  continuation patents 8–9, 12, 215–39
  counterbalancing rights 61

Digital Millennium Copyright Act 52–3
Doha Declaration veto 77
Drug Price Competition and Patent Term Restoration Act 1984 227
governance of public science 26–7
Hatch Act 1887 208
links between patent examiners and judges 267
Morill Act 1862 208
Omnibus Trade and Competitiveness Act 1988 47
Patent Act 1952 220
1995 changes 218, 221–2, 227–8, 229, 234–5
public and private institutions 245, 252, 258
IPR system compared with France's 266–70
technology and copyright 52–4
Trade Act 1974 47
TRIPS Agreement 47, 55, 61
universities and scientific commons 37–42
video market 51
United States Patent and Trademark Office (USPTO) 208
continuation patents 8–9, 215–39
Universal Copyright Convention 244
Universal Studios v. Corley 63
universalism 30
universities 29, 208
policies and research findings 37–42
research exemptions 36–7, 42
university innovation systems 324, 329–32
Uruguay Round 2, 4, 74, 110
user behaviour 259–60
user rights, copyright and 48
'usus' rights 250, 264, 265, 268
utilitarian classical economics 117–18
utility 35
utilization ratio of patents 323

value
created by inventor 115
indicators of 152, 153–4, 161–2, 163
Venice 314
venture capitalists 120–21
Verspagen, B. 286
Viacom Inc. 50
video market 51–2
Videx 88, 89
Vincenti, W. 24, 34
Vinding, A. 184
von Hippel, E. 323

Waldron, J. 46, 58, 59, 60
Walsh, J. 25, 32–3
Walt Disney Prods v. Air Pirates 58
Warner Home Video 51
Watal, J. 72, 74
WEA 50
weak ties 184
Williamson, O.E. 247, 248, 266
Willoughby, K. 151
Winter, S. 25, 124, 126, 136
Wisconsin, University of 41
World Bank 89
World Commission on Culture and Development 59–60, 64
World Health Organization (WHO) 89, 92
3x5 Initiative 94
treatment guidelines for AIDS/HIV 94, 95–6, 97
World Intellectual Property Organisation (WIPO) 73
Performers and Phonograms Treaty 1996 61–2, 63
World Trade Organisation (WTO) 73–4, 244
implementation of Doha Declaration 77–8, 100–101
TRIPS *see* Trade-Related Aspects of Intellectual Property Rights (TRIPS) Agreement
World War II 26, 117
Wyatt, S. 152, 153, 154, 159

Zerit 88, 89
Zhang, S. 73, 74
Zidovudine 89, 94, 95, 96
Ziedonis, R.H. 235
Zigani, W. 91
Ziman, J. 18, 24